GATEWAY TO *America*

AN ILLUSTRATED HISTORY OF ST. LOUIS

KIRSTEN N. HAMMERSTROM

dedication

FOR DAVE AND TOM

Published by

Heritage Media Corp.

Heritage Building

1954 Kellogg Avenue, Carlsbad, California 92008

www.heritagemedia.com

ISBN: 1-886483-73-6

Library of Congress Control Number: 2002114292

Kirsten N. Hammerstrom *Author & Photo Editor*

Charles E. Parks *CEO/Publisher*

Lori M. Parks *Editorial Director*

Stephen Hung *Executive Vice President*

Randall Peterson *CFO*

Editorial	**Design**
Betsy Baxter Blondin *Editor-in-Chief*	Gina Mancini *Art Director*
Betsy Lelja *Softcover Managing Editor*	Robert Galmarini
Mary Campbell	Chris Hamilton
John Woodward	Marianne Mackey
Staff Writers:	Charles Silvia
Julie Gengo	
Gregory Lucas	**Administration**
Victor Menaldo	Kelly Corcoran *Human Resources Manager*
	Lisa Barone
	Melissa Coffey
Production	Juan Diaz
Deborah Sherwood *IT/Production Manager*	Cyndie Miller
Dave Hermstad	Stephanie Stogiera
Arturo Ramirez	Vicki Verne

Profile Writers

Vicki Bennington

Arthur Goldgaber

Barbara Ponder

R. Jonathan Rehg

Joan Thomas

Michael Tsichlis

Printed in cooperation with the

St. Louis Regional Chamber and Growth Association

www.stlrcga.org

Printed by Heritage Media Corp. in the United States of America

ACKNOWLEDGMENTS

Thanks are due to the people who taught me to write: my mother, Frederica Hammerstrom, and the erstwhile editors of *Gateway Heritage*, Martha Kohl, David Miles, Tim Fox and Katherine Douglass. For patience and fortitude while the book was written, my husband, David Schultz, and my father, Frank Hammerstrom.

Charles Brown, Assistant Director of the Mercantile Library, and his staff deserve special thanks for patience and encyclopedic knowledge of their wonderful collections. Every library in St. Louis has wonderful collections that have inspired and informed my work, and I thank every librarian and archivist who has helped me over the years.

CONTENTS
part one

CONTENTS
part two

INTRODUCTION

by Kirsten N. Hammerstrom

St. Louis is one of my favorite cities. No matter where I have lived, I always think of St. Louis as home, perhaps because it's where I was born, where I went to college, where I met my husband and started a family. Even though I was born in St. Louis, I grew up in Chicago, leaving me with no good answer to that typical question, "Where'd you go to high school?" Like so many residents throughout St. Louis' history, I came to the city from someplace else and found myself staying. My years in the city are more fondly remembered now, since I left for a job in another city. It is still "home," and I think it will be for a long time. The view of the swiftly running rivers and green fields that flashes through the window of an airplane coming into Lambert thrills me; like many before me, I am drawn to the rivers.

The geography of St. Louis is, in many ways, the reason she exists. Built on the low bluff at a bend on the Mississippi River just below the confluence with the Missouri, St. Louis sits well protected from flooding and convenient to transportation networks and fertile agricultural land. Her location is as compelling today as it was in 1764. At that time, her position between the rivers made her a transportation hub, while today, it is her airport, a primary hub for TWA/American and Southwest Airlines.

She sits at the center of air, rail, road and river networks that bring business travelers, vacationers, commuters and goods into her offices, museums, schools and stores. She is the headquarters of a Federal Reserve Bank District and a regionally important financial center. The city is the host of countless major league sports events every day as the home of the Cardinals baseball team, the Blues hockey team and the Super Bowl-winning Rams football team. St. Louis is one of the few cities that have always been home to a professional baseball team, almost since the sport was invented. She has been the site of one of the largest real estate transactions in the history of the United States and the focus of landmark Supreme Court decisions on real estate policy.

From the Louisiana Purchase Transfer to Shelley v. Kraemer, St. Louis has played an important role in American history.

There are echoes in the city's history, currents that run through time as the river runs from Baden to Carondelet. In 1778 Don Fernando de Leyba wrote, "the classes of people are so mixed up that one cannot tell who is a farmer and who is a merchant," the first expression of a rural-urban conflict that would continue until the city-county separation of 1876. Her position below the confluence of the Missouri and Mississippi rivers and above the confluence of the Mississippi and Ohio rivers, gave St. Louis an incredible trade advantage in the early years of the 19th century before steamboats made travel up and downriver less of a physical feat. When steamboats replaced keelboats and canoes, the city's merchants were well established with trading and credit networks that reached south to New Orleans and east to Philadelphia, New York and Boston.

These same networks would provide direction for the railroads that soon spread across the country. Her influence was felt across the country, and although it would diminish as Chicago rose to prominence, St. Louis remained a pioneer. She made advances in city planning and reform, only the second city after New York to enact zoning codes. Her World's Fair celebrated American ingenuity and progressive reform and remained a lasting influence in the beautiful Art Museum and the system of lagoons and lakes that ran through Forest Park. She could be mercantile and magical at the same time.

Her history of supporting exploration — not just Lewis and Clark, but also Ashley and Henry and John James Audubon — for both commercial gain and scientific interest was richly rewarded in the early 20th century. A tall, slender young man from Minnesota settled on St. Louis as a home, impressed by the city's new, if rustic, airport and the spirit of camaraderie that infused her pilots. St. Louis rewarded his faith and bankrolled one of the most famous flights of all time. After Lindbergh, St. Louis would be "Aviation City," the home of international airways and one of the few city-owned and operated airports in the world. Her connection to exploration did not end with Lindbergh but continued as space capsules were made at McDonnell-Douglass.

Today, St. Louis is more than the acres confined within the 1876 boundary, as she always was. She is her people and her place; she is the buildings that stand downtown, reminding us of a time dominated by streetcars and high-rise office building, just as she is the steel and glass buildings of the suburbs where the new economy is shaped. St. Louis reaches along the river and back from the banks, from historic neighborhoods to modern suburbs. Her people reach from elderly descendants of the first French settlers to the newborn children of her most recent Bosnian and Vietnamese immigrants. She is a city of contrasts and continuities, looking toward a future built on her past.

one
1764-1825

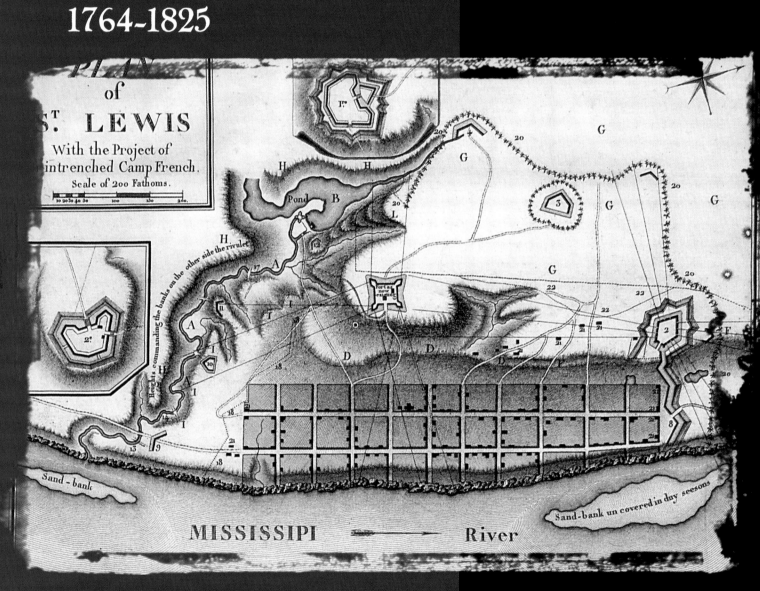

PLAN of S.T LEWIS With the Project of intrenched Camp French. Scale of 2oo Fathoms.

Pond

Heights commanding the banks on the other side the rivulet

Sand - bank

Sand-bank un covered in dry seasons

MISSISSIPI River

French Village, Frontier Capital:
DISCOVERY & FOUNDING

The story of St. Louis runs from the East to the West. From her settlement by Auguste Chouteau in 1764 to her streets spreading westward from the shore, the city stretches west, her story unfolding from the riverbank. Founded as a commercial depot for the French colony based in New Orleans, St. Louis quickly became a frontier capital and financial center in her own right. Chouteau had been sent by Pierre Laclede and placed in charge of an exploratory party charged with the task of constructing a new village on the shores of the Mississippi, just below the mouth of the Missouri River. Laclede had chosen the site some three months earlier, pleased with the gentle rise of the bank from the river's edge and the bluff that protected the site from flooding, as well as its proximity to other, earlier settlements. Upriver from Ste. Genevieve, Cahokia and Kaskaskia, the new settlement would occupy an ideal position for the exchange of goods up and downriver.

The first buildings constructed at the new site were crude cabins and storage buildings, temporary structures to house the party as Chouteau and his men laid out village streets and began work on a stone house for Laclede. Families were recruited from Cahokia, and from Fort de Chartres, where they were concerned about the impending British takeover. With

Plan of St. Louis
Engraving by Tardien L'aine from Victor Collot, A Journey in North America, Paris, 1826
The St. Louis Mercantile Library at the University of Missouri-St. Louis

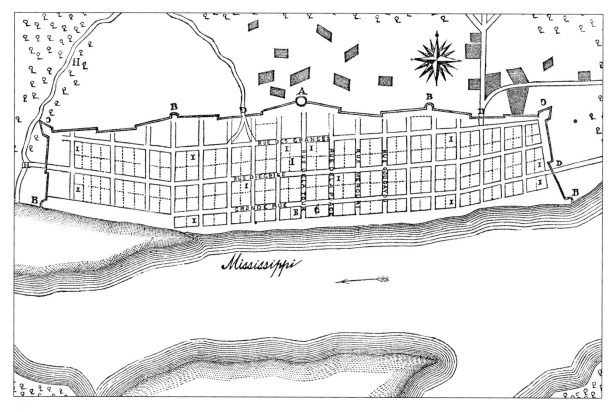

Mississippi

promises of land at St. Louis, many families opted to accompany Laclede across the river, despite the Indian threat. A band of Missouri Indians arrived at St. Louis during construction and frightened settlers away. The Missouri, whose women and children were enlisted by Chouteau to dig the cellar for Laclede's house, left after they were finally convinced of the impending threat of the British and their Indian allies from the north.

With the Indians returned to their villages upstream, the work of creating a new village began again. Captain Louis St. Ange de Bellerive arrived in 1765 to assume the civil and military authority for the new settlement and the surrounding territory; he brought with him additional settlers, artisans and traders from Fort de Chartres. Lots were assigned along the gridded streets of the village, which had been laid out in a deliberate plan, unlike other Creole villages. The plan was centered on an open plaza, *La Place d'Armes* on the riverfront, facing east. The Place was planned for settlers to use variously, for markets, militia practice and large public gatherings.

From this central plaza to the north and south, building lots stretched along three north-south streets: First Street, which ran along and faced the river, Second Street, and Barn, or Third Street, which ran between First Street

and the Common Fields, establishing both the city limits of the time and the manner in which the city would grow.

Narrower east-west streets intersected these: just to the north of The Place ran *La Rue de la Place*, or Market Street, while *La Rue de la Tour*, or Walnut Street, ran to the south. Laclede's stone house and headquarters occupied a prominent place on the block directly west of the market, with a block dedicated to the church directly behind his house. Every other block of 240 feet by 300 feet was divided into four building lots, 120 feet by 150 feet. Until the arrival of St. Ange de Bellerive and the establishment of a more regularized colonial government, Laclede distributed the lots without charge to encourage settlement. Eventually, land transfers became regularized, and the government required that paper deeds and transfers be recorded in the *Livres Terriens*, or land books. Lots were granted contiguously, to maintain a compact and secure village.

Each owner was expected to enclose his lot with upright palisades called *pieux debout*; on contiguous lots, these seven foot stakes topped with sharpened points provided the settlement's best defense against attack.

Behind the palisades, houses were, for the most part, simple. One-room cabins housed boatmen and engagés;

larger homes of several rooms housed traders and artisans. Creole houses were typically built of vertical logs set into the ground and chinked with a limestone plaster, then coated with whitewash. Steep thatch or shingle roofs sloped down to porches that ringed the houses, providing shade from the hot summer sun and shelter from bitter winter winds. Interior furnishings varied with the status of the owner; merchants would have wooden floors and glass windows, while farmers would have dirt floors. The Creoles' small houses and the city's generally pleasant weather encouraged outdoor activities. Longtime resident Frederick Billon recalled these times in his later years, describing a village where men played billiards and women amused themselves with "fiddling and dancing and the usual amount of gossip." Horse racing was a popular sport, and though Lieutenant-Governor Don Francisco Cruzat would issue ordinances prohibiting racing in the village streets, its popularity did not diminish.

Everyone kept a kitchen garden and grew vegetables and herbs to support the household. Grain crops were grown in the common fields in a shared agricultural pattern based on feudal customs. Long, slender fields stretched back from the village, in contrast with the eastern colonial American pattern of large, rectangular fields. Creole planting and tending patterns contrasted with the Anglo-American system as well. After plowing and planting, Creole farmers practiced a laissez-faire style of agriculture, leaving weeds and crops alike to grow until harvest. While the American system produced a larger yield, the Creole settlers of St. Louis usually managed to produce enough for their needs and Indian trade. Importation of grain was required in years when crops were poor or demands high, and this earned the village the nickname *La Ville de Pain Court* or Short of Bread.

Both the nickname and the need for imports would be attributed to village residents' mercantile focus and fascination with the fur trade, which left little time for farming. The unhurried pace of life in early St. Louis would later be construed as indolence by American immigrants unaccustomed to Creole agricultural methods and livelihoods based on the rhythms of the rivers or Native American trading patterns.

Most of St. Louis' early settlers, like the majority of people at the time, were illiterate. Even if they had been able to read, little reading material made its way upriver from New Orleans, and news was slow to spread. When village residents finally learned of the transfer of Louisiana from France to the Spanish, it was too late to protest. News of the exchange reached Louisiana in September 1764, almost two years after the cession; it would be nearly two years more until Don Antonio Ulloa arrived in New Orleans to assume Spanish control of the territory. Ulloa remained in New Orleans with two companies of infantry, leery of taking full control of the territory with so few men and an unwilling population.

Tension increased as he tried to restrict trade with France and finally placed the territory under Spanish trade law, a system that limited the colonies' mercantile exchanges to Spanish ships with Spanish crews from Spanish ports. For a territory accustomed to trading with France — and to which no Spanish boat had ever come — this seemed a death knell. Ulloa fled for Havana as angry citizens petitioned for repeal of the cession and restoration to France. Ultimately, the Spanish refused, preferring to use the area as a buffer against the British traders from the north. In St. Louis, St. Ange de Bellerive remained commandant of Spanish Illinois, the territory along the western bank of the Mississippi from the Ohio River to

Fragment, Auguste Chouteau Journal
The St. Louis Mercantile Library at the University of Missouri-St. Louis

St. Louis. At the same time, Ulloa had ordered Captain Don Francisco Riu to the territory with instructions to construct forts and manage a monopoly of the Indian trade along the Missouri River. This policy proved ineffective because Riu possessed neither the mercantile supplies nor the military strength to trade with or repel Indians. By default, trade returned to the St. Louis merchants.

Following the Ulloa debacle, Spain sent Lieutenant General Count Alejandro O'Reilly to govern her new territory in 1769. With a strong military backing, no-nonsense policies toward insurrection, and a free-trade policy with Havana and Spain, O'Reilly brought Louisiana firmly under Spanish control. He appointed Don Pedro Piernas Captain and installed him in the newly created position of Lieutenant Governor of Spanish Illinois (upper Louisiana). Piernas was charged with forestalling British trade and incursion and limiting purchases and shipments between territorial towns to New Orleans. To maintain cordial relations with St. Louisans, St. Ange de Bellerive was appointed Piernas' assistant, advising him on Indian affairs and formally transferring all of his powers to Piernas in 1770. Peaceful relations with the Indians (primarily the Osage and the Missouri) were maintained by a system of reward and punishment. Piernas, for Spain, refused to trade unless the Indians refrained from attacking traders, settlers and Spanish allies. This system worked well enough with the Indians, and Piernas kept the peace in St. Louis by accommodating the French instead of challenging them. By 1775, Piernas' reputation as a fair and able governor earned him a promotion to colonel of a regiment at New Orleans. At St. Louis, Lieutenant Colonel Francisco Cruzat replaced him and continued the accommodating regime.

St. Louis flourished in her trade with New Orleans, shipping deerskins and other furs down river in exchange for tafia, a crude form of rum, fabrics, metal ware, mirrors and other trade goods. Food was plentiful, in game and in the gardens and fields residents cultivated. Class differences existed as those with greater wealth had received larger land grants from Laclede in a pattern that persisted under the Spanish. Still, outsiders like the new Spanish governors were sometimes frustrated by residents' lack of outward markings of social class. Fernando de Leyba would complain that "the classes of people are so mixed up that one cannot tell who is a farmer and who is a merchant."

Despite his difficulties in seeing them, there were definite classes with an aristocracy of wealthy, land-owning Creoles like the Chouteaus and Papins. The Creole elite, originally from France or New Orleans, occupied positions of political leadership and were the engines driving much of the local government and economy. Artisans and traders with smaller holdings supported these leading merchants. Both groups employed engagés and voyageurs — usually single men, and usually without much, if any property — on a seasonal basis. These rivermen and trappers occupied the lowest rung of Creole class, but they were sometimes joined by free blacks with substantial property or trades. The very lowest class residents were slaves, mostly black, but some Native American, mulatto or mestizo. This structure remained in place when the government changed as trade monopolies were maintained. The bulk of the proceeds went to Spanish authorities and their licensees, primarily wealthier and more influential merchants; this pattern had existed under the French. Life in St. Louis was comfortable, and little change was expected when Captain Fernando de Leyba replaced Cruzat in 1778.

Far removed from the East Coast battlegrounds of the American Revolution, St. Louis nonetheless occupied a strategic position. As the Eastern terminus of Spanish holdings in North America, and with Spain and France newly allied with the Americans against the British in 1779, de Leyba faced an increasing British military threat. He responded by fortifying the village with two stone towers and enlisting male residents into a militia supporting his regulars. In an attack on St. Louis in May 1780, the British were successfully repelled with only a few casualties among the defenders.

St. Louis merchants, along with those at Cahokia and Kaskaskia, aided the Revolution's cause in extending credit and supplies to General George Rogers Clark, the elder brother of the famed explorer, William Clark. George Rogers Clark had been operating in the Northwest Territories against the British from a base at Vincennes. St. Louis and Kaskaskia merchants like Gabriel Cerre supplied Clark on the strength of promissory notes and bills of exchange, of which many would never be repaid. Indeed, years after his return from the Pacific Coast, William Clark continued to sort out his brother's tangled financial affairs. At the time of the Revolution, however, the elder Clark benefited from the personal trust — and animosity toward the British — displayed by St. Louis merchants.

The ultimate effect of the end of the Revolutionary War and the coming of American rule to the lands opposite St. Louis was an exacerbation of Indian tensions by British activities to the north at Detroit and Michilimackinac. The British had long been an aggressive force in the fur trade, playing Indian tribes against one another in a relentless quest for increased quantity and quality of peltries. Secure in the north, British traders maintained crucial advantages over St. Louis and other down-river merchants with a large, secure market for furs in London, backed with inexpensive trade goods.

Auguste Chouteau rose to prominence as a savvy businessman and shrewd politician. *Oil on canvas, c. 1800 The St. Louis Mercantile Library at the University of Missouri-St. Louis*

The northern trade had another advantage over the New Orleans trade: furs were less likely to spoil in the cooler northern weather, while the hot, humid climate of lower Louisiana spoiled many a valuable shipment. Fortunately for St. Louis merchants, the British would buy furs from anyone, while Spanish authorities ignored the illegal trade.

Auguste and Pierre Chouteau, leading fur traders and merchants by 1790, capitalized on Spanish fears of British, American and Indian incursions, promising to build a fort at the Great Osage village to the southwest of St. Louis in return for a monopoly on the Osage trade. The Chouteaus delivered on their promise, completing Fort Carondelet — named for the then Governor Baron de Carondelet.

This shrewd move assured the Chouteaus a large portion of the Osage trade even when their monopoly was not in force. Living with the Osage for several seasons of the year, Auguste, and later Pierre, would become well respected in the tribe, eventually taking Indian wives and participating in village life. This intimate knowledge of Indian life and the subsequent respect the brothers earned from the tribe later proved invaluable. Auguste and Pierre would maintain strong trade relationships with the Osage and under American authority, Pierre held the position of Indian Agent as a result of these connections.

Spain continued to view the Americans to the east with unease, if not alarm, worried by rumors of American conspiracies to acquire Louisiana, and by the territory's emotional ties to revolutionary France. The Louisiana Territory constituted Spain's defense — through sheer enormity of size — against what she perceived as an American threat to her Mexico and California holdings. Still, the expense of governing the Territory outstripped her revenues, and Spain had contemplated selling Louisiana back to the French as early as 1795.

Eventually, economies prevailed and in the October 1800 Treaty of San Ildefonso, Spain ceded the territory to France, after securing a "right of first refusal" if France ever wished to sell the territory. The Americans, under President Thomas Jefferson, had heard rumors of the impending retrocession and were poised to act. The prospect of a Napoleonic empire on the American continent was too unnerving to let pass. While the Americans intended to purchase only New Orleans and the Floridas, Napoleon offered them all of Louisiana, and in an audacious move, American diplomats led by James Monroe accepted and signed a treaty in April 1803. News of the purchase shocked and angered Spain — and surprised St. Louisans. A formal transfer was completed at New Orleans in December 1803.

St. Louis remained substantially unaffected by the transfer until March 1804 when Lieutenant Governor Carlos de Hault de Lassus surrendered upper Louisiana to the American Amos Stoddard, who acted for the French. Stoddard then signed the final transfer documents the following day, cementing the transfer to the United States. Stoddard assumed the role of commandant at St. Louis, acting in civil matters and attempting to allay residents' fears about their new masters. For some time after the transfer, the future form of government — civil or military — remained in debate.

While fur traders and merchants, represented by Pierre Chouteau, petitioned Washington for a military government, eventually the territory was divided in two. The Louisiana Territory to the south had its capital at New Orleans, and the Missouri Territory to the north had a capital at St. Louis. American immigrants flooded the newly opened territory that had been closed to them under Spanish conditions, which included allegiance to Spain and until quite late, conversion to Catholicism. Spain had loosened immigration rules and granted large tracts of land to American immigrants in a last-ditch effort to forestall an American takeover. Among the settlers who took advantage of Spain's generosity was Daniel Boone, already famous for his exploits and leadership in Kentucky.

Boone was known for his exploratory abilities and his taste for unsettled country. He was promised a large grant

Map showing the plan of St. Louis in 1780
The St. Louis Mercantile Library at the University of Missouri-St. Louis

The Colonial Spanish government invited Daniel
Boone to settle in the Louisiana country and
encouraged Americans to settle in Spanish territory
to fend off an American takeover.

Daniel Boone, Lithograph c. 1820
The St. Louis Mercantile Library at the
University of Missouri-St. Louis

of land (more than a square mile) and freedom from the religious requirements in exchange for a promise to lead settlers to the territory and to settle there himself. His son, Daniel Morgan Boone, applied for a grant and selected land along the Femme Osage River. Daniel Boone and his family, including his wife, Rebecca, son, Nathan, and Nathan's new wife, Olive Vanbibber, crossed into Missouri in October 1799 and established themselves along the Missouri River near St. Charles. Boone and his son, Nathan, spent much of their time hunting along the Femme Osage River, the Pomme de Terre and Niangua rivers.

The house known as Daniel Boone's Home, actually the Nathan Boone homestead, was built on the site of Nathan's original cabin. During his absence while on the winter hunts, his young wife, with the help a young slave girl, made extensive modifications and additions to the original cabin. In 1805 Daniel and Rebecca Boone moved into a cabin of their own on Nathan and Olive's land; Daniel Boone's failing health prevented him from joining the winter hunts until 1808. It was during these years that Daniel Boone struggled to prove the validity of his Spanish land grant in the American courts. Following the Transfer, Spanish land grants became suspect, all the more so because so many had not been confirmed in Havana, a process considered both cumbersome and unnecessary to inhabitants. These court battles left Daniel Boone a bitter man who did not see his claims settled until 1814. His experience was an altogether common one for landowners in the years after the Louisiana Transfer.

The Louisiana Purchase more than doubled the size of the young country, opening vast amounts of land to settlement and exploitation. In order to understand this monumental acquisition, President Jefferson detailed the 1803-1806 Voyage of Discovery, under the leadership of Captains Meriwether Lewis and William Clark, to complete a survey of the purchase and locate the fabled Northwest Passage to the Pacific Ocean. Jefferson intended the Corps of Discovery to survey the Upper Missouri territory of the new acquisition for both scientific and commercial (specifically, fur trading) potential and to establish strategic relations with the northern tribes. His instructions to Lewis were specific: "The object of your mission is to explore the Missouri river, & such principal stream of it, as, by it's course and communication with the water of the Pacific ocean, whether the Columbia, Oregan, Colorado or any other river may offer the most direct &

practicable water communication across this continent for the purposes of commerce."

Dispatched to St. Louis in 1803, then-Governor Carlos de Hault de Lassus requested that Lewis not proceed with his expedition until formal news of the Transfer arrived. Official word did not reach St. Louis until January 1804. Joined by William Clark, Lewis gathered supplies and hired men to make the trip. Departing from St. Louis for St. Charles in May 1804, Clark wrote of his first steps on the lengthy voyage that he was accompanied by many of the "neighboring inhabitants," and indeed, many contributed to the expedition. Lewis obtained foodstuffs, trade goods and other supplies from local merchants who were only too pleased to be able to establish friendly — and profitable — relationships with the new government. Both Lewis and Clark were invited to dine and stay at the homes of the local elite, commenting upon the luxuries and refinement of St. Louis leading citizens, the Chouteaus, Soulards, Cerres and other well-established French families. During their two-year absence, Lewis and Clark were feared dead by the same citizens who had feted them before their momentous journey, and there was great surprise and excitement upon their return in 1806.

During those years, Americans struggled to settle into governing the new territory and its leading city. Jefferson first appointed General James Wilkinson as the governor. Wilkinson, with careful astuteness, established himself with the important families, the Chouteaus, Soulards, Gratiots, and Lisas. Unfortunately, his land policies earned him the enmity of newly arrived Americans, Rufus Easton, William C. Carr, and J.B.C. Lucas, a French lawyer who had immigrated to the United States in 1784. Wilkinson's liberal policies regarding Spanish land grants (he proposed to honor nearly all claims) clearly favored well-established families, who may or may not have possessed entirely legitimate and certifiable claims.

Wilkinson was removed to New Orleans in 1806 and was eventually succeeded by Meriwether Lewis, with Frederick Bates as acting governor. Wilkinson's term had been contentious. Lewis' would nearly exceed that, as he remained embroiled in personal and financial difficulties and resisted Bates' influence, preferring to turn to William Clark for advice. Lewis' death in 1809 again threw the territory and the town into political confusion, as factions jockeyed for power and place. Frederick Bates remained the de facto governor as the newly appointed candidate, Benjamin Howard, distinguished himself primarily by his absence. Continuity was established after the 1812 advancement of the territory to second class status (the step just prior to statehood), with the appointment of longtime Indian agent William Clark as governor. Clark had earned great respect among the Indians as a fair and trustworthy trader and representative; his skills at negotiation, and friendships with leading citizens would serve him well as governor of the Missouri territory.

During Clark's years as governor, St. Louis enjoyed a position of importance that fueled her growth. The new territorial capital increased in geographic size, while her leading citizens expanded or improved their homes or built new mansions to reflect their increased wealth and importance. The Chouteaus continued to occupy a place of importance, both as civic leaders and merchants. Their long association with the Osage Indians and near monopoly of the Missouri fur trade ensured their comfortable lifestyle.

Newcomers like William Clark joined established merchants like Manuel Lisa, Pierre Menard and the Chouteaus in commercial ventures like the Missouri Fur Company, founded in 1809. When Lisa returned from an extensive trading expedition that ranged up the Missouri River and into the Rocky Mountains, he brought back an impressive collection of highly valuable furs. Impressed by the quantity and quality of his peltries, Auguste and Pierre Chouteau decided to join Lisa, overcoming their decades-long resistance to the Upper Missouri trade.

The Missouri Fur Company's rivals included John Jacob Astor's Pacific Fur Company; Astor was intent on capturing the fur monopolies for himself, despite the challenges posed by St. Louis merchants. While the Missouri Fur Company failed to make a profitable return on the partners' investments, traders continued to travel up the Missouri and deeper into the territory every year, increasing their knowledge of the land and whetting American appetites for the rich western lands.

During the early years of American government, St. Louis changed in ethnic concentration and physical appearance. The look and fabric of the city changed as new housing styles — primarily English and German houses — replaced the Creole cabins of early days. Frame or brick houses with simple gable roofs and a Georgian sort of symmetry replaced the hip-roofed, upright log-walled Creole cabins. At the same time, merchants began to shift their enterprises out of their living rooms and into spaces built solely for commercial purposes. These two-story brick buildings combined stores or offices with living space but began the separation of functions that would eventually lead to the establishment of a separate commercial district. Most residences and businesses alike remained near the river, with only a few — like that of Judge Lucas — built in the Common Fields on the bluff above.

Still, by 1808, St. Louis had spread west to Seventh Street. With a population of 1,400 and incorporated as a village, St. Louis was now large enough to command a newspaper of her own. Joseph Charless founded the *Missouri Gazette*, later the *Louisiana Gazette*, in 1808 — the first newspaper west of the Mississippi River. With a circulation still limited by widespread

William Clark
Oil on canvas by Chester Harding c. 1813 The St. Louis Mercantile Library at the University of Missouri-St. Louis

Old Chouteau Mansion, St. Louis
Ink and wash on paper The St. Louis Mercantile Library at the University of Missouri-St. Louis

illiteracy, Charless still maintained lively opinion columns, which he wrote himself. Some of his targets answered his columns with the stinging rebuke of physical assault. A letters column ran spirited responses to Charless' articles and was sometimes used to carry out verbal battles between readers. His readership was primarily English speaking and American; the Creole French elite had little use for most of Charless' opinions. They did, however, join their American contemporaries in placing ads in the paper for various commercial enterprises. Charless eventually gained a competitor, *St. Louis Enquirer*, edited by the sometimes-bombastic Thomas Hart Benton.

Benton was one of the new immigrants to St. Louis, young American men of learning and ability who came West seeking fortune and power just as farmers came seeking land and opportunity. Like so many others, Benton came from the south — Tennessee — where he had studied law. In St. Louis he quickly joined the landed elite, who were impressed by his abilities. Later, as a Senator, Benton would convince the U.S. government to finance and construct an overland railroad that would cross the continent from St. Louis to the Pacific Coast.

In his early career in St. Louis, he was perhaps best known for his 1817 series of duels with Charles Lucas that resulted in the young Lucas' death. Lucas made the initial slight, asserting that Benton had not paid his poll tax before voting in a special election. Benton, notoriously short of temper, was enraged and allegedly called Lucas a puppy; Lucas demanded satisfaction. The first time the contestants met on "Bloody Island" — an island in the Mississippi River, removed from St. Louis where duels were technically forbidden — Benton merely wounded Lucas. The second time, Benton killed the young man. Duels were common events in St. Louis in the 1810s, as young men used them to settle quarrels, some of which had begun in the pages of the *Missouri Gazette*. The Benton-Lucas duel cemented Easterners' view of St. Louis as a lawless and violent place. St. Louisans felt that this new lawlessness was the fault of newly arrived Americans. Some of the more violent and mythologized characters were the riverboatmen, epitomized by Mike Fink.

Mike Fink was the "King of the Riverboatmen," who plied the Mississippi and Ohio rivers and achieved a reputation for strength and ferocity that has passed into legend. Fink boasted, "I'm half wild horse and half cock-eyed alligator and the rest o' me is crooked snags an'

Keel Boat on the Mississippi
The St. Louis Mercantile Library at the University of Missouri-St. Louis

red-hot snappin' turtle... I can out-run, out-jump, out-shoot, out-brag, out-drink, an' out-fight, rough-an'-tumble, no holts barred, any man on both sides of the river from Pittsburgh to New Orleans an' back ag'in to St. Louis." While these qualities earned him respect on the river and among his compatriots, they tended toward chaos and anarchy when in port.

Riverboatmen brought their rough ways to St. Louis where boats arrived daily at the bustling levee. Furs came downriver from the hinterlands, floated in canoes and keelboats to St. Louis' fur markets, while cloth, grain, and luxuries came upriver from New Orleans. These boats would then travel back to New Orleans carrying furs. The return trip, made with the river current, could take as little as half the time of the upriver journey. At the time, most goods were carried on keelboats, squarish and some-what awkward craft with a small cabin or shelter in the center. While some keelboats might carry a sail — cordelles — most were pulled and poled upriver by sheer manpower, with boatmen towing the craft upriver by rope from the slippery banks. Rafts were used as well, primarily traveling downriver from more forested areas; these had a financial incentive in that the logs which composed the craft could be sold along with the cargo. The only diffi-culty would then be in obtaining a craft for the return journey upriver. The physical strength of the boatmen was required to move these boats up and down stream and then to unload their cargoes in port.

Steamboats run on wood- and later coal-fired power eventually supplanted these inefficient and exhausting modes of transport. The first steamboat to arrive in St. Louis was the *Zebulon Pike*, named for the famed explorer. The crude little *Pike* arrived in August 1817 after a six-week trip from Louisville, Kentucky. Steamboats made upriver travels far more practicable, although the rivers claimed their share of boats, and each had its own dangers. Missouri River boats, for example, were of shallower draft and lighter build than their Mississippi River sisters; these construction variations accommodated the shallower, swifter Missouri waters.

Even so, many boats were lost every year to snags and sandbars, with occasional explosions taking their toll as well. As late as 1828, 110 keelboats arrived at St. Louis from the Missouri River, although steamboats had largely taken over that trade. For many years, keelboats, flatboats and steamboats alike arrived at the St. Louis levee, carrying a variety of goods. Small manufactories in St. Louis produced copperware and tinware, shoes, furniture, pottery and bricks. By 1817, tobacco factories are been founded; later factories included white lead works and tanneries. Agricultural products including apples, oats, flour, and corn were shipped out of St. Louis to eastern and southern markets. The steamboat trade expanded St. Louis' market and her population, and wove her closer into the fabric of American life.

The coming of American immigrants changed the nature of the city as well. Once a proudly Creole town, St. Louis became more of an American melting pot, though she benefited from increased trade. While the Creole elite was taken aback by American brashness and braggadocio, these new immigrants were startled in turn by Creole customs. Protestant Americans were unaccus-tomed to the Sunday worship and celebration styles of the Creoles. Raised in more austere and Puritanical households, newcomers found the noisy Sabbaths shocking and even irreligious. These celebrations and fetes were part of the Creole week in which Sunday was a day when most of the villagers were together and free of work. Their customs did not require the more solemn observances of Protestants, who might spend the entire day in reflective mediation, prayer or Bible reading after a morning service. Still, these groups adjusted to each other and learned to coexist, though anti-Catholic prejudices did not disappear.

The Catholic population had lost its resident priest, who left with the Spanish government in 1804. Under Spanish rule the government had paid all church fees, which now devolved to the parishioners who were unac-customed to these new expenses, and without a priest to lead them, let the old log church fall deeper into disrepair. The site of the ramshackle wooden structure disheartened Bishop DuBourg when he arrived in 1818 to head the new Diocese of Louisiana and the Floridas, headquartered in St. Louis. DuBourg initiated a building campaign, raising funds for the construction of a new brick church to be the Cathedral of St. Louis.

Construction work began in 1818, and while the interior was not completed, the first Mass was held on Christmas Day 1819. DuBourg was also committed to education, and schools were sorely needed in early St. Louis. Under his guidance, the St. Louis Academy was established, upgraded in 1819 to the College of St. Louis. The Order of the Sacred Heart responded to his invitation, and five nuns arrived in St. Louis in 1818. Under Mother

Philippine Duchesne, the nuns established a girls' school and novitiate in Florissant. These, and a number of Protestant schools, provided the only opportunities for formal education in St. Louis; a public school system would not be established until the 1850s. Still, Protestant and Catholic churches provided both stability and social contacts, reinforcing existing networks while establishing new bonds.

As the St. Louis population expanded and became more American, natives and newcomers alike pressed for Missouri statehood. Eager for representation in Congress, with an eye toward influencing federal policy affecting the fur trade, even the conservative Creole elite favored statehood. Speaker of the House Henry Clay presented the Missouri legislature's petition for statehood to the House in December 1818, igniting a national debate over slavery. Missouri maintained a pro-slavery position, but she had become a pawn in a national movement to abolish slavery. A rider to the bill, proposed by a congressman from New York, proposed that no further slaves be introduced into Missouri, and that those born into slavery after Missouri statehood be freed at age 23. Debates raged in Washington and in St. Louis where much of the fighting was carried out in the newspapers. Charless and the *Gazette* held the anti-slavery position, while Benton and the *Enquirer* were pro-slavery.

After two years, the Missouri Compromise admitted both Missouri and Maine to the Union: Missouri slave and Maine free, to maintain a balance of slave and free states in the House. Additionally, slavery was prohibited in the rest of the Louisiana Purchase territory above 36 degrees, 30 minutes, the approximate southern boundary of Missouri. The Missouri Compromise laid the groundwork for later debates in the House and Senate over slavery and abolition and created bitter animosities along Missouri's western border with Kansas. Civil War guerilla warfare between Bushwackers and Jayhawkers would be incredibly fierce. Still, in 1820 Missouri became a state. St. Louis would lose her prominence as a capital, only to gain in commercial and cultural importance.

Slavery remained in St. Louis, though free blacks had been among the earliest residents. French and Spanish governments had the *Code Noir*, or "Black Codes," designed to regulate the relationships and behavior of black and white residents. Under these laws free blacks could own property but were restricted in their behavior and interactions with slaves. Still, the code provided, at least on paper, some protections that were not afforded under British or American systems. Legally or common-law married slaves could not be sold; old and ill slaves could not be freed and thereby removed from their master's financial responsibility, and punishments for various crimes were described.

These codes were by no means

First Cathedral of St. Louis, 1823: Bishop DuBourg raised funds for a brick cathedral to replace the dilapidated wooden church he saw on his arrival in 1818. *The St. Louis Mercantile Library at the University of Missouri-St. Louis*

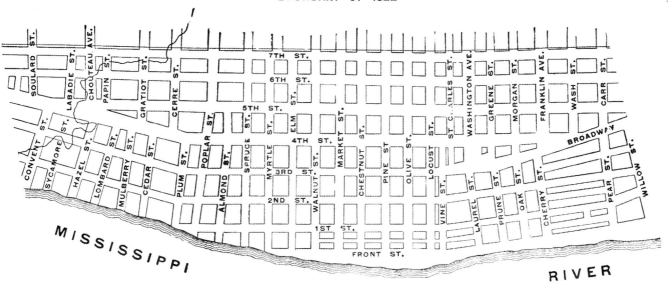

St. Louis, Mo.

BOUNDARY OF 1822

MISSISSIPPI **RIVER**

ACT OF LEGISLATURE, DEC. 9th, 1822

POPULATION 5,000   0.74 SQUARE MILES

humanitarian, but they did provide both slaves and freedmen with a kind of legal status. Free blacks were allowed, under the French legal system, to take advantage of legal rights including marriage contracts, wills and appraised inventories of estates. Under French and Spanish rule, some free blacks attained a relative prosperity and status in St. Louis. For example, Jeannette Forchet, born sometime in 1731, was one of the free blacks who took advantage of her legal rights. Prior to her second marriage, in 1773, Forchet had an inventory of her property prepared in preparation for a marriage contract, an unusual step for a free woman of color, but one that indicates how prosperous she was. Jeannette's industry and savvy acquisition of land were probably leading factors in her free status: like most other free blacks, she either purchased her own freedom, or was freed by a white master after serving as his concubine.

Though the sexual exploitation of slaves was prohibited under the Code Noir, it was certainly practiced. Perhaps Forchet's master freed her as a reward and a salve to his own conscience. For slaves, however, land deeds,

inventories and marriage contracts were far removed from their lives. After 1820, Missouri state laws addressed these issues. As in the Code Noir, free blacks were restricted from owning guns without a permit; black apprentices were forbidden to learn to read and write, and traveling slaves were required to carry passes from their masters. The difference was in a stricter enforcement of these rules with harsher punishments more widespread.

With the achievement of statehood, Missouri was prepared to enter fully into the Union and to participate in the great debates and discoveries of the coming decades. In St. Louis new technological advances and increased steamboat traffic exploded her commerce, creating a boom. Immigrants came from Germany and Ireland, swelling her population and contributing to her culture in a myriad of ways. Eastern merchants established trading links and satellite operations, strengthening ties to the rest of the country, while the city grew in geographic area, architectural splendor and cultural sophistication. By 1825, St. Louis was beginning to be the city recognized today.

two
1825-1855

Entrepreneurs and Emigrants:
THE ESTABLISHMENT OF THE "GATEWAY CITY"

Proudly cosmopolitan as the largest city in the American West, St. Louis proved she was equal to her eastern sisters in 1825 when she was included on Lafayette's tour of the country. Like the other cities he visited, St. Louis hosted balls, receptions and cotillions in the hero's honor. Local luminaries like William Clark attended the parties, honoring the man and his contributions to American liberty. But while the city celebrated her past, she looked to her future as well, and that lay to the west.

"Wanted: Enterprising Young Men" read the ad in the *Missouri Republican* for Ashley and Henry's proposed expedition to the Rocky Mountains. William Ashley and Andrew Henry formed a partnership in 1822 with the intention of exploiting the rich fur resources of the Rocky Mountains, despite competition from other St. Louis traders and John Jacob Astor's company. While the partners may have been prepared for interference from other traders, they were less prepared for the Indians.

William H. Ashley had come to Missouri sometime between 1803 and 1805, originally to Ste. Genevieve. Ashley had both a political and a military career in Missouri, serving as a justice of the peace and as a captain in the Missouri Militia. During the War of 1812 he manufactured

St. Louis sat at the center of trading networks that followed the rivers as illustrated in this color lithograph, "The Mouth of the Missouri River," by Henry Lewis, c. 1848, from Das Illustrite Mississippithal, Dusseldorf, 1865. *The St. Louis Mercantile Library at the University of Missouri-St. Louis*

gunpowder in Potosi; and in 1814 he was commissioned Lieutenant Colonel in the Washington County Militia. He moved to St. Louis in 1819 and continued his political career as a candidate for lieutenant governor and president of the senate. None of these experiences necessarily prepared him for his experiences in the field as a fur trader.

Ashley and his men met with disasters and setbacks of many kinds, much from the intense competition of other fur traders that led to horse stealing, bribing engagés and scouts with liquor, and the theft of Ashley's dog. This was an expedition that generated the kind of incredible-but-true stories that fueled the Mountain Man myth: Hugh Glass, savaged by a grizzly bear and left for dead, crawled out of the mountains to what is now South Dakota, surviving on a diet of wild berries and roots.

Endurance and tenacity were required that season and for several more to come. Supply trains had a difficult time reaching trappers, challenged both by terrain and Indians; winters were harsh, and took their toll on men and equipment. After several years in the mountains with a lower return than he had expected, Ashley sold his interest to Smith, Jackson and Sublette.

Ashley may have had trouble in the West, but merchants in St. Louis were thriving. The expanding fur trade increased their sales volume, and statehood encouraged immigration and drove up sales of supplies and goods to new settlers headed for outstate Missouri, as well as settlers and traders headed for New Mexico, which was newly opened to Americans following Mexican independence in 1821.

Mercantile families from New England and eastern seaboard commercial centers like Boston and Philadelphia sent their sons west to St. Louis where they established and expanded trading networks. Branch offices were opened in St. Louis and if they proved successful, were maintained, often by younger brothers who were sent west to replace the elders. These branches founded the relationships between St. Louis merchants and manufacturers and eastern capital and suppliers that helped fuel the city's growth and began to shift the economy away from the fur trade and toward manufacturing and industry. These merchants and their families, along with European immigrants, also had a profound effect on the culture of the city as the final step in the assimilation of the Creole culture, a process that had begun with the Louisiana Purchase.

The first wave of immigrants to reach St. Louis was the Germans. Gottfried Duden published his *Report of a Journey to the Western States of North America* in 1829, describing the lush river valleys and fertile grasslands of Missouri and comparing the land to the Rhine. His glowing depiction encouraged many Germans — disheartened by the political situation at home — to risk the journey. While some, like Isidor Bush, settled along the Missouri River on farms and raised grapes for wine much as they had at home, others stayed in St. Louis, attracted by the city's vitality. Others were resigned to urban life without funds to carry them farther, or they stayed to earn enough money to purchase their own land. In the city, Irish immigrants fleeing the Potato Famine added to the population, which doubled in just five years between 1835 and 1840. German immigration would increase again after the failed revolutions of 1848.

All of the immigrants had an effect on the city. Yankee merchants sought to influence the city's appearance and atmosphere, to tame her and make her more rational. The Germans changed the city politically, heightening a debate over slavery and politics that would rage for decades. The Irish added a new dimension to the Catholic Church and brought their own customs and political views. Many in St. Louis were willing to leave the Irish to themselves as a permanent underclass; and discrimination was as unavoidable

here as anywhere. Through language barriers and different customs, all could agree: St. Louis was a place of opportunity.

Located at the heart of the central network of the Missouri, Mississippi, Ohio and Illinois rivers, St. Louis commanded a impressive array of natural resources and equally impressive means of transporting them to other markets. Steamboats brought immigrants to the city's riverfront where many found employment as stevedores, hauling apples, cotton, lumber, pelts and other goods up from warehouses and onto boats bound for the east. They unloaded barrels and boxes and crates and trunks packed with manufactured goods from the east and Europe: silks and printed cottons, woolen goods and blankets, jewelry and silverware, books and newspapers. With these durable goods, they unloaded an intangible cargo of eastern values and institutions.

Upper- and middle-class immigrants were shocked by the confusion of St. Louis' city streets, by the brawling, tumbling, noisy mess of her voyageurs, riverboatmen and immigrants. They proposed solutions that were often based on reforms instituted by their home cities. Sewers and crime, libraries and libations all became subjects of their zeal; street improvements, a police force, a mercantile library and temperance societies were all put in place by eastern transplants striving to remake St. Louis according to

The busy waterfront seen in this view highlights St. Louis as a place of opportunity, a magnet for merchants and immigrants alike as they sought their fortunes on the new frontier.
The St. Louis Mercantile Library at the University of Missouri-St. Louis

their ideals. Since these newcomers were largely uninterested in real political power or office holding, the Creole elite encouraged these activities. A new culture with reforms and entertainments came to the city. Stirred by the expansion of the city, theatrical groups began not only to frequent St. Louis on their circuits, but also to establish themselves in newly constructed theaters.

In 1837 partners Noah Ludlow and Sol Smith built the St. Louis Theatre. This Greco-Roman temple at Third and Olive streets maintained high standards for its patrons, refusing to admit any unescorted women. Typically, unescorted women attending the theater in the first half of the 19th century were assumed to be prostitutes; they had traditionally occupied the seats in the gallery, which was now the province of the colored audience. Ludlow and Smith's exclusionist policies, which extended to the partners' refusal to include a saloon, attested to their moral and literary standards.

At the time these standards did not extend to the racist content of the dramas, which included minstrel or black face shows that exploited stereotypes of African Americans. Still, in addition to Dan Rice, the originator of the black face character Jim Crow, in June 1844, the St. Louis Theatre hosted Edwin Forrest in *The Gladiator*,

in which he played Spartacus to a packed house. Other dramatists adopted heavily stereotyped roles in which they portrayed recent immigrants, notably the Irish. George Handel "Yankee" Hill specialized in impersonating and lampooning Yankees, simple characters with names like Jedediah Homebred (in *The Green Mountain Boy*) and Jonathon Ploughboy (in *The Forest Rose*). Hill came from Massachusetts and was more similar to these characters than one might assume. While he exaggerated the speech and vocabulary of his characters, they were firmly based on the provincial New England characters he had grown up with. St. Louis' new Yankee residents would have been comforted by those familiar stereotypes, while remaining happily superior to them.

While new Yankee residents enjoyed the theatre and other new customs, St. Louis' Catholic population, which had replaced their original log church with one of brick in 1819, began construction again. With an affiliated academy and seminary (the roots of St. Louis University and the Kenrick Seminary) and a congregation swelled by immigration, St. Louis was declared its own diocese in 1826.

In 1834, after three years of construction, a limestone cathedral built in the spare Greek revival style replaced the brick church. While under the direction of Bishop Joseph Rosati, the cathedral was granted special indulgence by Pope Gregory XVI. Pilgrims who visited the cathedral's three altars would obtain an indulgence usually reserved to the visitors of the seven Basilicas in Rome. As the city grew, new Protestant congregations were forming to meet the spiritual needs of the newly American town. One of the city's earliest Protestant churches was the Baptist, organized in 1818 by John Mason Peck and James Welch with a church built at the southeast corner of Third and Market streets. Presbyterian churches followed, as well as

Methodist, but the most elite church, which attracted more members from the city's upper class, was the Episcopal Church, founded in 1825. St. Louis became the center of the Episcopal diocese, organized under Bishop Jackson Kemper and seated in the Christ Church.

While churches were built to meet the spiritual needs of the city's residents, politicians and businessmen argued for streets, sewers and wharves to meet their commercial and physical needs. The city's first mayor, William Carr Lane, was elected in 1823. A physician, Lane understood the need for clean water, drainage and sewers to make the city healthy. Recurrent epidemics also convinced businessmen that change was needed, or the city would decline. Lane's charge to the city included recommendations for a board of health, a mandate for the widening, straightening and paving of streets, and the construction of a hospital.

Improvement was slow as aldermen and builders faced the twisted streets of the original village. While these had been laid out in a grid by Chouteau, 50-odd years of construction and incursion by property owners had left them irregular. Streets that could be were widened, and paving projects financed by property taxes based on total street frontage were undertaken. Paving was irregular and slow because many owners left their taxes in arrears. Mud remained the medium of the streets, and St. Louis' reputation as an unhealthy city was hardly dented as small epidemics of cholera and fever occurred almost every year.

At the city's southern edge ran the Mill Creek and Chouteau's Pond, raised by damming the creek. Chouteau's Mill had ground flour for city residents for many years. Other industrial sites along the stream and pond included the Collier White Lead Company, a two-story red brick factory. The factory's process for recovering white lead was to place lead plates in ceramic vessels filled with vinegar and covered with manure; the white lead was then ground with linseed oil to create a paint pigment. Not only were factory workers exposed to lead, but smokestacks also released harmful vapors and liquids were released into Chouteau's Pond, which was part of the city's water supply. At the same time, cows were permitted to graze and drink along the shores of the pond.

The 100-acre pond provided a bucolic retreat from the city's teeming center and was used by residents for much of their recreation — boating, swimming, fishing and picnicking. For the first half of the 19th century,

View of cows in drained area of Chouteau's Pond
Copy of a daguerreotype
The St. Louis Globe-Democrat Collection,
The St. Louis Mercantile Library at the University of Missouri-St. Louis

Chouteau's Pond was a city jewel. After the devastating cholera epidemic of 1849, however, the pond was finally recognized as the city's largest health hazard.

Immigrants, some of whom worked in the factories surrounding the pond, had constructed simple houses — shacks and hovels — near the shores along Ninth and Tenth streets. As the spring of 1849 warmed, cholera began to claim its victims in the city. Hardest hit were the blocks near the pond, especially those along Ninth and Tenth, Clark and Walnut. The neighborhood came to be known as Shepard's Graveyard, in damning reference to a major owner of the surrounding property, Elihu Shepard. As spring and summer wore on, cholera caused the deaths of the majority of residents in the area closest to the pond, often in excess of 60 percent of a shanty's residents.

By the time the disease had run its course, slightly more than 6 percent of the city's total population of 64,000 was dead. The pond was clearly a cause. As the *Daily Missouri Republican* reported in August 1849, "Around this natural 'slop-bowl' are interspersed at short intervals, breweries, distilleries, oil and white lead factories, flour mills and… residences. Into this pond goes everything foul. No cauldron ever filled by the worst of witches… can boast of such a stew." The pond was routinely used as a garbage dump by factories and citizens alike, not just the immediate residents. This recipe, combined with run-off from privies, was surely the worst combination of ingredients possible for public health.

While the link between cholera and human waste was not completely understood at the time, the public health committee did understand that improper sanitation was clearly linked to the spread of the disease. By the fall of 1850, the Board of Health had ordered that the pond be drained. The pastoral scenes of the pond recorded by Thomas M. Easterly capture the pleasant beauty of the landscape and the momentous change signaled by the Board's order. St. Louis would no longer be just a trading city where goods manufactured in the East were exchanged for the raw materials of the West. Now she would become an industrial city, with her labor based not only on manpower, but also on the mechanical power of the steam engine in steamboats, railroads and factories.

After the arrival of the *Zebulon Pike* in 1817, steamboats began regular journeys to the city, competing with keelboats for cargo and berths in the city's harbor. In the 1820s and 1830s, keelboats still competed favorably with steamboats, which had not yet reached the levels of power and capacity that would convince investors of their worth. Still, while keelboats took up to 100 days to travel from New Orleans to St. Louis, even the early steamboats could make the journey in as few as 14 days. Goods shipped by steamboat were considerably cheaper: they required less labor cost in transport and were far less likely to spoil on the trip.

Steamboat arrivals at St. Louis skyrocketed, particularly after 1831 when the city was declared a port of entry for foreign goods. Immigrants and goods alike traveled on the steamboats, bringing cheap labor, more affordable supplies, luxury goods and new ideas to the city. Merchants were able to lower their prices — or raise their profit margins — in proportion to the decrease in wholesale prices occasioned by more efficient shipping.

Landings increased every year after 1817; in 1827 alone, 259 landings were recorded, more than doubling in six years to 573. Each successive decade brought additional landings and more boats; by 1844 more than 2,000 landings were made, with each boat averaging 300 tons in capacity. Auxiliary industries developed to serve the burgeoning trade. Foundries, boatyards and machine shops spread along the waterfront to join warehouses and wholesalers. Boats were unloaded and loaded, outfitted and repaired at St. Louis, increasing her trade and economic success.

This success did not always extend to her infrastructure. Stevedores struggled to unload boats in the mud of the unpaved levee and hauled loads through the muck of unpaved, ungraded streets. Steamboats and an inadequate infrastructure contributed to St. Louis' greatest disaster, which struck the same year that cholera raged.

In May 1849 the steamer *White Cloud* caught fire, the blaze started by a spark from her stack or perhaps from a neighboring boat. Flames quickly spread to adjacent boats, which, when cut loose from their moorings, spread the conflagration down the levee.

Soon, 24 boats and 15 city blocks were lost to the flames, and Thomas Targee, head of the volunteer firefighters, gave his life to stop the conflagration's spread. Fire jumped quickly from the steamers to piles of goods left on the levee; winds fanned the flames and shanties, and offices and warehouses alike succumbed to the flames. The narrow, and by now irregular streets of the original village facilitated the spread of the fire; and in order to halt the inferno, firefighters resorted to blowing up buildings. Targee was killed setting off the charge that finally halted the fire's progress. In the morning, little remained of the bustling riverfront but empty brick shells and heaps of smoking ash. Miraculously, the Cathedral of St. Louis and the Second Presbyterian Church both escaped the flames.

Despite losses estimated between $3 million and $6 million, St. Louisans found a benefit in the destruction. The widespread losses hastened the spread of the "American Improvements" the oldest part of the city desperately needed. With so many buildings destroyed and such compelling evidence of their structural failings, civic leaders had little trouble enacting civic and building improvements like fireproof masonry construction that included the new and fashionable cast-iron facades, wider streets and wharf improvements. Difficulties in containing the fire and the extreme hardships the firefighters had faced, pointed to the need for regularization and modernization of the volunteer firefighters, improved water mains and wider streets.

Modernization came in transportation, as well. By the 1840s and 1850s, St. Louis commanded the great network of Midwestern rivers. Steamboats plowed upriver from New Orleans, west from Cincinnati and Louisville, south from the Upper Mississippi Valley and east from the upper Missouri, converging on St. Louis and her booming economy. As a reporter wrote in 1850, "for two miles a forest of smoke stacks is seen towering above the arks from which they seem to grow. All between this and the line of warehouses is filled with a dense mass of apparently inextricable confusion and bustle, noise and animation."

But St. Louis' great rival rose at this time, too, and began competing with the riverboat economy to the south through the efficient, and less risky, railroads. As Chicago's

St. Louis, Mo.

BOUNDARY OF 1841

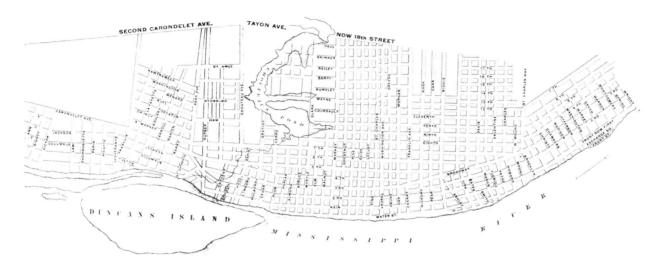

influence spread to the west and north, gathering the rich natural resources of Wisconsin lumber and Michigan iron, St. Louis businessmen nervously anticipated their next move. When the Illinois Central and Rock Island lines spread southwest and diverted the interior Illinois trade north, away from St. Louis, civic leaders were forced to take action.

Railroads began investing in St. Louis in the early 1850s and by the end of the decade, three companies had laid track connecting the city to her hinterlands. The Union Pacific, running west from the river, later connected to the Missouri Pacific and Kansas Pacific lines; the North Missouri, running north from downtown, followed the Mississippi to Hannibal; and the Iron Mountain, running south along the Mississippi, targeted the rich iron ore deposits of southern Missouri. The Iron Mountain Railroad was designed specifically to exploit the resources of Iron Mountain, Shephard's Mountain, and Pilot Knob, as St. Louis' business elite eagerly sought the means to compete with Pittsburgh and Cincinnati manufacturers.

Chartered in 1851, the Iron Mountain received a grant of $750,000 from the state legislature, which combined with $200,000 in private investments and $100,000 in municipal funds, provided an ample construction fund. The company still faced a number of obstacles, from the rocky bluffs at the river's edge that required blasting to

make room for tracks, to the claims of private landowners along the right of way. Expenses rose as the railroad company had to make expensive purchases to acquire adequate right-of-way along its chosen route through South St. Louis and neighboring Carondelet. Land speculators took advantage of any delays, and riverfront lots skyrocketed in value as construction plans were formalized. Manufacturers also purchased land adjacent to the line, planning to take advantage of lower shipping costs and convenient drayage to offset the initial cost of the land.

By 1856 the Iron Mountain railroad was making regular trips between St. Louis and southern Missouri. That same year, Carondelet's first ironworks opened. James B. Eads' ship works operated out of Carondelet, eventually building a fleet of ironclad ships for the U.S. Navy during the Civil War. Even before this, foundries and zinc works opened in the little town that had once been nicknamed *Vide Poche* (Empty Pocket) for the poverty of her residents. To the north, soap works, lumberyards and breweries all took advantage of the convenient riverside railroad.

While the city modernized her streets and new technologies transformed her riverfront into an industrial enclave, St. Louis retained her fur-trading heritage. Pierre (Cadet) Chouteau Jr. had assumed responsibility

The Author painting a Chief at the base of the Rocky Mountains.

G. Catlin.

Cadet maintained his family's tradition of learning, libraries and scientific interests. Fort Union's busy traders were joined in the 1830s by some of the most notable artists of the time. George Catlin published several famous books describing his years in the West, each lavishly illustrated with lithograph copies of his paintings depicting Indian people, villages and activities. Cadet Chouteau provided Catlin with passage from St. Louis to Fort Union in 1832, effectively underwriting his travels and research.

In 1833 another artist made the journey, this time in even more illustrious company. Karl Bodmer, a German artist, accompanied the world-renowned naturalist Prince Maximilian of Weid as he explored the Upper Missouri valley. Bodmer's watercolors of the Mandan Indians and Upper Missouri scenery remain some of the clearest and most beautiful depictions of the early West. Chouteau enlisted the help of his fort managers, including Alexander Culbertson, in assisting various naturalists and artists. Culbertson accompanied John James Audubon on his 1843 explorations into South Dakota, while the naturalist conducted research, made sketches and collected samples for the *Viviparous Quadrupeds of North America.*

for the western division of the American Fur Company in 1822 and ruthlessly pursued the business with Kenneth McKenzie. The American Fur Company pushed deeper into the West with each succeeding year, opening trading forts far up the Missouri River, including Fort Union at the mouth of the Yellowstone in 1828. Fort McKenzie at the mouth of the Marias and Fort Cass at the Bighorn opened in 1832. From these outposts, the company launched exploration and trading parties, challenging its rivals through the acquisition of not only furs, but also geographic knowledge and Indian allies.

Cadet Chouteau's interest in the Rocky Mountains and Upper Missouri River valley extended beyond furs and into archaeology. Shrewd as he was in business,

The partnership of fur traders and managers, naturalists and artists, was more natural than it might seem. Traders knew the unmapped terrain of western territories, the unusual plants and animals and their common names, while artists and naturalists, unfamiliar with the terrain and conditions, needed experienced guides to direct their efforts and preserve their lives. Pierre Chouteau, Jr. offered valuable assistance in the form of his guides, as well as in the free passage he provided on American Fur Company steamboats. Cadet Chouteau's leadership expanded the control and range of the company, which profited from new markets in buffalo hides and the increasing dependence of the Indians upon trade with the Americans.

Keokuk led a delegation of Sauk and
Fox to St. Louis.
Lithograph c. 1847
The St. Louis Mercantile Library at the
University of Missouri-St. Louis

St. Louis was the seat of the Federal Court in Missouri and this view
of the St. Louis Courthouse shows the completed dome.

As Chouteau's trade supported both the changes in the West and the artists who recorded them, a St. Louis artist was busy recording momentous changes closer to home. Thomas M. Easterly came to St. Louis in 1847 and operated a temporary gallery for six months until he settled permanently in 1848. He then operated a studio and gallery on Fourth Street well into the 1870s. Easterly not only recorded those citizens who commissioned portraits but also set about systematically recording the growing — and vanishing — landscape of St. Louis.

As Chouteau's Pond was drained in the early 1850s, Easterly made a series of plates depicting the pond as it changed from a glassy-surfaced, sylvan lake to a muddy-banked puddle surrounded by busy factories. His portraits captured the changing faces of the city's residents and visitors as well, from German immigrants rising to prominence like Ernst Angelrodt, to the new Yankee elite like Massachusetts-born William Greenleaf Eliot, the Unitarian minister who founded Washington University in 1835. Some of the most unusual portraits Easterly made were those of Keokuk, leader of the Sauk and Fox Indians, and members of the party that traveled with him to St. Louis in 1847.

St. Louis was a seat of federal government, home to the headquarters of the Indian Superintendent assigned to manage the affairs of the western Indians, including those of the Nemaha Agency tribes, which included the Sauk and Fox. St. Louis was prominent in administering and supplying the bureaucracy of the federal government. Her location provided access to the best transportation available at the time, favorable trade rates, and ample supplies of foodstuffs and trade goods. Indian agencies were supplied from St. Louis, and tribal leaders and business managers journeyed to the city to negotiate trade agreements with government agents and merchants alike.

St. Louis was also home to the federal courts, notably the U. S. Circuit Court. The courthouse at St. Louis was first housed in a brick building completed in 1833, but an expanding population and increase in legal activity made the space inadequate in just a few years. By 1839, construction had begun on a Greek Revival building in the style of the Pantheon, later capped with a more decorative Renaissance-style dome. By 1851, both new and old courthouses were sharing the site between Fourth and Broadway, Market and Chestnut streets. Henry Singleton designed the first phase of construction, the east wing, in 1839 while Robert S. Mitchell completed the rest of the building in 1851. Alterations to plans for the dome, delayed completion to 1861 after William Rumbold's 1859 plans for a cast-iron dome were accepted. In the meantime, the courthouse was the scene of battles with far-reaching consequences not just for the participants, but for the nation as a whole.

St. Louis courts and judges had been hearing slave suits for freedom for decades before the Dred Scott case reached national prominence in 1857. Under an 1807 territorial statute, which became state law in 1824, slaves with evidence of wrongful enslavement could petition a court for permission to sue their owners for freedom. At the time, such evidence could include manumission papers or proof of birth to a free mother; but the doctrine employed by most slaves, as by Dred Scott and his wife, Harriet, was "once free, always free." Under this principle, slaves who had lived in a free state, even for a short period of time, and even with their owners, could claim they were free.

Liberal interpretations of the 1807 statue made this principle a viable route to permanent, legal freedom. Among the slaves who sued for their freedom prior to Dred Scott was Lucy Delaney, who, at the age of 12 was the subject of an 1842 court petition filed by her mother. Delaney was born into slavery in St. Louis and worked as a nursemaid and house servant; her mother, Polly Crockett, based her suit on the principle that she had been kidnapped from freedom in Illinois and sold into slavery in Missouri. Polly Crockett was eventually successful in her suit, obtaining permanent, legal freedom for herself and her daughter. Lucy Delaney's memoir of her life, *From the Darkness Cometh the Light; or, Struggles for Freedom*, published in 1891, described her life as a girl in St. Louis and the progress of her mother's suit.

Under the law of the time, Delaney was held in the St. Louis jail for more than 18 months as her case was argued, after which Judge Mullanphy finally declared her

yours truly
Lucy A Delaney

Lucy Delaney was the subject of a petition by her mother for her freedom.
Steel engraving by the American Engraving Company, 1890, from Lucy Delaney, From the Darkness Cometh the Light; or, Struggles for Freedom, St. Louis, 1892 The St. Louis Mercantile Library at the University of Missouri-St. Louis

free. Edward Bates, a prominent St. Louis lawyer, argued her mother's position. Bates came to St. Louis from Virginia in 1814 and began to practice law; he was appointed Missouri's first Attorney General. Bates was anti-slavery, though considered a moderate; his abilities as a lawyer and politician made him a promising candidate for the presidency in 1860.

At the time that Bates represented Lucy Delaney's mother, he was in his early 50s, and a leader of the St. Louis Bar. His arguments describing Polly Crockett's Illinois childhood and how a free woman could not give birth to a slave compelled the court to grant Lucy her freedom. Many other slaves, less fortunate in their representation, would not be successful. They found alternate paths to freedom, like William Wells Brown, who escaped slavery in St. Louis to become an accomplished author and playwright, second only to Frederick Douglass. While in St. Louis as a boy, Brown had been hired out by his owner in a number of different trades; working for Reverend Elijah Lovejoy, the abolitionist editor of the *St. Louis Observer*, made a lasting impression on Brown, despite its ironies. Lovejoy was an unpopular editor, considered fanatical by some of his opponents for his unwavering attachment to his opinions.

The 1836 lynching of a free black man, Francis McIntosh, launched the debate that would end both Lovejoy's career in St. Louis, and his life. McIntosh, arrested on the levee for a minor offense, was so frightened by the teasing threat of hanging that he attacked and killed one of the arresting officers. After he was taken to the city jail, a mob gathered, overcame the sheriff and captured McIntosh, whom they slowly burned to death.

A debate erupted in the papers, as some defended or excused the mob action, and others condemned it. The German *Anzeiger des Westens* took the side of law and order, condemning the violence and chastising citizens not only for participating, but for failing to stop the violence. Lovejoy joined the fray, declaring in the *Observer* that "we

must stand by the Constitution and laws or *All Is Gone*." The problem with his position, which was relatively moderate to begin with, was that he would not drop the issue. The participants were never brought to trial because the lynching was judged an unpunishable act, perpetrated by an unidentified crowd. Lovejoy raged against the decision, attacking the judge and the court system with a vengeance, and finally descending into personal attacks and character assassination. His written rage was met with violence when his printing equipment was destroyed. Lovejoy decamped to Alton after a second attack, only to suffer the loss of two presses before he died in November 1837 while attempting to save his remaining press. His martyrdom did not end the debates, and St. Louis remained divided over the issue.

Free blacks had lived in St. Louis almost since the city's founding and had amassed sizable fortunes in the fur trade and in real estate; some were artisans and practiced trades and crafts. Cyprian Clamorgan, a descendant of the early settler and fur trader Jacques Clamorgan, described a "colored aristocracy" whose members, unable to vote and not even considered citizens, still influenced the politics of the city and state by their various campaign contributions. Clamorgan specifically stated that the Emancipation Party rose to prominence as "the result of the unwearied and combined action of the wealthy free colored men of St. Louis, who know that the abolition of slavery in Missouri would remove a stigma from their race, and elevate them in the scale of society."

While St. Louis' free blacks and newspaper editors debated the rule of law and end of slavery, they constituted a microcosm of the larger slavery debates that consumed the country in the early 19th century. Even before the Civil War, slavery contributed to the Mexican War. James K. Polk, who had made annexation of Texas part of his presidential campaign platform in 1844, declared war when Mexico refused to sell California to the United States. With the news of war, there was a rush of volunteers from St. Louis and Missouri. Stephen Watts Kearny and John C. Fremont, both with local connections, were already serving in the Army of the West. Dispatched on an exploratory mission to California with Kit Carson, Fremont was given the task of stirring subversion among American residents. He worked to encourage Californians to agitate for annexation to the United States, ultimately inspiring an uprising that proclaimed the formerly Mexican territory an independent republic. Fremont then served as the new republic's military governor.

Meanwhile, volunteers from St. Louis and Missouri marched under the command of Alexander Doniphan to Fort Leavenworth to join the prairie-hardened troops of Stephen Watts Kearny. Kearny, born in 1794 in New Jersey, began his military career in the War of 1812 as first lieutenant in the 13th United States Infantry. Brevetted major in 1823 for 10 years of loyal service, Kearny accompanied General Henry Atkinson to the headwaters of the Missouri in the 1825 Yellowstone Expedition. He was stationed at Jefferson Barracks just south of St. Louis but lived in the city with his wife, Mary; and his sons, Charles and William Kearny, attended St. Louis University. Shortly after the outbreak of the Mexican War, Kearny was promoted to brigadier general commanding the Army of the West, which took possession of New Mexico and California. In this capacity, after Doniphan's brigade joined Kearny's regular troops, he resigned himself to two weeks hard drilling of the new troops to provide them with the discipline and training they would need to survive in the field. Kearny's resolve was rewarded as the Army of the West marched over the Santa Fe Trail to capture the capital of New Mexico. They occupied Santa Fe in August 1846 after encountering no resistance.

Kearny then left for San Francisco and replaced John C. Fremont as governor. Fremont, married to Thomas Hart Benton's daughter, Jessie, was never easy to command; he disobeyed Kearny and was promptly court-martialed. Doniphan and his troops were left to face the Mexican Army, defeating a force of 4,000 at Sacramento Creek, just north of Chihuahua in February 1847. The war finally ended in September when General Winfield Scott occupied Mexico City. In February 1848 the Treaty of Guadalupe Hidalgo ended the war, awarding the United States ownership of California, Nevada, Utah and Arizona, as well as much of New Mexico.

With so much new territory to assimilate, the rules of statehood and the Missouri Compromise were hotly debated. Many southerners saw the new territories as a means to expand and thereby protect slavery; they advocated expanding the Missouri Compromise line of 36 degrees, 30 minutes west to the Pacific. Southerners saw the cotton-growing lands of Texas and New Mexico as land prime for the slave-based plantation economy; the fertile lands of California beckoned as well. Members of the Free Soil party, mostly northern abolitionists, but also including some southern politicians, agitated for the admission of the new territories as free states. In the Compromise of 1850, California was admitted as a free state, though allowing slaveholders to retain their slaves for some time. Utah and New Mexico were granted territorial status, with the slavery question to be decided when they applied for statehood, while Texas, a slave state, ceded a portion of its territory to New Mexico. St. Louisans felt the mixed blessings of the aftermath of the Mexican War: trade with Santa Fe was eased and expanded, benefiting merchants, but the slavery question had not been decided. The uneasy settlement of 1850 left neither free-soilers nor pro-slavery interests satisfied. The storm clouds gathered in the next decade, presaging the war to come.

The attack on Mexico City by Gen. Winfield Scott, shown here in a steel engraving, was a decisive battle in the Mexican War.
The St. Louis Mercantile Library at the University of Missouri-St. Louis

three

1855-1870

Storm Clouds:
ANTE-BELLUM AND WAR

St. Louis looked upon the Compromise of 1850 with mixed emotions: her merchants, fur traders and investors saw the West as their special purview, with St. Louis both gateway and gatekeeper to the resource-rich lands of the territories. From the grassy plains of Kansas, to the gold deposits of northern California, to the fur-rich plains of Nebraska and South Dakota, St. Louis sought a position to benefit from them all. She could ignore, for a time, the divisions between free states and slave states, pro-slavery and pro-emancipation forces, even at home, in pursuit of wealth and expanded markets.

Through her leading senator, Thomas Hart Benton, St. Louis declared her intentions for the West: a railroad to the Pacific, starting with a line from St. Louis to Jefferson City, and from there to Kansas City. Benton's proposed line ran into intense competition from Iowans, anxious for a line that would connect them with the fertile Western lands and north to Chicago. The battle turned to wrangling over the Kansas territory and whether Missouri slave-owning interests would succeed in expanding slavery west into new states.

The Kansas-Nebraska act of 1854 was designed to allay Northern and Southern fears, splitting the territory into Kansas, just west of Missouri, and Nebraska, west of Iowa. These territories

The battle at Wilson's Creek, Missouri, was a defining moment for Confederate sympathizers in St. Louis and Missouri.
Hand-colored steel engraving by V. Balch after F. O. C. Darley, 1862
The St. Louis Mercantile Library at the University of Missouri-St. Louis

could both be exploited for railroad lines, and with each permitted to decide the slavery question for itself, the balance of free and slave states might be maintained if Kansas were to decide as a slave state. The Kansas-Nebraska Act of 1854 effectively repealed the Missouri Compromise and replaced it with popular sovereignty, whereby the citizens of the new territories would decide by vote for slave or free status. Thus, the groundwork was laid for the border conflict between Missouri and Kansas that raged before the Civil War even began. St. Louisans maintained their interests in the debate, anxious to expand the railroad and retain their influence over territorial politics.

The contest for slave or free supremacy was waged in St. Louis as well. German Abolitionists and American slave owners argued in their newspaper columns for and against the extension of slavery to the territories, and sermons were preached on the issue. There seemed to be

no clear answer or end to the debate. *The Anzeiger des Westens*, as edited and published by Henry Boernstein, adopted an anti-slavery position that extended to challenging the elite, and immovable, power structure of St. Louis.

Like many German immigrants of the mid-19th century, Boernstein was a liberal who came to America after the failed revolutions of 1848. Five German immigrants had purchased the *Anzeiger* newspaper in 1836 from its editor in Belleville, Illinois, and moved its offices to St. Louis as the first German-language newspaper west of the Mississippi. The first editor of the *Anzeiger* was Wilhelm Weber, who wrote the paper's first columns on race issues when he scooped his competitors with the story of Francis McIntosh's lynching in 1836. Weber chastised the citizens for their actions and implied that the violence was racially motivated and would not, perhaps, have been perpetrated against a white man. In the storm that followed, Weber did not repeat his assertion of racially motivated violence, choosing instead to defend his honor and the independence and equality of the Germans in America.

The *Anzeiger* retreated from discussing slavery in the St. Louis area, or even Missouri, until the paper was sold to Henry Boernstein in 1850. Boernstein's position was more radical than that of his predecessors. He swung his paper's allegiance to Thomas Hart Benton, who was voted out of his long-term Senate seat in 1850, and endorsed Benton for the House of Representatives in 1852. Benton had, by this time, become outdated. He clung to the Missouri Compromise and the Compromise of 1850 as the means to preserve the Union and failed to see that his desire to preserve the Union would inevitably lead to war. Benton's desires to maintain a middle ground and to preserve the Union without openly addressing emancipation were futile. Even backed by the growing German American population that supported emancipation, Benton could not regain his political throne.

The *Anzeiger* maintained its strong support for a free economic and political system and supported Benton's political descendants, Frank Blair and B. Gratz Brown. Blair and Brown founded the *Missouri Democrat* to compete directly with the *Missouri Republican*, the descendant of the city's first paper, the *Louisiana Gazette*, originally founded by Joseph Charless in 1808. The *Republican* was the voice of the Whig, soon to be Democratic, Party and supported slavery, while the *Democrat* was the voice of the nascent Republican Party and supported Bentonites and Free Soilers. Gratz Brown shocked St. Louis and the nation in 1857 when he proposed the abolition of slavery in Missouri before the state General Assembly. Brown's position was economic rather than moral. He understood the East-West loyalties of the Yankee immigrants who had come to dominate St. Louis and the state's mercantile empires; he understood, too, the distaste for slavery in the North and its identification with the pre-industrial, antiquated South.

Brown's position was not unusual in its ambivalence. Many St. Louisans, like many Americans, could claim no easy position on the issue. Contradictions were common. Early American immigrants from the Northeast who had intermarried with the original Creole elites became indistinguishable from them in their political views, as they adapted to local positions of social and political prominence. William Carr Lane, though St. Louis' first mayor, had emigrated from Pennsylvania. Lane assimilated completely, adopting a hard-line pro-slavery and pro-secession attitude. Frank P. Blair and B. Gratz Brown were from Kentucky, a strongly agricultural state with pro-slavery leanings; both adopted anti-slavery and pro-Union positions.

Many St. Louisans chose not to address the issues at all, though some were forced to confront it by their ministers. William Greenleaf Eliot came to St. Louis from his native Massachusetts in 1835 and built the Unitarian Church of the Messiah in 1851, where he served as pastor. Despite his stated position that the pulpit was an inappropriate forum for political issues, in 1857, Eliot brought his congregation to the slavery question in an indirect manner. He preached against sin and wickedness, and for the righting of wrongs by "the great Christian method, to strive against sin."

It was in this electric atmosphere that the Dred Scott case broke, a case that would eventually shake the nation as it did the city. The players reflected the curious mix that was St. Louis, and the legal journey mirrored the changes taking place across the nation. In 1830 Scott's owner, Peter Blow brought him from Virginia to St. Louis, where he was sold to Dr. John Emerson; Scott traveled with Emerson to the free state of Illinois and the free Wisconsin Territory. While owned by Dr. Emerson, Scott married Harriet Robinson, who was also a slave; Emerson brought them both back to St. Louis in 1842.

After Dr. Emerson's death, Scott sued his widow Irene for his and Harriet's freedom in a petition filed by Francis Murdoch, an abolitionist lawyer from Alton. Ironically, Peter Blow's sons, Taylor and Henry T. Blow, represented the Scotts in their suit. The Blow brothers advised Scott that he was entitled to his freedom after his residence in free territory, an extension of the "once free, always free" doctrine that had been written into law with the Missouri Constitution of 1820. In the state constitution, a liberal interpretation of an 1807 statute barring wrongful enslavement permitted even brief residency in free states or territories to be considered emancipation.

In June 1847 a judge of the St. Louis County Circuit Court denied the Scotts their freedom on a legal technicality but immediately ordered a new trial. The second trial ended with the Scotts granted their freedom in January 1850. But Irene Emerson, represented by her brother John Sanford, immediately appealed to the Missouri Supreme Court, which reversed the decision in 1852. The court ruled that the Scotts had lost their freedom when they returned to Missouri in a ruling that effectively negated the "once free, always free" principle that had held for decades throughout states courts; only Hamilton R. Gamble dissented.

Scott and his supporters did not give up; they remained in St. Louis where Charles E. Labeaume, who had supported them in their original suit, employed them. The Scotts' lawyers appealed to the federal courts, this time naming Sanford as Scott's owner. Sanford's lawyers claimed that Scott, as a "Negro of African descent," was not a citizen of Missouri and therefore could not file a suit. In May 1854 Judge Robert Wells of the U.S. Circuit Court at St. Louis ruled against the Scotts but committed a deliberate procedural error to

Broadway in St. Louis
Color lithograph, c. 1850
The St. Louis Mercantile Library at the University of Missouri-St. Louis

permit their lawyers to appeal to the U.S. Supreme Court on a Writ of Error. In the case of Dred Scott v. Sanford, the Scotts' suit for freedom was overshadowed by the larger politics.

The decision that was rendered March 6, 1857, addressed two critical issues: the citizenship of blacks and the constitutionality of the Missouri Compromise. In a three-part ruling, dominated by the opinion of Chief Justice Roger B. Taney, the court found that slaves or free blacks could be citizens of a state, but not of the United States; as a result, Dred Scott could not file suit in a federal court. The court also found that slaves who voluntarily returned from a free territory to any slave state placed themselves under the laws of that state, as interpreted by the state's courts.

The court's final ruling was that travel or transport to a free territory would not free a slave, citing the Fifth Amendment guarantee of property rights. The Fifth Amendment argument led the court to the opinion that Congress had no authority to pass legislation forbidding slavery in the territories, making the Missouri Compromise unconstitutional. Scott had lost his suits and his health. Ill with tuberculosis, he was sold to Taylor Blow, who immediately freed him. Scott died of tuberculosis in 1858, only 18 months after the Supreme Court decision.

The issues raised by the Supreme Court's provocative decision would not die, and the Dred Scott case became another step down the path toward war that began with the Compromise of 1850 and the Kansas-Nebraska Act of 1854. In St. Louis Frank P. Blair was elected to Congress in 1856, and B. Gratz Brown to the Missouri legislature. Both were Republicans who supported emancipation, and both attempted to maintain a center position, which would prove increasingly difficult as the slavery debates progressed.

St. Louis Germans were strong supporters of Blair, sharing his anti-slavery position; many accompanied him almost everywhere. After South Carolina seceded from the Union in December 1860 to protest the election of President Abraham Lincoln, Blair organized his German followers into a Home Guard. The Guard formed a paramilitary group that would later participate in the Camp Jackson incident, St. Louis' own Civil War battle. Meanwhile, Southern states followed South Carolina in leaving the Union; by Lincoln's inauguration in March 1861, 10 states had left the Union, including Missouri's close neighbors, Arkansas and Tennessee.

Missouri Governor Claiborne Fox Jackson was a secessionist. Following the lead of other pro-secession governors, Jackson called a convention to consider the question of Missouri's relationship with the Union, openly declaring his belief that "the destiny of the slaveholding states is one and the same." By February the convention's delegates had convened, the majority of whom were slaveowners, though pro-Union slaveowners. After the convention moved to St. Louis, secessionist Sterling Price was voted president, but Hamilton R. Gamble dominated the proceeding. Gamble, a former Supreme Court Justice who had rendered the minority opinion in the Dred Scott case, was a dedicated Unionist and held to the rule of law. Under his influence, the convention voted against secession but attached opinions recommending the extension of the Missouri Compromise line to the Pacific and opposing the coercion of seceding states.

It was too late for these sorts of measures, though, which had barely succeeded 10 years earlier. The majority of people in St. Louis were pro-Union, pragmatically accepting the mercantile realities that connected the city to the northeast and upon which the city relied. Even so,

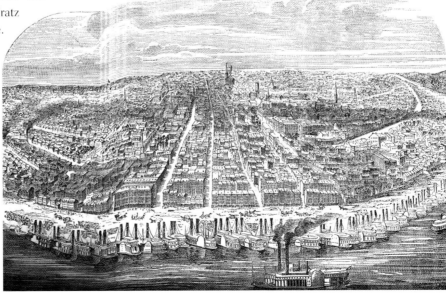

Bird's Eye view of St. Louis, 1860
The St. Louis Mercantile Library at the University of Missouri-St. Louis

that had previously battled through newspaper columns and senate-floor speeches.

The forces that met that day reflected the variety of opinions and positions in St. Louis. Regular U.S. Army troops were commanded by Captain Nathaniel Lyon, later a Brigadier General; several troops of volunteers marched with Lyon's regulars. Among these were the 1st U.S. Volunteers, commanded by Colonel Frank. P. Blair; the 2nd U.S. Volunteers, commanded by Colonel Henry Boernstein, the former editor of the *Anzeiger*; and the 3rd U.S. Volunteers, commanded by Colonel Franz Sigel.

Lyon's troops were largely American, while the volunteer troops were mostly German; Blair's Home Guard was the nucleus of his Volunteer company. Numbering nearly 6,000 together, these federal troops — followed by curious civilian onlookers — marched to Camp Jackson and surrounded it on all four sides. Despite a force numbering fewer than 1,000 men, Frost initially rejected Lyon's request for an unconditional surrender, but realizing he was greatly unnumbered, gave in. His officers joined him, with the notable exception of John Knapp, who broke his sword on a stump as a point of honor. Knapp later served in the Union Army, a testament to the tangled nature of St. Louisans' sympathies.

After Frost's surrender, Lyon intended to take the prisoners in custody to the arsenal; but action was delayed for at least one half-hour after Lyon was rendered unconscious by a kicking horse. The troops grew restless and as civilians swelled the ranks of the crowd, tensions increased dramatically. Taunts began to fly — many directed at the Germans — and were followed by dirt clods, rocks and bricks. Feelings intensified; after Captain Blandowski, an officer in Sigel's Volunteers, was struck and wounded by a bullet, the skirmish began. In the end, 34 soldiers and civilians were dead or wounded, including women and children.

Some of the casualties, like Blandowski, eventually would die of their wounds. None of the regulars fired; and whether civilians or volunteers started the shooting, blame fell squarely on the Germans. The Missouri Volunteer Militia was paroled from the arsenal the next day. Just a month after Fort Sumter, St. Louis' only battle was over. The city never saw armed conflict within her limits, but she witnessed plenty of the effects of war, most of them ill. Her citizens were divided, and war swirled around her, filling her hospitals and prisons, sharply reducing her trade and threatening the rest of the state.

there were active secession supporters in the city and in the government. Daniel Frost, the commander of the Missouri Volunteer Militia, made plans to seize the St. Louis Arsenal from federal troops. As the largest stockpile of weaponry in the slave states, the arsenal was considered vital to the Confederacy. Although his attempts failed, Frost was given command of several pro-southern militia companies at St. Louis and directed by Governor Jackson to train them. Under General Frost, these troops were sent to take a position on the bluffs above the arsenal but prevented in their attempt by then-Captain Nathaniel Lyon, commanding federal troops.

Frost established a camp just inside the city limit at Lindell Grove, east of Grand Avenue along Olive Street, south to Laclede and east to Garrison Avenue. The camp's streets were laid in a grid and named for Jefferson Davis and General Beauregard; Frost named the camp for his commander, Governor Jackson. The Camp Jackson incident of May 10, 1861, was a clash between two factions

Missouri's allegiance to the Union undoubtedly saved St. Louis from the destruction and hardship Baton Rouge and New Orleans experienced. Still, the embargo against southern ports noticeably limited her shipping, and the loyalties of her citizens were sharply divided. After the Camp Jackson incident, men joined up on both sides to prepare for war. The action moved southwest, as the Confederate Army of the West led by Brigadier General Benjamin McCulloch sought to protect southern interests from Union bases in Missouri. The Missouri State Guard under General Sterling Price, who had assumed command of the unit formed from the Volunteer Militia after Camp Jackson, aided him.

Missouri's Governor Claiborne Fox Jackson was strongly pro-Confederate, and rural portions of the state agreed as well as some of St. Louis' leading families. For example, William Clark's descendants were proudly pro-Confederate. Meriwether Lewis Clark and his son,

William Preston Clark, joined the Confederates although both were graduates of federal military academies. William Preston Clark resigned his commission and returned home from overseas to join the Confederate Army, afraid of arrest all the way from New York. The Clarks' cousins, the Glasgows, were largely pro-Confederate, though William Glasgow confounded his family when he remained loyal to the Union.

Missouri's governor was not as loyal. In June 1861, less than a month after the Camp Jackson incident, Governor Jackson presented General Lyon with an ultimatum, demanding the dissolution of the U.S. Volunteers and the removal of Union troops from Missouri. Lyon was irate and refused. As a result, Jackson and his supporters left St. Louis for Jefferson City. As Lyon marched his troops west along the Missouri River, Jackson fled to southwest Missouri where he declared Missouri an independent state and was accepted into

Misunderstanding, more than military action, caused the Camp Jackson incident.
"Terrible Tragedy at St. Louis," wood engraving, New York Illustrated News, May 25, 1861 The St. Louis Mercantile Library at the University of Missouri-St. Louis

the Confederacy. Loyal to the Union, Hamilton R. Gamble remained in Jefferson City and served as provisional governor of the state.

The dual governments remained in effect throughout the war, and the Confederates maintained their shadow administration first in Arkansas and later in Texas. The bitter feelings came to a head in August 1861, as Sterling Price's State Guard met Nathaniel Lyon and his U.S. Volunteers at Wilson's Creek just outside Springfield, Missouri. Lyon was killed and the Union troops defeated. The news encouraged St. Louis' Confederate sympathizers, who anticipated a quick and favorable resolution to the war. They were shortly to learn otherwise, when John C. Fremont was appointed to command the Western Department of the U.S. Army.

Fremont had enjoyed a varied, if somewhat rocky, career to this point. He was married to Jessie Benton, the outspoken daughter of the late Senator Thomas Hart Benton. Benton had protected him after his court martial for insubordination in the Mexican War, and Fremont had enjoyed a renewed military and political career. Fiercely anti-slavery in his views, Fremont was arrogant in his dealings with St. Louisans and inclined to punish the Southern sympathizers. He acted swiftly and harshly, declaring martial law in St. Louis on August 14, 1861, an act intended to squash Confederate activity and silence dissension. Southern-leaning newspapers were forbidden to publish, and "seditious" out-of-state papers were banned from circulation. Saloons were closed and curfews established.

Fremont meant business, and he intended to prove it. Two weeks later he declared martial law in Missouri, limiting movement and forbidding the bearing of arms north of Jefferson City and Cape Girardeau, on pain of trial and execution. His most daring act was his declaration, in the same order, that the property of any persons rebelling against the Union was forfeit and that "their slaves, if any they have, are thereby declared free men." Fremont's emancipation of slaves in Missouri was effective immediately; he preceded Lincoln's own Emancipation Proclamation. The city and the state were in an uproar: abolitionists and the Germans rejoiced, pro-slavery

Unionists were shocked, and Governor Gamble was outraged. Lincoln rescinded Fremont's orders to shoot armed secessionists and asked Fremont to modify his emancipation terms.

With his uncanny ability to irritate his superiors, Fremont replayed his California mistake: just as he had irritated and disobeyed Kearny, so too he disobeyed Lincoln, refusing to alter the emancipation decree. Lincoln rescinded the orders and sent cabinet member Montgomery Blair to investigate Fremont's behavior. Montgomery was the brother of Frank Blair, the prominent St. Louis lawyer and politician and commander of the Home Guard. Fremont retaliated against Lincoln by jailing Frank Blair for insubordination. It was a costly political move from which he never recovered; Lincoln removed Fremont from command in November.

From start to finish, Fremont commanded the Western Department of the Union Army for only five months, but within that time he provided ample cause for comment. His wife, Jessie Benton Fremont, was probably the more intelligent of the two and certainly a driving force behind his successes. They had married when she was 17, and she had assisted him throughout his career, tempering his impulsive actions with her keen intelligence. She was a staunch abolitionist and supported Fremont's decisions. In 1861 she was delighted to return to St. Louis and immediately adopted an active role in local activities. With William Greenleaf Eliot, she helped organize the Western Sanitary Commission and brought the prominent reformer Dorothea Dix to the city both as an adviser and to help recruit women to serve as nurses in local military hospitals. Jessie may well have contributed more to the Union cause by her dedicated reform action in St. Louis than her husband's bold military orders.

The Western Sanitary Commission was founded to provide care for wounded soldiers, refugees and civilian casualties. The federal government lacked the resources to adequately supply, house and care for so many people. Staffed by volunteers like congregational minister William Greenleaf Eliot and James Yeatman, a prominent St. Louis banker, the Western Sanitary Commission met the needs of many victims of war. At the same time, the

Ladies' Union Aid Society was formed with the similar, but more focused purpose of caring for wounded soldiers. As the war dragged on, both organizations had to extend their care to include refugees of Missouri's bloody guerilla warfare, newly freed slaves in need of work, and children orphaned by war. The two organizations eventually came to work together, with the Union Aid Society responsible for daily operations, and the Sanitary Commission devoted to fundraising. Both were noticeably successful.

The Union Aid Society supplied 15 hospitals in St. Louis in addition to floating hospitals for the Mississippi fleet and railroad cars outfitted as ambulances for transporting the wounded. The amount of work these volunteer organizations undertook and successfully completed was phenomenal. These groups provided Union women with public and useful means of supporting their immediate male relatives and the political cause. Under the Martial Law decree, Confederate women in St. Louis were unable to voice their opinions and had to be clandestine in their activities.

Those who were not cautious risked imprisonment in the Gratiot Street Prison, a former medical college converted to penal use in 1861 upon the departure of the owner and operator, Dr. John McDowell, a fiercely Confederate sympathizer. The Gratiot Street Prison usually held men as prisoners of war. Women were imprisoned most often for spying, mail running or other partisan activity. Some St. Louis men were also imprisoned for aiding the Confederacy or voicing their opinions too loudly. In an ironic twist, federal authorities seized the "slave pen" at Broadway and Clark streets that belonged to Bernard M. Lynch and converted it into a military prison. Outfitted with barred windows and bolts, this prison-like structure had been used to hold slaves until they were sold at Lynch's Market on Locust Street between Broadway and Fourth streets. Pro-emancipation Unionists undoubtedly took pleasure in the irony of using the property to imprison their pro-slavery, secessionist enemies. In this atmosphere Confederate sympathizers were faced with difficult choices. Some served in the military while others, unwilling or too old to serve, moved to Confederate held states, or to Canada, where they found life more comfortable, far removed from the uncomfortable border position.

The people who came to St. Louis during the war were often those attempting to escape its effects farther

Run by the Ladies' Union Aid Society, floating hospitals provided remarkable and badly needed care. *"The Ward, Floating Hospital on the Mississippi," wood engraving after Theodore Davis from Harper's Weekly, May 9, 1863 The St. Louis Mercantile Library at the University of Missouri-St. Louis*

could be moved someplace safer, most often across the river to Illinois. Freed slaves became refugees as well after the federal Emancipation Proclamation went into effect on January 1, 1863.

Federal authorities generally refused to provide for those freedmen and women who were not directly employed by the government, so local aid societies established networks to find or provide jobs for thousands of former slaves. Between January and March of 1864 alone, nearly 1,000 black refugees passed through Benton Barracks. The numbers were astonishing, and voluntary organizations like the Ladies' Union Aid Society and the Western Sanitary Commission met their needs until the establishment of the Refugee and Freedmen's National Bureau in 1865.

Perhaps the crowning achievement of the Western Sanitary Commission was the Mississippi Valley Sanitary Fair held at St. Louis in May 1864. Organized to benefit the Ladies' Union Aid Society and the Ladies' Freemen's Relief Association, the month-long Fair was held in a temporary building on Twelfth Street between Olive and Washington. Something like a church bazaar, the fair offered a range of activities. Needlework and foodstuffs were sold along with art and china. There were activities for children, and dramatic tableaux as well as auctions and lotteries. All of the special events and exhibits were listed in the *Daily Countersign* newspaper, published on site as a guide and fundraiser for the fair. All told, the Sanitary Fair netted more than $550,000. St. Louis women rose to meet the needs of civilians and soldiers alike and formed lasting bonds and organizations as a result. After the war, the women of the Ladies' Union Aid Society gathered again to found the Women's Suffrage Association of Missouri, strengthened by their work together and the visible, positive role they had played in easing the discomforts of wartime conditions.

Despite the best efforts of the Ladies' Aid and other societies, the war ravaged rural Missouri, and few families escaped the pain of losing sons, husbands, brothers or fathers to death or disability. Slave families were profoundly affected as well, as they fled slavery following the Emancipation Proclamation of January 1863. Technically, Missouri's slaves were not affected by the Proclamation, as Confederates did not hold the state, but runaways

Refugees flooded St. Louis, and women's groups strove to accommodate them. *"Union Refugees from Western Missouri Coming into St. Louis,"* wood engraving from *Harper's Weekly*, December 28, 1861 The St. Louis Mercantile Library at the University of Missouri-St. Louis

afield. Guerilla warfare raged in outstate Missouri, and border clashes intensified as the war ground on. These raids did not reach St. Louis, but news of them and the refugees did. The Ladies' Union Aid Society established a relief auxiliary for the refugees and opened its first home, with 60 beds, on Elm Street. Black refugees were housed in separate quarters in the rear of the building. Funds were provided by taxes on Confederate loyalists, who were punished for their views and even held responsible for distant events.

Refugees flooded the city as guerilla warfare intensified — "Bloody Bill" Anderson and his partisans visited deadly raids on towns as close as Clarksville and Louisiana upriver — and the aid societies sheltered more than a thousand refugees in one year alone. For the most part, refugees were housed, fed and clothed only until they grew bolder and more frequent, and owners recognized the increasing futility of pursuing them. Treatment and conditions grew harsher, and frictions increased as the economic climate worsened in a cycle that led to increasing numbers of runaways. Many escaped slaves came to St. Louis where some found work on the riverfront and others joined the Union Army to earn a certificate of emancipation.

As the guerilla warfare of rural Missouri escalated, the flood of runaway slaves and refugee freedmen grew. Confederate masters, seeking revenge for property loss and the effects of war, often treated families that the runaways left behind with especial severity. While no mechanism or agency existed to care for or administer to the refugees, and there was no official policy beyond non-intervention between master and slave, Union soldiers often assumed the initiative and assisted slaves on their own. As Confederate property, runaway slaves were considered contraband and were therefore able to be "confiscated" by the Union. The Union Army may have been fighting to end slavery, but African Americans still felt the blows of racism.

The Emancipation Proclamation, though widely celebrated, failed to change the typically racist, paternal and often unjust relations between blacks and whites. Free or slave, blacks still earned less for labor and were charged more for goods than whites. Full Emancipation for St. Louis' slaves was achieved by an amendment to the Missouri Constitution. The state convention met in St. Louis at the Mercantile Library on January 6, 1865; five days later the convention passed an ordinance abolishing slavery and involuntary servitude, with the exception of criminal punishment. The Governor proclaimed that "no person… shall know any master but God"; and the deal was struck. January 14, 1865, was an official day of celebration and observance as crowds composed of blacks and whites paraded along downtown streets, and buildings were hung with flags. In the afternoon, a 60-gun salute was ordered, and the proclamation was read to an approving crowd. Slavery in Missouri had ended, and St. Louis' slaves were permanently free, more than 11 months before the Thirteenth Amendment to the United States Constitution was ratified.

There would be other lasting effects of the Civil War in St. Louis as well, in the redirection of northern trade firmly to Chicago and her hinterlands. The old Philadelphia-St. Louis network was replaced, irrevocably, by a Chicago-New York link forged in the steel of railroad tracks and bridge trusses. Manufacturing and mercantile trade declined noticeably when southern ports were blockaded, and citizens felt the pinch.

With New Orleans shut down and the river patrolled by Union forces, shipping was severely curtailed and dangerous. These risks forced upper Mississippi businessmen to turn to Chicago for trade. Just before the war, St. Louis had begun to lose this trade as a disappointing result of the Hannibal and St. Joseph Railroad. This line, running across the northern edge of the state, had been promoted in St. Louis as a means of drawing agricultural produce to the levee at Hannibal where it would be transferred to riverboats headed south to St. Louis for distribution east and south. Instead, the railroad diverted trade to the north, effectively drawn into Chicago's network by its connection with the Chicago, Burlington and Quincy line, which linked Chicago with the agricultural riches of western Illinois and eastern Iowa.

The railroads had a number of advantages over riverboats even without factoring the difference in shipping costs. Railroads were subject to far fewer risks: steamboats confronted rapids and ever-changing snags and sandbars, winter ice that could freeze solid across the entire width of the Mississippi at St. Louis and the unpredictable schedules that resulted. Goods were also loaded and unloaded only once on the railroad and could be shifted from one

The successful Mississippi Valley Sanitary Fair raised funds to support the aid societies that were helping refugees, soldiers and their families. This is the auction of General Lyon's last letter. *Stereograph by Robert Benecke, 1864 The St. Louis Mercantile Library at the University of Missouri-St. Louis*

line to another in a box car in contrast to goods shipped by water, which were loaded and unloaded by hand at several ports, adding labor costs to the wholesale price. For commodities that had to be shipped overland as far west as Santa Fe, these additional fees did not add significantly to the wholesale price. They did, however, make St. Louis-based wholesalers and suppliers dependent on steamboats unable to compete with Chicago-based brokers who shipped by rail.

St. Louis had begun construction on railroad lines well before the war. In addition to the Iron Mountain line, the Pacific Railroad began construction in 1851 on a line that ran west from downtown through the Mill Creek valley to Kirkwood on its way to Hermann. This piece of the line opened to traffic July 1853 and was

extended to Jefferson City in 1855. Railroads were not without their own risks, and the Gasconade disaster, in which the bridge over the Gasconade River collapsed under the force of the new locomotive *Missouri* traveling at 15 miles per hour, was typical. More than 100 passengers were killed or injured when the engine and two passenger cars pitched into the river. Construction continued despite the blow to the Pacific's reputation, and the line reached Kansas City where it joined the Missouri River Railroad that ran from Kansas City to Leavenworth.

Throughout the Civil War, as the steamboats faced threats from gunboats on the Mississippi, the railroads were subject to guerilla attacks. Both the Pacific and the Iron Mountain Railroads suffered damage inflicted by rebels hoping to disrupt Union shipping. These attacks also weakened St. Louis' position relative to Chicago as investors shipped north to avoid Missouri routes that risked total loss. St. Louis' wartime economic climate was a continuation and extreme variation of the larger economic

VIEW ON LUCAS PLACE.

shifts taking place in the nation. The war simply catalyzed these changes, for even the rail lines extending from St. Louis were firmly linked to markets based on river connections and to the geometry of the rivers' influence. This geometry extended to the city's appearance, dictating the long expanse that spread north and south along the Mississippi and the arc of her growth to the west. Within the city, though, the geometry was changing.

Residential streets had been taken over by industrial areas as manufacturing and wholesaling enterprises grew in size and number from the 1840s through the Civil War. Neighborhoods that had been the home of the city's Creole elite and wealthy newcomers grew unpleasant as they were taken over by soot, runoff, noise and the working class. Homeowners moved west, only to be caught up again in the industrial expansion. Population growth and fear of disease made the once-fashionable row houses, a style transplanted from Philadelphia and New York by Yankee immigrants, seem unpleasantly crowded.

Expanding industry and a growing population fueled homebuilders' desire to protect their investments, a desire that found expression in Lucas Place. Laid out and subdivided by James H. Lucas in the 1850s, Lucas Place provided a pleasant respite from the busy commercial streets crowded with peddlers, dray vans, transients and hustlers. Deed restrictions prohibited any commercial uses, and a covenant required a 25-foot setback from the street on a minimum lot width of 25 feet. Lucas Place was the first experiment with what would become the grandest neighborhoods of all in St. Louis, the private places of the Central West End.

The houses of Lucas Place were part of a transitional period in the domestic architecture of high-ranking St. Louisans; while wealthy immigrants from the northeast had lived in fashionable row houses, these were less appealing as the city's character around them changed. Two blocks of row houses built in the mid-1840s were quickly surrounded by the growing commercial clatter: Walsh's Row on South Seventh Street, built in 1845, and Hart Row at Seventh and Pine, built around 1846. These attached homes had very small front yards; typically opening directly to the street front as houses did throughout the United States and Western Europe. Five years later, in 1850, residents were ready to remove themselves from the confusion of public streets; the 25-foot setback required on Lucas Place created a middle zone between the public street and the private home, symbolically protecting the home and family from unwanted incursions.

The first resident of Lucas Place was the fur trader Robert Campbell, who completed his house in 1851, although in a style clearly derived from the row house style, with windowless sidewalls that anticipated nearly contiguous neighbors who never arrived. Campbell eventually added bays to the side of his house, opening the rooms to light and air. After Campbell, Samuel C. Davis built the third house on Lucas Place in 1854, also in a lightly modified row house style. The first house

Wealthy residents enjoyed new homes removed from the grime and confusion of downtown streets. *The William M. Morrison House, engraving, 1860 The St. Louis Mercantile Library at the University of Missouri-St. Louis*

the mound was probably 50 feet from base to crest. Scientists, naturalists, historians and curiosity seekers debated the origins of the mound, and a few voiced concerns over the destruction of such a mysterious landmark. Progress was slow and accomplished entirely by hand at a desultory pace, until 1868. With the end of the war, railroad expansion was renewed, and the Big Mound stood in the path of progress embodied by the North Missouri Railroad.

While still accomplished by hand, excavation and leveling proceeded at an accelerated pace, as the railroad paid the wages of a larger work crew. As the mound was excavated, skeletons that were assumed to be bodies of "modern Indians" were exhumed, along with grave goods of beads, disks, and scant "ear jewels." Some observers correctly assumed a connection between the Big Mound of the city's northern riverfront and the mounds found at East St. Louis and Cahokia, Illinois; others, despite the evidence of man-made artifacts, firmly believed the mounds were accumulated piles of river silt. With the railroad financing the work, the destruction that had slowly moved but little of the mound since 1852 was completed within a year. By 1869 only a slender shaft of the original mound remained, soon to be carted away to make room for the new railroad.

designed to be completely independent of its neighbors was the Sarah Collier house of 1858, attributed to George I. Barnett, the best architect in St. Louis at the time. Lucas Place was established as a quasi-private residential enclave that provided the wealthy with spacious, and gracious, living.

As the city built up, she also tore down. Thomas M. Easterly, the daguerreotype photographer who had come to St. Louis in the 1840s recorded the enormous new changes to the landscape. Easterly had made a successful career taking portraits of St. Louisans, both wealthy and poor. His patrons included many of the wealthy and powerful citizens, along with ordinary people and visiting Indians. He also turned his camera to the historical, purposefully recording the structures of old St. Louis that remained, capturing French colonial structures in advanced states of decay, abandoned industrial sites and the beginning of the end of the steamboat era.

What captured his attention in these decades was the destruction of the Big Mound, an Indian mound on the north side of the city that stood in the way of urban expansion.

The Big Mound stretched 319 feet long, 158 feet wide, and 34 feet high from its base. Streets were graded around the mound, and by the time clearance began in earnest,

The Civil War remade St. Louis as it remade the nation. Loss of southern markets forced her to turn increasingly to the North and the Southwest, to direct competition with Chicago. The Mississippi River was at once a connector, by boat, and a barrier to rail. Shipping interests had blocked a bridge for years, effectively strangling the eastern trade. Railroads were the game now, and as soon as the war ended, construction boomed. All that St. Louis needed was a railroad bridge, but she had the man to build the best.

four
1870-1900

The City Where the Mississippi Flows:
GILDED AGE ST. LOUIS

As the age Mark Twain called Gilded dawned in St. Louis, her citizens recovered from the war and took stock of their city's place. She had escaped physical damage during the war, but her trade losses had been substantial.

A variety of solutions and approaches were suggested and tried, ranging from an unsuccessful war of words favoring removal of the nation's capital from Washington to St. Louis, through novel techniques in packing and shipping goods, to the desperately needed railroad bridge across the Mississippi at St. Louis.

The debate over a rail bridge had raged for years as railroad boosters, merchants and manufacturers had wrangled with steamboat captains and owners over the merits and safety of a bridge at St. Louis. Steamboat interests strongly opposed a bridge as a threat to their business and as a hazard to navigation. Steamboat interests imposed strict standards on the width and height of the bridge spans, believing that a satisfactory and affordable bridge simply could not be designed or built. They required that the bridge be high enough to allow steamboats to pass safely underneath at normal water levels and that the supporting piers be far enough apart to allow safe navigation.

St. Louis, Missouri — the new railroad bridge gave St. Louis an economic boost after the Civil War.
Wood engraving by Schell and Hogan after C. A. Vanderhoof, 1876, from Harper's Weekly, July 8, 1876
The St. Louis Mercantile Library at the University of Missouri-St. Louis

These stringent design limitations convinced most that the job could not be done. The financial implications for the river men were serious as shipping by rail had proved to be less expensive and less risky than shipping by river. Chicago's rise had proven that, and it was Chicago's prosperity that finally united St. Louis' river and rail men. By the end of the Civil War, even the riverboat interests could see that a bridge-less St. Louis could never compete effectively with Chicago's wholesalers, manufacturers and investors, who tapped the natural resources of the northern Mississippi Valley and practically maintained a trade monopoly in the region.

Bridge companies scrambled for the contract. Congress passed a bill authorizing construction and when the dust settled, the St. Louis and Illinois Bridge Company led the field. The project required constructing a bridge to cross the river at Washington Avenue that would meet the stringent requirements. Riverboat interests demanded that all bridge spans be at least 50 feet high, with one span 500 feet wide, or two of at least 350 feet. As the company prepared to begin construction, James B. Eads was appointed to plan and direct construction of the bridge.

Eads was neither an architect nor an engineer, but he knew the river better than anyone else did, particularly the critical riverbed and currents that dictated the design and materials of the bridge piers. He had gained this expertise in the dangerous pursuit of salvage, combing the riverbed in a crude diving bell. During the Civil War, he had demonstrated an audacious kind of brilliance, constructing seven slender ironclad gunboats in just over two months, tailored to the Union Army's war on the Mississippi.

The success of the fleet garnered Eads a nationwide reputation as an engineer. In constructing the bridge, he was assisted by Henry Flad, a former St. Louis water commissioner, and Charles Pfeifer. Both were trained engineers, which lent credibility to the project. The design

was unveiled in 1867: Eads proposed a bridge with a center span of 515 feet, and two side spans of 497 feet, easily surpassing the steamboat operators' requirements.

Massive stone piers sunk into bedrock supported the spans of tubular steel arches. The arches also supported the iron beams of the bi-level roadbed to carry foot, wagon and railroad traffic. In all, Eads that estimated construction costs would total $4.5 million. His crews began work in the summer of 1867, tearing out the wharves near Washington Avenue to clear the land prior to starting construction on the western approach.

By February 1868 they were ready to lay the limestone foundation, and St. Louis could watch the long-awaited bridge begin to cross the river with a sense of wonder at the methods employed. Workers labored inside caissons designed to hold out water and sand, supplied with compressed air at surprising depths; on the east side, 68 feet of sand covered the bedrock. The caissons had to reach below the river's surface all the way to bedrock, at depths approaching 100 feet. Many laborers became ill with what they called "caisson disease." They suffered from the bends, poisoned by nitrogen bubbles in the bloodstream that resulted from too-rapid decompression.

Dr. Alphonse Jaminet was commissioned to study the disease after a worker's death in 1870. Jaminet concluded that rapid compression and decompression were to blame and recommended a longer decompression period than the five minutes that had been in effect. A formula was developed that required only one minute for six pounds of pressure above normal. At the east pier bedrock, Jaminet prescribed less than 10 minutes of decompression for the men working at the east pier, consequently lessening but not eradicating the effects of caisson disease. By the time pier construction was complete, 14 men had died from rapid decompression. Under the rapid construction schedule, piers were completed and ready for the superstructure by 1871.

It was in the superstructure that Eads, despite his lack of formal engineering training, excelled. Andrew Carnegie watched with interest, calculating the gain to his Keystone Bridge Company if it could land the contract to supply Eads' steel. What Carnegie could not calculate was Eads' exacting standards, which ultimately led to a revolution in steel-manufacturing standards. Keystone had been prepared to supply iron for the St. Louis project, but Eads insisted upon high-quality steel. Under his direction, Henry Flad had designed a machine to measure and test the dimension and tensile strength of all the steel members shipped from Keystone's foundries and rolling mills.

Flad routinely rejected pieces that failed to meet his exacting standards. Eads had designed his bridge to last, and he intended that the genius of his design would be matched by the quality of its construction. He developed chrome-alloy steel of a higher quality than the carbon steel typically supplied but only shared his specifications and requirements, not his recipe, with manufacturers.

At the beginning of the project, Carnegie had bought stock in the bridge, but he grew angry at Eads' cost to his company in returned goods and sold his shares in protest. Eads maintained his standards, and engineers watching the construction progress came to agree with him. Carnegie began producing high-tensile steel in addition to iron. If the bridge's engineer and his construction methods changed the engineering and steel-manufacturing world, the bridge itself revolutionized St. Louis, becoming an elegant symbol of the city's optimism, verve and financial acumen when it opened with great fanfare on Independence Day, 1874.

The entire city turned out to see the bridge and watch the triumphant parade in honor of the birth of the nation, St. Louis' rise and prominence, and the bridge itself. Gun salutes were fired throughout the day and numerous speeches delivered in praise of the endurance, strength and beauty of the bridge, and by extension, the city. Within a year, however, the bridge company was bankrupt, a victim of the panic of 1873. Unable to pay construction costs that overran initial estimates by at least 50 percent, the company that had started an engineering revolution now began a financial revolution. Debt-ridden

Construction of the innovative Eads Bridge was both rapid and difficult.
From a stereograph by Robert Benecke, 1873 The St. Louis Mercantile Library at the University of Missouri-St. Louis

investors turned to New York's Jay Gould to rescue them. In defense, local railroads joined to form the Terminal Railroad Association, which leased the bridge and its adjacent tunnel in perpetuity. The bridge was St. Louis, physically and symbolically, and St. Louis interests were determined to control it.

The railroads that ran over the bridge were many: the Missouri Pacific, the Wabash, the Ohio and Mississippi all used the bridge to connect eastern and western markets. The Union Pacific Railroad's Eastern Division president, John D. Perry, was headquartered at St. Louis. In 1867 the Union Pacific was lobbying for a southern route to the Pacific, which would reach from St. Louis across Kansas to Denver to end at San Francisco and link the Missouri River and the Pacific Ocean. The Union Pacific commissioned Alexander Gardner to accompany surveyors and photograph the southern route. He compiled images of St. Louis in 1867, the same year that bridge construction began. Ultimately, the northern route through Nebraska prevailed; the line that ran from St. Louis to Denver was the Kansas-Pacific.

Robert Benecke photographed St. Louis in 1867, creating a panoramic image of the city as she stretched north and south along the riverfront, steamboats clustered at her wharves and warehouses cramming the narrow streets of the levee. Benecke captured the city before the bridge and continued his chronicles with a series of stereographs documenting bridge construction.

After completion he again photographed the levee, with the happy chaos
of river shipping signaling prosperity
augmented but not threatened by the
elegant but sturdy bridge stretching across
the background. A panoramic view of the
bridge and the river graced the title page of
Compton and Company's publication of
Camille Dry's *Pictorial St. Louis: A*
Topographical Survey Drawn in Perspective
A.D. 1875, a large-folio book collecting
hundreds of pages of bird's eye views of the
entire city. Page by page the book documented a thriving metropolis, singling out
factories, lumberyards, department stores
and breweries in an impressive catalogue of
Gilded Age booming industries.

All along the waterfront, businesses
thrived. Local companies adapted to the

postwar economy and the railroads with innovations. The St.
Louis Compress Company,
formed in 1873, was the
largest compress plant in the
world. Using hydraulic and
steam presses, the company
flattened 500-pound bales of
cotton to nine-inch slabs,
which could be loaded onto a
railroad car 50 at a time. With
compressed cotton cancelling
the bulk factor, steamboats
no longer had the edge over
railroads in shipping cotton
bales. St. Louis used this
edge and strong rail con-
nections to New York and
New England to establish

new trading partners in the textile mills of New Hampshire, Massachusetts and Rhode Island. By 1880, St. Louis trailed only New Orleans and Savannah as a national cotton market.

While new industries were born, others adapted and expanded. Along the riverfront and west toward the city limits, St. Louis' industries were modernizing. Brickyards, common in South St. Louis, turned from hand molding to machine techniques in the 1870s. Machine-made bricks were pressed in steel molds by hydraulic rams, making cheaper, denser, more uniform bricks that were also more weather-resistant. These advances in brick making created a national demand.

The Hydraulic Press Brick Company, located near Manchester Avenue and River Des Peres, was the largest American supplier of bricks and burned more than 10 railroad cars of coal a day to fire its kilns. St. Louis-made terra-cotta ornaments and fire clay products for industrial and construction uses were also in high demand

St. Louis manufacturers used new hydraulic presses to make more uniform bricks and became national suppliers. *Cheltenham Brick Works is seen in this wood engraving, 1879. The St. Louis Mercantile Library at the University of Missouri-St. Louis*

nationwide. Brewers also created a national market for St. Louis' products. Anheuser-Busch occupied a large brick complex in South St. Louis, with property stretching from the river to the top of the bluff and from south of Arsenal Street north for several city blocks.

Long a producer of aged German-style lager beer, the company, under Adolphus Busch, introduced a new, light-bodied beer in 1876. Budweiser was marketed nationally and designed to appeal to a multitude of

Hard-nosed principles of efficiency were the foundation for the imaginative and elegant department stores that tempted women with a lush variety of goods. These same principles produced the abundant and whimsical advertising cards of the day that with witty or sentimental scenes, often in collectible series, touted the benefits and necessities of the maker's products. Advertising cards sold soap, sewing machines, shoes, canned beef, clothing and cotton threads. They permeated the culture and created memorable sales images that worked. This was the face the public saw, which masked the infrastructure of modernization that made the products available.

Changes in marketing were paralleled by changes in production methods, and if the marketing images affected people, so did the production methods. While workers benefited from industrialization's ability to make goods more affordable, they also suffered from the methods. The most effective form of protest was the strike, which had been used nationally since the 1820s to protest wage cuts and speed-ups in the textile plants of New England.

palates. The great changes were not so much in product manufacturing as in marketing and distribution. Anheuser-Busch's Budweiser was still beer; the difference now was that New Yorkers could drink St. Louis-made beer shipped east by rail, with little cost difference between the local and the national.

The Meyer Drug Company supplied regional pharmacists and encouraged their professional development so they could keep pace with advances in the drugs available. Pharmacists could better appreciate Meyer's products, and the firm became the nation's largest drug company. Brown-Bryan, the precursor to Brown Shoe Company, was nationally advertised; shoes made in St. Louis were shipped by rail across the country. Brown-Bryan was able to undersell eastern manufacturers in the work-shoe market through the application of modern manufacturing techniques in their new, larger plants.

St. Louis manufacturers applied the principles of rational management, national marketing and saturation advertising to establish strong product positions across the country. Similar principles were applied to retailing, and proprietors like William Barr modified their establishments or moved to newly designed facilities to take advantage of streamlined processes for the movement of goods and information. Barr built a new department store in 1878 complete with electric lighting, telephones, steam elevators, tea-rooms and illustrated fashion catalogs — all designed to entice and impress the female customers to whom the store catered.

In St. Louis, carpenters, tinners and other craftsmen had organized unions in the 1830s; like unions across the country, the St. Louisans' rallying points were the 10-hour workday and stable wages. Unions waxed and waned with immigration, as cheap labor both weakened their positions and bolstered their mission. The Gilded Age, with successive depressions, was a period of deflation. When wages dropped faster than the cost of living, many workers were forced into penurious existences that increased the appeal of unions. St. Louis workers were primarily employed in small craft shops despite the growth of industrial complexes like the breweries and shoe factories. These workers favored exclusive craft unions over the more open Knights of Labor. Strikes were common, but usually small and short-lived, until the 1877 General Strike.

The nation's first General Strike happened in St. Louis, precipitated by a national railroad strike. It was something of an anomaly and may have been the result of the well-timed political machinations by the city's Workingmen's Party, a satellite organization of the Marxist First International Workingmen's Association.

With no more than 1,000 members, the St. Louis branch was predominantly German speaking and usually committed itself to acts no more radical than pamphleteering and refusing to march in Independence Day parades. The Railroad Strike of July 1877 presented an unusual opportunity, and the Workingmen's Party seized it. Just across the river in East St. Louis, on Sunday, July 22, 1877, rail traffic had halted and stockyard and meatpacking workers had taken up the strike, walking out in sympathy with the freight workers. News of the strike reached St. Louis, and on Monday, a mass meeting was held in downtown St. Louis. The crowd, estimated at 8,000-10,000 people, filled the site of the old Lucas Market on Twelfth Street between Olive and Chestnut.

Over the following days, workers in various industries walked off the job to demand an eight-hour day and the end of child labor. In response, factory owners and other well-to-do citizens organized a Committee of Public Safety that was in effect a citizen's militia. By Friday, the militia was backed by federal troops from Fort Leavenworth and the strikers had lost general support. Late that afternoon strikers were arrested in their headquarters in Schuler's Hall on Biddle Street. Workers would not see an eight-hour day or an end to child labor for some time, but small gains were made. As a result of the strike, Missouri established a State Bureau of Labor Statistics in 1879, and the following year saw proposals to build the first public baths in St. Louis. Labor unrest resonated at low volumes for years, and subsequent depressions would have their protests. Over the years, gains of various sorts were made and lost through workers' efforts at reform and change through protest.

The Gilded Age, with intensified urbanization and industrialization, and a surge in the immigrant population, brought structured reform and intensified infrastructure to St. Louis. The two were not entirely distinct, as reformers sought to improve city life through water quality, public transportation and open space. As politicians debated the city limit, they welcomed generous land grants and purchases that expanded the city's area and provided much-needed green space for her citizens.

Henry Shaw had donated 190 acres in 1868; the land stretched from Grand Avenue west to Kingshighway Boulevard between Arsenal and Magnolia streets. Shaw named the expanse Tower Grove Park and agreed to plant 15,000 trees, plants and shrubs, while the city contributed $360,000 for park improvements. Shaw's privately maintained gardens were adjacent to the park, which he named Tower Grove. During his lifetime his gardens were open to the public free of charge, which greatly expanded the appeal of Tower Grove Park next door. Farther north and stretching west from Kingshighway to Skinker Road was Forest Park, almost 1,300 acres bounded on the north by Olive Street Road and undeveloped land on the south.

The park was purchased by the city after legislative authorization, though this was challenged by several taxpayers' groups unwilling to assume the immediate debt and long-term maintenance of such a large undertaking. While Forest Park added substantial recreational green space to the city's area, in 1876 it was a 40-minute carriage ride from downtown, placing it out of reach of most of the city's residents.

The original design for the park, which was heavily wooded when it was acquired, emphasized scenic plantings suitable for passive recreation. Carriage drives provided paths to enjoy the changing views, and, along with a hippodrome for horse racing, served to benefit wealthy residents and not the city's poor. A streetcar line was added in 1885, finally making the park

William Barr Dry Goods was the city's first true department store, housing thousands of products under one roof, c. 1890.
The St. Louis Mercantile Library at the University of Missouri-St. Louis

accessible to almost all residents. Active recreational areas were added, too, as progressive reformers stressed the link between healthy bodies and healthy minds. In the 1890s, bicycle paths provided venues for the new craze made easier with the introduction of the safety bike, while tennis courts were added for that newly popular sport. Baseball diamonds followed as the game spread in popularity and practice. Forest Park became the city's pre-eminent park, the crowning emerald jewel in her infrastructure.

Less glamorous, but just as necessary, were the paving and sewer improvements that brought order to city streets and lessened the risk of disease. Throughout the 1840s and 1850s, drainage had been an important topic in circles of leadership. After the cholera epidemic of 1849, sewage was taken seriously, and an ordinance providing a "General System of Sewage" was passed in 1850. Drainage progressed on Chouteau's Pond, the source of much of the dangerous run-offs and wastes that polluted the city's water supply and streets, but storm water could still flood the area and send filthy water pouring through downtown streets.

It was clear to city engineers that a sewer was required to drain the Mill Creek Valley. They planned the Mill Creek Sewer, a sewer 21 feet high and 13 feet wide that would run from the Mississippi River five miles west to Vandeventer Avenue. The project, begun in 1857, eventually cost St. Louis taxpayers $3 million by the time

it was completed in 1889. In addition to the Mill Creek Sewer, main sewers ran along the ridgelines of the city, using natural runoff patterns and gravity to carry excess water to the Mississippi in orderly, covered channels.

Developers raced west of sewers, constructing homes and waste sewers before the city's main sewers reached the neighborhood. Property taxes did not always keep pace with the high cost of sewer construction, and the city struggled until the turn of the century when the World's Fair brought sufficient funds and focus to the project. Fresh water supplies, brought by separate pipes and systems, had been a municipal concern for at least as long as the sewers. St. Louis drinking water came from the Mississippi River well north of the Mill Creek Sewer but was rarely clear, given the strong currents, fluctuating levels and muddy bottom of both the Mississippi and Missouri rivers.

After the Civil War, city engineers addressed the city's growing needs with the Bissell Point pumping station, which incorporated mud-settling basins designed to clarify water drawn from the river. Powerful steam-driven pumps sent the water from the settling basins uphill to the water tower on North Grand Avenue. Designed in 1871 by George I. Barnett, the city's premier architect, the gigantic Corinthian column acted to moderate the surges from the Bissell Point station. The column held water 175 feet above the street to create a head of pressure that pushed water uphill to the Compton Heights reservoir on Grand Avenue in South St. Louis.

Schnaider's Beer Garden photographed by Robert Benecke, 1880
The St. Louis Mercantile Library at the University of Missouri-St. Louis

From the reservoir, water flowed into a series of ever-smaller pipes until it reached customers in their homes. For a few years after the construction of the Bissell Point Station, city water ran clear, shocking some old-time residents but delighting most. The settling basins could not keep pace with demand as the city grew, and the water was soon muddy again and flowed with only a weak pressure. Engineers built a second water tower on Bissell Street near the North Grand Tower, alleviating the problem for a short time. Not until the World's Fair was planned could city politicians appropriate the funds needed to construct a water plant

German Beer Garden,
wood engraving from
Every Saturday
magazine, October 1871
*The St. Louis Mercantile
Library at the University
of Missouri-St. Louis*

with a filtration system and pumping capacity adequate for the growing city.

As St. Louis' physical infrastructure grew, so did the social infrastructure of informal associations and formal organizations. These organizations were strictly segregated by gender so that women and men moved in separate spheres. Fraternal organizations had auxiliaries for women, but men and women typically followed separate social paths. By 1880 the *St. Louis City Directory* listed 41 Masonic organizations alone, including the African American Prince Hall Lodge.

Many other organizations were mutual-benefit societies founded to provide insurance to their members, as much as social entertainment. These groups provided disability and death benefits from their subscriptions and dues and were often the only safety net many industrial workers had. The city's German population had a large network of social clubs tailored to specific interests. The *Turnverein* mixed physical fitness with somewhat radical politics, while the *Frei Gemeinde-Verein* drew many members who had fought in the failed revolutions of 1848. Other groups, like the *Sangeverein*, concentrated on retaining cultural memory in a new country. They celebrated the music and culture of more than 35 separate groups reflecting the varied backgrounds of the German population in St. Louis.

The Turnverein was perhaps the most popular, offering a wide variety of classes and programs for all ages. Although primarily focused on gymnastics, the Turners also advocated social and political reforms, including the end of child labor. Turner halls became community centers; their members were so populous and influential that they were able to convince the St. Louis Public Schools to add physical education to the curriculum in the 1880s.

By far the most socially prominent and important organization was the Mystic Order of the Veiled Prophet of the Enchanted Realm. Founded in March 1878, the Veiled Prophet solicited 20 prominent St. Louis businessmen to found an organization dedicated to promoting the interests of St. Louis. The fledgling organization limited its membership to 200, with a membership fee that increased from $25 to $100 within a few months.

Members included men born in St. Louis and elsewhere, but most were merchants and all were well to do; some were lawyers, real-estate agents or capitalists, as stock traders were known. They planned to launch a Mardi Gras-like parade in conjunction with the city's Agricultural and Mechanical Fair held every year in October. Members intended to create a grand spectacle for their first outing in 1878; they hoped to impress the farmers and traders who visited the fair with positive

The Veiled Prophet debutantes' ball became the most important
event of the social season.
Lithograph, October 1891
The St. Louis Mercantile Library at the University of Missouri-St. Louis

visions of a happy and unified St. Louis, especially after the city's infamous General Strike of 1877.

The Veiled Prophet planners conceived a complex event that included a parade culminating in the crowning of the Veiled Prophet before an audience of thousands. The first Prophet crowned "King of St. Louis" was Police Commissioner John G. Priest, a choice undoubtedly made to resonate with the strikers of the previous year. The Veiled Prophet's celebrations grew to include a ball, which became the pinnacle of the social calendar and the highlight of the debutante season.

Although social expectations and pressures limited women's roles in Gilded Age St. Louis, many women were interested in roles that brought them outside the home and into the public sphere. For middle-class women, the expectation was that the home was their proper sphere where they cultivated a refuge from the increasingly turbulent industrial city and raised children to exacting moral standards. This was not every woman's reality — some women had to work, and some were simply too poor to pursue the ideals published in women's magazines and books.

Most working women were employed as domestic servants or laundresses, although some worked in industrial jobs. A smaller percentage worked as teachers, secretaries or shop clerks. Professional women and nurses accounted for the smallest numbers of working women, despite recent strides in women's education.

In St. Louis, the most politically active women joined the Woman Suffrage Association of Missouri, founded in 1867 at a meeting in St. Louis Mercantile Library. Most of the founding women had been active in the Ladies' Union Aid Society during the Civil War, an experience that taught them the power of organized action. The Woman Suffrage Association argued that the 14th Amendment, which granted former slaves citizenship, gave all United States citizens, male and female, the right to vote. This argument was the focus of petitions drafted by Virginia and

The Veiled Prophet was one of the most important and influential groups in St. Louis, and the Veiled Prophet parade and fireworks provided much excitement.
Wood engraving, 1882
The St. Louis Mercantile Library at the University of Missouri-St. Louis

The Veiled Prophet parade featured Mardi Gras-like floats and displays.
Wood engraving from Frank Leslie's Illustrated News, 1882
The St. Louis Mercantile Library at the University of Missouri-St. Louis

Francis Minor that were presented to the Missouri Legislature, argued before Missouri courts, and eventually pled before the U.S. Supreme Court.

The Minors argued that the 14th Amendment guaranteed that no U.S. citizen should be subject to state laws that abridged the privileges of citizenship. Since women were citizens and subject to the responsibilities of citizenship in paying taxes, the Minors reasoned that they should also exercise the rights of citizenship, namely suffrage. These and other arguments were placed before a national suffrage convention held in St. Louis in October 1869, attended by such suffrage movement luminaries as Susan B. Anthony and Julia Ward Howe. While the petition and principles were reprinted in *The Revolution*, the suffrage movement's newspaper and distributed to every member of congress, state and federal legislatures refused to act.

Frustrated, the Minors pursued litigation: in 1872 Mrs. Minor attempted to register to vote in her St. Louis district, asserting that she was "a native-born, free white citizen of the United States and the State of Missouri." As expected, the district registrar, Reese Happersett, refused her attempt and the Minors sued him in St. Louis County Circuit Court. As the case wound through the court system and up to the Missouri Supreme Court, arguments were made on both sides of the 14th Amendment, with the courts declaring that the Amendment was passed only to protect former slaves from "unfriendly legislation." When the U.S. Supreme Court delivered the final opinion in 1875, the Minors' arguments were rejected. The Court declared, "The Constitution citizenship does not confer the right of suffrage upon anyone." The Minors were defeated, and suffragists nationwide dropped the use of litigation as a tactic.

The Minors had ignored the 15th Amendment, considering that it merely confirmed the right of suffrage assumed by the slaves freed and made citizens under the 14th Amendment. Whatever their opinion on the matter, newly freed slaves were the subject of similar suffrage suits and battles. The 1865 Missouri Constitutional Convention had issued the state's emancipation ordinance without granting the full rights of citizenship.

The 14th Amendment prohibited the restriction of rights based on color, legalized state-funded schools for African Americans, and guaranteed the right to own property and testify against whites. These provisions directly responded to the pre-Civil War laws that prohibited slaves from learning to read and write, owning property and testifying against whites in court. But the Amendment stopped short of granting full suffrage to the former slaves and freedmen. For some, denying African American men the right to vote denied them their manhood and their citizenship; the question was whether they would be equated with women, incapable of responsible voting, or if African American men could really be men, equal to whites.

The arguments for full citizenship and suffrage for freed slaves followed some of the same logic as the arguments for women's suffrage. Arguments were made that military service during the Civil War proved the African American commitment to American ideals of citizenship and service and that "taxation without representation" was unjust. Only a very small number of politicians supported unrestricted African American male suffrage in the immediate postwar years; one of the leaders, though, was Missouri senator B. Gratz Brown.

Based on his pre-war Free Soil stance, Brown saw full suffrage as necessary to prevent the extension of a racial caste system, which would inhibit Missouri's economic growth. He was on dangerous ground when it came to assembling allies; some free soilers, while admitting that slavery was an impediment to progress, also despised African Americans and were loathe to associate with them. Even Brown's longtime associate, Frank P. Blair, was convinced of the dangers of association with African Americans. These fears fueled the debate over suffrage, as politicians and their supporters confronted the difference between political ideals and practical realities. Anti-Brown newspapers argued that full enfranchisement led down a path to "Negro equality, Negro intermarriage, Negro school teachers for children, Negro constables, Negro judges and juries, Negro legislators."

Empowering African Americans with full voting rights and full citizenship endowed them with membership in the community and made them an undeniable part of the national identity. A statewide referendum granting full suffrage to African Americans failed the 1868 elections; free soilers and abolitionists could not all reconcile themselves to voting for equality with the men they had labored hard to free. Suffrage for former slaves in St. Louis and Missouri would not come until the 1870 passage of the 15th Amendment to the United States Constitution.

The 15th Amendment did have an effect on equality, if only at election time, as one St. Louis African American observed in 1870. "Streetcar conductors cannot tell if you are black or white. I take a look in my glass sometimes to see if by some hocus pocus I have turned white, but it gives back the same old face, and tells me I am a citizen and not chattel now." This freedom and equality was not universal; segregation remained in place, but there were no poll taxes nor grandfather clauses to prevent St. Louis' African American community from participating in elections. Full equality for African Americans and an end to segregation in parks and schools would remain fighting points for St. Louis' black and white citizens for decades to come.

Ironically, six years after the 15th Amendment was ratified, St. Louis embarked upon an act of segregation that would resonate for over a century and is debated even today. In 1875 a Missouri constitutional convention approved the separation of the city from the county, and the establishment of home rule in the city. The relationship between city and county had been contested for years before the legal separation and led directly to the split.

One of the earliest arguments for separation was made in 1843 when St. Louis citizens petitioned the Missouri General Assembly to request division from the county. In its response, the Legislature called an advisory referendum, on which only residents of St. Louis County could vote. With little interest in the matter at the time, voters turned down the proposal. As the population of the city increased rapidly, at a far greater rate than the county, the issue intensified for city residents.

The immediate issue was taxation. In 1858, as the city enacted taxes to cover the costs of municipal improvements to sewers, water supplies and streets, the county court levied a special tax to cover its own debt. Outraged city voters and politicians complained loudly to Jefferson City and gained greater city representation on the renamed county commission. The two sides could not be reconciled, though, and the city chafed under the county's rural legislature. Bitterness increased throughout the Civil War, as the demands of refugees and martial law taxed municipal resources.

The heart of the issue was St. Louis' quest for home rule and the desire for freedom from the cumbersome process of submitting charter amendment to the General Assembly for approval. The sophisticated politicians and leaders of the city scorned the rural bumpkins of the county and saw the county as an unwieldy tax burden and the source of inefficient practices. Property tax assessments were duplicated for city and county until consolidated under county authority after protest by St. Louis Mayor Daniel G. Taylor in 1862. Appropriations for rural projects seemed too high to city officials, who accused county officials of graft at the expense of city residents. The debate was fierce and reached a high point of violence when Joseph Pulitzer, acting as both state legislator from St. Louis and *Westliche Poste* reporter, shot Captain Augustine Edward in the leg during an altercation over Pulitzer's printed allegations of Edward's lobbying activities as a county official.

Cooler heads prevailed as officials began studying several options. Some favored merging the city and county into one corporate entity to eliminate duplication of tax assessment and overlaps of political and legal jurisdictions. This plan offered a simplicity and fairness that editorialists considered worthy of support. The draft reached the Missouri Legislature in 1871, and while it was passed in the Lower House, it never reached the Senate. This effectively ended the consolidation movement.

Reorganization of the county government was one alternative, but by 1871 this tactic held little appeal after the failures of preceding decades. Separation it would be, and supporters stood firm as newspapers editorialized "a government would then be got rid of which costs an immense amount of money and contributes nothing to the welfare and prosperity of the city. Of every five dollars raised by the county four dollars is contributed by the citizens of St. Louis, and nothing ever comes back." This was the attitude that forced the issue at the 1875 constitutional convention, which was considering the question of home rule for St. Louis. Consolidation was discussed, persuasively, and a provision was adopted but not implemented; a majority of the delegates favored separation and would not be moved.

Separation meant complicated negotiations over boundaries, properties and debt. Despite the potential for disagreement, on July 30, 1875, the convention voted overwhelmingly to approve the separation of St. Louis City and County. The authorizing legislation assured the city full possession of Tower Grove and Forest Parks; city officials who had but lately approved the purchase of the Forest Park tract would not have sanctioned their loss. The entire park tax would become the city's responsibility; in exchange for all the county buildings within the city limits that reverted to the city, St. Louis City was required to assume the county's debt.

On August 22, 1876, the separation scheme was put to all voters in the county, and while early returns showed the proposal had passed, final counts, based upon heavy rural opposition, defeated it. Angry supporters charged county election officials with fraud and following an investigation and recount, both separation and city charter were declared to have legally won the vote. By October these provisions were in effect, and the rural-urban squabbles of the city's first half-century were thought to be over.

Essentially, rural territory had been included within the city limits to allow for expansion. There was concern that even these "rural" areas would constitute a tax drain on the city, failing to provide a return on the municipal improvements they would require. Despite a jump in overall area from almost 18 square miles to more than 61 square miles, the city soon grew to bulge against her boundaries. No one could have anticipated this growth, or the complex inter-relations between the populations, businesses and schools of the city and county, but still, no provisions for altering the standards of separation existed.

St. Louis railroads brought suburban residents to the city to work, but the city lost the revenue of commuters' property taxes to the county. In the same way the city would lose businesses to the county in the 20th century, as mergers created the need for expanded headquarters for which downtown had no room. Ultimately, the city-county split was a shortsighted solution to the urban-rural debates and the city's resentment of the corrupt county court system of the time.

St. Louis City could hardly be blamed for resentment of the county; the city had experienced a building boom that would continue until the Depression. Downtown buildings grew in height and mass, decorated with terra cotta ornaments derived from organic forms in the style of the beaux-arts. The city and county found a point of unifying pride in the new Union Station, built to replace the small station at Market and Twelfth streets. In 1891 Theodore Link's design for the new Union Station was accepted by the Terminal Railroad Association, and construction began on what would become the multi-block complex of passenger station, hotel and terminal. It stretched west on Market from Eighteenth to Twentieth streets, with 10 acres of train yards spreading south into the Mill Creek Valley.

Link's building, with a façade of gray Indiana marble and a gray Spanish tile roof, was the best example of

ceiling, multi-level perimeter and fanciful ends incorporating bas-relief female figures holding glass globes, glittered with the electric promise of the future.

Skeptics called the station overbuilt, but even the original grandiose scale required expansion by 1930. Two years after the station was built, 19 miles of track in the yard handled 950 passenger cars on an average day, with more than 1,500 daily ticket sales. Even with its enormous capacities, Union Station was only a passenger station; the sheer volume of rail traffic in St. Louis at the turn of the century required separate freight and passenger terminals.

Union Station's striking architecture was a landmark for travelers and residents alike. This view is from Eighteenth and Market Streets, c. 1950.
The St. Louis Mercantile Library at the University of Missouri-St. Louis

the Romanesque style of Henry Hobson Richardson in St. Louis at the time. A clock tower reached up to the sky from the Eighteenth Street end of the station, reminiscent of a castle tower, while the deep-silled windows that punctured the façades heightened the castle reference. Union Station was the gate to the city, the monumental entrance that impressed travelers outside and in. The station's interiors were decorated with murals, mosaics and bas-relief figures depicting the 22 railroads arriving daily. The Grand Hall on the second floor, with its barrel-vaulted

In 1891 Samuel Cupples with Robert S. Brookings built the Cupples Station complex, a multi-block set of seven-story buildings on 30 acres with more than one million square feet of warehouse space. Between Seventh and Eleventh, Spruce and Poplar streets, the Cupples Station Warehouses housed wholesale goods of the Moll Grocery store, the largest distributor in St. Louis, with outlets in five states, as well as national concerns like the Western Tea and Spice Company. Most of the city's heavy wholesale trade passed through Cupples Station, consolidating facilities, reducing drayage costs, and decreasing shipping time. Goods could be off-loaded from railcars for processing and shipped back out again within the limits of the complex, increasing suppliers' control over their goods at an economy of cost.

Union Station and the Cupples Station Warehouses were part of a larger building boom in St. Louis, best symbolized by her finest skyscraper, Louis Sullivan's Wainwright Building. Built in 1891, the Wainwright stands as Sullivan's — and St. Louis' — first skyscraper. Designed by the Chicago firm of Adler and Sullivan with local architect Charles Ramsey for St. Louis brewer Ellis Wainwright, the 10-story office building was the architectural firm's first use of a steel and iron skeleton covered by a masonry skin, foreshadowing the "curtain wall" construction of the mid-20th century. As the building's advertising brochure stated, "the columns are of extra heavy wrought steel, and the floor beams are of extra size, thus giving the greatest amount of strength and durability."

The Wainwright, at Seventh and Chestnut streets, was a harmony of form, material and function. With a

super-columnated façade, rhythmic piers, and spandrels decorated with floral tracery, it was an elegant addition to the city, efficient and beautiful at the same time, glowing in rosy hues of pink granite, brick and sandstone. Her lower floors housed barbershops and restaurants, retail establishments meant to serve the tenants who were offered rental offices of varying size and status. The large plate glass windows of the street level tempted passers-by with views of the goods and services for sale, while lobby entrances, wrapped with floral tracery and bas-relief ornamentation endowed a sense of wonder and a heightened purpose upon the tenants and their clientele. From the cornice to the latch plates, Sullivan's Wainwright Building was a testament to a new age of architectural design, realizing the principles of commodity, firmness and delight in steel and stone.

The Title Guaranty Building, designed by local architects Eames and Young, joined the Wainwright Building in 1898, across the street at 706 Chestnut. Three stories taller, the Title Guaranty echoed the Wainright's elegant columnated façade and circular attic windows, with Roman arches worked into the terra cotta of the attic floor and leafy terra cotta ornamentation at the street level. Taller and sparer than its neighbor, the Title Guaranty achieved a greater affinity to the modern skyscraper, while sacrificing the elegant massing of Sullivan's building. St. Louis had grown up, with a downtown office-building boom smaller than Chicago's, but substantial nonetheless.

Architecture and growth, beauty and business all combined to make St. Louis the fourth city in the United States after New York, Chicago and Philadelphia. She was poised for a new era, ready to move from national to international importance. New York had the World's Fair and Crystal Palace in 1853, Philadelphia hosted the Centennial Exposition in 1876, and Chicago held the World's Columbian Exposition in 1893. St. Louis had bid for the 1893 World's Fair and lost, but she was ready again by the century's end with proposals for the Louisiana Purchase Exposition. Intended to commemorate the 100-year anniversary of the Louisiana Purchase, the 1904 World's Fair celebrated America's ingenuity and promise along with her history. For St. Louis, the fair was a chance to show just how far she had come — after a few changes were made.

Local architects Eames and Young built the Title Guaranty Building
at Seventh and Chestnut to complement its neighbor, the graceful
Wainwright Building. Title Guaranty or Lincoln Trust Building, 1944
The St. Louis Mercantile Library at the University of Missouri-St. Louis

five

1900-1927

A City Worth Seeing:
THE WORLD COMES TO ST. LOUIS

In 1900, St. Louis stood poised for the new century, ready to transform herself into a suitable hostess for the world. She had a thriving business community, a well-built and beautiful downtown, and a handsome park system. But she also had deep internal conflicts, a reputation for corruption, and a crying need for improved and expanded infrastructure. All of these problems would be addressed before the fair opened in 1904. Shortly after reform Mayor Rolla Wells was elected in 1900, he faced the first of his challenges.

The Streetcar Strike of 1900 was one of the longest and most disruptive strikes in St. Louis, but it also unified the city in unexpected ways. Its roots were in the Missouri legislature's decision to permit municipal street railways to acquire, either by purchase or lease, another street railway's property, effectively opening the door to the monopolization of the streetcar system.

In St. Louis, the United Railways Company moved to acquire all the rail lines, property and franchises of every railroad system in St. Louis except for the Suburban Street Railway Company and then operated the new, expanded company as the St. Louis Transit Company. Riders in St. Louis were already unhappy with the casual and careless service provided by

The Slope of Art Hill, Festival Hall and W. Pavilion are on the left; the machinery building is at right.
Underwood & Underwood, c 1904, St. Louis Public Library, Louisiana Purchase Exposition collection, Special Collections

many of the independent street railways, and news of the conglomerate increased their complaints. Workers, afraid of the huge corporation, acted to protect themselves through unionization, organizing and campaigning to increase membership in the Amalgamated Associate of Street Railways Employees of America, Local 131.

The management of the St. Louis Transit Company resisted employees' efforts to unionize, rejecting the workers' demands for union recognition, a 10-hour day and a standard wage structure. In March 1900, though, the company agreed to recognize the union in an attempt to prevent an immediate strike, but by late April, relationships between the union and both the Suburban and St. Louis Railway Companies had deteriorated to a critical point.

On April 29, workers walked out at the Suburban Street Railway Company in protest over union recognition; police commissioner Harry Hawes set the tone for the strike when he authorized non-striking workers to carry weapons. On May 8 more than 3,000 employees of the St. Louis Transit Company went out on strike, creating havoc in downtown St. Louis. Newspaper commentators declared that the strikes were a question of "unionism, pure and simple." City residents were frightened by the consolidation of the streetcar lines, and enraged by eroding service, they strongly supported the strikers. Just one day after the strike, citizens could be seen wearing buttons pledging their commitment to "Walk until the strike is

settled." Despite strikers' fears, many citizens supported the strike. William Marion Reedy noted in the May 17 edition of *The Mirror* that "however the leading businessmen may feel about the strike, the sentiment of the greater number of the people, who are not leading businessmen, is with the strike."

Reedy's audience was overwhelmingly educated and affluent, and despite his reputation for muckraking, he was no rabble-rouser. Indeed, in this strike, the rabble roused itself: men and women alike turned out to harass the conductors and motormen still running cars. The *Post-Dispatch* reported that one woman tried to strike a motorman with a dead frog tied to a string. This level of chaos continued for a short time, but by late June the strike was weakening as donations to the strike fund failed to meet even subsistence level needs for the workers. The boycott, however, remained firmly in place. A settlement was reached on July 2 only to be broken within the week, renewing both the strike and the boycott. Neither would finally end until September 1900. The streetcar companies had promised that consolidation would improve service, ease congestion and increase efficiency, but when these promises failed to materialize, citizens not only complained but also took action. The poor service offered by the St. Louis Transit Company united ordinary citizens with the strikers, and investigations by the mayor's office supported their complaints. Mayor

Rolla Wells himself stood on street corners to witness the crowds of would-be-riders left standing in the cold as the streetcars raced to keep their schedule. Wells was a reformer, and it was his steady guidance that led the city to make the improvements necessary to support the World's Fair.

As mayor, Rolla Wells recognized the need for change in the city as well as the powerful ability of her citizens to unite around critical issues. Looking forward to the promise of the World's Fair and determined to disprove Lincoln Steffens' unflattering portrait of St. Louis in *The Shame of the Cities*, Wells systematically began to address the city's needs. He initiated a system of business management for the city that promised efficiency and greater revenues, an improved water supply and filtration system, reliable municipal services in street lighting and garbage collection, and a wide-ranging plan for civic improvements and beautification to be accomplished in concert with the Civic Improvement League. It was an impressive agenda, and Wells, true to his campaign platform of reform, delivered most of his promises.

An improved water supply was deemed one of the most urgent projects needed to prepare for the World's Fair. Demand had long outstripped supply, and clear water was almost unknown in the city. After more than doubling in size with the 1876 city-county split, the city's demand for water rapidly outstripped the capacity of the Bissell's Point Waterworks. The waterworks had seemed adequate when operation began in 1872, but no one had anticipated the sudden gain in area four years later. Not only did the waterworks fail to maintain a supply of clear water, but the reservoirs were also pumped dry on heavy-demand days. Money to construct the Chain of Rocks plant was authorized in 1886, and in 1894, when the plant began operating, the intake tower stationed in mid-river channeled water into the settling basins where simple gravity filtered the muddy water. The supply and clarity were adequate for almost a year, but then the water quickly reverted to its customary murkiness.

Water and health commissioners maintained an almost ironic detachment regarding the water, which began to acquire the trappings of mythology. In 1888 an eel was supposedly found in a downtown sink. Later, the water commissioner reported that marine life in the Bissell's Point settling basins improved, rather than corrupted, the water quality. As plans for the World's Fair proceeded and decorative waterfalls were planned as a central attraction, fair directors feared that cascades of thick, muddy river water would make a mockery of not only their planning but also the $10 million investment of city government and citizens.

In June 1901 the Municipal Assembly authorized the appointment of a commission of "three expert hydraulic engineers" to study the problem and prepare a solution. The engineers discovered that Quincy, Illinois, had successfully used ferrous sulfate and calcium carbonate to clear its water. The chemicals were tested on St. Louis' embarrassingly silty water and proved successful. For the first time in decades, city water ran pure and clear. This treatment, along with the increased supply and improved filtration, ensured an ample supply of clean, clear water for citizens and visitors alike.

Mayor Wells had cleaned up city water, and he tackled the question of garbage collection as well. For years the St. Louis Sanitary Company had maintained a "garbage monopoly" with an annual contract worth $65,000. Ed "Boss" Butler, who had a reputation for crookedness, fraud and cronyism, owned the company. Wells vowed to break Butler's hold on the city. He tried and failed to prevent the 1901 renewal of Butler's contract at the incredible yearly fee of $130,000, but he succeeded in 1903. Wells was wealthy enough to purchase the small Chesley Island just down the Mississippi River from the city, and he stocked the island with hogs. Then, in 1903, he gleefully informed Butler that his services were no longer required. The city hauled the garbage to barges and then to Chesley Island where the hogs did the rest. Mayor Wells broke the back of the bribery and graft system of municipal government and defeated its most shameful practitioner, Ed Butler. The city management could now dedicate itself to the production of the World's Fair.

Mayor Rolla Wells applied business principles to city government with positive results, c. 1903. *The Mercantile Library at the University of Missouri St. Louis*

The Louisiana Purchase Exposition had excited St. Louisans hopes for nearly a decade after losing the 1893 World's Columbian Exposition to their hated rival, Chicago. Under the direction of former St. Louis mayor and Missouri governor David R. Francis, the city would realize one of the most successful world's fairs ever held. Francis was a consummate politician and organizer. Under his direction, private subscriptions of $5 million were raised, $4 million in just one night at a mass meeting. The subscriptions were not just donations, as stock in the Louisiana Purchase Exposition Company was issued at $10 dollars a share. The city pledged an additional $5 million dollars, and an equal amount of federal funding was sought and eventually acquired after intense lobbying.

Organizers argued over the location and form of the fair. Pierre Chouteau, a direct descendant of the founding family, proposed a "Museum of American Genius." Chouteau imagined the fair would permanently re-create the original village of St. Louis on the riverfront, with French colonial cabins housing exhibits of the latest inventions. Landowners promoted various sites in Carondelet and O'Fallon Park before the company settled on the western half of the city-owned Forest Park. In addition to the park, the LPE Company leased acreage just west of Skinker Road in St. Louis County. The fairgrounds

occupied more than 1,200 acres in all, substantially more acreage than even the Columbian Exposition. Francis had his land and his financing; he proceeded now to assemble a board of directors to organize the planning and construction of fair buildings and the necessary exhibits. The board leased Washington University's new Cope and Stewardson buildings just west of Skinker Road as its headquarters, since the area around the fair site was largely undeveloped, and they saw no point in wasting money.

The Director of Works and Chief Architect was St. Louis' Isaac Taylor, who hired George Kessler to plan the grounds. In keeping with the city's spirit of reform, Kessler, the mind behind the Kansas City parks and boulevards program, conceived the fair not only as a successful commercial undertaking but a true City Beautiful in miniature. Kessler's approach followed the best city-planning principles of the time and later influenced the development of St. Louis' Civic Improvement League.

For the fairgrounds, Kessler devised a system that followed the natural topography of Forest Park and rejected a strict gridded structure for the plan. Isaac Taylor had decided that the architectural style of the St. Louis Fair would be like that of Chicago's 1893 Fair; the neo-classical beaux-arts style was seen as the most appropriate style to

Kessler's "Main Picture" featured the stylish Festival Hall and sparkling waters of the Cascades. *Gardens of the Cascades*, Keystone View Company, c.1904 *St. Louis Public Library, Louisiana Purchase Exposition collection, Special Collections*

link European cultural traditions with American construction ingenuity. The style gave the fair an air of uniformity and elegance, however conservative or contrived.

The Main Picture, as Kessler called it, was focused on the neoclassical rotunda of Festival Hall, located at the top of Art Hill and flanked by the colonnaded Terrace of States. The Cascades descended the hill in orderly tiers, culminating in the Grand Basin. This decorative waterfall ran crystal clear with "water of diamond transparency," thanks to the new Chain of Rocks treatment plant. Exhibit palaces, neatly categorized and grouped by type, fanned out from this central point.

To the north of Festival Hall were the Palaces of Machinery, Transportation, and Electricity. East from these, in an arc, spread the Palaces of Education, Manufactures, Mines and Metallurgy, and Education. The Palace of Fine Arts, the only building constructed of steel and stone rather than wood and plaster, stood behind Festival Hall. On an axis to the west of the Main Picture were the Palaces of Horticulture and Agriculture, with the monumental Floral Clock running in front. The numbers on the clock's 100-foot diameter dial were floral plantings 15 feet across; every half-hour, a two-and-a-half ton bell struck the time, and an immense hourglass turned over. Scattered throughout the grounds were state buildings, foreign buildings, and the separate Philippine Exhibit. The exhibition palaces and overall scale of the fair celebrated Jefferson's Louisiana Purchase and its central city, St. Louis, in a truly grand style.

President Theodore Roosevelt dedicated the fair on April 30, 1903, in ceremonies that included 12,000 regular and state troops and a dedicatory speech. One year later, David R. Francis opened the fair as he shouted, "Swing open, ye portals. Enter herein, ye sons of men. Learn the lessons here taught and gather inspiration for still greater accomplishment." President Roosevelt tapped a telegraph key in the East Room of the White House, and the fair's machinery was set in motion: the modern era was upon St. Louis, and she was the focus of the world. Forty-three foreign nations constructed buildings for their exhibits, and the third modern-era

Olympics were held at Washington University's Francis Field on the Exposition grounds. The fair was educational in intent, entertaining and uplifting in its realization. Visitors — more than twelve million — came to see the wonders of the machine age and to study the people of the Stone Age.

The St. Louis World's Fair hosted one of the largest "anthropological" exhibits, an effective human zoo displaying Native Americans, African Pygmies, Japanese Ainu and other indigenous peoples to curious fairgoers. One Inuit girl at St. Louis was named Nancy Columbia; she had been born at the Chicago World's Fair while her family was displayed there. Even the defeated Apache leader Geronimo appeared at St. Louis. Native people were arrayed in villages constructed with traditional methods, intended to both educate and validate modern American visitors.

Anthropological displays were a popular feature of early World's Fairs.
"Singwa as a photographer"
Photograph by Jessie Tarbox Beals, Beals album 2, St. Louis Public Library,
Louisiana Purchase Exposition collection, Special Collections

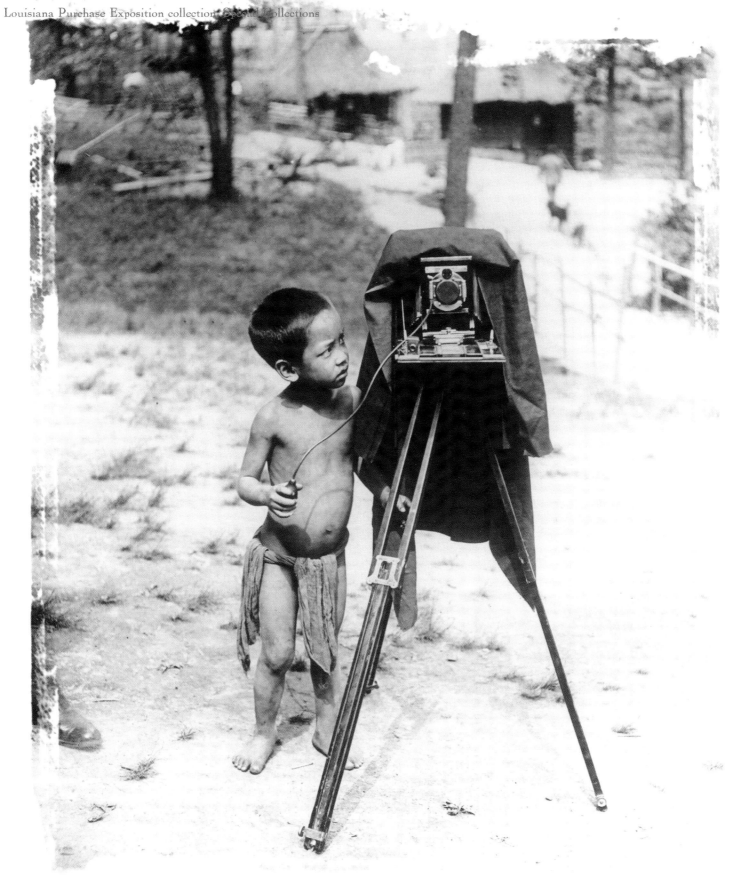

Among the highlights was the Anthropology Department's "Anthropology Days" attraction, intended to answer the question of athletic prowess among the races. In the "Tribal Games," indigenous visitors were asked to compete in classical Olympic events like the shot put, running broad jump and foot races, but American and European athletes were not asked to engage in "primitive" sports. The poor performance of the competitors proved conclusively to James Sullivan, the head of the Department of Physical Culture, that "the savage is not the natural athlete we have been led to believe." Native games were organized on the last day of the anthropological Olympics, and the performances of some of the contestants managed to impress even Sullivan, though he continued to chide the head of the Department of Anthropology, Dr. W. J. McGee, for his support of the "primitive peoples."

The regular Olympic Games were well attended and well covered in the local and national press. Most of the contestants were Americans, and the contests took on an urban-versus-rural flavor instead of an international character. The marathon excited considerable interest as athletes followed a circuitous and dusty course through St. Louis County. Thomas Hicks from Massachusetts won

135- pound wrestling championship
St. Louis Public Library, Louisiana Purchase Exposition collection, Special Collections

The third international Olympics were held at the St. Louis Fair. Here is the start of the 1500 meter run.
St. Louis Public Library, Louisiana Purchase Exposition collection, Special Collections

the marathon race, though his path was unusual. Hicks and the other runners were monitored by physicians and trainers who followed the course in a convoy of 20 automobiles and Hicks was the subject of a strenuous experiment to prove the performance-enhancing ability of some drugs. The drug in question was strychnine, which was administered to him in an egg white solution twice during the race. As a result, he was not allowed to drink water on the marathon course but was limited to having his mouth sponged out. His trainers also bathed him in warm water, even though the temperature that day was well over 90 degrees. Hick's primary trainer, while impressed that he ran the course like a well-oiled machine, noted that he showed "more or less hallucination." The fair's immense size and fanciful planning combined a practical aspect of Progressive-era planning with a hallucinatory sense of scale and wonder.

Massive exhibition palaces covering acres of ground housed sewing machines and locomotives; Parisian gowns and Japanese vases; McCormick Reapers and cows sculpted from butter. The Pike housed the boardwalk-like attractions of Hagenbeck's performing animals, re-enactments of the Galveston Flood, and the scenic

Tyrolean Village. Within the fairgrounds, visitors could take a round-the-world trip, visiting Europe, Asia, the Middle East and the American West all in one journey. The grand scale of the fair and the exhibits could make a one-day trip exhausting, and many visitors returned again and again.

There was just too much to see and do: the Ferris Wheel lured riders into its massive gondolas to enjoy panoramic vistas as they rose high above the fairgrounds. For 50 cents, riders could look to the southeast and see Japanese Pagodas, the re-created Mosque of Omar in Jerusalem and the splendid dome of Festival Hall. Beyond these lay the city, the mansions and private places of the fair's benefactors, a low hum on the horizon beyond the magical white buildings. The fair had its own hotel, the "Inside Inn," an elegant but temporary structure; it had a police force, a firefighting force, and its own medical corps. Vendors sold souvenir ruby glass butter dishes and cake plates, penny postcards and elegant books of photographs.

There were many places to lunch, from elegant dining terraces to humble hot-dog vendors. Ice cream cones and iced tea were sold; in the hot St. Louis summer, visitors relished the refreshing coolness of iced drinks and the

Oriental displays, including this Japanese salutation, gave visitors an "around the world tour" right at home. *Photograph by Jessie Tarbox Beals, Beals album 1 St. Louis Public Library, Louisiana Purchase Exposition collection, Special Collections*

delicious, tongue-tingling cold of sweet ice cream. By the time the World's Fair closed on December 1, more than twelve million paid visitors had thronged the wide promenades and marveled at the range of exhibits. The park had changed from forest to city, and the marvels of the fair were recorded by hundreds of expert and recreational photographers. The World's Fair gave the city a fabulous seven months of entertainment and wonder in return for the years of preparation.

For St. Louis the lasting legacies of the fair were more than just fond memories and butter dishes. Government reform, paved streets that ran as far west as Skinker Road, and park improvements were physical inheritances. From Kessler's "Main Picture" to the daily management of thousands of employees, this brilliantly planned production was a living model of a city in its arrangement and facilities. Together with Mayor Rolla Wells' goals for civic reform, the fair provided an impetus for St. Louis' leap into modern city planning.

In addition to solving water and garbage problems, Wells had plans to remake the very image of the city. He appointed a public buildings commission, and in 1904, the commission published a report that outlined the need for new municipal buildings to replace the small and deteriorating structures in place. Though primarily concerned with the Four Courts and Jail buildings, the Commission's report laid out a plan for a group of municipal buildings centered on city hall, using Twelfth Street as an axis. Commissioners reported that the consolidation of buildings, which would occupy property already owned by the city, would provide both "the convenience of the conduct of public affairs," and "a dignified architectural effect." This north-south plan also suggested that the "small blocks between Market Street and Chestnut Street should be acquired and devoted to smaller buildings, such as Public Records and Historical Museum, and would afford ample space and surroundings for monumental buildings."

All of the commission members were architects, members of the St. Louis Architectural League and trained in the traditions of the beaux-arts. They drew plans based on European capitals before settling on the Washington Mall as frame of reference. All of their plans included vistas with plazas and green space in front of monumental structures. Axial, and very linear, these plans were intended to bring a formal, ordered beauty and repose to the urban landscape. In the public buildings group plan, beautification and planning extended beyond

Festival Hall, fountain of central cascade in operation — the harmonized buildings and well-landscaped grounds of the fair gave planners a life-size model of City Beautiful techniques. *Louisiana Purchase Exposition Company, c 1904, St. Louis Public Library, Louisiana Purchase Exposition collection, Special Collections*

the landscape. The City Beautiful Plans in the *Report of the Public Buildings Commission* might have been influenced by the fair plans. The plazas and lagoons, the monumental buildings and statues were models the commissioners could observe for themselves. The harmonized style and careful planning of the World's Fair buildings and grounds are echoed in the Commission's plans. The classical building style symbolized both Mayor Wells' reformed government and St. Louis' position as a leading American city. The long tree-lined parkway punctuated with monuments and ending with a domed public library was designed to replace the grimy commercial buildings of Market Street with an architectural style suited to the international importance St. Louis had earned with the World's Fair.

The Civic League, a group that included businessmen and civic leaders in addition to architects, was the city's first official planning group. Like the Public Buildings Commission, the league imagined a new St. Louis, united by a clear plan that would erase (or at least soften) the divisions between ethnic groups and classes to achieve a "unity of civic life." In 1907 the Civic League published the groundbreaking *City Plan for St. Louis*, addressing

almost every aspect of municipal reform in one publication, from street paving and riverfront improvements to the idea of a civic center as the heart of the city.

Despite the practical need to tailor the city's infrastructure for new technology and heavier use, the public buildings group remained a part of the city plan. The league argued that the grouping of homogeneous public buildings "will serve as splendid example of the advantages to be gained by the proper arrangements of buildings about an open park space, which will have its influence on all subsequent private as well as public building operations in the city."

City government, by law and by example, would change the workings and the look of the city for the better. The public buildings group plan would combine the best of the old European examples and the fresh, democratic visions of American planners. Like most other progressive reformers, those in St. Louis tried to make a city with a physical environment that would gently encourage and mold her citizens. They believed that honest government, modern architecture, and improved city services could make residents more civil, virtuous and civic minded. Even though class and ethnic differences would persist, righteous persuasion through the subtle influences of grass, statues of heroes and scholars, and the wholesome effects of democratic architecture would endow the population with the necessary values for success and citizenship.

Among the most popular reforms instituted were the public baths, designed to provide access to bathing facilities as well as to encourage American standards of cleanliness among a growing immigrant population.

Longtime working class residents used the baths as well, augmenting crowded and inadequate bathrooms at home. Reformers hoped that the baths would cleanse the body politic and remake immigrants and working class Americans in the image of the city's middle class.

The Civic League of St. Louis had made a survey of city housing conditions in 1908 and was shocked to find out that in some neighborhoods, only one person in 200 had a bathtub. The statistic meant that most people were trying to keep clean with nothing more than a basin and a sponge. For progressive reformers like William Marion Reedy and Charlotte Rumbold, dirty residents, dirty streets and dirty politics were all related problems. Rumbold had completed the 1908 housing survey for the Civic League and was joined by Mrs. Louis Martin McCall, who was also a member of the Wednesday Club, in the campaign for public baths.

The first step the influential women's club took was to establish a "vacation playgrounds" program for poor and immigrant children. The vacation playgrounds combined games, lessons and showers for "little tenementers," who flocked by the thousands to the Open-Air Playgrounds run by the Civic League and the Wednesday Club. Reformers intended that the organized play would encourage middle-class values in the children, and that the availability of the free showers, so tempting and refreshing in the hot, sticky St. Louis summers, would accustom them to higher standards of cleanliness. The incredible success of the program, the enthusiasm of the children and the impending World's Fair all combined in 1902; the Municipal Assembly authorized construction of several bathhouses. In 1907 the very first public bath opened in St. Louis, on Tenth between Biddle and Carr streets. Public Bath No. 2 opened two years later in the Soulard Neighborhood, just across from the market. In all, St. Louis built six stand-alone public bath buildings, along with numerous others included in comfort stations, recreation centers and public pools.

Working-class St. Louisans were often suspicious of the elite reformers, puzzled and irritated by the sometimes-patronizing attitudes of the West End matrons. The public baths were at first no exception, but the practical use and simple pleasures of the baths made them, in the end, one of the most successful and popular reforms ever undertaken in the city of St. Louis. People could use the baths and ignore the reformers' intentions. They came and enjoyed the baths but maintained their own personalities, cultures and values; in short, they made the baths their own. Although separate facilities were maintained for each sex, they were not at first segregated by race, reflecting the typically integrated neighborhoods the baths served. This situation changed as race relations grew more tense. When city voters passed a housing segregation ordinance in 1916, racial segregation in the baths became the rule not by custom but by law.

The housing ordinance became a divisive issue in the city, which had maintained inconsistent segregation of services primarily by custom. For example, while African Americans did not attend school with whites, libraries were not segregated, nor were streetcars, department store elevators, or theaters. Residential areas were customarily segregated in middle and upper class neighborhoods, but the wards downtown in the poorer areas were more nearly integrated as immigrants — both African Americans from the Deep South and whites from eastern Europe — found affordable, if crowded, housing. Many lived in the decrepit buildings of once-fashionable areas long since abandoned by the middle class.

Some reformers could not separate cause from effect and assumed that the new residents had caused the deterioration of these neighborhoods, rather than expanding industrialization and the inevitable aging of poorly maintained pre-Civil War row houses. Sanitation in the crowded districts was typically substandard and again, this appeared to be the residents' fault. To many, it seemed that the new African American migrants created the decay of the neighborhoods they lived in. In 1916 this logic produced a plan for a housing segregation ordinance designed to protect white neighborhoods.

St. Louis was following a pattern set by Baltimore in 1910 when that city had successfully passed a residential segregation act. In St. Louis the plan was to require "separate blocks for residence" and to legally segregate churches and dance halls. The National Association for the Advancement of Colored People was vocal in opposing the act and was joined by the St. Louis *Post-Dispatch*, the *Globe-Democrat*, and the *Republic* newspapers, as well as Mayor Kiel and the majority of the city aldermen. Even so, the legislation was on the ballot for March 1916 and despite the opposition of so many leading politicians and businessmen, the petition was approved by almost 75 percent of voters.

The new law worked in both directions, prohibiting anyone, white or black, from moving onto a block where 75 percent of the residents were of another race. An injunction against the segregation ordinance was passed in April 1916. After the U.S. Supreme Court declared a similar law in Louisville unconstitutional, the St. Louis injunction was made permanent in March 1918. It was a hollow victory: restrictive covenants were still legal, and white real estate agents and homeowners alike used deed restrictions to prevent the sale of houses to African American buyers in a practice that would continue until the 1947 *Shelley v. Kraemer* decision.

As St. Louis reformers waged their war against dirty politics and dirty streets, and while segregationists fought the battle of the block, the war in Europe loomed ever larger. What had begun in the warm weather of August 1914 and stretched on for months and years remained distant from immediate concern for many in St. Louis until the chilly April morning in 1917 when President Woodrow Wilson announced that America had entered the war.

As St. Louis' men and boys volunteered and were drafted, many took the war to heart. Even before the declaration of war, the city had been divided on the German question. While August Busch and other leading merchants marched in the Preparedness Day parade of

William Marion published *The Mirror*, a magazine that criticized government and encouraged reform in St. Louis. Sketch, c. 1905 *The Mercantile Library at the University of Missouri St. Louis*

The virulent influenza epidemic of 1918 forced Mayor Henry Kiel, c. 1915, to close schools and churches in an attempt to stop the spread of the disease. *The Mercantile Library at the University of Missouri St. Louis*

1916, other Germans were loudly anti-British. German and Irish immigrants dominated the Neutrality League, fiercely advocating American non-intervention, while on the other side of the issue, Four Minute Men gave strongly pro-war speeches.

Germans were persecuted for their language and background and after America entered the war, those who were not full citizens were required to register as enemy aliens. This anti-German frenzy continued unabated throughout the war. German language newspapers were required to submit their news, war reports and editorials to the postmaster for approval, and the finished columns had to be printed in both German and English. St. Louis public schools stopped teaching the German language after decades of commitment to the subject. In addition, city streets were renamed, the most notable being the change of Berlin Avenue to Pershing.

Decades of German influence were eradicated in only a few years, despite the typically respectable and pro-American sentiments of the population. Even without radio and television, newspapers brought intense American propaganda and nationalism to the city. Liberty Loan posters encouraged sales with lurid images and intentionally emotional captions. Artists prepared cartoons promoting the Third Liberty Loan with images of German soldiers taking women captive as the spoils of war; a Fourth Liberty Loan Poster depicted the Statue of Liberty silhouetted against the Manhattan skyline in flames, encouraging bond sales "That Liberty Shall Not Perish From the Earth." The Third Liberty Loan parade was held in Forest Park on Sunday April 7, 1918, with entertainment that included bands playing on Art Hill. Businesses and residences alike decorated for the event with eagles and flags, banners and posters.

Despite pro-war propaganda and the best efforts of civic leaders to unite the city in the war effort, a streetcar strike was declared on February 3, 1918, which lasted only a week. After bitter conflicts including riots and assaults, the car strike ended on February 8. The *Republican* reported that the strike was an enemy plot to halt war work, quoting United Railways Company allegations that the strike was "organized by 'outsiders' bent upon crippling the nation's preparations for war."

In truth, United Railways had again tried to break the new reorganized union, which claimed 2,700 members from the company's employees. Demonstrations by strikers throwing vegetables, coal and rocks at streetcars and the forced removal of motormen from their cars brought out 1,100 policemen, who "shot their way through crowds" and arrested strikers for rioting. In the atmosphere of suspicion and patriotism, "radical" organizations were especially suspect; these fears resulted in a raid on the St. Louis headquarters of the Industrial Workers of the World.

Federal agents had planted an agent within the IWW to gather evidence of sedition. Policemen hauled away materials that the *Republican* described as "a patrol wagonload of socialistic literature and other propaganda of a very seditious nature." In addition to the streetcar strike, clerks at the five major department stores went out on strike in late February, along with workers at Wagner Electric and Simmons Hardware. Even though store clerks picketed on the sidewalks in front of the department stores and the Retail Clerks Local Number 80 prepared a contract, the clerk's union was essentially broken.

On March 28, 300 striking clerks agreed to return to work "on the condition that retailers will agree in writing to the new labor policy of the United States Government." As part of emergency war measures to ensure production by limiting strikes and increasing efficiency, the federal War Industries Board adopted strict new labor standards. Companies with War Department contracts were required to pay mandated minimum wages, accept an eight-hour workday and submit to inspections of working conditions. Many employers were also required to permit employees to bargain collectively.

Other wartime measures included food rationing. Under the direction of Herbert Hoover, the United States Food Administration declared limits on food. Wheatless and meatless days were adopted, food hoarders were raided and arrested by police, and limits were placed on cheese, butter and sugar. Families and restaurants were required to purchase wheat substitutes like corn meal, barley and oats for baking. Under these guidelines, families bought equal amounts of cereals and wheat flour. Even school children joined in the war effort, as the St. Louis chapter of the Junior Red Cross encouraged them to participate in thrift stamp drives, knitting projects and the collection of fruit pits and nut shells for manufacturing carbon gas mask filters. City newspapers reported on the amount of money St. Louis area children had raised in one week selling thrift stamps — over $8,000 when receipts from all schools were combined. By March 1918 more than 92,000 school children were members of the Junior Red Cross, and they joined together to hold pageants and parades, sell stamps and distribute pamphlets to promote the war effort.

The confusion and stress of the war were increased when the influenza epidemic reached St. Louis in early October 1918. Mayor Henry Kiel cancelled school, church services, theatrical performances and public gatherings to prevent spread of the deadly virus. Jefferson Barracks was quarantined, leaving drafted soldiers drifting about the city with no place to report. St. Louis lost 1,700 citizens to the flu before it was over. In the midst of the worst weeks of the epidemic came the news of peace — though at first, it was news of a false peace.

On Thursday, November 7, church bells suddenly rang out, and whistles blew across the city at 11:30 in the morning. Soon after, newsboys began hawking "extra" editions of all the newspapers with bold headlines declaring "Peace!" Office workers spilled into downtown streets, overcome with joy, thronging streets strewn with confetti. Flags were hung out, and people decorated themselves in red, white and blue. The following day, rain added to the dreadful gloom that the reports were false. When the armistice finally came for real, the celebrations were almost muted. That Monday, November 11, the city woke to whistles and noise just before 3 a.m., as factory, train and steamboat whistles blew in a chorus that signaled the end, at long last, to the dreadful war.

Cheering crowds throughout the spring of 1919 greeted the soldiers who came home, as St. Louisans thronged the Court of Honor on Twelfth Street. Draped with red, white and blue bunting and lined with the honorary shafts and arches, the Court of Honor provided a patriotic and comforting backdrop to the parade of servicemen. Amid these symbols of community, nation and democracy, the civilian population mourned the dead and celebrated victory.

The *Post-Dispatch* described the parade of the "Gallant 89th" on May 30, 1919. "Two trucks of flowers, with young women scattering a white and red floral trail, moved ahead of the parade into the Court of Honor. Behind the mounted police escort came Uncle Sam and Saint Louis, costumed figures, and then a grotesque marching representation of a side of bacon, following a banner which read, 'We brought home the bacon, Rhine and all.'"

A Gold Star service flag followed at the end to commemorate the dead of the regiments. St. Louisans celebrated together in the Court of Honor and mourned together on Art Hill in Forest Park. On Sunday, June 15, 1919, the city held a Memorial Honor Roll Service for the Heroic Dead of St. Louis and St. Louis County. This was under the auspices of the Memorial Honor Roll Committee and the Missouri Historical Society and was the only mass service planned to honor the dead. The program was organized with the intention of reuniting citizens, "regardless of creeds and schisms and factions." Open to the public, the quasi-religious service included community singing of the "Battle Hymn of the Republic," "Keep the Home Fires Burning," "America" and "The Star Spangled Banner."

Politicians and women's groups attempted to reunite the city with the service, focusing on the patriotic unity that had won the war, rather than the jingoist passions that had inflamed anti-German passions. The 1919 Prohibition Amendment dealt a heavy blow to the predominantly German brewing industry. Many breweries closed forever, and Anheuser-Busch survived by concentrating on non-beer products like Bevo and Malt-Nutrine, beverages with a negligible alcohol content touted as "conditioners" and healthful tonics. The end of the war brought an end to the authentically German flavor of the city. The Turnverein still practiced, but the passionate forces of patriotism had forced the German community into greater assimilation.

Women's groups had made some gains, however. They had joined the workforce at defense plants where

stalwart women formed a silent gauntlet, shaming the delegates as they walked from the hotel to the convention site. Groups of women enacted a tableau at the halfway point. Here, suffragists dressed in stages of mourning symbolized states where women had either partial or no voting rights at all; 13 demonstrators wore white and gold to symbolize the 12 states and sole territory that granted women full voting rights.

The demonstration was counted a fabulous success when the Democratic Party added suffrage to its platform. After 1917, war work occupied most women more than suffrage demonstrations, and even the suffrage newspapers published more news about women's contributions to the war effort than editorials favoring suffrage. This devoted attention to patriotic duties earned women the respect of President Wilson, though wartime fears of the immigrant vote and subsequent isolationism also fueled support for women's voting rights. By the spring of 1919, the Missouri legislature granted the state's women the right to vote in presidential elections; in June, at long last, full suffrage was achieved with the 19th Amendment. Missouri ratified the amendment within the month, taking a place in the forefront of support for women's rights just as the state had for African American Emancipation. While women won a long-fought, permanent right, Prohibition gave St. Louis pause, as the new act threatened a traditional industry.

they replaced men suddenly called into the armed forces. Some women made detonators and firing pins at the Wagner Electric Company while others joined the Mallinckrodt Chemical Company. Shoe and clothing manufacturers had traditionally hired women, but now women had some chance of moving into better-paying and more diversified positions, even if temporarily. They were still underrepresented in the unions and sometimes ignored by union officials.

Even with wartime labor shortages, many employers continued to see women as cheap labor, often paying women less than half the wages earned by men in comparable jobs. Still, the war offered opportunities, and many women took advantage of new openings. For many women the greatest opportunity was offered when Congress passed the 19th Amendment, ending decades of effort to achieve suffrage for women. St. Louis women had long been in the forefront of the struggle to earn the vote for women.

One of the most striking demonstrations was held in St. Louis in 1916 when the Democratic National Convention met at the St. Louis Coliseum. That June, more than 2,000 women lined the streets in a "walkless, talkless parade" that stretched east along Locust Street from the Coliseum at Twenty-third Street to the Jefferson Hotel at Twelfth Street. Dressed in white and draped with yellow sashes lettered with suffrage slogans, the

Throughout the 1920s other industries, many as long-standing as the brewers, kept St. Louis in the forefront of American manufacturing cities. She could no longer be "first in booze," but she could still be "first in shoes," as Brown Shoe and other companies made fully five percent of the nation's shoes in St. Louis. Rail and river connections served the city well and manufacturing industries were widely diversified.

St. Louis became the second-largest automobile-manufacturing center in the United States after Detroit. The Ford Motor Company entered the St. Louis market first, building a plant on Forest Park Parkway in 1914. Competitors soon followed: Chevrolet and Fisher Body opened plants in 1916 followed by another General Motors plant at Goodfellow and Natural Bridge Road in 1920. Local manufacturers also played a role in the expansion of the automotive market. Wagner Electric manufactured brakes, brake fluid and starters.

Other manufactures included Carter Carburetor, a division of William K. Bixby's American Car and Foundry, McKay-Norris and Moog Automotive. All of these companies manufactured parts for both assembly-line and after-market use. St. Louis-based designers and manufacturers competed with Detroit's "Big Three" makers until the end of the 1920s. The Moon Motor Car Company began as the Moon Brothers Carriage Company. Later renowned for its elegant touring cars and coupes, the company had made the first "Moon Motor" car in 1906. All of the cars were designed and manufactured in St. Louis, where the company had six plants.

But perhaps the most exciting new development in the city was the aviation industry. St. Louis had actually been a center for aviation since the turn of the century and was home to Thomas Benoist. A pioneer in aircraft development, he was one the first aviators to design and build a "flying boat" or seaplane and began manufacturing airplanes in 1911.

During World War I, St. Louis manufacturers joined in producing a new weapon of war: the airplane. Subcontracting for the Curtiss Corporation, the St. Louis Car Company and Huttig Sash and Door manufactured the Curtiss JN4D or "Jenny." Huttig Sash and Door retooled its factory to produce the wooden struts and frames over which canvas was spread and "doped" to make the fuselage. St. Louis Car Company produced metal work and completed the assembly. Curtiss continued to manufacture planes in St. Louis after the war and joined other

aircraft companies that were beginning to cluster around Lambert Field. Major Albert Bond Lambert first leased the 170-acre tract in 1920; and by 1923 the International Air Races were held at the eponymous Lambert Field. The spirit of the new industry infected the city as flight schools and manufacturers flocked to the new airfield. Among these was the slender Minnesotan who would become the city's most prominent aviator, a hero for the new age: Charles A. Lindbergh.

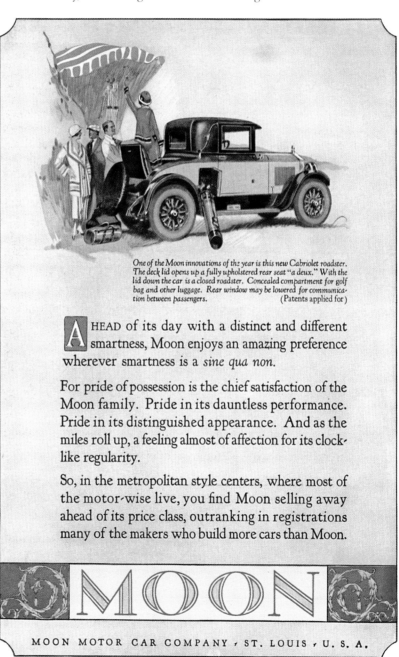

One of the Moon innovations of the year is this new Cabriolet roadster. The deck lid opens up a fully upholstered rear seat "a deux." With the lid down the car is a closed roadster. Concealed compartment for golf bag and other luggage. Rear window may be lowered for communication between passengers. (Patents applied for)

AHEAD of its day with a distinct and different smartness, Moon enjoys an amazing preference wherever smartness is a *sine qua non*.

For pride of possession is the chief satisfaction of the Moon family. Pride in its dauntless performance. Pride in its distinguished appearance. And as the miles roll up, a feeling almost of affection for its clock-like regularity.

So, in the metropolitan style centers, where most of the motor-wise live, you find Moon selling away ahead of its price class, outranking in registrations many of the makers who build more cars than Moon.

MOON

MOON MOTOR CAR COMPANY · ST. LOUIS · U. S. A.

Advertisement for Moon Motor Cars, c. 1925 — Moon Motor Cars were elegant and well-made local cars with a national reputation. *The St. Louis Mercantile Library at the University of Missouri-St. Louis*

six

1927-1945

City of Flight:
ST. LOUIS GOES TO THE WORLD

The man who became the city's favorite son wasn't even born there; he was born in Michigan on February 4, 1902, the only son of a free-thinking man and his independent wife. Charles August Lindbergh and his wife, Evangeline Lodge Land Lindbergh, were decades apart in age but similar in approach: they raised their only child, Charles Augustus Lindbergh, to be independent and resourceful, qualities that would serve him both as the nation's hero and on his quest to conquer the sky. His father was a congressman from Minnesota, so the young Lindbergh spent much of his time in Washington, D.C. where his estranged parents maintained separate residences; he would live much of the time with his doting but undemonstrative mother.

His adolescence was spent primarily in Little Falls, Minnesota, where he devoted more attention to running the family farm than to his schoolwork. Mechanical things like cars and motorcycles fascinated him from a young age; and he learned to drive as a young teen-ager. Lindbergh was captivated when his father took him to the Aeronautical Trials at Fort Myer, Virginia, in the summer of 1912.

Charles A. Lindbergh and the *Spirit of St. Louis* at Lambert Field, 1927: Lindbergh named his plane for the city where backers trusted his ability to fly nonstop across the Atlantic.
©Arteaga Photos, LTD

He enrolled in the University of Wisconsin at Madison only to drop out — rather than flunk out — in February 1922. Lindbergh remained fascinated with aviation. Since the usefulness of airplanes in reconnaissance had been proven in World War I, air companies and flight schools sprang up across the country. Instead of returning to Little Falls, Lindbergh signed up for the Nebraska Aircraft Corporation's flight school in Lincoln, Nebraska, arriving as the sole student in April 1922. Reorganized as Lincoln Standard Aircraft, the company promised a complete education in all aspects of aviation.

Lindbergh's first task was to dismantle a Hispano-Suiza engine; he would learn to "dope" wings, recondition airplanes and replace engines. This hands-on education gave him a practical foundation and thorough understanding of airplane construction and efficiency. He also had his first flying lessons, accompanied by 16-year-old Harlan "Bud" Gurney, who would come to be one of his closest friends. As Lindbergh progressed to solo flights, it became clear that he was a natural pilot; that spring and summer, he was able to make a living flying with barnstormers in Nebraska. His first airplane, purchased in May 1923, was a surplus U.S. Army Air Corps Curtiss JN4-D or Jenny — the training plane made in St. Louis.

The Jenny was a reliable biplane with an open tandem cockpit that allowed for paying passengers. As he flew through Minnesota in the summer of 1923, carrying passengers for a usual dollar-a-minute fee, someone suggested that he enlist as a cadet in the Army flying school. He would have access to the most up-to-date equipment, excellent instruction and the chance at a coveted officer's slot. On the way to take the physical and mental exams required for admission, Charles Lindbergh stopped in St. Louis to visit the St. Louis Air Meet held October 4 through 6, 1923. He met Bud Gurney again; Gurney was flying out of Lambert Field, and along with 125,000 other people, the two friends watched the Pulitzer Air Races of the last day. Lindbergh would continue to return to St. Louis: just as the city had been a hub at the center of steam and rail transportation networks, so it was now becoming a hub for air transport.

The Air Meet convinced him to enroll in the Air Corps flying school, and while he studied at Brooks Field outside San Antonio, Texas, Lindbergh applied himself more diligently than ever before. Anything related to flying interested him, and he became a devoted student,

desperate to avoid the "Benzene Boards" that washed fliers out of the school. He did well and progressed to Kelly Field, 10 miles away, for advanced training in the fall of 1924. By the time he graduated, it was clear that Charles Lindbergh flew better than any of his classmates. Of his entering class of 104 cadets, 19 remained, and Lindbergh graduated at the top of the class. As graduation day neared and he had no solid job offers in Texas, he thought again of St. Louis, where he had been so impressed by both the air races and the camaraderie of the pilots at Lambert Field.

The field was the property of Major Albert Bond Lambert, a native St. Louisan who had commanded and taught balloon pilots in World War I. Dedicated to aviation, Lambert bought 170 acres of farmland northwest of St. Louis, in what was then Anglum. With only a triangular landing area at the center, and no real runways, Lambert was open to any aircraft operator free of charge. Lambert operated the field at his own expense and promised to do so until the city of St. Louis could take it over. When Charles Lindbergh arrived in the spring of 1925, Frank and William Robertson offered him position of chief pilot for airmail service — to start as soon as Robertson received the contract. The Robertson brothers were still waiting to hear from the Postmaster General on the newly opened service routes.

In the meantime, chief pilot Lindbergh continued to barnstorm and test pilot aircraft. He began surveying the St. Louis-Chicago airmail route that summer, and when Contract Air Mail awards were made in October 1925, Robertson was ready to operate under C.A.M.-2. They had a fleet of five mail planes, all Army surplus DeHavilland observation planes with fabric-covered, silver-painted wings, plywood fuselages painted maroon and lettered U.S. Air Mail in stark white letters. With a cruising speed of 90 miles per hour, the DeHavillands were piloted from a rear cockpit, allowing the pilot to keep a watchful eye on the mail sacks in the front seat. The planes had been nicknamed "flying coffins" by Army pilots who knew them only too well; as chief pilot, Lindbergh insisted that all Robertson pilots be issued new silk parachutes, and that nothing be held against the pilot who needed to use one. With a route surveyed — often following railroad tracks — the Robertsons were ready to fly the mail. In a public dedication ceremony held April 15, 1926, Colonel Lambert's 13-year-old daughter, Myrtle, strewed flowers on Lindbergh's plane and announced, "I christen you the *St. Louis*. May your wings never be clipped."

The *St. Louis* flew one of the most dangerous airmail routes in the country, plagued by unpredictable weather. In the winter, even pilots who took off before sunset flew much of the route in total darkness. Even so, Robertson Aircraft Corporation pilots completed more than 98 percent of the C.A.M.-2 scheduled flights. Chief pilot Lindbergh grew tired of the predictability of the flights, as he had known he would. He took the Army physical and looked for an opening in the Army Air Corps.

In the meantime, with a great deal of solitary airtime, Lindbergh spun his thoughts further and further into aviation problems. How far could he fly in one of the newer, more efficient planes? How could he break endurance records, transcontinental records? And then he realized that if he could fly across the continent non-stop, he could also fly nonstop from New York to Paris. Raymond Orteig, a French-born Manhattan hotelier, had first offered a $25,000 prize for this flight in 1919, but revised criteria placed the award under the auspices of the National Aeronautical Association and opened it to aviators of all nations. Pilots around the nation knew about the prize, and Lindbergh turned it over in his mind during the long hours between St. Louis and Chicago. He would fly alone, with minimal supplies, in a single-engine plane built for fuel efficiency and load.

The new Wright Bellanca, a small-bodied high-wing monoplane powered by the air-cooled Wright Whirlwind engine, was his first choice. Lindbergh set out to find the funding to buy the plane; he knew that he could fly it. His first contact was St. Louis insurance executive Earl Thompson, who had taken some flying lessons from Lindbergh. Thompson was open to the project and intrigued by the young pilot's intention to fly alone, but Thompson couldn't fund it himself. Lindbergh then met with Colonel Lambert, who pledged $1,000 and promised a matching sum from his brother Wooster Lambert. Together the brothers matched the pilot's contribution of his life savings.

Although the Robertson brothers were losing money on the C.A.M.-2 route, they had first-hand knowledge and faith in Lindbergh's flying ability. They offered all the support they could give including the prestige of their

St. Louis was a leader in aviation innovation, buoyed by the airfield Colonel Lambert operated at his own cost. Shown is the Administration Building at Lambert Field, c. 1935.
©*Arteaga Photos, LTD*

name and support and an introduction to the editor of the St. Louis *Post-Dispatch*, who pointedly declined to participate. Finally, the young pilot's persistence paid off; he approached Knight, Dysart and Gamble, a St. Louis firm, where the founder's son, Harry Hall Knight, was also president of the St. Louis Flying Club. Knight was enthusiastic and immediately contacted his friend Harold Bixby, president of the St. Louis Chamber of Commerce. The two determined to raise the $15,000 Lindbergh estimated the flight would cost, with $10,000 for the airplane and $5,000 for expenses.

With financial backing, Lindbergh returned to the task of finding an airplane and finally received a positive

response from Ryan Airlines in San Diego. Ryan offered to build a plane — minus engine and instruments — for $6,000 and deliver it in 90 days. In February 1927 Lindbergh flew to San Diego to negotiate with Ryan Airlines' owner B.F. Mahoney and his chief designer and engineer, Donald Hall. As they talked, Hall sketched rough plans and Mahoney made mental calculations; in the end Ryan Airlines promised to deliver one Special Monoplane with a Wright J-5 motor within 60 days for $10,580; the plane's specifications were a fuel capacity of 400 gallons, a cruising radius of 3,500 miles, and the inclusion of an oil gauge, temperature gauge and altimeter. The order was signed on February 25, 1927, with $1,000 down.

He was on his way: Charles Lindbergh had established contacts in St. Louis that allowed him to assemble eight

backers, including E. Lansing Ray, the owner of the St. Louis *Globe-Democrat*; Colonel Lambert and his brother; Harry Hall Knight and his father; the Robertson brothers; and Harold Bixby. Representing the Chamber of Commerce, Bixby had asked if Lindbergh thought he could name the plane "*Spirit of St. Louis*," a request to which the pilot readily complied.

As the technicians built the plane in San Diego, Lindbergh watched every step. Plans were modified, as the wingspan had to be increased to accommodate the 2,800 pounds of fuel. When construction was complete, the silver high-wing monoplane was elegant in her simplicity. With a machine-finished engine cowling adding a circular texture to the smooth, silver-painted canvas structure, *Spirit* simply expressed her mission to fly one man as far and as fast as he could go.

In late April Charles A. Lindbergh climbed into the cockpit of the *Spirit of St. Louis* to fly her to St. Louis, his first stop en route to Paris. In his rented room he packed up his belongings, stripped his gear to its barest essentials, and prepared to take off for New York. He would leave from Roosevelt Field, taking off early in the morning of May 20, 1927, to fly more than 3,600 miles to Le Bourget airfield outside Paris. As he left New York, reporters watched from a muddy field. Lindbergh had been delayed for several days by rain and lack of visibility; now he flew east, into the unknown. Not many believed he would succeed; two French aviators had recently been lost in their attempt to cross the Atlantic, and it was rumored that Lloyd's of London refused to give any odds on the young pilot.

From Nova Scotia, though, came radioed reports of a small silver plane, and then reports came from ships at sea. Lindbergh could see little of this, and he had no radio. The weight had seemed extraneous, especially when crossing the naked expanse of ocean. He took only five drugstore sandwiches and a quart of water, and he wore a nine-pound zippered flight suit. Throughout the long night that followed several sleepless days, he struggled to stay awake. The open windows of the plane brought in blasts of cold air, which helped; and the wide-wing design and extra weight required manual correction, which also helped to keep him alert.

Finally, he saw the green and rocky coast of Ireland below him. Reports were radioed from Ireland to America; he was seen near the Channel. The French lit the great lamp at Cherbourg to light his way, and then, as the news spread, they traveled by the thousands to Le Bourget to wait. More than 150,000 Parisians were on the ground at the airfield when he was heard and sighted. As Harry Crosby, an American expatriate publisher recorded, the plane appeared first as a "white flash against the black night...and then another flash (like a shark darting through water)...then nothing. No sound. Suspense... then sharp white hawk of a plane swoops hawk like down and across the field — C'est lui — Lindbergh. LINDBERGH!" He landed on May 21, 1927, at 10:24 p.m., after flying alone for 33 hours, 30 minutes and 30 seconds. Charles A. Lindbergh was 25 years old, and the world's hero — and St. Louis had put him there. Celebrations in Paris, Belgium and London continued for days, followed by an ocean crossing on the Navy ship *Macon*, and crowded, joyous parades and celebrations in New York and Washington, D.C.

Lindbergh would not return to St. Louis until June 1927, when he flew back in the *Spirit of St. Louis*, landing at Lambert Field on the evening of Friday, June 17. A crowd of 5,000 people greeted him; they had waited patiently in the rain just to see him land. The next morning, Lindbergh was treated to a seven-mile parade that wound through the city and downtown St. Louis. The route was lined with American flags and posters of Lindbergh's image; a crowd of 500,000 people watched and cheered as their hero was driven by in an open car. At an official dinner that night, Charles Lindbergh was handed a

The entire city turned out to greet the returning hero at Lindbergh's Welcome Home Parade. *The St. Louis Mercantile Library at the University of Missouri-St. Louis*

dedicatory scroll and the keys to city; he had already won the hearts and admiration of the people. He rewarded his fans on Sunday morning with a display of aerial acrobatics performed in the trans-Atlantic plane. The *Spirit of St. Louis* swooped and soared above the 100,000 citizens who crowded Art Hill to watch the display. In a final gesture of thanks to the city that had launched his successful flight, Charles Lindbergh laid a wreath at the base of the Crusader King statue in front of the St. Louis Art Museum.

Lindbergh had brought the modern era right into the center of St. Louis. The celebratory parade wound its way through a city of contrasts. Downtown remained a mixture of architectural styles as new corporations grew and created a new building form: the corporate office tower. Many of the downtown buildings were no more than 25 years old. In the late 19th century, major wholesalers and retailers had established headquarters in St. Louis where they could take advantage of the convenient railroad lines, river traffic and central markets. Some, like the Rice-Stix Dry Goods Company, were originally wholesale companies. Rice-Stix moved to Sixth and Washington in 1906, opening the "Grand Leader" department store. The Grand Leader eventually occupied the entire city block bounded by Sixth and Seventh, Washington and Lucas streets, and the company, now called Stix, Baer and Fuller, became an important retailer in St. Louis and the nation.

One of the largest department stores in St. Louis, the Stix Company, was a local reflection of national changes in retailing. As a large department store, Stix provided a number of services to its customers with a philosophy of service and fair treatment that owners extended to employees through discounts, vacation pay, sick leave and other benefits. Stix promoted service, encouraging sales staff to expand sales through various techniques. The firm also maintained mail and telephone ordering services designed to increase customer loyalty. Along with other St. Louis department stores, Stix published *Modes and Manners* for local customers.

This magazine provided fashion forecasts and stories about fashion designers in addition to photographs and stories about home and garden design. Along with the city's other two retail giants, Scruggs, Vandervoort and Barney and Famous-Barr, Stix sold ideas as much as objects. Each of the three companies had a city-block size store housing tens of departments stocked with goods for every income level. The stores hosted special events like book signings and exhibits, sometimes even incorporating historic fashions and costumes into their sales floor displays.

While the Grand Leader on the northern edge of the central business district housed the retail store and corporate office, the Famous-Barr store was firmly placed in the center of downtown. Occupying the first eight floors of the Railway Exchange Building, Famous-Barr was sheltered from unpredictable markets by the upper 14 floors, all of which were designed for lease to the railroads for executive suites. Famous-Barr was the city's largest department store, and the Railway Exchange Building was a dominant feature of the skyline. Occupying the block bounded by Sixth and Seventh, Olive and Locust Streets, 22 floors clad in ornate white terra cotta decoration, the building would not be joined by a comparable landmark until the rise of new corporations brought new architectural styles to St. Louis.

By the late 1920s, corporations had replaced proprietorships and partnerships as the dominant business form. The success of this new business form helped generate new architectural forms — the true skyscraper corporate headquarters — and new architectural styles. St. Louis had city-block sized buildings, but these were typically squat, low-rise buildings most often used as wholesalers' warehouses. Corporations involved with new technology were far larger in size and required far greater amounts of office space than older businesses. The corporations housed accounting, hiring and advertising functions under one roof to centralize control of business functions and expenses.

The common elements among major office tower consumers of the 1920s were large fixed capital investments, in the form of both technology and distribution networks, which necessitated large numbers of employees. In St. Louis these were, notably, Southwestern Bell, Laclede Gas, Union-Electric, and the

Missouri Pacific Railroad, all utilities or common carriers. As St. Louis grew and new businesses formed, competition for commercial and office space in the central business district was intense. Offices needed to be close to each other before widespread use of telephones, so that information could travel quickly; they also needed to be relatively close to transportation networks.

As a result of this increased demand, land value increased to a point where owners and developers needed to erect taller buildings on smaller lots in order to realize a return on the initial land investment. Consequently, they hired architects to design and supervise the construction of buildings that utilized new steel structural elements that could carry the loads of a tall building. The flexible interior space achieved with columns and lightweight partitions was particularly useful in attracting tenants who wished to customize their office space. In order to amass enough space, it was often cheaper to buy land and erect a building than to attempt to rent enough space; a new building might also be the only way to accumulate enough space. Any space within the building not dedicated to the corporation could be leased to defray construction costs, and eventually turn a profit. The corporate office tower also provided a corporate symbol, a method of advertising success and prestige, especially when designed by a prominent firm.

In St. Louis one of the most prestigious firms was Mauran, Russell and Crowell. This firm had designed the earliest corporate office buildings in St. Louis, the Railway Exchange Building of 1908-1911 and the 1911 Laclede Gas and Light Building at Eleventh and Olive streets. The Laclede Gas Building, like the Railway Exchange, used classical and beaux-arts forms to endow the buildings with a sense of grandeur and style, an enduring grace. Modernized uses of classical styles had served the firm well since the turn of the century; they had designed churches and elite clubs before winning the

Railway Exchange and Laclede Gas contracts. Then, in 1922, Southwestern Bell Telephone and the Kinloch Telephone Company merged. The telephone companies had competed for decades since the expiration of the basic Bell Company permits; by 1920 Kinloch had 30,000 customers in the immediate St. Louis area. The merging of the two companies made Southwestern Bell Telephone one of the largest employers in the city and ended residents' need to keep two telephones to have full city coverage.

The new corporation also needed headquarters to celebrate a newly won status and merge all the employees and functions. Mauran, Russell and Crowell were awarded the contract for their design of a 29-story skyscraper-gothic tower unlike anything else in St. Louis. Tall piers emphasized the height of the tower, and floors stepped back in symmetrical pairs on either side of the Pine Street entrance to stretch like buttresses lifting up the central tower. The various rooflines were edged with vertical motifs reaching ever higher: the Southwestern Bell Telephone Building was truly a "cathedral of commerce" or as the promotional brochure put it, "a monument to communication." St. Louis' most modern building was completed in 1926, and increased its land value by a phenomenal 340 percent. Mauran, Russell and Crowell repeated the magic for the Missouri-Pacific Railroad. The architectural firm designed a simpler deco-gothic office building for the railway on Thirteenth between Pine and Olive streets. The form and massing were remarkably similar to the Telephone Building but smaller and less magnificent in scale. Once again, however, the land value jumped — this time, by 350 percent.

St. Louis was a winning town: home to major corporations and manufacturing concerns as well as renowned universities, birthplace of the *Spirit of St. Louis*, and the city just couldn't lose — unless the Browns were playing. St. Louis' American League team, the Browns had been organized in 1874 as the Brown Stockings. The city's first

Construction of the Railway Exchange building, c. 1910 — also designed by Mauran, Russell and Crowell, the Railway Exchange combined rental office space above the Famous-Barr department store. *The St. Louis Mercantile Library at the University of Missouri-St. Louis*

Rogers Hornsby managed the St. Louis Browns (shown here in March 1934) from 1933 to 1937, though his spectacular hitting ability could not lead the team to the World Series, as it had for the Cardinals in 1926.
The St. Louis Mercantile Library at the University of Missouri-St. Louis

professional team, they played at the Grand Avenue Park baseball diamond, a forerunner of Sportsman's Park. The famous stadium had its genesis in the Sportsman's Park and Club Association organized in 1880 by Alfred and William Spink to promote and improve the playing grounds.

By 1881 the Spinks and Chris von der Ahe, a northside grocer and saloonkeeper, had combined the Sportsman's Park and Club Association with the St. Louis Browns baseball team. The new team played in the American Association from 1882 to 1891, starting out poorly but eventually becoming renowned as a skillful and speedy team. Von der Ahe failed to retain control of the team, which was sold at auction in 1899 to the Robison brothers of Cleveland; they kept the team in St. Louis but renamed the club the St. Louis Cardinals, playing for the National League.

The new Cardinals proved little better than the original Browns, sliding into a mediocrity they would maintain for decades. In 1902 the new American League fronted a St. Louis team called the Browns, who despite fronting better teams than the Cardinals, proved inconsistent at living up to the reputation of von der Ahe's early team. But it was the Cardinals, lineal descendants of St. Louis' original baseball team, which finally provided the city with professional baseball teams to rival the best teams of the East.

The change in the team began not just with the 1915 acquisition of Rogers Hornsby, a phenomenally good hitter, but also with Sam Breadon, who bought a majority interest in the team in 1920. Breadon demoted then-president Branch Rickey but retained him as manager. He also negotiated with Browns owner Phil Ball to allow the Cardinals to use the Sportsman's Park stadium on a lease basis, shedding the decrepit Robison Field in the middle of the 1920 season. With the rickety old stadium sold, Breadon and Rickey were able to launch the innovative farm system, which was designed to develop the best players possible. This ensured the Cardinals a chance against wealthy eastern teams like the Giants, who routinely outbid all others to secure the best minor league players.

Rickey and the Cardinals used the profits from the sale of Robison Field to purchase interests in Texas, Arkansas and western New York state teams, creating a base for training and scouting that would eventually provide some of the best talent in baseball. The next step in revitalizing the

Cardinals was Breadon's 1924 replacement of Rickey with Hornsby in the dugout. Rickey moved into the front office as general manager, and Rogers Hornsby — batting .403 in 1924 — assumed the day-to-day management of the team. The move paid off in 1926 when the Cardinals beat the Yankees and brought home the city's first World Series Pennant. The Cardinals won the final game on the third out when catcher Bob O'Farrell tagged Babe Ruth as he attempted to steal second base. The city was triumphant: St. Louis had bested New York and proven the strength and worth of the west to the stodgy eastern giant.

The Cardinals remained a strong team and won the League pennant in 1928, 1930, 1931 and 1934 as well as the World Series in 1931 and 1934. The team was an assortment of irrepressible personalities in the late 1920s and 1930s, home of the popular "Gas House Gang." Rogers Hornsby, despite his excellent abilities as a hitter and a manager, was a compulsive gambler weighed down by his debts. His unrelenting crankiness got him traded from the Cardinals to the Giants in December 1926. In return the Cardinals got Frankie Frisch, the "Fordham Flash" who went straight from college to the major leagues.

After joining the team in 1927, Frankie Frisch managed the Cardinals and helped the team win pennants in 1931 and 1934. Frisch is shown here with Sam Breadon in spring 1934. *The St. Louis Mercantile Library at the University of Missouri-St. Louis*

Dizzy Dean and his brother, "Daffy," each won two games in
the 1934 series, gaining the Cardinals the Championship. Dean
is seen here with Frankie Frisch in October 1934.
The St. Louis Mercantile Library at the University of Missouri-St. Louis

The Gas House Gang, August 1935 — the St. Louis Cardinals team
of the 1930s was arguably one of the best in baseball history, despite
the antics and aggression that earned the team its nickname.

While St. Louis fans mourned the loss of the "Rajah," team members who appreciated Hornsby's abilities had also felt his steely gray eyes and sarcastic tongue at practice and in the game. Frisch could be sharp-tongued as well, but he was a good all-around player. He faced unhappy fans, bitter and resentful at losing Hornsby, but he had a unique and aggressive playing style that won them over. In 1930 a young farm-team schooled player joined the Cardinals in St. Louis. With an irrepressible style, Jerome "Dizzy" Dean made his debut against the Pirates, pitching a 3-1 game. The following year, Johnny "Pepper" Martin joined him. Martin helped the Cardinals best the Athletics in the 1931 World Series; and by the end of the Series, Martin had 12 hits and a .500 batting average.

The farm system had paid off. Rickey's innovation provided the team with incredible talent and gave young players both a paycheck and the luxury of playing baseball in the midst of the Depression. By 1933, Frankie Frisch managed the team, and Dizzy Dean, joined by his brother Paul, along with Pepper Martin and Ripper Collins, led the Gas House Gang. They didn't just play excellent baseball; they also entertained fans and distracted

their managers with a seemingly endless round of exploits on and off the field. From grass-skirted dances by Pepper Martin, to exploding cigars and the tableau they presented one summer — wearing fur coats and lighting a fire in front of the dugout on a typical 100 degree St. Louis summer day — the Gas House Gang delighted fans and brought home pennants.

Baseball in St. Louis had always been entertaining, and now it was innovative. Rickey's farm system was one in a line of innovations beginning with Ladies' Day. Instituted in 1908 by then-Browns owner Robert Hedges, Ladies' Day increased attendance and "softened" the image of rough-and-tumble, scandal-ridden baseball. Hedges stood at Sportsman's Park's entrance gates, pockets stuffed with reserve tickets that he handed out to any male patron accompanied by a woman. Even though Ladies' Day guaranteed free admission to all women, in

1932 the St. Louis *Argus* reported that African American women were required to pay admission, even on Ladies' Day, and called for a boycott. It was a small salvo, but it had been fired.

The "color line" would have to be crossed in baseball at some point. Integration came to baseball only after World War II, and later in St. Louis. Oddly enough, it was the Cardinal's own former manager, Branch Rickey, who first signed Jackie Robinson to the Montreal farm team of the Brooklyn Dodgers, finally changing baseball. In St. Louis, the Browns integrated first. Cardinal players had declared that they would not play Robinson, but in 1947 the DeWitts, brothers who owned St. Louis' American League team, signed Henry Thompson and Willard Brown.

The Browns had fronted uninspiring teams for years and had never won a league pennant, let alone played in the World Series, until 1944. That year the Browns played the Cardinals in the only all-St. Louis World Series ever. They lost four games to two — the Cardinals had Stan Musial, after all — but tried hard. The Browns achieved a kind of notoriety again in 1951 when Bill Veeck Jr. bought the team. He brought in Satchel Paige, who had played for Veeck's Cleveland Indians. He instituted a number of promotional changes and innovations designed to rebuild team confidence and position as well as fan interest.

Veeck saw St. Louis as a one-team town, and he planned to make it his. When August Busch bought the Cardinals in February 1953, Veeck looked elsewhere, knowing that he could compete with neither Busch's financial nor his hometown status. In April 1953 Sportsman's Park became Busch Stadium, sold to the Cardinals for $800,000 dollars. Veeck was desperate to get out of St. Louis, and baseball was desperate to get rid of him. He planned to move the Browns to Baltimore, but when it was clear the team could only move without him, he sold the Browns to a Baltimore syndicate, ending St. Louis' proud run as a two-team town. The Cardinals played baseball well enough for two teams, but an era had ended.

For many city residents, a new era was needed for the riverfront. As early as 1912, real estate magnate John Gundlach had complained to George Kessler and the Civic League about the condition of the St. Louis riverfront. Housing the oldest part of St. Louis and the earliest business districts, the levee had been neither refurbished nor well maintained. To Gundlach's eyes, it was shabby, seedy, rundown, and in need of change, perhaps even clearance. In 1927, just two months before Lindbergh took off for New York, the St. Louis *Globe-Democrat* published a reminiscence of the riverfront, painting a picture of a long-gone time "when the levee was the chief attraction to the sightseers, with a mile or so of steamboat smokestacks... in belching activity, and with the paved slope from the river's edge up to the first row of buildings the busiest scene in the Mississippi Valley." The reporter was convinced that visitors from 1857 would be disappointed with the scene 70 years later, "because the levee scene would be found exceedingly dull and prosy today — only a short-trip packet or two to be seen lying in the water's edge and hardly any activity at all on the upslope to the front street."

As early as 1917, the City Plan Commission had recommended that the central riverfront be substantially improved. The riverfront would linger, unchanged and deteriorating, until civic leader and lawyer Luther Ely Smith took up the cause, settling on the riverfront as the best site for his proposed memorial to Thomas Jefferson. Smith called the riverfront "historically sacred ground" and wrote of a monument to Jefferson and the Louisiana Purchase that would be "a memorial not to any one man, but to the Territorial Expansion of our Great country, and to the men who made it possible."

Although steamboat and barge traffic had continued to compete with the railroads,

(Left and below) These buildings stood on the levee before clearance, c. 1930. Architectural historians recognized that the cast-iron fronted buildings on St. Louis' levee were some of the finest examples in the nation. Clearance of the waterfront proceeded anyway, as the city worked to change and modernize its image. *The St. Louis Mercantile Library at the University of Missouri-St. Louis*

Once used as Manuel Lisa's fur warehouse, the Old Rock House — now a saloon — was one of only three riverfront buildings that survived the 1849 fire. (1935 photo) *The St. Louis Mercantile Library at the University of Missouri-St. Louis*

the advent of truck lines and the construction of the Municipal Bridge pushed the levee to the sidelines of St. Louis business. Its history seemed long past, as well, since few French colonial era buildings had survived either the 1849 fire or the decades of disdain and neglect as the city expanded to the west. By 1935 the only pre-fire buildings that remained on the riverfront were the 1818 "Old Rock House" at Chestnut and Wharf streets, the 1840 Matthew Rippey House at 217 Valentine Street and the 1842 Howard Building at 408 North Wharf Street. Only the Rock House, used by Manuel Lisa as a fur warehouse, predated Missouri Statehood; by the 1930s, it housed a bar. Other buildings, many of them some of the finest examples of pre-Civil War cast iron facades and construction, were home to small businesses — cafes and saloons, music halls and lunch counters — that supported both the diminishing numbers of levee workers and a small artists' colony.

Still, in Depression-era St. Louis, jobs for many were far more important than the studios of a few. Luther Ely Smith's successful campaign earned the support of Washington and federal grant money. By 1934, Civil Works Administration Project 104 had been authorized and work had begun, as the Jefferson National Expansion Memorial Association had secured Congressional approval of a bill to finance the acquisition and clearance of riverfront property. Workers began tearing down the old buildings, preparing the site for the planned Louisiana Purchase Monument and reflecting pool. By the time clearance work was complete, only the severely linear Cathedral of St. Louis and the Rock House remained east of Third Street.

This was not the only clearance and memorial building project in St. Louis to benefit from federal relief funds. The long-planned Soldier's Memorial and Public Buildings Group was finally under way. Local women's and veterans' groups had succeeded in convincing the City Plan Commission to include a Soldier's Memorial Building in the civic center planned for the area opposite City Hall. The official campaign began with the 1918 document *St. Louis After the War*, in which the City Plan Commission equated new civic buildings and parks with patriotism, making the reformed city a memorial to the soldiers.

As the "City Beautiful" movement became the "City Practical," proposed memorials included a municipal auditorium dedicated to all the men who had served. The Kiel Auditorium on Market Street alludes to this notion in the quotations from Woodrow Wilson inscribed on its north façade. Funds for the memorial had been included in the 1923 bond issue for city improvements, but land acquisition had eaten up most of that money. The project languished until federal relief money became available.

The Civilian Conservation Corps put local men to work clearing the plaza and park area between Market and Olive streets that would connect City Hall and the Public Library. Old brick mercantile buildings that had been home to boarding houses, tailors and tobacco shops were torn down, their basements filled in. Workers laid out walkways and planted trees, shrubs and grass to bring green space into the city center. At the same time, architects Mauran, Russell and Crowell completed designs for the Soldier's Memorial. The firm worked as part of the Plaza Commission Architects, a committee of leading practitioners assembled to ensure both quality and consistency in publicly funded downtown building projects. The commission worked with an advisory panel

Planners and designers focused on the riverfront as the birthplace and symbol of the city.
The St. Louis Mercantile Library at the University of Missouri-St. Louis

of veterans to establish an interior program that would satisfy the mandate to commemorate the dead and carry on with the living.

By the summer of 1935, the design had been formalized as it stands today: behind the simple Art Deco walls of the temple, the space was divided into ground-floor museum rooms with second-floor meeting rooms and an auditorium. The central loggia housed a black granite cenotaph listing the names of all 1,075 St. Louis city and county men who died overseas, under a dramatic red-and-gold canopy of stars set in a mosaic dedicated to the Gold Star Mothers. The memorial to the dead provided much-needed work for the living.

Dedicated in 1937, the Homer G. Phillips Hospital increased the quality of medical care available to St. Louis' African American population and served as a premier teaching hospital for African American nurses and doctors.
The St. Louis Mercantile Library at the University of Missouri-St. Louis

Federal relief funds finally provided the money to construct a long-promised hospital for the city's African American population. Homer G. Phillips Hospital was dedicated on February 22, 1937, the result of a long struggle by African American citizens to achieve parity in health care and physician training. While the city's 1923 bond issue allocated funding for "Negro Hospital," it was included only after several years of protest and despite voter approval, no funds had been made available. Black physicians were prohibited from training in white hospitals, even when these hospitals were funded by taxes collected from citizens of all races. This inequity and the lack of

reconstituted, with Homer G. Phillips again spearheading the effort to persuade the city to build a new, larger hospital with modern medical technology. As a result, $1 million of the $87 million civic improvement bond of 1923 was earmarked for the new "Negro Hospital." Louis Aloe, president of the city's Board of Public Service, allocated an additional $200,000. Still, construction was delayed for nine years after funding was available, despite the city's desperate need for improved hospital services for its African American community.

Homer G. Phillips was mysteriously murdered in 1931 before construction began on the hospital for which

The Admiral excursion boat was a perennial favorite for daytime excursions and evening dinner-and-dancing tours. ©Arteaga Photos, LTD

adequate patient facilities led to the creation, in 1915, of a community group to lobby for the necessary funding. Homer G. Phillips, a Howard University educated lawyer, was a leading member. The city purchased the old 177-bed Barnes Hospital at Garrison and Lawton streets, and converted the vacant building into City Hospital No. 2, the only facility dedicated to the care of African American patients.

When the hospital opened in 1919, the first patients were African Americans transferred from the segregated wards of City Hospital No. 1. By 1921 even the new facility was inadequate. Patients were crowded into hallways for lack of rooms, creating dangerous fire hazards and undermining their treatment. The community group

he fought. As a memorial, the five-building complex, which included a home and training school for nurses, was named for him in a cornerstone laying ceremony in December 1933. Homer G. Phillips Hospital quickly became the pride of the Ville Neighborhood and the St. Louis African American community. A source of quality health care and excellent training for nurses and doctors, the hospital helped strengthen the local African American professional class, providing a means to a better life.

For many African American St. Louisans, the Depression amplified their difficulties in finding well-paid employment. Whites and blacks alike suffered layoffs as the national economy failed. By 1933 the value of St. Louis manufactures and wages had dropped by half compared to 1929, and by the end of 1931, 25 percent of all St. Louis workers were unemployed, with 40 percent of black workers jobless. Locally, the St. Louis Provident Association attempted to provide assistance but was overwhelmed with applicants. By 1933 more than 100,000 St. Louisans were on the relief rolls, grateful for President Roosevelt's New Deal.

As in other large cities, a shantytown known as Hooverville grew along the riverfront. Many of the people who built Hooverville shanties were simply trying to maintain a sense of home and community life in the face of disaster. It was an orderly city within the city with streets laid out in a regular grid, four churches and an ad hoc government. Residents built shacks and planted gardens in fenced yards. They worked together to meet their needs and established their own post office and community center, as well as a kindergarten. The Works Progress Administration cleared the shantytown as the riverfront site for the Jefferson National Expansion Memorial was prepared. Impoverished citizens worked together to survive the desperate years of the 1930s, sometimes peacefully as in Hooverville, and sometimes more forcefully as strikes were staged in protest of wage cuts, layoffs and discriminatory hiring practices.

"Do as the nut-pickers did!" cried workers after the Funsten Nut Strike in 1933. Black and white women alike struck the Funsten Nut Company after five wage cuts in two years. In 1933, at the peak of the Depression, more than 30 percent of all St. Louisans and 60 percent of African Americans were unemployed. Drastic wage cuts intensified the misery of those who still had jobs. One group of workers — African American women in the nut factories whose salaries fell to $1.80 a week — had had enough.

On May 15, 1933, after the fifth wage cut dropped their pay to three cents a pound for picking nuts from shells, the women workers walked out of the four Funsten Nut Company factories. The women protested not only the wage cuts but also Funsten's discriminatory practice of paying white women four cents a pound and requiring them to work fewer hours. Five hundred strikers demanded a restoration of their pre-Depression wages and equal wages for equal work. In 1929 the average wage had been almost $10 a week; the precipitous drop to $1.80 by 1933 had forced many workers to seek assistance from the Provident Association.

Outraged by the less-than-living wages, workers with friends in the Communist Party began organizing workers into a local of the Food Workers Industrial Union. Twelve women demanded higher wages and equal pay for white and black women. When the company did not respond to their demands, the workers walked off the job; and within a week of the initial strike, more than 1,200 women were on strike. Even some of the white women joined strikers whose ranks included almost every African American worker in the company. As the wages became public knowledge, the *Post-Dispatch* editorialized on the Funsten Nut Strike, citing it as justification for a uniform minimum wage to prevent excessive wage cuts. Finally, Mayor Dickman was called in to appoint an interracial municipal committee to help the union negotiate an end to the strike. On May 23, 1933, strikers voted on and unanimously approved a settlement promising to pay all workers double the usual wage for white women. The success of the nut-pickers strike was acknowledged to be an incentive for other Depression-era strikes in the city, as "Do as the nut-pickers did!" became a rallying cry.

As long as the Depression lasted, St. Louis workers and their families worried about local and national problems. They were as shocked as the rest of the country when radio reports brought the news of the Japanese attack on Pearl Harbor into their homes. December 7, 1941, was a frightening day, with events that would change both St. Louis and the nation forever. Local manufacturers prepared to retool their factories for defense work, while everyone prepared to contribute to the war effort.

The Depression had forced many local automobile manufacturers to close; by 1939 only Ford and Chevrolet made cars in St. Louis. Now the war would change that, as the plants switched from cars to personnel carriers and tanks. Women were hired in large numbers to replace the white, male workers drafted by the military. Mobilization had begun by mid-1940, when the draft was reintroduced, while the Lend-Lease act was pivotal in causing manufacturers to begin planning for the switch from domestic to military products; contracts to supply the Allies began the process. Mobilization was characterized by the erection of large new plants in addition to conversion of existing plants.

One of the largest producers in St. Louis was the U.S. Cartridge Small Arms Plant at Goodfellow and Bircher avenues in Wellston, a small suburb just to the northwest of St. Louis. The plant occupied 291 acres in an area that was soon crowded with other war materials plants and war worker housing. The Small Arms plant, which created more than one-third of all the defense jobs held by women in St. Louis, employed almost 21,000 women. The work was repetitive but light and far better paid than traditionally female occupations like domestic service and retail sales. Women filled bullets with gunpowder, performed quality-control inspections and cleaned bullet sleeves. Men ran the heavy machinery and performed all ammunition tests.

Despite the pressures of wartime production, women still performed "women's work." The U.S. government issued pamphlets praising the natural abilities of women to perform repetitive, "finger-nimble" tasks, helping to reinforce a division of labor along gender lines. The women at the Small Arms plant were not, of course, the only defense workers in St. Louis. Women worked at the

Amertorp Torpedo Factory on south Kingshighway in the torpedo assembly line; they worked at the Scullin Steel Company on Manchester Avenue where the "Earthquake" bombs were made; and they worked at the Curtiss-Wright Airplane Corporation just north of Lambert field where the SB2 Helldiver was made.

The Curtiss plant was a small community itself, and the company hosted both recreational opportunities and patriotic events. In January 1945 actress Jane Ball and Captain Herschel Melvin, a veteran of the Ploesti raids, participated in a War Bond Rally at the Curtiss-Wright plant. Ball and Captain Melvin spoke in the plant cafeteria to an appreciative crowd of workers. As plant workers listened to the speakers that January, they may have wondered, "What will I do after the war? What job will I

Gen. Omar Bradley was welcomed with a parade when he visited St. Louis on June 11, 1945. Bradley came to promote bond sales and encourage citizens through the last days of the war in the Pacific.
The St. Louis Mercantile Library at the University of Missouri-St. Louis

have?" Wartime prosperity couldn't last forever, particularly for women and African Americans in manufacturing jobs previously closed to them.

Despite the increasing needs for workers across the nation, African Americans were often excluded from hiring. In response, A. Phillip Randolph organized the March on Washington Movement. Local African Americans joined the movement, picketing the Small Arms Plant and other defense contractors in St. Louis. Pressure from the organization forced both the federal government and local defense contractors to increase the number of African Americans they employed. As St. Louisans joined the armed forces, they encountered segregation again.

The city was proud of all who served as men like Wendell O. Pruitt joined the prestigious Tuskegee Airmen. Throughout the city, increasingly sophisticated communications technologies allowed St. Louisans to follow overseas events more closely than before. The war came home even harder after the federal government lifted some censorship rules, releasing photographs of Pacific Theatre casualties. The *Post-Dispatch's Pictures* magazine, newsreels, posters and radio programs flooded St. Louisans with news of the war and homefront propaganda. Rationing programs, and scrap and bond drives affected nearly everyone — while not fought on American soil, the Second World War probably affected more Americans than before.

As the war drew to a close, St. Louis hosted rallies and parades that featured national heroes and celebrities. St. Louisans could be as proud of General Omar Bradley as the rest of Missouri. Bradley, who was born in Higbee, Missouri, grew up in Moberley before he attended West Point. As commander of the 12th Army Group — the largest U.S. field army ever put into combat — Bradley was largely responsible for victory in Europe. After the German surrender, President Truman appointed the four-star General to head the Veteran's Administration. Bradley arrived at Lambert Airport aboard a C-47 transport plane, landing shortly before 2 p.m. on June 11, 1945.

A celebratory parade began just after 3 p.m. at Seventeenth and Washington streets. St. Louis police reported a crowd of about 250,000 people, even though the general had requested that no one engaged in combat training or war work be required to visit the parade, as he did not wish to detract from the war effort. Many employers followed his wishes, and the crowd was composed largely of women and school children dismissed early for the occasion. As the parade, which included military bands and units, wound through downtown on Washington and Olive streets, office workers leaned from windows and cheered the general, tossing paper, ticker tape and confetti into the street. A reviewing stand had been erected at Soldier's Memorial where the Court of Honor for World War II dead was already under construction. Bradley spoke there in tribute to the men still fighting, and in the hope that the new Memorial stele would be in honor of "as few dead as possible." In the end, St. Louis lost more men in World War I than in World War II, a mixed blessing for the devastated families.

When the war finally ended, St. Louisans couldn't even read about the Japanese surrender in the *Post-Dispatch,* the *Globe-Democrat,* or the *Star-Times* because the daily newspapers were on strike. Soon after that other unions went out on wildcat strikes, and 60,000 St. Louisans stood in unemployment lines. Emerson Electric's war plant was for sale and Curtiss-Wright executives, after reassessing the situation in St. Louis, closed the aircraft plant. The factory at Lambert Field, a point of pride for the city since it was built in 1941, was sold to McDonnell Aircraft in late 1945. Like previous wars, World War II brought immense changes to the city. Along with the rest of the country, St. Louis suffered from the unemployment and confusion that followed the immediate end of the war but looked forward to a promising future. Building projects halted by the war would be taken up with a renewed sense of purpose and accomplishment in the flush of victory.

When the long war finally ended with the U. S. victory over Japan, St. Louisans celebrated along with the rest of the nation.
The St. Louis Mercantile Library at the University of Missouri-St. Louis

seven

1945~present

The City Spreads:
POSTWAR EXPANSION

Returning GIs who crossed the Mississippi River into St. Louis after World War II saw a desolate riverfront and an aging downtown business district. St. Louis' problems were typical of other large industrial cities: aging downtown construction and an as-yet-incomplete shift in economy. Traffic congestion became a problem again, as gas rationing ended. All these challenges had been put on hold by the war effort, but St. Louisans operated on faith that progress on these and other problems would be best made through basic, physical improvement of the urban landscape.

On the riverfront, work on the Jefferson National Expansion Memorial had halted during the war years and the levee became a gigantic parking lot, watched over by the graceful Cathedral of St. Louis. National Park Service plans for the site included connecting the Cathedral and Court House by new walkways to museums of fur trading, architecture and national expansion.

After the end of the war, when city and country looked forward to a better future, a modern memorial seemed more appropriate than ever, symbolizing American youth, freedom

Aerial View of St. Louis from the East Side showing the cleared riverfront site of the Jefferson National Expansion Memorial, c. 1948 —
when soldiers returned to St. Louis from overseas, they saw a city in need of revitalization.
©Arteaga Photos, LTD

and leadership. By 1944 Luther Ely Smith called for a new kind of memorial, "national in scope and interest, inspirational and educational in character, contributing to the practical and aesthetic life of the community."

When a national design contest was held in 1948, Eero Saarinen's revolutionary design was selected. The gleaming stainless steel catenary arch soars 630 feet above the riverfront, its triangular legs and gentle curve a modern reflection of James B. Eads' elegant bridge just to the north. In the early 1960s, as his stunning monument to the Louisiana Purchase began to rise on the St. Louis riverfront, architect Eero Saarinen explained that "more

Aerial view of St. Louis showing the cleared riverfront used as a parking lot, c. 1950
©*Arteaga Photos, LTD*

and more it began to dawn on us that the arch was really a gateway and gradually, we named it the Gateway to the West." Finished in 1965, the arch became an instant civic symbol. When Pierre Chouteau proposed a riverfront "Museum of American Genius" and re-created Village of St. Louis, he could not have imagined how Saarinen's soaring monument, with a historical museum in its base, would fulfill that dream.

While the arch rose above downtown St. Louis, the county's formerly sleepy suburbs became thriving commercial districts. In the late 1950s, Clayton emerged to challenge the established central business district's role as a center of commerce. The first expansion in Clayton after World War II came from the retail trade. Late in 1944, St. Louis department stores began to conduct branch store location studies based on current and predicted demographics and spending patterns analyzed by census

district. Clayton, University City, Webster Groves and Richmond Heights all showed over $5 million each in residents' disposable income. Studies of cash and charge receipts from 1940 and 1944 showed that Scruggs, Vandervoort and Barney depended on St. Louis county for a major portion of its gross incomes; sales to people traveling between 6 and 12 miles to the downtown stores accounted for 40 percent of the store's volume.

As store planners studied how people traveled downtown to shop, they realized that the amount of automobile traffic would continue to grow. Stix, Baer and Fuller provided inexpensive parking in a 275-car garage; and Famous-Barr was building a 600-car garage. Scruggs' only available parking spaces were in a leased building several blocks from the store, and these spaces were neither publicized nor widely used. Figures showed that of the three leading department stores, Scruggs received the largest portion of its volume from St. Louis County shoppers, particularly from the portions of the county with a large purchasing power.

Realizing that between 80 and 90 percent of all shoppers would travel by car to reach stores in the county, retail planners began to seriously consider Clayton as a new Scruggs' location. Boyd's opened the first Clayton branch in 1946 but was quickly overshadowed when Famous-Barr's modern branch store at Forsyth and Jackson opened on October 8, 1948. Scruggs followed suit on September 15, 1951, with a new brick-and-glass store at 7700 Forsyth, complete with two parking levels. After merging with the Wohl Shoe Company, the newly enlarged Brown Shoe Company moved into modern headquarters at 8300 Maryland Avenue in 1952, preferring to house all operations in one building. Today, Clayton remains a vital business district. The old department stores have been converted to new uses not only by new retail chains, but also by local universities. Border's Books and Music occupies the old Scruggs store, while Washington University has converted the Famous-Barr building into a "west campus," housing the University Archives in addition to administrative functions.

Just as Clayton was the site of the first branch stores, St. Louis County led the nation with new shopping centers adapted to the automotive suburban lifestyle. These retail satellites in the county eventually displaced the centralized downtown retail district. One of the nation's first planned shopping centers, Northwest Plaza has embodied all the ideals of the suburban shopping experience — from open-air plaza to enclosed shopping mall — since 1965. Its landscape designer, Lawrence Halprin, told the *Globe-Democrat*, "Northwest Plaza was designed as a complete city. It is complete with pedestrian streets, parks and plazas."

After Northwest Plaza, both the city and the county built prestigious new shopping malls as postwar prosperity made it possible for more and more families to afford a middle-class lifestyle. Homeownership increased rapidly as returning soldiers took advantage of favorable loan rates. The new single-story, two- and three-bedroom homes erected in Florissant and other suburbs did more than accommodate practical needs. They also gave their residents a social blueprint for the lives that they might lead. Open-space plans, family rooms and eat-in kitchens encouraged informal, collective activity; picture windows and sliding doors linked interior space to the outdoors.

St. Louis is the headquarters for many national companies and continues to contribute to the national economy and culture. This view is of Central Street in Clayton.
Photo by Kirsten Hammerstrom, 2000

Modern design and new housing construction were not limited to suburban developments. City planners turned to the housing problems that had plagued St. Louis since the 1908 report prepared by the Civic League. Initial attempts to improve housing conditions in the city focused on legislation. Minimum housing standards were to encourage landlords to conform to the laws. Unfortunately, sunless and unheated rooms and exposed sewers persisted in the poorest districts.

During the Depression, city planners recognized that new approaches were needed, and they prepared some of the earliest slum clearance and housing reconstruction projects in the nation. Using the able draftsmen of the

City Plan Commission, the Slum Clearance Committee recommended two neighborhoods where clearance and new housing construction would be of greatest benefit. Projects in these two areas were completed in early 1941 and 1942 as Clinton-Peabody on Chouteau Avenue for whites, and Carr Square Village on Carr Street for African Americans. Both projects were composed of low-rise two- and three-story garden apartments finished in brick. The planners created new neighborhoods, refashioning streets into super blocks and clustering houses in groups around open park land and play space. During the war, Clinton-Peabody was used to house war workers, and plans to revitalize additional neighborhoods were suspended.

The first postwar project was Cochran Gardens, a residential project consisting of mixed-height buildings; and the Pruitt-Igoe Homes followed in 1953. Postwar public housing in St. Louis brought welcome relief from embarrassing and dangerous conditions. When residents moved into their new apartments, they had appliances, central heat and hot water, working toilets, and new interiors ready to be decorated. The apartments offered a better life, a chance to succeed and a piece of the American Dream. All too quickly, however, "public housing" became synonymous with "slum." Pruitt-Igoe, the most infamous of all projects, became a national symbol for the failure of public housing to achieve planners' goals of creating better housing — and better lives — for the urban poor. St. Louis had led the nation in building public housing, and she led the nation again in tearing it down. Since 1972, the city has been tearing down high-rise apartment buildings and replacing them with smaller garden apartment units in addition to single-family homes.

The city continues to address housing problems with innovative solutions like the Eads Homes — new, single-family residences — near Lafayette Park.

Just as she led the nation in housing, St. Louis also led the country in planning for expressways and highways for cars. City Plan Engineer Harlan Bartholomew wrestled with how to move people around the metropolitan area. Traffic congestion had begun to reach unbearable levels in the early 20th century when automobiles and trucks shared city streets with horses, wagons and trolleys. Suburban commuters clogged main arteries like Lindell Boulevard and Market Street as people began to switch from streetcar commuting to driving. The City Plan Commission, recognizing the need to ease traffic congestion, attempted to solve the problem in 1912 by proposing a Central Traffic Parkway. This and other early highway plans were based on the parkway model, providing green space, trees and occasional comfort stations, as planners combined city beautiful ideals with practical

After the war many corporations moved west to Clayton, consolidating offices in spacious, modern facilities. Here is the entrance to Brown Shoe Company Headquarters on Maryland Avenue in Clayton.
Photo by Kirsten Hammerstrom, 2000

needs. The Express Superhighway was constructed and St. Louis entered the automotive age full speed — 45 mph. Under the Major Street Plan, downtown streets were widened and cutoffs eliminated; but even with these changes, congestion remained unbearable.

Missouri and St. Louis highway promoters, blueprints in hand, had been waiting for federal funding since the 1940s. Harland Bartholomew, one of the architects of the national interstate system, viewed St. Louis as a planning laboratory. Civic leaders welcomed interstate construction as an opportunity to boost the economy, ease traffic congestion, lure shoppers back from the suburbs, and counteract the urban fragmentation caused by city-county separation. The 1956 Federal Aid Highway Act may have had greater economic and social consequences than any other piece of 20th-century domestic legislation. The St. Louis area received two of the first three construction contracts awarded under the Highway Act, and a portion of I-70 was the first section of the national system actually constructed. The federal government ultimately invested $250 million in St. Louis interstates. Plans were laid out for I-64, locally known as Highway 40, and for I-44. Today, these and newer highways connect St. Louis with her suburbs, bringing thousands of people to work every day.

As St. Louis-based planners worked to ease transportation difficulties within the region, new immigrants arrived in the city, drawn by jobs in new postwar industries. Many of the new immigrants were African Americans coming north. As residents, they would participate in the long struggle for equality that had begun more than a century earlier with Lucy Delaney and William Wells Brown. For the new migrants, Union Station best symbolized the city's historical status at the crossroads of American race relations. Here, African Americans traveling south had to change into Jim Crow cars, while those traveling north were allowed to leave their seats at the back of the train and sit wherever they chose. Everyone could eat at the Harvey restaurant. Outside the station, blacks found a city that still projected the ambiguities and ambivalence of its southern border heritage. Public accommodations were segregated, but one rarely found a sign to indicate which restaurants, restrooms or drinking fountains were accessible.

After the war St. Louis faced new challenges in race relations. The history of direct action for integration in St. Louis can be traced to 1944 when the Citizens Civil Rights Committee, an interracial group of women, began holding sit-ins at downtown department store lunch counters. Local members of the Congress on Racial Equality and the NAACP continued the sit-ins for over a decade, working to integrate restaurants, hotels and theaters. CORE members handed out wallet-sized cards indicating which restaurants served blacks. When St. Louis outlawed discrimination in public accommodations in 1961, it essentially endorsed what local citizens had already achieved. Local actions had a national effect when J.D. and Ethel Shelley challenged the restrictive covenants in 1946 by attempting to buy a home on a white block in North St. Louis.

In 1948 Thurgood Marshall argued the case before the U.S. Supreme Court. *Shelley v. Kraemer* declared racial restrictive covenants unenforceable and became a linchpin of the national civil rights struggle. The St. Louis Archdiocese integrated its schools in 1947, and when the Supreme Court outlawed "separate but equal" schools in the 1954 decision in *Brown v. Board of Education*, St. Louis integrated its schools with little protest. African Americans continued to work for equality as Washington University integrated in the mid-1960s, and more professional education and employment opportunities became available. Homer G. Phillips Hospital continued to be a leader in educating African American doctors and nurses until it was finally closed in the 1980s. Today, African American politicians and civil servants occupy important positions in city government, earning the support or derision of St. Louisans of all races depending on their performance, not their race.

Long a destination for a network of railroad lines carrying immigrants and new ideas, St. Louis now occupied a central position in new broadcasting networks. KMOX had been leader in radio broadcasting, making the Cardinals the home team of the western half of the nation. After World War II, local programming decisions articulated the changing relation of the city to the nation. In 1947 KSD broadcast the first television program in St. Louis; the station would be the city's only television broadcaster until 1953. In its early years, KSD offered no daytime programs and relied on KSD-radio for announcers and the St. Louis *Post-Dispatch* for news. When the station was not broadcasting network shows, it filled airtime with talk shows, cooking shows, current affairs and game shows. An appliance store sponsored "What's the Price," where viewers won appliances by calling in and guessing

Old Courthouse, St. Louis, c. 1965 – court cases like Shelley v. Kramer
changed the racial and social landscape of both the city and the nation.
©Arteaga Photos, LTD

the price. The show was so popular that when viewers' calls overloaded three phone stations, KSD quickly installed 15 more lines.

Local television stations continue to broadcast a combination of national and local programs, providing the city and the region with historic overviews, in-depth coverage of regional emergencies and a sense of pride. As television brought the look of the nation to the city, music took the sound of St. Louis to the nation. Musicians like Chuck Berry, Albert King, and Ike and Tina Turner forged their styles at clubs like the Sunset and the Imperial, where they played before teenaged audiences from throughout the metropolitan area. A city known for the blues became known for rock-n-roll, the newest of American national music forms.

Like other American cities, progress in St. Louis depended upon its position in a larger national culture and economy in the postwar era and benefited from Cold War spending. Military spending during World War II revitalized the St. Louis economy, and in the postwar years defense spending continued to have a dramatic effect on the local economy. St. Louis firms supplied the government with everything from desk chairs to space capsules. The city was the home of the nation's two largest military contractors, General Dynamics and McDonnell. St. Louisans could proudly boast that the Mercury, Gemini and Apollo space capsules were locally produced. McDonnell engineers worked closely with National Air and Space Administration scientists and astronauts to produce the spacecraft that would successfully launch both city and nation into the next era of exploration.

From the jumping-off point for western explorers, to the center of important networks for steamboat and railroad lines, to the hub for international airlines, St. Louis has remained in the forefront of travel and exploration. From the stainless steel Gateway Arch commemorating Lewis and Clark's Voyage of Discovery, to the silvery *Spirit of St. Louis* replica that hangs in the Missouri Historical Society, to the gleaming gold-leafed bases of the Mercury space capsules, St. Louis has always looked to the future as she remembers her past.

Downtown St. Louis is seen from the east in 2001. Historic and vibrant, the city faces the future while building on the past. ©*Arteaga Photos, LTD*

TABLE OF CONTENTS

Partners in St. Louis

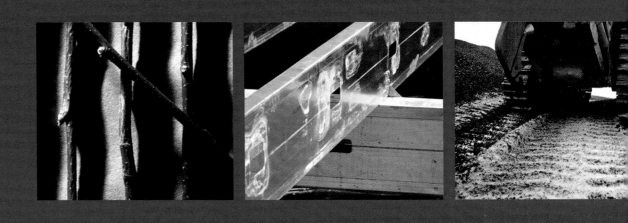

St. Louis real estate and construction industries and unions and business development organizations are bringing life back to the central city.

BUILDING A GREATER ST. LOUIS

Located on the banks of the great river, St. Louis is a city where the north meets the south, the east meets the west, and the past meets the future. The historic Eads Bridge, Lacledes Landing and the Old Cathedral share the levee with the Saarinen Arch, a gleaming example of the technology of tomorrow. The Arch frames the Old Courthouse, which is part of our Civil War history.

As the city grew west from the river, it left a record of the changing lives of its people. The early city on the banks of the river became the center of commerce. The advent of the automobile led to the development of the rolling countryside to the west as a residential area. As the population center grew westward, commerce followed.

The St. Louis real estate and construction industries are bringing life back to the central city. Grand Center is being redeveloped as a theatre district combining existing concert halls with outstanding new museums. Great universities are expanding their campuses. Corporate campuses are growing in the Old Mill Creek Valley. Warehouse buildings are being redeveloped to house apartments, hotels and condominiums in the central city. The picturesque railroad station has become a highly successful shopping center, flanked by a fountain by Carl Milles whose theme is the meeting of the rivers. The historic City Hall faces the new Thomas Eagleton Federal Building rising above the skyline.

St. Louis continues to be a mixture of the new and the old. The masonry architecture of the early days continues to bring scale and harmony to the everyday lives of its people.

Thanks to the real estate and construction industries and unions and businesses development organizations, the Saarinen Arch, intended as the Gateway to the West, has become a Gateway to the Future as well.

RAYMOND E. MARITZ
President • Raymond E. Maritz & Sons Inc.

M.L. Johnson and Company, Inc.

M. L. Johnson and Company, Inc. (MLJCI), a multi-dimensional construction management company, is led by a close-knit management team that insists on the consistent delivery of the highest-quality service.

Founded in 1991 with the basic goal of delivering sound construction management services along with excellent customer service, M.L. Johnson and Company has been involved in many high-profile construction projects and renovations in and around the St. Louis area.

With a background in architecture, President Marvin L. Johnson envisioned a company that could provide complete construction management services to both the public and private sectors. He and his wife, Renee, executive vice president, took a personal dream and made it both a reality and a shared vision among the team that Johnson assembled during the firm's first decade. Johnson now says, "We are on a journey that few have traveled. It's not about Marvin's dream anymore. It's a shared vision."

The building of direct relationships with end uses, and the challenge to the company to grow its capability and capacity is an excellent fit in the basic philosophy of competing "outside of the box" of a "minority business." Johnson says the company must ultimately be known more for its ability to deliver the highest quality than for the fact of its African-American ownership.

Rough framing work of the M.L. Johnson and Company at-risk construction management project of the BJC St. Peter's facility

M.L. Johnson and Company provided at-risk construction management services in the renovation of Saucers, the St. Louis Science Center coffee bar.

In addition to the ownership group, the corporate vision for success has enabled the company to recruit a group of world-class professionals in their respective fields that has helped the company to grow in capacity and capability along the lines of the vision of its principals, remain ready to commit and deliver quality services to its clients.

Realizing that the most difficult aspect of starting a new business is in its early years, Johnson characterizes the growth of M. L. Johnson and Company with the story of the fabled Chinese bamboo tree. It is said that the giant Chinese bamboo tree begins quite humbly with a hard nut planted in the ground. After it is planted, it must be watered each day, and must be fertilized routinely. Both are essential to the growth of the tree. In those first critical years, nothing is apparent above ground. However, the care regime must continue. If at any time it stops, the tree will die unseen, below the earth. In the fifth year, the tree breaks through the surface and grows to be 90 feet tall within six weeks. The proverbial question is; did the tree grow 90 feet in five years or in six weeks? Marvin Johnson knows it took five years of unwavering faith in an outcome and persistent, diligent action to bring about that growth.

After completing its first decade in business, much like the bamboo tree, M. L. Johnson was growing consistently in the beginning and is now growing in leaps and bounds with its roots firmly apparent in the St. Louis community. Through careful nourishment, the company's management team has brought the company to the forefront of the construction management industry.

What is now a thriving business with 60 employees began in a home basement with one phone line. Through several levels of growth, the company moved to a one-room office, then to a bigger office and finally to the Bank of America building, which the company eventually purchased, now occupying about 16,000 square feet of office space.

Renovation of the building has not only provided M.L. Johnson with luxurious and functional space but also provides ample space for Bank of America, in addition to rentable areas on each level. The company's plans to redevelop portions of the Benton Park neighborhood include a public park as well as commercial and residential renovations with the intent of spurring economic growth and an opportunity for revitalization of the surrounding community.

Staff diversity is an important part of the M.L. Johnson and Company group. The company believes that true diversity brings a richness, broadness and depth to professional solutions. The company has created jobs and leadership opportunities for young St. Louisans. The company believes that it has a distinct advantage in its recognition that creativity, excellence, boldness, brilliance, and even genius, have no racial or gender preferences. "We intend to be a magnet for talent, without racial or gender limitations," says Johnson.

Marvin L. Johnson believes strongly in continuing education for all employees. By keeping everyone in the company continuously prepared to meet future needs of clients, Johnson says that opportunity and growth will follow. One of his favorite sayings is, "Chance favors the prepared mind."

The entire management team believes that one of the most important aspects of being in business is to be perceived simply as providers of high-quality services with no limitations as to who the players are.

Using a hands-on approach to management, Marvin and Renee Johnson are still very involved in day-to-day business operations. Though each has his or her own areas of specialization, cross training among upper management allows the partners to keep a finger in every aspect of the business, providing a safety net of support and guidance. This filters down through the organization,

creating a networked team environment filled with initiative, creativity, leadership achievement, solutions and on-time delivery of projects.

Mike Brown, contract administrator; Marvin Woods, Director of Technical Services; Viola Pancratz, Senior Controls Manager; Lee Duarte, finance manager; Gwen Albritton, director of organizational development and human resources; and Floyd Simms, director of project services, are all strong and vital members of the management team. Each plays a major role in the continued success and viability of the company.

The corridor of the elegant Chase Park Plaza Hotel, a joint venture renovation project in which M.L. Johnson and Company was construction manager

M. L. Johnson and Company was the subcontractor for structural concrete in the construction of the Chuck Knight Education Center at Washington University.

Experts in civil, structural, mechanical and electrical disciplines, as well as finance, business, real estate and human resources make up the company's intensely qualified staff, along with senior-level project managers, skilled labor and seasoned superintendents who all strive to provide superior value to customers. Marvin Johnson states, "It is the responsibility of this company's

The Chuck Knight Education Center dining hall at Washington University

The company stresses four primary elements for the successful execution of projects:

1. Cooperation within a fully integrated project team committed to the success of the project
2. Commitment from a team that remains intact during the course of the project
3. Continuity of quality in all project phases through a consistent vision of a dedicated staff
4. Control through evaluation of planning, design and construction elements to ensure value of the ultimate project

All projects are given day-to-day attention by an assigned project manager and continuous oversight by the company's principals, giving clients a personal and direct contact throughout all phases of construction.

Several other critical strategies have also provided basic guidelines for the success of M.L. Johnson and Company. Recognizing that understanding expectations is the main element in a successful project, listening is strategy No. 1. Experienced staff, effective organization, state-of-the-art management tools and a proactive approach to providing quality in the most cost-effective manner possible are further means of achieving the desired outcome. The M.L. Johnson construction process is client-focused, goal oriented and success driven.

M.L. Johnson and Company has been involved in such projects as the Alton Belle Casino renovation, BJC campus integration, the Cupples Station renovation and several projects for the Forest Park Master Plan, St. Louis Science Center, Washington University School of Medicine, and Hilltop Campus Earth and Planetary Science facility.

leadership to make leaders out of each our staff members. It is a welcome task for each of us."

Continuous training and mentoring in the latest estimating and scheduling software and technology keeps the company on the cutting edge of construction management. The professional staff maintains ethics and policies established by corporate principals and each possesses broad technical and administrative abilities that allow the firm to operate at peak efficiency, resulting in greater value for the client.

The pursuit and achievement of excellence in construction from start to finish of a project is the primary goal of MLJCI. Effective management, field safety, project controls, planning, issue resolution and cost-containment are brought to every project the company is involved in. MLJCI also provides constructability review, value engineering, construction administration, quality assurance, quality control and pre-construction services.

Developing and growing self-perform capabilities in general carpentry, heavy equipment operation and general labor has helped the company to maintain a realistic understanding of construction issues.

The Bank of America building in the Benton Park neighborhood of St. Louis houses 16,000 square feet of luxurious office space for M.L. Johnson and Company.

The $50 million Cupples Station project is a redevelopment in downtown St. Louis that included renovation of the Westin St. Louis Hotel. The project included conversion of five existing buildings to a five-star hotel facility.

M.L. Johnson was the construction manager for the $9 million River's Edge Area III at the St. Louis Zoo. This project includes nine new animal exhibits. The St. Louis Science Center project involved major upgrades to the Omnimax Theatre, the Infant Care Facility, multi-purpose room and the Saucers Coffee Bar.

Other major projects include participation on the $133 million Renaissance Grand Hotel project, the $80 million facility expansion for the St. Louis Public School System, and the Renovation of the Chase Park Plaza Hotel and Schnuck's Markets, Inc.

The firm partnered to complete the renovation of the Adams School and Community Center, a turn-of-the-century K-12 public school. Numerous renovations at various St. Louis Connect Care locations, the Homer G. Phillips display at the Missouri History Museum and many additional projects in the St. Louis area are examples of M.L. Johnson and Company's outstanding accomplishments showing the care and expertise that has become the company's hallmark.

M.L. Johnson was the recipient of the Minority Business Enterprise of the Year Award in the construction category in 1995. It has received the *St. Louis Business Journal* notation as the 6th-Largest Minority-Owned Business in St. Louis, the Special Achievement Award-St. Louis Sentinel and the AGC Keystone Award for partnering excellence. In 2000 and 2001 the firm was recognized as one of the top 25 African-American-owned businesses in St. Louis. In 2001 the St. Louis Counsel of Construction Consumers recognized the firm with its "Construction Cost Effectiveness Award" for its team performance on the Adams School Renovation.

M. L. Johnson and Company actively participates in organizations and programs that promote self-esteem, awareness and success-building activities. Company principals are involved in an ongoing mentoring relationship as part of the AGC of St. Louis Stempel program and have served on the AGC of St. Louis board of directors and on the board of trustees of the AGC of St. Louis Education Foundation. It supports the Joe Torre Foundation, The Learning Tree and the Life Sources, Inc., among many other community organizations. The company participates in the St. Louis Internship

Marvin and Renee Johnson founded M.L. Johnson and Company in 1991.

Program and is a member of the National Society of Black Engineers-St. Louis Chapter.

The ultimate goals for M.L. Johnson and Company are to be self-sustaining, self-perpetuating and self determined. Five principals to the firm plan to develop a foundation to work and help support community-based nonprofits and a scholarship foundation for African-American engineers.

Entering the new century, MLJCI has a clear vision of the future: consistent development in all areas. This will be achieved by consistently providing clients with excellent customer service and cost-effective management from pre-construction to post-construction, based on the solid foundation of successful projects that the company's reputation has been built on. With continuous education and ongoing opportunities for its employees along with proactive research and planning for future success, M.L. Johnson is sustained by the very philosophy that Marvin L. Johnson built it on — "Chance favors the prepared mind."

The M.L. Johnson and Company team provides expertise and quality in all projects, large or small, that the company undertakes.

Clark Properties

*M*aking a difference in neighborhoods by creating jobs, revitalizing economic development and breathing new life into formerly booming areas can bring a wealth of personal as well as professional satisfaction.

Harold Clark became instrumental in such changes in 1983 when he began buying and refurbishing properties whose better days seemed to be behind them. What's more, Clark discovered he had a knack for this type of redevelopment, and before long, Clark Properties, now a full-service real estate development and property management company, began to grow.

Clark's first company, Clark Painting Company, began in the 1960s working for major corporations in St. Louis and eventually around the world. Clark became one of the nation's largest and most successful industrial painting contractors. In addition to bridges, pipelines, refineries and manufacturing plants, he regularly performed major restoration and redevelopment work for many national and area developers. After retiring from the painting business in the late 70s, Clark quickly grew restless and started investigating redevelopment opportunities to keep busy and so began his next career.

He knew that industrial redevelopment takes many different forms depending on the condition of the existing facilities, former use and the intended new use. Selective or complete demolition, environmental cleanup, refurbishing older facilities and building new facilities may be required. In many cases, completely replacing the sites' utilities and streets are necessary.

While things started small for the company, work began to snowball and opportunities to purchase some very significant industrial sites began to come Clark's way.

One of the first major redevelopment projects undertaken in the 80s by the newly established Clark Properties was the former GAF Industrial facility in St. Louis. This 28-acre, 211,000-square-foot project, now known as Riverview Industrial Center, required more than $3 million of improvements and has become a major distribution center.

One of the most challenging and satisfying opportunities for Clark was the redevelopment of the former General Motors Assembly Plant in north St. Louis. This 161-acre property, now known as Union Seventy Center Business Park, is an ongoing project that continues to stimulate economic activity in and around the park. Major cleanup, renovation, street additions and overcoming the former image of the property proved to be obstacles that Clark Properties was willing and able to overcome.

The investment in the Union Seventy park exceeds $100 million. Attention to every detail has attracted major corporations such as Pepsi-Cola, Save-A-Lot, Smurfit-Stone, MFR Tire and United Rentals, which have located production/distribution centers and office/warehouse facilities in its boundaries. The site includes a 2.2-million-square-foot multi-tenant office and warehouse building as well as several additional refurbished and new buildings.

The common theme among Clark Properties redevelopment sites is underutilized property that is environmentally challenged with buildings that are deteriorating, sometimes requiring demolition and environmental remediation. In many cases, the surrounding community is also in decline. The properties are then put into re-use through master planning of the site, which includes redevelopment and the creation of an environment that will bring people back into the area.

Harold Clark, founder of Clark Properties

Alton Center Business Park in Alton, Illinois, before development work began at the site of the old Owens-Illinois Inc. glassworks

The company is involved in all phases of the redevelopment process, including initial site selection, feasibility studies and utilization analysis. Its services also extend to financing and procurement of governmental incentives, environmental assessment, the redevelopment itself and property management.

In 1997, Clark's son, Michael, who was a partner in Clayco Construction Co., joined Clark Properties and became president and owner in 2000 when Harold Clark retired. Picking up where his father left off, Michael Clark continues to work with further development of Union Seventy Business Park, which Harold Clark started more than 10 years ago.

Clark Properties' first step into Illinois is the current redevelopment of the former Owens Illinois Glass plant in Alton, now known as Alton Center Business Park. This project is helping a once-thriving area to again reach its potential as an economic center in the community. Development of the park has involved demolition of more than 1 million square feet of buildings. In its first phase, the development has already attracted the largest private water utility in the country.

Within the business park, Clark Properties has created a memorial site in honor of former employees of Owens Illinois Glass, consisting of Owens' memorabilia, including a 4,000-pound piece of carved glass and a walkway featuring bricks and granite stones engraved with past employees' names.

Other major Clark Property developments in and around St. Louis include Southwest Industrial Center, a former U.S. Army ammunition plant; 1920 Beltway and 170 Center and Northwest Industrial Center, the former Boise Cascade facility.

Clark Properties and its principals have been very involved in contributing to the viability of the Mathews-Dickey Boys' and Girls' Club where Harold Clark served on the board for many years. Michael Clark continues on the Mathews-Dickey board today. Clark Properties is also active in numerous civic and community development programs. The company is a member of the Leadership Council of Southwestern Illinois, St. Louis Regional Commerce and Growth Association, the Illinois Public Affairs Committee, and the National Brownfields Associations.

The company and its developments have been the recipient of many prestigious awards. The Phoenix Award

The reflection pond at the Union Seventy Center, one of Clark Properties' developments at the site of the former General Motors plant in St. Louis

for Community Impact, the region's top Brownfield Redevelopment, the River Bend Growth Association's Chairman's Award, The Southwest Illinois Development Authority's Outstanding Development of the Year and The Captain of the River Bend Award have all been received for Alton Center Business Park. The Union Seventy Center Business Park has also been recognized with numerous achievement awards.

Clark Properties plans to continue Brownfield developments, creating a level playing field for distressed sites, enabling the surrounding communities to compete with Greenfield sites for economic development and job opportunities.

Harold Clark's driving philosophy in all his years of business were: to remember that your word is your bond; pay your bills on time; build up a reputation with subcontractors; and always have impeccable credibility — then you can't go wrong.

Alton Center Business Park's refurbished warehouses, which are now the home to American Water Company

First American
Title Insurance Company

First American Title Insurance Company, now one of the largest title insurers in the world, also is one of the oldest. It can claim a history in St. Louis dating back to 1854.

First American's history can be tracked on two separate timelines.

In St. Louis the company traces its history from 1854, when Henry Williams compiled the first private index to the city's public records for his firm. Williams' indexes and abstracts changed hands many times before ultimately becoming the property of Title Insurance Corporation of St. Louis, which was incorporated in 1927. Title Insurance Corporation of St. Louis later became St. Paul Title Insurance Company. In 1901 Land Title Insurance Company of St. Louis was formed and operated as a competitor of St. Paul Title Insurance Company.

Across the country in California, Orange County Title grew out of the 1894 merger of the area's original two abstract companies. By 1963 the firm had taken the name "First American" and was operating in four states. Four years after going public in 1964, the California-based firm became a general holding company — The First American Corporation — and First American Title Insurance Company became a wholly owned subsidiary.

First American Title Insurance Company then executed an aggressive expansion plan, and by the early 1980s it had gained a national presence through the acquisition of selected firms. It purchased both St. Paul and Land Title at that time, bringing these great firms with their extensive history into the fold.

Movement defined this period of the 19th century in America, particularly in Missouri and California — the gateway to the West and the Wild West itself. Immigration and westward migration stimulated the real estate market in both areas and spurred the need for abstract companies, which initially provided only title searches. At the time, a prospective property owner usually retained an attorney to render an opinion on the abstract, but holding anyone liable for the information proved difficult. Title insurance arose to reduce the long-term risks associated with real estate transactions and thus facilitated the entire process of purchasing property because it indemnified the owner or lender against loss.

A policy of title insurance issued by First American, available for a one-time premium and remaining in effect until the property is sold or refinanced, provides protection against defective title, undisclosed liens, unreleased mortgages and other claims, such as easement and adverse possession issues. In the event a claim arises, First American will defend the insured at its own expense, compensate the owner for any loss that results from an unsuccessful defense and when possible, correct or clear the title. The company also offers a rider that increases coverage in accordance with the inflation rate.

Like other underwriters, First American's standard policy indemnifies property owners and lenders against mistakes or misdeeds arising prior to issuance. Its EAGLE policy, created in 1997, goes beyond that to take the industry-leading step of offering coverage for events that occur after the policy is purchased, including forgeries and encroachments as well as some subdivision law and building permit violations.

The company broke new ground again in 1999 when it introduced the first standardized

First American Title Insurance Company evolved from the Hall-Evans Company, pictured here in 1914. *Missouri Historical Society*

international policy to meet the need for title insurance in the numerous countries where none is available. The product, which insures property worldwide, has been well received and demand is expected to grow. First American, which operates directly in 10 countries, has brought title insurance to many of those countries, including Canada and Hong Kong.

First American holds a tradition of investing in technology to improve its operations. In the early 1970s the company completely automated the real estate records of St. Louis city and county. First American's state-of-the-art title production and delivery technology now offers customers worldwide the convenience of online ordering of its products and services.

In addition to title insurance, First American provides everything needed to complete a home purchase including a property profile, real estate appraisal, flood-zone determination, mortgage document preparation, and property and casualty insurance. Escrow or settlement services, which engage a neutral third party to close a real estate transaction pursuant to the terms of the sales contract, are available. The company also issues title reports to individuals, banks making equity loans or lawyers filing liens, and insures lenders of commercial loans secured by personal property under the Uniform Commercial Code. Another wholly owned subsidiary, Midwest Disbursing, offers a full line of construction disbursement services.

Recognizing that each real estate market is different, The First American Corporation affords each office of First American Title Insurance Company the authority to make decisions locally, and this autonomy contributes greatly to the title company's success. Customers enjoy the convenience of working with insurance and real estate professionals versed in the local market but gain the security only a national company can furnish.

At a time when the title insurance industry is undergoing rapid consolidation, First American already is adept at acquiring successful firms in selected markets, integrating them into its corporate culture and providing them with the technology and autonomy to best serve its customers. First American leads the industry in developing new products to serve and protect the parties

Orange County Title (shown here about 1900) is the predecessor to The First American Corporation, which operates First American Title Insurance Company in St. Louis and nationwide. *Historical Collection, First American Financial Corporation*

to real estate transactions. It is committed to improving its national and global operations through investments in technology designed to deliver products and services with increased convenience and efficiency.

Today, First American Title insurance Company products are available directly or though a wide network of agents, including Land Title. In addition to insuring residential properties, the underwriter has insured many of the area's major construction projects including roadways, shopping malls, sports venues and the St. Louis Gateway Arch. The First American Corporation is now a diversified, international provider of information services and boasts an expanded product line that includes consumer information, such as credit and public records reporting, screening of prospective renters and employees, and trust and banking services.

First American Title Insurance Company's office in Clayton, Missouri *Historical Collection, First American Financial Corporation*

McCormack Baron

*I*n the fall of 1968 Richard D. Baron, a young Legal Aid attorney, met Terence McCormack, a housing consultant for the Teamsters Local 688. Baron was representing public housing residents involved in a rent withholding action against the St. Louis Housing Authority, protesting rent increases and living conditions in nine public housing developments. McCormack was working with Teamster leader Harold Gibbons, who was asked by Mayor A.J. Cervantes in 1969 to mediate the strike, which he successfully did in October of that year. Baron and McCormack worked together from 1969 to 1972 in reconstituting the Housing Authority and in 1973 jointly founded McCormack Baron & Associates, a company recognized today as the pre-eminent developer of quality affordable housing.

The company initially was established as a consulting firm providing services to community-based organizations dealing with issues related to housing, community development and capacity building. The firm undertook its first housing development in 1977; renovating the historic Washington Hotel into a 99-unit residence for low-income families in St. Louis.

Since its inception, McCormack Baron has focused on inner-city neighborhoods and downtown locations. It has distinguished itself as the leading for-profit residential development and management company committed exclusively to rebuilding urban neighborhoods. The firm has moved from restoring single historic buildings to undertaking multi-block development projects that involve both market-rate and affordable housing. Its large-scale residential projects are designed to stimulate new private investment in the community, either by single-family homebuyers, or by retail and commercial businesses.

McCormack Baron developments are characterized by a blend of financing sources — both public and private. Its financing techniques incorporate a variety of funding approaches that utilize federal programs, tax-exempt bond financing, tax-increment financing, conventional loans, pension funds, foundation loans and grants, and equity from the private sector. During the course of the firm's development activities in local communities, it has successfully created relationships with local government, the private sector, community-based organizations and foundations.

Richard Baron was invited in 1990 to serve on the National Commission for Severely Distressed Public Housing, which developed recommendations for the Congress in dealing with severely deteriorated public housing sites. The commission focused on three areas: physical improvements, management improvements, and social and community services to residents. The commission proposed that Congress authorize a new, targeted initiative, now known as HOPE VI, that would create new partnerships among Public Housing Authorities, nonprofit organizations, the private sector and resident organizations. The grant funds would provide physical improvements including demolition, replacement housing, home ownership opportunities and off-site development, using the grant money to leverage private capital. Congress

McCormack House at Westminster Place

George L. Vaughn Residences at Murphy Park

enacted the new legislation in 1991. McCormack Baron played a key role in designing the HOPE VI program with former HUD Secretary Henry Cisneros.

To date, the firm has completed the lease-up of four phases of the first "HOPE VI" site in the country (Centennial Place in Atlanta, Georgia). It has completed similar projects in St. Louis, Missouri, including the Residences at Murphy Park Phases I and II; as well as in San Francisco, California; Kansas City, Missouri; and Little Rock, Arkansas. The first phase of a multi-phased development in Minneapolis is underway. McCormack Baron was selected in St. Louis as the lead developer of the Blumeyer public housing site, which recently received $35 million in HOPE VI funds. Other firm HOPE VI developments are in process in Pittsburgh, Pennsylvania; Los Angeles, California; Gary, Indiana; and Jersey City, New Jersey. All of these developments initially involve a master planning process that includes neighborhood, public housing authority and city participation.

McCormack Baron recognizes that the success of any development depends on community support and involvement. The approach is evident at the Residences at Murphy Park on the near north side of St. Louis. Once the site of the George L. Vaughn public housing development, McCormack Baron has created a new neighborhood that offers attractive garden and townhome apartments to draw residents from a broad economic base. During construction, Baron enlisted the support of both the St. Louis Board of Education and local corporations to renovate the Jefferson Elementary School to serve neighborhood families and transform its operations.

McCormack Baron also has extensive experience in developing both commercial/retail and community facilities. The firm has developed approximately 1 million square feet of commercial space. McCormack Baron's commercial development portfolio includes the Hadley Square Building and Lindell Marketplace in St. Louis; Quality Hill in Kansas City, Missouri; and Ninth Square in New Haven, Connecticut. In March 2001 McCormack Baron opened the Westin Hotel at Cupples Station in St. Louis, beginning the Cupples Station redevelopment, a renovation project involving nine historic warehouses located just west of Busch Stadium.

In addition to traditional redevelopment activities, McCormack Baron has undertaken other community projects. The Center of Contemporary Arts (COCA) was founded in 1986 by Richard Baron. From the beginning, COCA has contributed greatly to the cultural and artistic education of St. Louis families and children. As part of its outreach, COCA provides after-school and summer programs to students at Jefferson Elementary and other city schools. Similar programs are planned for the recently renovated Adams Elementary School and Community Center. Adams Elementary reopened as a neighborhood school in September 2001 through the joint efforts of the Washington University School of Medicine and the St. Louis Board of Education with McCormack Baron acting as program manager. The school is integrated with a 33,000-square-foot community center that was dedicated in October 2001.

To date, McCormack Baron has developed 84 projects with total development costs in excess of $1 billion. Its management portfolio includes 15,000 apartments. From its founding, McCormack Baron has been dedicated to the production of affordable housing of the highest quality. It has consistently approached housing development within the framework of preserving existing neighborhoods, recreating communities and strengthening families.

Jefferson
Elementary School

Westin St. Louis at
Cupples Station

Office of the Mayor
of the City of St. Louis

*I*n the nearly 180 years since St. Louis was incorporated as a city, the Office of the Mayor has played a key role in advancing the interests and well-being of its citizens. Whether in times of crisis or peace, depression or prosperity, it is the calling of the city's chief executive to provide vision and leadership to the community.

St. Louis' first mayor, an energetic young physician named William Carr Lane, set the standard for subsequent mayors. Elected in 1823, Lane envisioned a great future for St. Louis and actively pursued initiatives that sought to transform the former fur-trading village into a city, proposing badly needed street and water supply improvements, the creation of a free school, and the establishment of a hospital for the sick and indigent. In a break with the city's Creole past, Lane recommended that the town's French-labeled streets be given English names, with a preference for the names of trees such as olive, pine and chestnut.

During the mid-19th century St. Louis grew at a frenzied pace, as waves of westward moving pioneers and immigrants from distant lands poured into the city. Mayoral leadership was more important than ever in providing stability during these rapidly changing and

Francis G. Slay, 45th mayor of St. Louis

tumultuous times. One of the most difficult tasks fell on Mayor James Barry, an Irish immigrant who served during the cholera epidemic and the Great Fire of 1849. Under Barry's leadership, the city's commercial district was rebuilt after the fire and the levee widened to ease congestion caused by traffic on the Mississippi River.

Substantial changes in city services occurred during the 1850s and 60s. After a political battle that stretched over the terms of three mayors, increasingly violent volunteer firefighting companies were replaced by the current city fire department in 1857. In the months leading up to the Civil War, the city's police services were reorganized and placed under the administrative control of the state, an arrangement that remains to this day. Although the city was deeply divided during the war, St. Louis mayors helped to keep the municipal government aligned with the Union.

During the last three decades of the 19th century, St. Louis continued to see an explosion of growth and change. But in a fateful move that would restrict future growth, the city separated from St. Louis County in 1876, limiting its size to the 62-square-mile area that exists today. A new city charter adopted the same year increased the mayor's term of office from two to four years, helping to bring greater long-term stability to city leadership. But other changes led to more fragmented government, where a number of "county" offices such as sheriff, treasurer and collector of revenue functioned independently of the city administration. These changes were later incorporated into the city charter of 1914 and have made mayoral leadership more challenging.

As St. Louis entered the 20th century it boasted the rank of fourth-largest city in America. Local leaders eagerly seeking an opportunity to showcase their city to the world found it in the centennial of the Louisiana Purchase held in 1904. Under the slogan "New St. Louis," Mayor Rolla Wells undertook numerous steps to

Historic St. Louis City Hall has been home to city government since 1898. The landmark building is representative of the French Renaissance Revival Style, similar to the city hall of Paris.

beautify the city and reform municipal services in preparation for the celebration, including the introduction of a new purification system to clear up the city's notoriously murky drinking water. But perhaps the biggest city booster at the time was former St. Louis mayor and Missouri Governor David Roland Francis, whose prodigious efforts as president of the Louisiana Purchase Exposition helped to make the St. Louis World's Fair the grandest ever seen.

Over the next several decades St. Louis mayors lobbied for numerous civic improvements. Popular three-term mayor Henry Kiel was among the most successful, pushing for the continued development of Forest Park, where he located the Municipal Opera and the St. Louis Zoo. Kiel also helped

WILLIAM CARR LANE

secure the construction of Homer G. Phillips Hospital, the only local health care facility at the time dedicated to treating African Americans. But Kiel's most far-reaching achievement was the passage of an $87 million bond issue in 1923 that led to a series of large-scale projects, including the widening of Market Street and other major roads, as well as the construction of the Soldiers' Memorial, Aloe Plaza (across from Union Station) and the Municipal Auditorium that later bore the mayor's name.

Despite progress, civic leaders continued to be concerned about the state of the city's aging and unattractive riverfront. Working with community leaders, Mayor Bernard Dickmann convinced President Franklin Roosevelt in 1934 to approve the clearance of 40 square blocks along the riverfront for the creation of a new national memorial to Westward Expansion. Development of the project continued under the 12-year tenure of Mayor Raymond Tucker and was topped off in October 1965 with the completion of the 630-foot Gateway Arch, the international symbol of the spirit and vitality of the St. Louis region.

After decades of population loss due to postwar suburban flight, a principal goal of recent mayors has been to renew St. Louis' urban landscape and to highlight the city as an attractive community in which to live, work and play. Programs such as Operation Brightside and Operation Safestreet, begun in the 1980s under Mayor Vincent Schoemehl, have helped to enhance the city's aesthetic appeal and reduce crime. An important watershed in the political life of the city occurred in 1993, when Freeman Bosley Jr. was elected the city's first African-American mayor.

Today, the Office of the Mayor of the City of St. Louis continues to play a vital role in shaping the city's destiny as it has for nearly two centuries. In 2001 the citizens elected Aldermanic President Francis G. Slay as their 45th mayor. Seeking to enhance St. Louis' position as a national urban center, Mayor Slay's chief goals are to revitalize city neighborhoods, encourage diversity, strengthen public schools, and attract and retain business investment.

Dr. William Carr Lane (1789-1863) was elected the first mayor of St. Louis by a margin of 52 votes. His policies helped set St. Louis on a path to urban growth.

The opulent City Hall Rotunda reaches four stories in height and is encircled by three balustrated balconies that overlook the ground floor.

Raymond E. Maritz & Sons Inc.

Throughout two generations, the Maritz family architects have been changing the face of St. Louis. In 1914 Maritz and Young, the firm now known as Raymond E. Maritz & Sons Inc., was in its infancy but hit the ground running. St. Louis was booming, the architectural community was just developing, and plenty of work was available for the talented new architect, Raymond E. Maritz, and his partner, Ridgely Young.

Maritz first became interested in architecture when he was a small child and his French grandfather took him to the site where construction was being done for the 1904 St. Louis World's Fair. He watched the engineers who were designing the French Pavilion and decided then that architecture would be his field. It also sparked a love of France and French architecture.

Maritz loved France so much that he volunteered as an ambulance driver in Paris during World War I, before the United States became involved. Through the years he made numerous trips to Paris, and years later he was given a membership in the French Legion of Honor for his service in France.

Maritz attended Washington University School of Architecture and L'Ecole des Beaux Arts in Paris. While still in school he was commissioned to build a country manor house at what became known as Hillcrest Farms.

In the early days Maritz and Young was primarily focused on large residential building in a variety of traditional styles. There are now about 40 houses designed by the firm on the National Historic Register, many of which are in the Carswold area of Clayton.

Maritz, known for what was later called "period" architecture, designed homes that were gracious but not ostentatious. His love for France came through in his work with touches of French style as well as other cultural touches that came together to create a style all his own.

During the 30s the firm's work branched off to a number of schools and churches, and Maritz's work was widely respected and admired. During World War II there was no practice of architecture, as only defense-oriented building was allowed, and the office was closed.

Maritz had twin sons, Raymond E. Jr. and George, who both came into the firm in 1950, and the company changed its name to Raymond E. Maritz & Sons Inc. Both sons attended the Massachusetts Institute of Technology.

Educated during a period when the first generation of modern architects was teaching, Raymond E. Maritz Jr. became a modernist, with a respect for traditional architecture.

During the 50s, the firm ventured into commercial projects including Clayton City Hall and Florissant City Hall. By 1968 the company began to grow and work shifted to a variety of office buildings, both large and small.

Maritz Sr. continued to work as an architect until he died in 1973. Our Savior Church in Jacksonville, Illinois, was a job started by Ray Sr. that Ray Jr. finished after the death of his father.

Ray Maritz Jr. continues to operate the firm in the lower level of the 140-year-old Cast-Iron Building at Laclede's Landing, also on the National Historic Register, which Maritz and Sons renovated.

When presented with an architectural problem, the firm first seeks an understanding of the client's needs and then searches for the best way to satisfy them. Consideration of the

The home of William Wenzel, built by Raymond E. Maritz & Sons, Inc. in Hermann, Missouri

site, economics and aesthetics all play a role in the final solution.

Maritz says that architecture is much like art, and architects take great personal satisfaction in their work, much as artists appreciate paintings or composers appreciate music.

An exhibit in 2001 at The Bernoudy Gallery of Architecture at The Sheldon Art Galleries featured the work of Raymond E. Maritz Sr. and Raymond E. Maritz Jr. From the senior Maritz's drawings and photographs to the "tools" of the trade, the exhibit showcased highlights of both father and son, including Raymond Sr.'s residential "period" homes and Raymond Jr.'s buildings found throughout the St. Louis area. The exhibit is now a permanent fixture in the lobby at Maritz, Inc. in Fenton, Missouri, a company begun by Raymond Sr.'s two brothers.

One unusual feature of Raymond E. Maritz & Sons is that although it is a relatively small office, it has designed some of the largest corporate campuses in St. Louis. The award-winning campus of A.G. Edwards & Sons has been an ongoing project for 30 years. The multitude of buildings, all designed by Raymond E. Maritz & Sons, are connected by a second-story walkway linking buildings together. The master plan for the campus was created one step at a time as A.G. Edwards grew and its needs expanded. The latest project at the site is a 1-million-square-foot office complex combined with the Benjamin F. Edwards Learning Center.

Maritz, Inc. has also been a longtime client and has had a relationship with the architectural firm for 50 years.

An overview of the expansive "country" campus of Maritz, Inc. in Fenton, Missouri, designed by Raymond E. Maritz & Sons, Inc. Maritz, Inc. has had a working relationship with the architectural firm for over 50 years.

Its sprawling "country" campus in Fenton is one of the largest in the St. Louis area and stretches across Interstate 44 with a connecting "bridge" allowing employees to walk above the traffic.

Raymond Maritz Jr. also designed The Sheldon Art Galleries building and the Fine Arts Building at John Burroughs School in Ladue as well as many other buildings throughout the St. Louis region. He also designed several unique vacation houses at the Lake of the Ozarks.

Since the firm's beginnings, technology has been constantly changing, now providing new manufacturing materials. Not only are there more available, but structural techniques have changed as well, and materials are being used in new ways. Masonry veneers, glass and granite "skins," stainless steel and terne metal are just some of the materials being used today that have changed the appearance of modern office buildings.

Ray Maritz Jr. has served on the Goodwill board for many years, the board of the Herbert Hoover Boys Club and the Mathews-Dickey Boys' and Girls' Club. The company has donated services to the same organizations. A Raymond E. Maritz endowed professorship was created several years ago at Washington University School of Architecture.

Raymond E. Maritz & Sons Inc. is a traditional architectural practice that has not changed a lot over its nearly 90-year tenure in St. Louis. Its dedication to design and client needs has worked for the company for many years, and as far as Raymond E. Maritz Jr. is concerned, the advent of the 21st century means "business as usual."

The John Burroughs Art Center is part of the prestigious John Burroughs School in Ladue. The center was designed by Raymond E. Maritz Jr.

Southern Real Estate & Financial Co.

hile ice cream cones and Dr Pepper were making their debut at the Louisiana Purchase Expedition, better known as the 1904 St. Louis World's Fair, Southern Real Estate & Financial Co. made its debut in St. Louis. Brothers Louis A. and Charles J. Cella came to the area from Chicago in 1890 and incorporated the urban real estate company the same year as the fair.

Interests in thoroughbred racing and vaudeville led the brothers into additional business ventures. During the World's Fair the company contributed a then-astronomical figure of $50,000 to the stakes of the thoroughbred horse race, the World's Fair Handicap that was run in what is now Fairgrounds Park.

The brothers decided to participate further in the fair with the purchase of 16 elephants for an exhibition. All went well until the fair was over and the Cellas were left with 16 elephants to care for and feed. With an entrepreneurial spirit, Louis Cella came up with the idea of dedicating the elephants to the development of agriculture. For a short time, this appeared to be a lucrative business but was eventually abandoned when it was found that uric acid was not beneficial to crops.

This did not slow Charles and Louis down and by 1910, in addition to the viable urban investment and management end of the business, the company owned 15 racetracks in North America. It became heavily involved

in the vaudeville circuit, eventually owning about 40 legitimate theatres across the nation.

Southern Real Estate proved to be a driving force during the "go-go" days of the theatre in the 40s and 50s and was involved in the production of many great Broadway hits, including *Oklahoma!*, *Bells are Ringing* and *Carousel*, among others.

With the advent of television, many theatres of the time went out of business, and over the years Southern Real Estate's legitimate theatre holdings declined. The American Theatre in St. Louis is the last one remaining under the company's ownership.

Horse racing tracks were an intricate part of Southern Real Estate & Financial Co. in the earlier days. The company developed Delmar Race Track, located in what is now University City. Accesses to the track were where Eastgate and Westgate residential areas now stand. The only remaining track under the Southern name is The Oaklawn Jockey Club in Hot Springs, Arkansas, which many people have referred to as "The Saratoga of the South." Innovation in technology made Southern the leader in simulcast broadcasting by being the first to broadcast a race from one track to another, across state lines to Arlington racetrack in Chicago. Today, simulcasting is used by every racetrack in the country.

Around 1910 three additional Cella brothers moved to St. Louis from Chicago and became involved in what had developed into the family business. The three brothers

The NCR Building on South Outer 40 in Ladue, Missouri, is another holding of Southern Real Estate & Financial Co.

The American Theatre in St. Louis is the only legitimate theatre still owned by Southern Real Estate & Financial Co.

served in specialized capacities at the company and by 1915, Southern Real Estate had grown to be the largest ad valorem taxpayer in downtown St. Louis. It still remains a major player in the St. Louis downtown business community.

When Louis died in 1917, Charles J. Cella took over the helm and ran the company until his death in 1942. As Charles J. was the only one of the five brothers with children, his son, John G., took over the company. In 1968, when John G. died, his son, Charles J. Cella, became president, CEO and chairman of the board and remains so today. Charles' sons, John and Louis, have continued the family tradition and have both been with the company for over 15 years.

While Southern Real Estate's original focus was on the investment and management of urban real estate, with a niche in the entertainment world, changing population shifts have in turn transferred Southern's interests to the suburbs and away from the urban and entertainment ends of the business. This population shift

began in the St. Louis area in the early 80s and was accentuated in the early 90s.

Regional expansion, along with foresight of the eventual migration of people to the suburbs, kept Southern Real Estate at the forefront of development but moved much of its assets outside the city of St. Louis. However, it still owns the 15-floor 705 Building, a landmark in downtown St. Louis, started in 1896 and completed in 1903. The 705 Building houses about 30 tenants, consisting mostly of lawyers and accountants. The company also has a second office location in Little Rock, Arkansas.

Southern Real Estate developed and still manages regional malls and strip centers in the suburbs of St. Louis, Florida, Arkansas, Tennessee and Nebraska. Simon Properties, one of the largest mall-developing companies in the country today, partnered with Southern Real Estate for Simon's first mall venture — the University Mall in Little Rock, Arkansas, in 1969.

Southern Real Estate continues in new mall development from the ground up, from establishment to the management of maintaining the completed facilities as intricate parts of the communities in which they stand.

Other endeavors have included investment in timber and the design, production and assimilation of log homes in Northern Michigan.

Throughout the years, generations of the Cella family have believed in good citizenship and giving back to the community. This has been achieved through the support of and service with many philanthropic organizations, including the establishment of the Dr. Norman P. Knowlton fund for patient care at Washington University Medical School and the Russell-Rice Scholarship for Sports Writing at Vanderbilt University in Nashville, Tennessee, of which Charles Cella is chairman. Each generation has also served on a number of boards throughout corporate America, ranging from banks to building material companies to electric companies.

Future plans include the continued lateral expansion of the company in a conservative but sound fashion while continuing the slant toward creativity and entrepreneurialism that has kept Southern Real Estate & Financial Co. a successful St. Louis business for almost 100 years.

The University Mall Shopping Center in Little Rock, Arkansas, is one of many malls developed by Southern Real Estate & Financial Co.

The 705 Building, a 15-story St. Louis landmark, was completed in 1903 and currently houses about 30 professional tenants under the ownership of Southern Real Estate & Financial Co.

St. Louis Regional Chamber & Growth Association (RCGA)

With "Growth" as its middle name, the St. Louis Regional Chamber & Growth Association (RCGA) has been a major force in the St. Louis region since 1836, although it has carried out its mission under several names over the past 166 years.

In 1973, with the merger of the Chamber of Commerce of Metropolitan St. Louis, the St. Louis Regional Industrial Development Corporation and the St. Louis Research Council, it became the St. Louis Regional Commerce & Growth Association. In 1999 it was renamed the Regional Chamber & Growth Association to better convey its role as the regional chamber of commerce, as well as the region's primary economic development organization.

With offices in the Metropolitan Square Building downtown, the mission of the RCGA is to unite the region's business community and to engage dynamic business and civic leadership to develop and sustain a world-class economy and community.

The RCGA serves the 12-county bi-state metropolitan area that comprises the City of St. Louis; St. Louis, St. Charles, Jefferson, Franklin, Warren and Lincoln counties in Missouri; and St. Clair, Madison, Monroe, Clinton and Jersey counties in Illinois. With nearly 4,000 member companies, RCGA members constitute 40 percent of the regional work force.

POSITIONING THE REGION FOR GROWTH

St. Louis, which began as a fur-trading center, became a major manufacturing center, was at the center of the garment and shoe industry, and was a primary

aviation and defense center, saw an economic downturn in the latter part of the 20th century. St. Louis was experiencing flat job growth.

In 1994 RCGA leaders launched a bold effort to revitalize the area's economy and stimulate civic energy, beginning with the recruitment of Richard C.D. Fleming as president and CEO of the organization. The Greater St. Louis Economic Development Council, composed of a cross-section of regional public and private sector leaders, was created through the RCGA, and the $12 million "Campaign for a Greater St. Louis" was launched in 1995. This campaign, which sought to generate 100,000 net new regional jobs by the end of the year 2000, surpassed this goal by some 15,000 jobs.

Subsequent to this successful campaign, the RCGA unveiled a set of specific, interconnected goals designed to encourage sustained economic growth and shape the region's direction, agenda, and its civic aspirations. A team composed of RCGA board members developed this "civic game plan" to position the St. Louis region as a competitive economic force in the 21st century.

This plan, "Shaping A Greater St. Louis: New Commitment, New Energy, New Economy," is a package of long-term regional initiatives addressing the region's most vital issues: identify and leverage distinctive industry clusters; build sound and predictable physical infrastructure; identify ways to enhance the region's work force competitiveness; close the economic disparity gap; revitalize the region's central city; establish a common regional legislative agenda; unite and engage the regional business community; and pursue and fund an

The fountain sculpture across from the restored historic Union Station in downtown St. Louis was sculpted by Carl Milles and dedicated in 1940. Union Station is full of unique restaurants and shops, a grand hotel and cocktail area in what was once a busy railroad station.

A bird's-eye view of the Jefferson National Expansion Memorial and the beautiful downtown St. Louis riverfront symbolizes St. Louis' position as the "Gateway to the West."

ongoing plan for business creation, attraction, retention and expansion.

The RCGA is committed to the development of high-tech industries in the St. Louis region and making Greater St. Louis a place where new firms can grow in an innovative and entrepreneurial environment. St. Louis is already a regional center for activity in the areas of plant and life sciences, information technology and advanced manufacturing.

Rapid growth in information and other technologies transformed the U.S. economy during the 1990s, and St. Louis' economy was transformed as well. St. Louis has a higher-than-average concentration of jobs in fields such as computer systems analysis, hardware engineering, software applications engineering, medicinals and industrial chemicals.

St. Louis' integration into the new economy can be measured in a variety of ways. The Milken Institute, an economic research think tank based in California, recently cited St. Louis as a regional "tech-pole" of new economy activity. Dr. Robert Atkinson of the Progressive Policy Institute and Paul Gottlieb of Case Western Reserve University ranked St. Louis in a variety of new economy indices. According to its work, St. Louis is 10th among all metro areas in the percent of workers in "gazelles" (fast-growing firms) and 20th in "job churning," a measure of voluntary employee movement between firms. St. Louis is unique in that it experienced success in the old economy as one of the largest American cities during the 19th and early 20th centuries, and it is committed to success in the new economy.

Paralleling the region's efforts to grow the number of companies in distinctive industry clusters, the RCGA is working to sustain and grow St. Louis' well-established role as a corporate headquarters location. St. Louis ranks 6th in the nation as a corporate headquarters location, with 8 Fortune 500 headquarters companies.

The RCGA also markets the St. Louis region's quality of life assets. The region has all the big-city

The St. Louis region is a major high-tech center — ranked No. 2 in the Midwest — with more than 23,500 high-tech jobs.

amenities with the charm of a smaller city — and the fourth-lowest cost of living among the top 20 metropolitan areas in the country.

A sampling of its quality of life assets includes: the world-renowned Missouri Botanical Garden, the Saint Louis Art Museum, the St. Louis Zoo, the Saint Louis Symphony Orchestra, top-ranked universities and medical centers, impressive bridges, the Jefferson National Expansion Memorial, as well as the Great River Road, Pere Marquette State Park and Lodge, Forest Park, hiking and biking trails, and many historical sites. First-class hotels are available to the many tourists and business travelers who come to the area, and a multitude of restaurants offering a variety of cultural cuisine delight residents and visitors alike.

Community and children's theatres, cultural organizations and a variety of professional societies give residents opportunities for volunteerism, networking and community involvement.

While valuing its rich history and great traditions, the St. Louis region has a progressive spirit, and the St. Louis RCGA is the driving force for progress and success in the 21st century.

The Great River Road traverses along the east side of the Mississippi River from Alton to Grafton, Illinois, flanked by mighty limestone bluffs. The road's spectacular scenery is enhanced with glimpses of nesting eagles during the winter months and local flora and fauna throughout the spring and summer. Brilliant fall colors lead visitors to historic Grafton and its antique shops, historic hotel, wineries and Pere Marquette State Park, one of Illinois' largest.

South Side Roofing and Sheet Metal Co., Inc.

Operating primarily in Missouri and Illinois, South Side Roofing and Sheet Metal Co., Inc. installs roofs that cover hospitals, protect shopping malls, span power and assembly plants, and shelter schools and homes. It offers built-up, modified bitumen, single-ply, slate, tile, shingle and wood shake roofs as well as waterproofing for commercial, industrial, institutional and residential structures.

South Side prides itself on innovative approaches to complex projects. Its roofers utilize the most modern equipment to perform their work or work at night to accommodate clients. Helicopters deliver materials and remove debris where the company's cranes prove inadequate.

Working at night is one way South Side accommodates clients' schedules.

The family business has come a long way since Henry Binder founded it in 1920. His small crew primarily installed flat roofs using a built-up method that layered roofing felt between applications of hot bitumen. The grueling work was devoid of labor-saving equipment, although trucks were beginning to replace horse-drawn wagons by 1923.

Binder guided South Side through the economic uncertainties of the Great Depression and on to tremendous growth. He twice moved the company to larger facilities. Upon Binder's death in 1962, his daughter and son-in-law, Henrietta and Robert Osterholt, became vice president and president respectively. About a year later, another established St. Louis roofing company closed its doors. The owner, who respected South Side's workmanship and integrity, gave the company much of his equipment and encouraged his employees to accept jobs there. His lead estimator, Ray Arnold, followed that suggestion and brought clients as well as expertise in clay tile and slate work to South Side.

As the industry developed, South Side tested and adopted new roofing systems. The 1960s brought the industry's first major change in about 100 years. Single-ply roofing, using synthetic materials and a new installation method, triggered an evolution that moved roofing from a simple trade to a highly technical craft. Like other construction trades, roofing felt the impact of inflationary pressures stemming from the Vietnam War. Labor shortages and high turnover created chaos. Wages climbed at double-digit rates and costs skyrocketed.

To address the issues, President Richard Nixon in 1971 enacted wage and price controls and established the Construction Industry Stabilization Committee to oversee separate craft union boards composed of industry and labor leaders. The boards reviewed

South Side's first location was only a fraction of the size of its current 25,000-square-foot facility.

and approved contracts under prescribed guidelines until 1974. Robert Osterholt traveled monthly to Washington, D.C. as a representative of the roofing and waterproofing industry.

South Side thrived despite the economic turbulence and by 1971 needed more room. As a result, it constructed the present 25,000-square-foot facility. Sadly, just three years later, Osterholt died.

During his career, Osterholt was president of the National Roofing Contractors Association, which recognized him with its highest honor, the Piper Award. He held offices with the Midwest Roofing Contractors Association and received its greatest honor, the McCauley Award. Osterholt also served as president of the Roofing Contractors of Greater St. Louis.

Osterholt's death hit his family hard but Henrietta Osterholt, as South Side's new president, took immediate steps to secure the company's future for the employees and her three children. She squelched "going out of business" rumors with a newspaper notice stating unequivocally that South Side would continue its tradition of quality. Ray Arnold again proved to be a valuable ally, cutting short retirement to return as executive vice president.

The 1970s heralded a new construction boom in the metropolitan area with South Side receiving many commercial contracts. Its crews installed thousands of red clay tiles at West Port Plaza and acres of flat roofs throughout the region. In 1974 a hailstorm kept South Side's 100-man work force busy for an entire year.

Family forms a strong core of leadership at the company. Each of the Osterholt children began working there during the 70s and now serve as officers of the corporation. Henrietta Osterholt's son-in-law, Douglas Jones, is executive vice president. Her sons, Robert and William Osterholt, are vice presidents and her daughter, Carolyn Jones, is secretary.

Like her husband, Henrietta Osterholt became an industry leader. She is a past president of the Roofing Contractors of Greater St. Louis and was the first woman board member of the National Roofing Contractors Association. The busy executive also serves her community. A longstanding member of the board of directors for Catholic Cemeteries, she has worked on the boards for Cardinal Glennon Children's Hospital, the YMCA and Fontbonne College.

The Equitable Building in downtown St. Louis is among the many office buildings South Side has roofed.

Following Robert and Henrietta Osterholt's example, their sons and son-in-law are involved with national, regional and local associations and volunteer countless hours to local community organizations. This community spirit prompted South Side and its employees to roof several residences for Habitat for Humanity and to partner with the union to replace a roof for a local parish.

The United Union of Roofers, Waterproofers & Allied Workers Local No. 2 ranks South Side as among the largest roofing contractors in the greater metropolitan market. Additionally, the St. Louis Business Journal placed the company seventh in its 1999 list of the largest businesses owned by women and minorities.

South Side has developed and maintained long-standing relationships with many of St. Louis' premier companies, roofing the Anheuser Busch corporate headquarters and numerous Stockhouses as well as vital Boeing facilities. Historic restoration projects are an integral part of South Side's business. The company completely restored slate and flat roofs covering unique buildings at the Boeing Leadership Center on the bluffs of the Missouri River. Similar to an earlier project at St. Anthony of Padua Church, the job entailed the duplication of new copper guttering, finials and other details along original designs. South Side is one of an elite group of roofing companies to undertake restoration projects.

As long as people need roofs of any type, South Side will meet that need. Armed with decades of experience, the company is moving confidently into the future and growth seems assured.

Taylor-Morley Homes

Celebrating 50 years in the building industry and in St. Louis development, Taylor-Morley Homes is well known for "building homes and neighborhoods where people want to live." Recently nationally recognized as "2001 America's Best Builder" by *BUILDER* magazine and The National Association of Home Builders, Taylor-Morley Homes has proven their passion for 100-percent customer satisfaction, and 100-percent customer service to be one of the reasons that sets them apart from the rest.

Taylor-Morley's roots began in 1952 when Benton Taylor and Roland Hitt started the company as Taylor-Hitt. In the company's early years, it gradually increased from building five to 10 homes per year to 30 to 40 homes per year. Then around 1965, Benton Taylor concentrated his efforts on working with the St. Louis County Highway Department, taking a hiatus from the construction business.

In the mid-70s, Taylor went back to building. He met and sold a home to Harry Morley. The two struck up a friendship, and the rest, as they say, is history. Morley joined the company after stepping down as president of the St. Louis Commerce and Regional Growth Association in the late 70s.

The current chairman and CEO, Taylor's son, Bill, joined the company in 1975, managing apartments. Morley's son, Mark, joined the company around 1987 and is now president and chief operating officer. Benton Taylor remained with the company until his retirement in 1995. Harry Morley is the chairman emeritus.

Over the years Taylor-Morley has been recognized for its many achievements with countless Homer Awards for excellence in design and craftsmanship, Excellence of Achievement Awards and Excellence in Community Development Awards. In addition, the company has received Bravo Awards recognizing communities five to 10 years old, the Better Business Bureau's World-Class Customer Service Award, the Golden Achievement Award for Excellence in Customer Service, with the previously mentioned 2001 America's Best Builder award as its crowning achievement. Taylor-Morley was the highest-volume builder to receive the award for 2001.

Benton E. Taylor started Taylor-Construction Co. He then went on to found, along with family members, Taylor-Hitt. He later formed a partnership with Harry Morley, and it became Taylor-Morley Homes, as it remains today.

In honor of Taylor-Morley's celebration they have raised the "quality bar" yet another notch by now including Pella® Proline® Series Wood Windows as a standard feature in most homes.

"Based on their superior product and workmanship, we've used Pella windows in our high-end custom homes for years. Since the Taylor-Morley name is synonymous with quality, we decided that including them in the majority of our communities and partnering with a company whose name is equally identified with quality would be a great way to celebrate our 50th anniversary with our customers," explains CEO Bill Taylor.

The builder is also leading the industry with the introduction of Taylor-Morley Service Plus, a unique program designed to augment the firm's award-winning customer service by offering additional home maintenance services to meet owners' needs.

Yet another first in the region, Taylor Morley Homes is now providing extended warranty coverage to homeowners with its two-year "Peace of Mind" program.

Throughout its history, Taylor-Morley has maintained that "quality over quantity" is what sets a company apart, and it continues to stand by this philosophy. The significance of curb appeal is a part of this same philosophy, and the company keeps an eye on the future of the property, assuring that it will maintain its current quality and appeal years down the road.

In 1998 the company targeted and planned sustained growth of annual gross revenue and number of units built and had three consecutive record years, with gross sales between $80 and $90 million. With a high percentage of its business from referrals, the company exceeds customer expectations and is proud of its high level of customer satisfaction.

Teamwork with trade partners, value engineering, a tremendous amount of technical training, cutting-edge software development and continuous quality improvement have prepared Taylor-Morley for further development in the 21st century.

Adding to the excitement of the firm's celebration, it has also announced the opening of its new Design Gallery. The first of its kind in the Midwest, the gallery is available exclusively to Taylor-Morley customers and provides a

single location where buyers can make all of the selections entailed in planning, designing and finishing their homes — from roofing and siding to home theaters and closet organization. Its headquarters also resides in the 60,000-square-foot office building.

Making inroads into Illinois, Taylor-Morley is developing the residential section of a golf community in Belleville with single-family and villa homes. A mixed-use master plan community in O'Fallon, Illinois, will include estate homes, first- and second-time "move-ups," and villas attached and detached.

The company's success and longevity is attributed to its quality orientation, attention to detail, streetscaping and the preservation of green space. Building neighborhoods with playgrounds, lakes, walking trails and swimming pools is a part of Taylor-Morley's commitment to families, and with its in-house architectural department, the company assists clients with home design and reduction of costs. A wide range of community developments offers customers a choice of locations and price ranges.

The company has developed over 120 neighborhoods in areas that have included Chesterfield, South St. Louis County, St. Peters, West St. Louis County, North St. Louis County and St. Charles County. Taylor-Morley is also becoming involved in residential housing development in the city of St. Louis.

Taylor-Morley's custom-home division concentrates on upper-end, one-of-a kind custom homes located in many upscale areas across the St. Louis metropolitan area, such as Town and Country, Olivette, Creve Coeur and St. Albans.

Expedition of production schedule is another area of which the company is proud. Through trade partner agreements, the company guarantees its partners a consistent number of houses. By slotting

new construction in the even-flow process, Taylor-Morley is now able to manage the cycle time; materials are readily available; and superintendents are able to spend more time with inspections and working with the customer.

The principals and staff at the company are involved in and support many community and charitable organizations, including the Sports Commission, St. Louis Commerce and Regional Growth Association, Home Builders Association, Habitat for Humanity, the Missouri Highway and Transportation Commission, the United Way, Children's Hospital and the Better Business Bureau, and have served on boards of many such entities.

Retention of employees, who receive a minimum of 80 hours of training per year, guarantees experience, knowledge and continuous education that benefits the client as well as the company. The company culture includes employee involvement in all aspects of the business, including future projects and financials, further solidifying the team environment. Total Quality Management challenges employees to become more involved, and Continuous Quality Improvement assures goal setting and the continued growth of the entire team that makes up Taylor-Morley.

For the future the company's attention remains on market research in order to continue to give people the size and type of home that they want with the amenities that are most desirable. "Knowing your customer" was a challenge that Benton Taylor presented to his employees. This challenge became the mission for Taylor-Morley — provide homebuyers what they want — in the places they want to live — with the service they deserve.

Through overall teamwork and recruiting and retaining the best, most capable people in the business, the company's greatest asset — its people — will continue to serve the community in the tradition that has sustained Taylor-Morley for over half a century.

AFRAM Corporation

From the geography of his native Africa, D. Solomon Akinduro unearthed a name for his company — AFRAM Corporation — that conveys its rock solid commitment to providing quality engineering design and construction management. AFRAM — meaning "rock" in the Ghana language — is the name of a river in that country distinguished by its steady flow even during the dry season.

Akinduro, originally of Nigeria, had over 20 years in construction management in 1993 when he founded AFRAM to capitalize on the opportunities he saw for a quality-oriented business capable of delivering excellent services. Four years later, Akinduro, who holds a bachelor's degree in civil engineering and a master's degree in construction management, took AFRAM fully operational and left his full-time job.

In 1998, AFRAM added engineering design to its offerings, and since that time has grown 200 percent annually. The engineering division is headed by Senior Vice President Kenneth Chandler, P.E. with over 40 years experience.

By the end of 2000 AFRAM had a branch in Memphis, where it had contracts with the city and the Memphis-Shelby County International Airport and opened another branch in Chicago in 2001.

AFRAM's highly qualified and diverse staff, whose backgrounds range from general contracting to engineering to certified materials testing, team with clients to maximize efficiency, function and economy. Akinduro, who trained in England as a quantity surveyor, accurately assesses costs on international projects as well as domestic ones.

Project analysis, inspection and evaluation, cost estimating and scheduling, quality assurance and control, and contract and claim administration are among the firm's services. AFRAM is qualified for civil, electrical,

D. Solomon Akinduro, founder and president of AFRAM Corporation

environmental, structural, transportation and mechanical engineering and can provide seismic evaluations and design.

Total Quality Management and customer satisfaction form the cornerstone of AFRAM's corporate philosophy, which aims to exceed a client's expectations. State-of-the-art technology and software combined with ongoing professional development keep AFRAM's staff on the cutting edge of their fields. The firm has spearheaded projects ranging in scope from universities and transportation to commercial, housing complexes and government facilities.

The early years of the 21st century found AFRAM involved in a number of important undertakings. As construction manager for many of the St. Louis Public Library's capital improvement projects, it was managing the renovation or replacement of several facilities. In connection with the expansion of Lambert St. Louis International Airport, AFRAM was providing services such as cost estimation, scheduling, design and quality assurance. On the international front, AFRAM is involved in the planning and construction of a township in Nigeria and an oil refinery project in Ghana.

AFRAM supports efforts to improve the city of St. Louis, where it is headquartered, and belongs to a large number of civic and community organizations including the Engineers Club of St. Louis, St. Louis Ambassadors, and the Regional Chamber and Growth Association Leadership circle. It is also a member of the National Minority Business Council and the Associated General Contractors of St. Louis.

AFRAM plans to open more branches nationwide as opportunities beckon, particularly those on large transportation projects. Customer satisfaction has driven AFRAM's past growth, and as this young company continues to deliver the innovative solutions and excellent services that are its hallmark, the future can only bring greater success.

Economic Development Center of St. Charles County

Go west, young folks; go west of the Gateway Arch, Gateway to the West and cross over the bridge to St. Charles County! For more than two decades, thousands of people have chosen to do just that. This energetic county, just across the Missouri River from St. Louis County, experienced a population explosion since 1980, virtually doubling in size (144,000 to 283,000) by 2001. Providing a strong, vibrant economy with a job base to meet the needs of this rapidly swelling population base is the mission of the Economic Development Center of St. Charles County (EDC). Its spacious modern office building, located 15 miles from Lambert International Airport, houses an incubator for early-stage businesses, offering a variety of finance programs for every size of business. Plus, in its resourceful quest to provide and retain jobs, the EDC supports programs designed to attract new business interests to the area.

A significant component to the greater St. Louis metropolitan area, St. Charles County bears a noteworthy history, sustaining archives as momentous to the past as those of its neighbors across the water. The city of St. Charles, its county seat, served as the first capitol of Missouri. The first Interstate highway project in the United States began in 1956 at what is now Interstate 70 and Fifth Street in St. Charles.

Established in 1990, while St. Charles County was experiencing its burgeoning population spurt, the EDC, a private nonprofit organization, was formed to help area businesses grow by providing small business loans and industrial revenue bonds. It inaugurated its incubator facility in 1993 and opened a second facility in 2001. Designed for the early-stage entrepreneur, the mixed-use facility provides premier offices and production/light manufacturing bays with competitive rent and flexible leases. Incubator clients share up-to-date office services and equipment and have access to professional amenities including a resource room; conference rooms; a reception area and shipping/dock areas. On-site business development counseling and assistance with financing and procurement affords an infant business a substantially higher than average prospect of survival beyond the critical first five years.

Another core program of the EDC is one that assists businesses interested in relocating to St. Charles County. The EDC set a goal in 1994 to create 20,000 new jobs by the year 2000. Working with local municipalities and the county, it surpassed this goal, growing the job base from 72,601 to 92,875 by the end of 1999. The High Tech Corridor along I-64 fueled this growth. Envisioned by the EDC board, it stretches from

> **Established in 1990, while St. Charles County was experiencing its burgeoning population spurt, the EDC, a private nonprofit organization, was formed to help area businesses grow by providing small business loans and industrial revenue bonds. It inaugurated its incubator facility in 1993 and opened a second facility in 2001.**

Weldon Spring to Wentzville and has attracted significant high-tech industries. Lured by the availability of campus settings, highly successful industrial parks in a natural setting and quality residential housing, large corporations, along with hundreds of smaller entrepreneurs, now find success in the Corridor.

With an eye to the issues facing a thriving community, the EDC works with area partners to develop action plans on employment issues such as work force development, life cycle housing and intra-county transit. Success on these fronts will ensure that St. Charles County continues to realize its vision as the place to "grow your business."

Fred Weber, Inc.

From hauling rocks with a rented dump truck in the 1920s, Fred Weber nourished his St. Louis home-based business, and grew it to become a dominant name in highway construction and materials. After adding reliable employees and more trucks, the company secured its first road contract in 1928 — excavation and pipe work on Fox Creek Road. Now, over 70 years later, the St. Louis metropolitan area views a transformed landscape, owing much of that change to Fred Weber, Inc. The "We" in Weber today remains the main ingredient in its ongoing success; in 1986 it became an employee-owned corporation. That same year Thomas P. Dunne Sr., who originally joined the company as a concrete crew laborer, eventually rising to field engineer, took over as chairman and CEO.

From the beginning, as the Weber company acquired additional contracts, it purchased the equipment necessary to perform the work. In the 30s its crews constructed brick sewers in the city and did excavation for sites that now host familiar landmarks, such as the stately Third Baptist Church and McKinley High School. Even in those Depression years, Weber paid his workers above the average scale and gained their loyalty.

During the World War II era, Weber added rock crushing to its operations and began to supply materials for military base construction, furnishing several thousand tons of rock aggregate for the building of Fort Leonard Wood. Near the war's end, it gained a major concrete job in St. Louis County — the enclosure of Cold Water Creek at St. Louis Lambert Airport.

The area's postwar growth put Weber to work building and widening roads, creating a need for construction materials. Purchasing 340 acres on Creve Coeur Mill Road, it began its Materials Division with the North Quarry. Soon adding the South Quarry on New Baumgartner Road, it kept pace with its increasing road construction contracts, including one to widen Highway 40. By the mid-50s, Weber

obtained contracts for paving the new interstate highways, beginning with I-70.

Fred Weber Sr. passed away in 1963, but the enterprise he started flourished into the 21st century with the increasing demand for highway work throughout the state of Missouri. Today, an aerial panorama of the region's highway network displays Weber's achievements; the company worked on virtually every interstate highway in the area. Additionally, it prepared sites for public places such as the Riverport Complex and Amphitheater, constructed in the 90s.

Fred Weber, Inc. now operates from its Maryland Heights headquarters. Its Missouri subsidiaries are Iron Mountain Trap Rock Company, Creve Coeur Trucking, Mehlville Haulers, Inc., Crystal Springs Quarry Golf Club, Limestone's Bar & Grill and Jotori Dredging Inc. Its Naples, Florida, subsidiary is Naples Dock and Marine.

By upholding the high standards established by its founder, Weber continually earns awards from fraternal and government organizations, most notably the Missouri Department of Transportation. Both the company and its devoted employees support innumerable community welfare programs, donating time and money to worthy causes. They "pave the way" for both ease of travel and prosperity into the new century.

Fru-Con Construction Corporation

The general contracting company that Jeremiah Fruin founded in 1872, now known as Fru-Con Construction Corporation, has come a long way. From its days of building much of St. Louis' infrastructure and downtown skyline, the company has expanded its offerings and target markets, as well as built a strong regional network spanning the nation and the heart of Mexico.

Fru-Con, which has perfected its name several times over the years, offers a comprehensive range of construction and engineering services to the industrial, commercial, institutional, environmental and civil markets. It also serves as developer for retail centers, assisted living facilities and resorts.

Fru-Con is known for its industry-leading safety record, which has garnered the company many honors, including a 4-million-hour safety recognition award from the Procter & Gamble Company for Missouri's largest industrial project, two safety awards from the Business Roundtable and several honors from Anheuser-Busch.

Having learned the construction business from his father, Fruin founded his own company after working independently in street and sewer construction for several years following the Civil War. After Fruin died in 1927, his son-in-law, Redmond S. Colnon, took over and guided the company through several decades of expansion.

In 1940 Fruin-Colnon Contracting Company formed Fruco Engineering from an existing division and in a move considered innovative at the time, began offering integrated engineering design, procurement and construction. The decade also marked the birth of the company's longstanding relationship with Procter & Gamble.

During the next two decades, Fruin-Colnon undertook projects as diverse as subways and soap factories. It completed Busch Stadium in 1966, a project that undoubtedly would have pleased Fruin, who some believe brought baseball to St. Louis.

By the 1970s Fruin-Colnon had become an extensive organization, so in 1975 it formed Fru-Con Construction Corporation to provide unity for its numerous operating entities. Fru-Con helped shape the St. Louis skyline during that decade, a period of downtown redevelopment. It completed the Spanish Pavilion, the Equitable Building and several other well-known structures.

Fru-Con in 1984 became a wholly owned subsidiary of Germany's Bilfinger Berger AG. The move linked it with firms in Australia, France, Poland, Nigeria and Hong Kong. In the 1990s Fru-Con acquired H.E. Sargent, an environmental construction firm. Fru-Con also expanded its regional office network, increased its industrial and commercial project base, and enjoyed a resurgence in the power market.

The company, with $500 million in annual revenue, employs 2,000 people full time, staffs several offices in the United States and Mexico, and consistently ranks as a top contractor in the magazine *Engineering News-Record*. Its services include development, engineering, construction, design-build, start-up and maintenance.

The organization supports numerous local and national charities, including the Family Resource Center (which aids abused and neglected children), United Way and the American Red Cross. Employees serve on various civic and community boards.

Fru-Con has mastered success through its strategy of offering a full menu of services to a diverse range of markets. The company looks forward to continued longevity and expansion during the 21st century using this same philosophy.

Fru-Con corporate headquarters, which the company built in 1987

Kaemmerlen Electric Company

Building a Greater St. Louis

Before the rise of America's throwaway society, fixing small appliances, rather than replacing them, was the norm and Kaemmerlen Electric Company led the nation in warranty work on blenders, toasters and other conveniences. Its repair business thrived and by the late 1960s, Kaemmerlen, which also served the construction and commercial food service markets, had topped $1 million in sales.

Kaemmerlen Communications provides a full-service approach to communications cabling, offering a turnkey solution to voice, data and video cabling systems. This approach begins with design and installation and continues through ongoing maintenance.

Unwilling to rest on his laurels, Thibaut Casper (T.C.) Kaemmerlen, who founded the company in 1924, foresaw the demise of the repair industry in the shrinking cost of appliances. In 1974 he closed the repair shop to focus on electrical construction and commercial kitchen appliance service. Around the same time, computers hit the business world and his son, Robert Kaemmerlen Sr., took the company into the computer room market. This emerging market involved the design and installation of the electrical systems that support a computer room's unique systems of power distribution, HVAC and fire alarm.

A 1987 reorganization split Kaemmerlen into two entities. Robert Kaemmerlen Sr. remained at the helm of the electrical contracting division while his brother, Bruce, established Kaemmerlen Parts and Service to cater to the commercial food service industry.

Kaemmerlen Electric offers contracting services to commercial, institutional and industrial markets. The company has a history of involvement in projects that are unique, challenging and demanding.

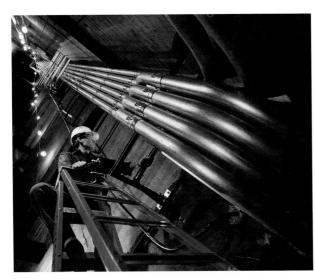

Kaemmerlen Electric serves industrial, commercial and institutional markets, particularly in the areas of health care, residential care facilities, emergency power and data centers. It offers design/build capabilities including project management and quality engineering. In addition, the company seeks out fast-track and unusual projects that present unique challenges to the firm. Kaemmerlen's responsiveness and sense of teamwork has led to the company's inclusion on many demanding projects. Kaemmerlen's sales in 2001 exceeded $25 million.

Kaemmerlen's strategy of adapting to the changing currents of American life and charging into new markets is a family tradition. In 1996 Robert Kaemmerlen Jr. founded Kaemmerlen Communications to design, install and service structured cabling systems for voice, data and video. This division of Kaemmerlen Electric offers a Registered Communications Distribution Designer (RCDD), a certified cabling team and experience in all types of media including Ethernet, UTP, STP, coax and fiber optics.

Seeking out new market niches is only one reason for the continued success of Kaemmerlen Electric. The development of long-term relationships is clearly a contributing factor. Building and maintaining close bonds — whether with a customer, vendor or employee — is top priority, and some of Kaemmerlen's relationships span the three generations of family leadership.

Giving something back to the industry is a company tradition. T.C. Kaemmerlen was a founder and the first president of the National Appliance Service Association (NASA). Bob Kaemmerlen Sr., a past president and governor of the St. Louis Chapter of the National Electrical Contractors Association, serves on a national committee that drafts the National Electrical Code.

Kaemmerlen's steadfast commitment to its employees, vendors and customers has afforded stability in an industry that is highly cyclical. The company respects its personal history and the traditions it has carried through the decades, as does the city in which it resides — St. Louis.

Kwame Building Group Inc.

The selection of Kwame Building Group Inc. in 1999 for the team managing the $5 billion expansion of the Orlando International Airport marked a turning point in the company's history. The contract, recognizing KWAME as a joint venture partner, promoted the small, minority-owned business to a new status in the industry and also increased overall minority participation on the job.

KWAME — meaning "born on Saturday" in the Akan language of Ghana — is reaching the heights that Anthony Thompson, its president, had envisioned when he founded it in 1991. Thompson, then an engineer with the Anheuser-Busch Companies, initially hired others to manage KWAME's daily operations, compiling reports and conducting presentations in his off-hours.

Thompson's experience in project management at the Fortune 100 level was a primary influence in KWAME's formation, particularly his observation that minorities held few, if any, key leadership roles in construction. Thompson addressed that issue through KWAME by building a diverse and talented team equipped with the skills needed to win major contracts.

Thompson's blueprint for success is working. St. Louis-based KWAME, with offices in Orlando, Jacksonville and Pittsburgh, boasts an annual average growth rate of 20 percent. Minorities compose about 67 percent of the 80-person staff; women fill about 38 percent of management positions.

KWAME provides "pure" construction management, putting the company squarely in the owner's corner. Its services include project and claims administration, an encrypted estimating system, comprehensive scheduling and value engineering.

KWAME's project management begins with a master plan establishing procedures, policies and other terms, and continues for the duration of construction with reports, productivity evaluations and quality controls. Detailed budget estimates factor in techniques, scheduling and special challenges; costs are monitored continually. An automated document control system maintains daily reports including schedule changes and photographs. KWAME, which employs Total Quality Management and ISO 9000, uses the Internet to allow authorized parties to access job information.

KWAME's excellent reputation and extensive experience — particularly in the construction of airports, transportation systems, hospitals and schools — reflects in its selection for long-term, costly projects. Among those are the expansion of Lambert International Airport in St. Louis, improvements to Pittsburgh's light rail system, and the renovations of the local Barnes-Jewish Hospital campus and the Orange County (Florida) Public Schools.

KWAME also builds communities, donating over $250,000 to charities from 1996 to 2000 and endowing an annual $10,000 scholarship at the Jackson State University School of Engineering. A major sponsor of the National Society of Black Engineers' annual Future City Competition, KWAME promotes engineering careers to elementary and high school students. Thompson serves on the boards of several organizations, including Focus St. Louis. As its first project, Kwame Constructors, a separate general contracting firm founded in 2000, constructed women's shelters at no charge.

KWAME is positioned to capitalize on the strong construction market that Thompson believes will continue through at least 2011. Population growth — like that of Florida, where KWAME has opened another office — is driving the need for more airports, schools, hospitals and other facilities.

The Cross County MetroLink extension in St. Louis is one of the transit projects KWAME has joint-ventured on.

Sheet Metal Workers Local 36

A vocation existing before colonial American times prospers in the modern world of ever-advancing technology. Today's sheet metal workers continue in the tradition of their forebears who joined forces in Toledo, Ohio, on January 25, 1888. In an effort to improve working conditions, they formed the nucleus of what is now the Sheet Metal Workers International Association (SMWIA). Those progressive individuals included organizers of Local 36, headquartered in St. Louis. In the forefront from the beginning, Local 36 produced the second and sixth general presidents of SMWIA.

Now more vibrant than ever, SMWIA shares mutual interests with its members and their employers, benefiting the community at large. Abandoning the conventional mindset of labor and management as natural adversaries, the union and its International Training Institute team with the Sheet Metal and Air Conditioning Contractors' National Association (SMACNA) to provide quality state-of-the-art training for a surprisingly diverse and fulfilling career.

Examples of sheet metal work surround people in everyday life, yet most fail to recognize the end result of the expertise and dedication of skilled craftsmen. The heating and cooling systems in homes and public buildings; stainless steel counters in restaurants and cafeterias;

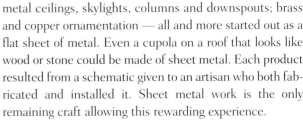

metal ceilings, skylights, columns and downspouts; brass and copper ornamentation — all and more started out as a flat sheet of metal. Even a cupola on a roof that looks like wood or stone could be made of sheet metal. Each product resulted from a schematic given to an artisan who both fabricated and installed it. Sheet metal work is the only remaining craft allowing this rewarding experience.

Earning a good living with excellent benefits, including ideal pensions, SMWIA's journeymen often advance to different facets of the field. Some eventually become union leaders, instructors, or join the ranks of contractors. Initially drawn to the craft by family example, a career-day presentation or job fair, or simply the need for employment, they all share the desire to exercise their mental as well as physical capabilities. Seeking a career beyond the stereotypical office setting, they use math and computer technology as well as industrial equipment in their work. SMWIA's outstanding five-year apprentice program allows new members to start drawing a paycheck from the onset. They learn at both its training facility and on the job.

After Local 36 instituted its own training center, its innovative leaders, in cooperation with SMACNA, doubled its St. Louis training facility space in 1999. Several years later, they realized a need for even further expansion. Noted nationwide for their superb craftsmanship, journeymen trained in St. Louis possess much-sought-after skills.

SMWIA Local 36 and SMACNA donate valuable time, skill and funds to many area causes. St. Vincent Home for Children, Habitat for Humanity and Christmas in April are just a few of those benefiting from their goodwill. In collaboration with other unions and area contractors, Both Local 36 and SMACNA are active members of PRIDE, a St. Louis-area group dedicated to providing quality workers and work to the local-area construction industry. As conscientious employees, employers and citizens, Sheet Metal Workers Local 36 and SMACNA members fortify the future of a great city.

Sheet Metal Workers Local 36 President David C. Zimmermann and Dan Durphy, co-chairman of the Apprenticeship Training Committee, pose in a sheet metal ribbon-cutting ceremony with sheet metal men, a dog and a model of the Gateway Arch — all created by members of Local 36.

(Left to right) Dan Andrews, coordinator of the Sheet Metal Workers Joint Apprenticeship and Training Program, examines schematics on the drafting board with Co-chairman Dan Durphy.

St. Louis County Economic Council

reating jobs, expanding their companies' operations, diversifying industry and creating wealth are just a few of the many goals that St. Louis County's 1 million residents and 36,000 businesses are striving toward each day. To make these goals a reality, many individuals and companies tap the resources available at the St. Louis County Economic Council (SLCEC), which has been committed to improving the region's quality of life through a myriad of economic development programs since 1984.

The St. Louis County Economic Council is a not-for-profit economic development organization responsible for creating high-quality business and employment opportunities, which in turn lead to long-term diversified growth throughout St. Louis County and the St. Louis region. SLCEC oversees several local and regional economic development programs, including various loan programs; World Trade Center Saint Louis; small business incubators; and real estate redevelopment.

SLCEC's loan and tax-exempt bond programs assist growing businesses in securing financing to purchase land, buildings, machinery and equipment. The funds, often at lower interest rates and longer terms than banks, also allow companies to finance growth capital, working capital, and receivables and inventory. Many of its customers are companies that could not obtain some or all of the financing they needed from a bank — new companies without a track record or those without a large amount of collateral. To date SLCEC has disbursed nearly 780 loans and tax-exempt bonds totaling more than $1.6 billion.

But today's marketplace is not just about competing locally or even regionally — it's also about successfully competing at the global level. World Trade Center Saint Louis is SLCEC's international business resource, offering innovative solutions to help businesses and the region compete on the world stage. Companies can turn to the World Trade Center for timely, reliable and relevant individualized market research, networking opportunities and international business information.

SLCEC's St. Louis Enterprise Centers (business incubators) help launch new businesses, expand existing businesses, create jobs and boost long-term regional

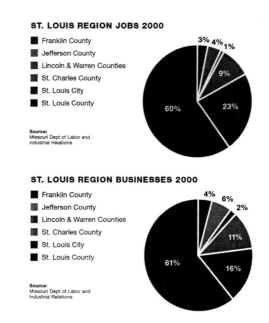

ST. LOUIS REGION JOBS 2000

- Franklin County
- Jefferson County
- Lincoln & Warren Counties
- St. Charles County
- St. Louis City
- St. Louis County

3% 4% 1%
9%
60% 23%

Source:
Missouri Dept of Labor and
Industrial Relations

ST. LOUIS REGION BUSINESSES 2000

- Franklin County
- Jefferson County
- Lincoln & Warren Counties
- St. Charles County
- St. Louis City
- St. Louis County

4% 6%
2%
11%
61% 16%

Source:
Missouri Dept of Labor and
Industrial Relations

economic development. The Enterprise Centers also nurture an entrepreneurial environment and provide new and expanding small businesses with nearly 100,000 square feet of affordable office, warehouse/production and retail space. But just a place to hang a shingle is not sufficient. These companies also benefit from a supportive professional environment that features mentoring by community business leaders, networking opportunities and links to resources.

Like other metropolitan areas, St. Louis County has opportunities for community reinvestment in many of its inner-ring suburban areas. SLCEC targets these sites and works to return them to productive commercial, industrial and/or residential use. From acquiring land for redevelopment to environmental remediation to infrastructure improvements, SLCEC often takes the first critical steps needed to attract private developers. It also coordinates the efforts of municipalities, community groups and business leaders while adding its own expertise and resources to redevelopment projects. These programs help stabilize and energize regional communities.

SLCEC hopes to continue these efforts into the future: "We are committed to continuing to provide companies and communities with innovative solutions," says Denny Coleman, SLCEC president and CEO.

Supreme Electric Company

Supreme Electric Company, which celebrated its 40th anniversary in 1999, today continues providing its customers with the quality workmanship espoused by its founder and owner, Bob Hepp.

Hepp graduated from the city's Roosevelt High School and cultivated his trade at its nationally renowned Ranken Technical College. While working for his father-in-law as an apprentice electrician, he foresaw the field as a good way to earn an honest living. He reasoned that by using the best materials and doing the work himself to ensure the best job possible, he could generate demand for his services. After earning an electrical contractor's license, he started his own business, then called Superior Electric, in 1959.

Operating out of his home for the first three years, he at first used one part-time employee. As word of his excellent craftsmanship and service spread, he eventually added more workers and moved his office to a commercial site. Incorporating in 1962, Hepp landed his first major job three years later when he took on the first five temporary buildings for Meramec Community College.

The company moved within the south St. Louis area several times over the years. For a long time it occupied a small building situated behind a venerable structure that always housed an eating establishment in St. Louis County's Grantwood Village. There, Hepp managed his business in a converted shed that had previously served as a chicken house — it mutated from chicken wire to electric wire.

The company name was changed to Supreme Electric Co. in the 1980s. Licensed to serve St. Louis city and county and St. Charles, by 2001 it required five electricians with four trucks. As in the beginning, Hepp insists on "superior" or "supreme" work and courteous service. A member of the International Association of Electrical Inspectors, he personally inspects each job prior to the city's inspection. Keeping in step with evolving technology, he considers the increasingly expanding National Electrical Code Handbook to be his bible. Bonded and insured, Supreme specializes in rewiring, 100-200 AMP service, room additions, and concealed renovation wiring for commercial and residential customers.

After working with Supreme's electricians for several years, Hepp's son, Joe, now uses the knowledge he acquired then, and combining that with his computer skills, he manages the company's office. Supreme moved on to its location on Watson Road early in 2001, and Hepp envisions Joe carrying on the family tradition well into the new century.

Hepp's traction orange business cards — like his company — stand out from the others. The color reflects his fervent interests in streetcars. A charter member of San Francisco's Market Street Railway Company, he used his trade skills to aid the recent resurrection of that city's Market Street streetcar line. Furthering the interest of his hometown, he is also active in St. Louis' Citizens for Modern Transit, a nonprofit advocacy group instrumental in the development of the city's Metro Link. Hepp's fervor for streetcars is exceeded only by his dedication to his brainchild — Supreme Electric Company.

The St. Louis Mercantile Library at the University of Missouri-St. Louis

Besides being headquarters for major corporations, the St. Louis area hosts many flourishing entrepreneurial businesses.

BUSINESS & FINANCE

How do I best introduce the business and financial section of the history of St. Louis? I can say it is an ideal market. It has been and continues to be a wonderful community in which to live, work and raise a family. It is a place that creates wealth of all kinds.

St. Louis has often been described as the nation's largest small town. While more than 2.5 million people live in the St. Louis region, which includes 12 counties covering 6,375 square miles in Missouri and Illinois, the focus for most residents is a close-knit bond of community and neighborhood. The combination of multiple neighborhoods, a wealth of large and small businesses and a high concentration of high-quality schools creates a strong economic base and adds up to form the 18th-largest metropolitan area in the United States. The St. Louis business and financial conditions are not characterized by over-concentrations or fits of starts and stops.

Historically, the economic drivers for the St. Louis economy have been similar to other markets, but what distinguishes the city from many other major metropolitan areas has been its ability to sustain balanced, stable growth for so many years. St. Louis is ranked as the 18th-largest market in the United States. But it is particularly telling that St. Louis is ranked 16th in total deposits and is flush with wealth and discretionary income. This is a strong market, and the people who live here and and run it have their financial fundamentals battened down tight.

Because St. Louisans run a tight financial ship, St. Louis is home to the "millionaire next door." The personal financial discipline that makes millionaires of the likes of office workers, craftsmen and letter carriers is common to the ethic in St. Louis. St. Louis embodies the Midwest work ethic and a balance of family values. The bond of communities and churches, schools and neighborhood associations reflects a character that not only produces enriched lives, but also is good for business and great for finance.

It's nearly the ideal climate for business, strong in its core base and both national and global in its reach and influence. In fact, St. Louis is home to 20 Fortune 1000 companies and ranks fourth in the United States as a headquarters location for Fortune 500 companies. The region's total number of Fortune 500 corporate headquarters stands at 10, just behind Atlanta, Chicago, Houston and New York.

Besides being headquarters for major corporations, the St. Louis area hosts many flourishing entrepreneurial businesses. St. Louis ranked second in the United States in *Entrepreneur* magazine's listing of the top places for small business, marking four straight years on that publication's Top 10 list. In addition, *Inc.* magazine placed the region among the Top 10 areas for growing firms and *Black Enterprise* magazine also named St. Louis as one of six new business meccas for African-Americans.

Commerce is what drives business and finance. We say commerce is good. Commerce is good for business. Commerce is good for families. Commerce is good for building and sustaining wealth. Commerce is thriving — in St. Louis. The fundamentals for long-lasting healthy growth are well in place. At Commerce Bank, we believe the strong success of our super community banking format is a direct reflection of the St. Louis business and finance landscape. We review and finance thousands of business plans every year in St. Louis. The ones that succeed are the ones that meet their market head on and deliver on its needs. The players in St. Louis business and finance prove worthy of the challenge each time "they raise the bar."

When concluding a review of the past and present St. Louis business and financial landscape, one sees the essence of American spirit, ingenuity and fortitude. A place with people of character, guts and imagination; a place abundant with people with ideas and the courage and wherewithal to put them into action is a place I'm proud to call home. The stability of our business and financial condition reflects and sustains a responsible freedom sure to stand the test of time.

DAVID W. KEMPER
Chairman of the Board
President and CEO. Commerce Bancshares, Inc.

Commerce Bancshares, Inc.

A venture founded in 1865 with just $10,000 by Francis Reid Long on the banks of the Missouri River in Kansas City has grown many times over the years to become Commerce Bancshares, Inc., a leading regional banking company in St. Louis with $11.4 billion in assets. Today, the registered bank holding company operates a network of more than 300 Commerce Bank locations and six subsidiary banks in Missouri, Kansas and Illinois.

The company attributes its impressive record of prosperity on a dedication to taking care of customer needs and serving each branch's community. In fact, community service is the focus of Commerce's mission statement directives: "Be Accessible. Offer Solutions. Build Relationships." The bank is also proud of its commitment to both investing in and advising entrepreneurial companies such as St. Louis-based Enterprise Rent-A-Car, now a billion-dollar corporation. Partnering with innovative companies and helping to create value has, in turn, reflected the bank's own entrepreneurial spirit.

Commerce Bancshares entered the St. Louis region in 1969 with the purchase of banks in the communities of University City, St. Charles and Kirkwood. Three years later, Commerce Bank's first city branch was opened on 500 Broadway in the heart of downtown.

While a wave of bank consolidations in the 1990s eliminated the local character of several St. Louis-area financial institutions, Commerce remained independent. In the late 90s it increased market share by gaining deposits from consumers and businesses that preferred a locally based institution. Commerce, publicly traded under the symbol CBSH, now ranks as one of Missouri's top banks by a number of customers and one out of four Missouri households is served by it.

Commerce Bank's three primary lines of business include consumer banking, commercial banking and investment services. Investment services comprise trust, brokerage and money management.

David W. Kemper, chairman, president and CEO, Commerce Bancshares, Inc.

In addition, five non-banking subsidiaries include mortgage banking, brokerage, credit-related insurance, venture capital and real estate.

To help deliver a more localized, community-driven approach, the bank innovated a Super-Community Bank strategy. The model has four components: competitive products, competitive pricing, superior service and superior knowledge of the market based on active local involvement.

Through one of its key management disciplines, called Managing Local Markets, Commerce empowers its people in each community it serves to analyze, plan and implement an active program of customer service, account retention and business development. Commerce officials think obtaining superior knowledge of a local market is impossible without knowing the lay of the land. To help attain that knowledge, Commerce has a board of community directors — individuals from many different professions — in each community who serve as the bank's "eyes and ears." Community boards meet regularly to hear local concerns and banking needs and relay them to local bank officials.

These guiding principals were already evident in the bank's earliest days when it was known as Kansas City Savings Association. Founder Long, who became Kansas City's mayor in 1869, was successful in developing long-term relationships with customers by offering both financial advice and capital to young companies. After just 13 years of operation, bank capital was $50,000 and deposits $250,000.

To reflect Kansas City Savings' vital role in funding commercial ventures, it established a new charter in 1882 as National Bank of Commerce. In 1906 William T. Kemper joined the company as president of a newly created, separate Commerce Trust Company (Commerce Trust Co. and the National Bank of Commerce merged in 1921 to become Commerce Trust Co.). This marked the beginning of his

family's century-long tie to the bank. With Kempers at the helm throughout the 20th century, Commerce continued on a path of consistent, strong and sound revenue and asset growth. The tradition continues to this day as David W. Kemper, William's great-grandson, is now chairman, president and CEO.

Giving back to the community is another important tradition. Ten times each year the bank presents a Community Service Award to an individual who is making a significant improvement to his or her community's quality of life through civic action or redevelopment efforts. A grant ranging between $5,000 to $10,000 is presented to the recipient's organization of choice. Commerce's community directors help to nominate candidates for the award. The bank also annually donates millions of dollars in gifts and grants through its foundations.

Another hallmark of the company — a commitment to technical innovation — began in 1928, when Commerce introduced the first 24-hour transit department in the country. This helped speed up the transit of checks between banks, reduce losses and was acclaimed for strengthening the banking system. Over the years, firsts for Commerce Bancshares include creating the first money market department in Kansas City and the first full-scale international department in the 1960s. In late 1984 Commerce Bank of Omaha — formed to issue enhanced credit card products — introduced "Special Connections," the first combined credit card and automated teller transaction card in the market.

To capitalize on fast-growing Internet technology, Commerce began offering online banking and bill-paying services using Intuit, Inc.'s Quicken software in 1996. Later improvements made Internet banking accessible through any Web browser — anytime, anywhere. Commerce Bancshares was recognized for these efforts when *United States Banker* magazine named it one of the Top 10 U.S. banks for technology.

A commitment to innovation has simply been a natural outgrowth of responding to customer needs and requests for new services, explains CEO Kemper. "Staying close to our customers and being responsive by innovating new services and products to take care of their needs is the theme that has run throughout our history," Kemper says. "Our employees get excited when we bring something new to market." Going forward, Kemper is confident that the "financial services market is still dynamic and growing and will yield great opportunities for companies that can manage change and stay focused on customer needs."

Stifel, Nicolaus & Company, Incorporated

The significance and impact of certain historical events have a way of getting watered down when viewed from the long-range perch of modern life. To help make sense of the past, it's a good idea to shuffle the cards into the right order.

For instance, simultaneous to the doors opening at the St. Louis investment firm of Stifel, Nicolaus & Company, Incorporated, in 1890, a couple of German inventors were hard at work tightening the lug nuts on a noisy but addictive little idea they called the automobile. And to the North an English chap was putting a new twist on an old idea that would soon revolutionize the way in which folks got themselves about town; the bicycle would forever alter the European landscape. And in the states, the telephone was only a much-talked-about new fad and the movies weren't even the movies yet.

That's how long ago St. Louis-born Herman Stifel and German-born Henry Nicolaus combined their financial expertise and pioneering spirit to give birth to Stifel Nicolaus. Dedicated to the betterment of the community in which they worked and lived, these financial visionaries set the tone for their company's thriving success with the simple but humane philosophy of "safeguarding the money of others as if it were your own."

What began over 100 years ago as an unassuming brokerage and underwriting business, but with strong leadership at the helm and a handful of dedicated employees to steer its course, has blossomed into a complex, full-service investment firm — providing securities brokerage, investment banking, trading and investment advice to individual investors, professional money managers, businesses and municipalities.

Since its inception, Stifel Nicolaus has held to the belief that it is more important to nurture long-term business relationships as opposed to turning short-term profits. This philosophy forged the foundation for its dedication to the St. Louis community as a whole, championing several infrastructure growth projects that it not only underwrote but philosophically supported as well. Several of St. Louis' most successful companies have also benefited from their relationships with Stifel Nicolaus.

But although it has always maintained its operating headquarters in St. Louis, by establishing itself early on as an underwriter of municipal bonds, Stifel Nicolaus quickly and effectively broadened its scope of operations and became a dominant player on the national scene. By lending its financial support to a little-known Oklahoma oil company in the 1930s that later merged with its New Jersey counterpart, Stifel Nicolaus helped give rise to one of the country's largest

The firm's headquarters at One Financial Plaza, in the heart of downtown St. Louis

oil refinery and gasoline companies: Conoco. It was also one of the original supporters and participants in the first commercial airline flight from St. Louis to Chicago in 1928.

During this country's prolonged and prosperous stretch of growth and expansion in the 20th century, Stifel Nicolaus was right in the fray, shouldering the responsibility for underwriting many of the nation's largest construction projects. From Chicago's O'Hare Airport to the Mackinac Bridge and the Maine and Pennsylvania turnpikes to St. Louis' Veteran's Memorial Bridge and the Rock Island Centennial Bridge, Stifel Nicolaus has always been a leader in the financial industry in its unwavering support of a growing and unfolding nation.

But it's the people behind the scenes who are the company's lifeblood, dedicating personal time, expertise and money to a multitude of charitable causes and organizations, including the United Way, the USO, The Boy Scouts of America and the St. Louis Zoological Society. Since the beginning, employees have always been encouraged to participate in community activities and join professional organizations. Through the years many Stifel Nicolaus associates have led by example while serving as president of one of the most influential and prestigious organizations of the investment industry, the Investment Bankers Association (IBA).

Its longtime relationships with political candidates and U.S. presidents is also well documented. From President Hoover to Wendell Wilkie to President Bush, the fight for democracy as well as the United States' continued role as a world leader have long been major concerns and beneficiaries of support of the Stifel Nicolaus family. In keeping with the philosophy that business is family and family is business, Stifel Nicolaus was a forerunner

in the idea and implementation of one of the nation's first Employee Stock Ownership Plans (ESOP), in which employees hold a stake in the company, fostering a desire to ensure their company's success and growth. It was also one of the first to install an employee profit-sharing plan, which it did in 1954.

But it has taken over 100 years for Stifel Nicolaus to position itself where it is today. With more than 70 offices strategically located in over 15 Midwestern states, Stifel continues to grow, but with the committed intention of "being the best, not the biggest."

For a company of its physical size and presence, and the immense impact it has had on the industry and community, Stifel Nicolaus surprisingly, but intentionally, maintains manageable broker/client ratio relationships. This benefits not only the client, but in the sometimes capricious world of investment banking, Stifel Nicolaus has earned the reputation as being the "firm of choice" to work for. With its "close to the client" approach to brokering, decisions are streamlined through the company without getting bogged down in a sea of middle managers.

And this distinguished practice will continue into the future. With the technological developments that are reshaping the entire world as well as the investment industry, Stifel Nicolaus sees the topsy-turvy technological revolution as more of a positive — another tool with which to "strengthen the personal relationship between brokers and clients." The firm also believes technological advancements provide a more effective means of communicating that will enhance dialogue and interaction.

And in keeping with Stifel Nicolaus tradition, the client will still come first.

U.S. Bank

If a 19th-century banker could visit a U.S. Bank branch, he'd delight in the "super" ATM dispensing postage stamps along with cash and marvel at the wide array of products and services now available. But he'd feel right at home with U.S. Bank's traditional business philosophy of nurturing personal relationships with customers and supporting the community.

U.S. Bank is a financial giant with a hometown attitude. While offering the resources that enable customers in 24 states to maximize present opportunities and achieve long-term goals, U.S. Bank forms a cornerstone in its cities by fostering revitalization, supporting charities, and participating in local organizations and events in the tradition of the proud community banks that preceded it. In St. Louis, U.S. Bank carries that baton for Mercantile Bank, a presence in the area since the founding of State Savings Institution in 1855.

Acquisitions drive the histories of both Mercantile and U.S. Bank. Mercantile grew extensively through the practice, gaining United Postal Savings, Mark Twain Bank, Roosevelt Bank and others before combining during the late 1990s with Firstar, itself an amalgamation of established community banks with roots stretching back to 1853. In 2001 Firstar, holder of the largest market share in St. Louis and Missouri, acquired the 149-year-old U.S. Bank and adopted the name.

The "new" U.S. Bank became the nation's second-largest bank in terms of territory and the eighth-largest bank holding company with assets of $165 billion, 2,200 branches and 5,200 branded ATMs. The transition occurred seamlessly for the financial institution's 10 million customers, who continued to conduct business with the same highly qualified personnel, but gained a broader spectrum of banking, lending, investment and insurance products and services. Advisory boards composed of civic and community leaders as well as representatives from businesses and industries ensured that decision-making would remain in the hands of people who live and work in the area.

Convenience and guaranteed service are the cornerstones of U.S. Bank, which offers around-the-clock customer service. Branches operate in stores, workplaces and schools, like Saint Louis University, where student identification cards double as ATM cards. Regardless of income level, U.S. Bank offers opportunities for free checking accounts. Small businesses may conduct business at any retail branch or open an account that "sweeps" excess funds into a savings account and provides for a simple line of credit. Commercial customers also enjoy tools such as treasury management and payment systems. The success of U.S. Bank's efforts to encourage business development reflects in the large amount of loans and credit lines it carries for companies of all sizes.

Each U.S. Bank customer, regardless of line of business, can rely upon the bank's commitment to efficiency and accuracy, which is backed by its exclusive Five Star Service Guarantee. Failure to deliver any part of that guarantee results in the bank crediting the customer's account anywhere from $5 to a few hundred dollars.

U.S. Bank, a multimillion-dollar civic contributor, donates to over 250 St. Louis metro-area charities each year, supporting a variety of enterprises including the arts, education, and health and community causes. Among the events U.S. Bank sponsors are the Saint Louis Jazz Festival, Senior Olympics, Wild Lights at the St. Louis Zoo, the Broadway Series at the Fox Theatre, Fair Saint Louis, and the St. Louis County Fair and Air Show. The generosity of its employees consistently places U.S. Bank in the United Way of Greater St. Louis' Million Dollar Club and their volunteer efforts are vital to the success of local organizations and events, such as Fair Saint Louis, where each year more than 160 employees staff ticket booths. U.S. Bank executives serve on the boards of numerous charities and youth groups as well as Civic Progress and the Regional Chamber and Growth Association.

In cooperation with Future Builders, U.S. Bank's Community Counts program underwrites service-learning projects developed by public school students in the sixth through twelfth grades who want to improve the communities. Another grant program offers money to organizations undertaking projects or programs to support the residents of North St. Louis and improve neighborhoods in that area. In recent years, U.S. Bank has played a major role in downtown St. Louis' revitalization projects including the Cupples Station complex, the City Museum, the Convention Center Hotel and many other historic rehabilitation projects in the Washington Avenue Loft District.

Through its Community Development Corporation (CDC), U.S. Bank makes equity investments in projects that provide quality affordable housing throughout the region. The CDC partners with local organizations and both for-profit and not-for-profit developers to provide safe and affordable housing for individuals and families with low and moderate incomes.

U.S. Bank is a leader in online banking and presents a suite of integrated payment solutions. The bank's ATMs, which sell phone minutes as well as

stamps, provide statements and offer ticket sale and coupon printing capabilities.

By embracing advances in technology, U.S. Bank continues a trend that Mercantile set when it established a data service center in 1962, a mere year after "automation" became an industry buzzword. By 1963 Mercantile customers could opt for a monthly automated service that transferred money from a checking account to a savings account. Fourteen years later, when St. Louis' first point-of-sale debit card debuted, Mercantile customers were among the first people who could use ATM cards at the participating service stations.

U.S. Bank's commercial clients operating in the global marketplace utilize foreign exchange services and lock in exchange rates for projects. Online reporting services and other products are available to institutional clients. U.S. Bancorp Piper Jaffray®, a nationally recognized investment management firm, opens the door on investment possibilities for retail and commercial customers.

U.S. Bank can accommodate anyone's financial needs throughout the course of a lifetime. Change is a constant in the banking industry but U.S. Bank customers can rest assured that their bank will remain true to its traditional business philosophy. Products and services will be delivered with convenience, efficiency and, most importantly, a smile and a personal touch.

U.S. Bank's commitment to community is evidenced by the countless hours its employees volunteer with local organizations.

With U.S. Bank behind them, communities and businesses grow.

St Louis has a strong manufacturing and distribution support base.

MANUFACTURING & DISTRIBUTION

The St. Louis metropolitan area is home to many manufacturing and distribution companies operating in a wide variety of different industries. Many of these local companies operate in very competitive markets both domestically and internationally. As a result, these companies have cultures that embody the best of class. We are fortunate to have such a strong base of companies in the St. Louis area.

Many local companies have a rich history of success here in St. Louis. In many ways, the success of the area companies parallels the growth and success of the city. Maintaining a strong manufacturing and distribution employer base will give the city strong advantages as we continue to grow.

St. Louis has a strong manufacturing and distribution support base. Our location near the center of the country provides unique advantages. The deep and diverse labor pool also supports local industry well. Additionally, the city has a strong educational presence, which further supports area employers. Our area also provides nationally recognized health care services.

While St. Louis offers significant advantages to our local companies, the city offers many advantages to our citizens. The affordable cost of living and strong family environment are two real assets of our city. The breadth and diversity of cultural events also defines our city. On the sports front, St. Louis has been called the "Best Sports City in America" and the "Best Baseball City." The success of all of our professional sports teams spoils us.

These benefits keep manufacturing and distribution employers in our area. The factors also attract new companies to St. Louis. These employers create excellent jobs and career paths for our citizens. The companies and their employees contribute to keeping St. Louis a vibrant and active community. We are proud to call St. Louis home.

JOE R. MICHELETTO
CEO & President • Ralcorp Holdings, Inc.

163

Anheuser-Busch Companies, Inc.

Since its founding in St. Louis in 1852, Anheuser-Busch has been marked by a constant, intense focus on one concept: quality. Today, nearly five out of every 10 beers sold in the United States is an Anheuser-Busch product. The company's beers have always been known for their fine ingredients and unmatched quality. From the company's choice of the finest-quality, freshest brewing ingredients, to its marketing efforts, to its environmental policies, Anheuser-Busch has always insisted on the highest standards. This tradition has enabled the company to grow to become the world's largest brewer and to be a leader in the container manufacturing and family entertainment industries.

The modernized brew house at the St. Louis brewery was originally completed in 1892 and is one of the major attractions of the St. Louis brewery tour. In addition to St. Louis, complimentary brewery tours are offered at the Anheuser-Busch breweries in Fairfield, California; Fort Collins, Colorado; Jacksonville, Florida; and Merrimack, New Hampshire.

A LEGACY OF QUALITY

Anheuser-Busch traces its roots in St. Louis to the Bavarian Brewery. In 1860 Eberhard Anheuser saw a diamond in the rough when he purchased a failing Bavarian Brewery in St. Louis along the banks of the Mississippi. The brewery became a family business early on when Eberhard hired his son-in-law, Adolphus Busch, as a salesman.

Adolphus became president in 1880 and used modern technology and marketing savvy to build the brewery into an industry leader. It was Adolphus who began transforming the company into an industry powerhouse and who is considered its founder. Today, developments in technology and marketing prowess have helped keep Anheuser-Busch at the top of its game.

A brilliant visionary and innovator, Adolphus dreamed of a national beer market and a national beer. As a first step in making that dream come true, he launched the industry's first fleet of refrigerated freight cars. From a business that had failed three times in its early years, Adolphus built the brewery into the industry leader through the application of modern technology and marketing. He was the first U.S. brewer to use pasteurization, artificial refrigeration and refrigerated railcars on a large scale and the first to bottle beer extensively. These technological innovations allowed him to produce a higher-quality beer more efficiently and to market it throughout the country in an era when most brewers were strictly local.

It was also under Adolphus in 1876 that Budweiser, America's first national beer brand, was brewed using traditional brewing methods and only the finest barley malt, hops and rice. Twenty years later, still under Adolphus' leadership, the company developed Michelob, which soon became the pre-eminent American super-premium beer.

Adolphus' son, August A. Busch Sr., led the company during the turbulent eras of World War I and Prohibition. During Prohibition, the company survived and protected the jobs of its employees by making such products as baker's yeast, soft drinks and Bevo, a non-alcohol, malt-based beverage.

When Prohibition was repealed in 1933, the Clydesdales became part of Anheuser-Busch. August A.

Busch Jr. presented a hitch of the mighty horses to his father, August A Busch Sr. to commemorate the first bottle of post-Prohibition beer brewed in St. Louis. The original hitch consisted of six horses. The eight-horse hitch debuted a year later. Following the repeal of Prohibition, the Clydesdales became an enduring symbol for the company, and Anheuser-Busch's focus shifted back to its core product, beer.

One of Adolphus' two grandsons, Adolphus Busch III, guided the company through the end of the Great Depression and World War II. The other grandson, August A. Busch Jr., then led the firm through the postwar era, during which the company first began establishing breweries outside of the St. Louis area.

Since its inception in 1852, Anheuser-Busch has been a company focused on the future. Today, that future includes an aggressive goal — becoming the world's beer company. The company is already the world's largest brewer, capturing 10.3 percent of the world market share. In the United States, the company commands more than a 48 percent market share and is twice as large as its nearest competitor

KING OF BEERS

In 2002 the board of directors of Anheuser-Busch Companies Inc. named Patrick T. Stokes as President and CEO of the corporation. Stokes succeeds August A. Busch III, who will continue as chairman of the board. Succeeding Stokes as president of the beer company, Anheuser-Busch, Inc., is August A. Busch IV.

August A. Busch III was the fourth generation of his family to hold the reins of the company. Under his guidance as chairman of the board and president of Anheuser-Busch Companies, the corporation continued to thrive with a market share approximately twice that of its nearest competitor. Anheuser-Busch is also becoming a growing force in the international beer industry. In addition, the company has major interest in the packaging and entertainment industries.

During his tenure, August A. Busch III developed a strong senior management team that has helped the company consistently deliver

Dalmatians have traveled with the Budweiser Clydesdale hitch since the 1950s. In the early days of brewing, Dalmatians were bred and trained to protect the horses and guard the wagon when the driver went inside a retail account to make deliveries.

shareholder value and maintain its commanding leadership position in the industry.

Quality ingredients and freshness are the keys to great beer taste. Anheuser-Busch uses only the finest natural ingredients selected through the most exacting requirements and specifications in the brewing industry. The best two- and six-row barley malt, highest-grade rice, imported and domestic whole hop cones, yeast and purest water used in the Budweiser brewing process are chosen with care and pride. Budweiser is brewed naturally, without artificial ingredients, additives or preservatives. The brewing process takes 30 days or more. Anheuser-Busch brews and ages the beer the old-fashioned way. Much of the 30 days is spent in large tanks lined with beechwood chips. It is here where the beer ages and produces natural carbonation — something unique to Anheuser-Busch beers.

Besides Budweiser, Anheuser-Busch now produces more than 30 brands of beer and malt beverages, including Bud Light, the world's second-leading beer.

Budweiser is brewed locally in 12 U.S. cities and at Anheuser-Busch-operated breweries in the United Kingdom and China, two of the company's largest international markets. Budweiser is also brewed under license in eight additional countries outside the United States under the direct supervision of Anheuser-Busch brewmasters.

Anheuser-Busch brands are sold in more than 80 countries, and the company continues to expand its global presence thanks to partnerships with local brewers

Anheuser-Busch founder Adolphus Busch laid the foundation for the company to become the industry leader.

Anheuser-Busch recycles more than 97 percent of its everyday operations waste.

Busch Entertainment Corporation, Anheuser-Busch's family entertainment subsidiary, is one of the leading theme park operators in the United States. Formed in 1979, it consists of nine popular and distinctive adventure parks and is the industry leader in thrilling entertainment, wildlife conservation and education. More than 20 million guests visit Busch Entertainment parks each year.

The parks' innovative approach to attraction design, groundbreaking veterinary techniques, and animal rescue and rehabilitation are well known. SeaWorld, Discovery Cove and Busch Gardens support wildlife conservation, education and research projects on all seven continents and the Arctic. Busch Entertainment is recognized worldwide for aiding animals in distress and has rescued more than 5,000 ill, orphaned and injured animals in just the past five years.

Each of the company's subsidiaries contributes to the success of Anheuser-Busch. The company's history of well-managed growth, diversified holdings and strong leadership has guided Anheuser-Busch into the 21st century as the clear leader in the industry.

As the world's largest brewer, Anheuser-Busch has a vested interest in ensuring that its beers are consumed as intended: responsibly and by adults. No company benefits when its products are misused, something acknowledged by the company's 25,000 employees who are raising children, living and working in this society, and driving the same highways as everyone else. Alcohol abuse, drunk driving and underage drinking are problems everyone would like to see solved.

in a number of countries including Canada, Ireland, Argentina, Japan, Mexico, Italy and Spain.

Increasingly, people the world over are becoming familiar with Budweiser through international advertising campaigns and sponsorships of global and regional sporting events, including the FIFA World Cup, the Olympic Games and the National Basketball Association.

Over the years, Anheuser-Busch has established several subsidiaries related to its beer operations. In 1973 Anheuser-Busch formed Metal Container Corporation, which operates 11 can and lid manufacturing facilities in the United States. MCC supplied 61 percent of Anheuser-Busch's domestic beer cans and 80 percent of Anheuser-Busch's domestic lids in 2000. MCC is also a major supplier of cans to Pepsi-Cola and, in 2000, added Coca-Cola and Grupo Modelo of Mexico as customers.

In 1978, Anheuser-Busch set up a recycling subsidiary, Anheuser-Busch Recycling Corporation, which has grown into the world's largest recycler of aluminum beverage cans. It collects more than 685 million pounds annually.

Throughout this growth and expansion, Anheuser-Busch has been committed to environmental initiatives. At the turn of the century, Adolphus Busch began recycling spent brewers' grains for use as animal feed.

Today, the company still recycles grain and undertakes numerous other innovative environmental campaigns. Since 1993, Anheuser-Busch has won more than 100 environmental awards in the areas of waste reduction, conservation, recycling and animal protection.

Tackling these problems requires a team approach: one that involves parents, teachers, community organizations, law enforcement officials, the alcohol beverage industry, treatment and prevention authorities, and many others. Anheuser-Busch and its network of nearly 700 independent beer wholesalers are committed members of this team through their awareness campaigns and educational initiatives, which include national advertising campaigns and more than two dozen community-based programs that fight drunk driving and underage drinking and that promote responsible drinking among adults who choose to drink.

Since the early 1900s, Anheuser-Busch has promoted moderation to its customers. Anheuser-Busch began its *Know When To Say When* campaign in 1982 and was the first in the industry to bring responsibility messages to network television (in 1985) with its *Know When To Say When* commercials. Anheuser-Busch's newest campaign to fight alcohol abuse is *We All Make A Difference*. This latest alcohol awareness initiative reinforces the good practices of drinkers who exercise personal responsibility, designate a driver or call a cab, and builds on the momentum of an almost two-decade decline in drunk driving fatalities. With a financial commitment of more than $350 million since 1982 alone, Anheuser-Busch leads the alcohol beverage industry in the fight against alcohol abuse.

PART OF LIFE IN ST. LOUIS

One of St. Louis' most popular attractions is the complimentary tour of the St. Louis brewery. The St. Louis brewery tour offers the public an opportunity to learn about the rich brewing heritage of Anheuser-Busch and how beer is brewed and packaged today. The historic 100-acre brewery is a rich part of America's brewing history. During the tours, guests who are 21 years of age or older are invited to enjoy complimentary tastings of Anheuser-Busch products in the Hospitality Room. Soft drinks and snacks also are served. Tours showcase Anheuser-Busch's time-honored brewing tradition and century-old commitment to quality.

The St. Louis brewery is home to three national historical landmark buildings, including the old schoolhouse where August Busch Sr. attended grade school; the Anheuser-Busch Clydesdales stable that was built in 1885 by Adolphus Busch; and the historic brew house that was built in 1891.

St. Louis residents and tourists alike flock to Grant's Farm in St. Louis County. Once the home of August A. Busch Jr., Grant's Farm today houses the only existing structure hand-built by an American president — Ulysses S. Grant. Grant's Farm is a unique blend of education and entertainment and attracts some 600,000 visitors each year. Guests enjoy complimentary open-air tram rides that roam the 281-acre farm, entertaining animal shows, spectacular wildlife and rich history.

Anheuser-Busch is proud to be part of life in St. Louis. The company has a long-standing tradition of giving back to the communities in which it does business, always seeking to improve the quality of life. And as it approaches the future, Anheuser-Busch will continue to support responsible corporate citizenship and to emphasize the bedrock of its success — its focus on quality.

For a century and a half, the company has stressed an unwavering commitment to quality while continually pursuing innovative ways to enhance quality in every segment of business — its products, services and relationships. That operating philosophy has served Anheuser-Busch well in the past — and will continue to do so in the future.

Anheuser-Busch celebrates the holidays by installing some 1 million lights throughout its St. Louis world headquarters complex. Anheuser-Busch's traditional spectacle of lights has become one of the metropolitan area's most popular holiday exhibits.

Busch Entertainment Corporation, Anheuser-Busch's family entertainment subsidiary, is one of the leading theme park operators in the United States. Busch Entertainment is recognized worldwide for aiding animals in distress. One of Busch Entertainment Corporation's many wildlife-assistance efforts involves work with manatees, an endangered species in Florida.

GlaxoSmithKline

*E*very year, the GlaxoSmithKline (GSK) facility in St. Louis manufactures billions of TUMS tablets. Millions of people around the world choose TUMS — whether by the bottle or by handy rolls — to relieve acid indigestion.

TUMS is a success story that is more than 70 years old. The story begins, however, far from St. Louis and even beyond the shores of America. TUMS is a product that found initial success on the high seas and was manufactured commercially because of popular demand.

TUMS was formulated by James Harvey Howe, a pharmacist, who after the death of A.H. Lewis in 1928 became president of the Lewis-Howe Medicine Company. Howe wanted to make a treatment for his wife's acid indigestion. He created a gentle antacid medication and flavored it with peppermint oil. The tablets were a big success with Mrs. Howe, so James ran his formulation through the Lewis-Howe tableting machine and kept a jar full of tablets on hand. When the Howes traveled, the tablets went with them.

Mrs. Howe saw the commercial potential for the tablets aboard a luxury ship. The Howes shared their tablets with passengers aboard ship, who liked them so well they awakened the Howes at all hours of the night to get the tablets that brought immediate relief. After one early morning awakening, Mrs. Howe remarked

to her husband that if people were willing to beg for the tablets, then they surely would pay for them.

Lewis-Howe started commercial production of TUMS in 1930. Within three years, TUMS was world famous.

The name TUMS was chosen in a contest conducted by the company on a local radio station. Listeners were invited to send in their suggestions with a prize of $100 being offered to the winner. A nurse submitted the winning entry, TUM, and the slogan "TUMS for the Tummy" was born.

The origins of Lewis-Howe date back to 1870 when A.H. Lewis opened the City Drug Store in Bolivar, Missouri. He developed a laxative called Nature's Remedy that helped the business grow and eventually led to relocation in St. Louis. James Harvey Howe, who eventually would create TUMS, went to work for his uncle in A.H. Lewis' Bolivar drugstore at the age of 14. Howe was certified as a pharmacist in 1890 and moved with the company to St. Louis in 1901.

Today, TUMS is one of the leading consumer health care products of GlaxoSmithKline.

Lewis-Howe continued to prosper with TUMS and Nature's Remedy. In 1964 the company entered the ethical pharmaceuticals market with the formation of Arch Laboratories. The first product of Arch Laboratories was a pleasant-tasting antacid called Dicarbosil.

The history of GlaxoSmithKline is even older than TUMS. Created in 2000 by the merger of Glaxo Wellcome and SmithKline Beecham, GSK traces its roots

(Left to right) An early picture of James H. Howe and A.H. Lewis in a meeting in what is still the TUMS building

The TUMS sign, known as a downtown St. Louis landmark, graced the TUMS building until June 2001.

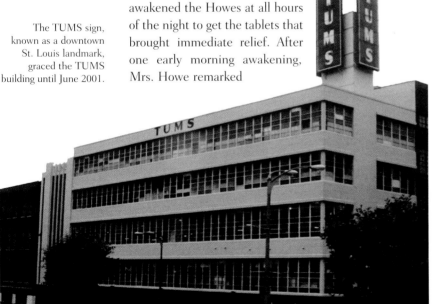

to 1715 when Silvanus Bevan first established the Plough Court Pharmacy in London, England. That pharmacy grew into a major pharmaceutical manufacturer that became part of Glaxo, a company known at the beginning of the 20th century for its powdered milk formula.

SmithKline Beecham dates back to 1830 when John K. Smith opened his first drugstore in Philadelphia, and to 1842 when Thomas Beecham launched his Beecham's Pills business in England. He also manufactured the famous Beecham Powders known as a "cure for whatever ailed folks."

Beecham and A.H. Lewis took similar paths to success. Just as Lewis in the United States had created Nature's Remedy, Beecham developed a laxative called "Beecham's Pills," which was launched in 1842. By 1913 production of Beecham's Pills had reached 1 million a day. In 1926 the company introduced Beecham's Powders, which was described as a treatment for influenza, colds, headaches, neuralgia, rheumatism and nerve pains.

The Beecham and Lewis paths came together in the 1970s and 80s. In 1978 Norcliff Thayer acquired Lewis-Howe. Eight years later, in 1986, The Beecham Group acquired Norcliff Thayer and with it TUMS and Oxy products. In 1989 the Beecham Group merged with SmithKline Beckman to form SmithKline Beecham.

Today, GlaxoSmithKline has more than 100,000 employees around the world. The St. Louis facility is part of GSK's Global Manufacturing & Supply organization, which has 107 manufacturing sites in 40 different countries.

The St. Louis TUMS plant of today has the same commitment to quality, customer satisfaction and service as it did when it made the first antacid tablet in 1930. TUMS remains one of the world's leading antacids and calcium supplements. During the mid to late century, other products were also manufactured at the site, but in 1996 the company made the decision to devote the entire plant to the production of the ever-popular TUMS, streamlining and updating the entire operation.

With calcium carbonate as a key ingredient, TUMS was also found to be a great source of calcium, which increased its popularity in the 1980s in the wake of the beginning of the osteoporosis epidemic. It is still considered today to be an excellent calcium source.

With a huge manufacturing plant, packaging process, extensive warehousing and a diligent quality control department, 229 employees produced more than 28 million pounds of TUMS in the St. Louis continuous process in 2000.

Some of the company's prescription products include Avandia for Type 2 diabetes, Advair for asthma and a number of vaccines for children and adults.

GSK has a strong commitment to supporting the global community. Since 1998 GSK has been working with the WHO on one of the most ambitious health programs ever undertaken to eliminate the disease lymphatic filariasis, also known as elephantiasis. The company's St. Louis facility Community Involvement Team has participated in local community activities and events with such organizations as the Komen St. Louis Race for the Cure, Big Brothers Big Sisters, St. Louis Children's Hospital, Juvenile Diabetes Research Foundation, MDA-Lock-Up, Disaster Relief-Red Cross-Sept 11th and Judevine Center.

On July 15, 1999, KMOX radio personality Charles Brennan unveiled this bronze marker near the employee entrance of the TUMS building. The building was the first to receive one of Brennan's historic plaques in downtown St. Louis.

The Nature's Remedy tablet started in the City Drug Store, depicted in this mural in Bolivar, Missouri, in 1890. The mural hung in the lobby of the TUMS building for many years.

L. E. Sauer Machine Co.

Moving from Kentucky to St. Louis in search of work early in the 1900s, Louis E. Sauer Sr. used his skills as a machinist, and his desire to be his own boss, to establish the machine company bearing his name. Sauer Sr. succeeded and his company flourishes today. After his two sons, Lou and Bob, joined the business, L. E. Sauer Machine Co. became a world leader in the development and manufacture of tooling for the corrugated box industry. It holds 15 patents in the field. Two additional companies, Centenary Central, Inc. and Dynasauer Corp., were subsequently formed to provide services and products for Sauer Machine. Bob Sauer's son, Warren, joined the company in 1977, and the future of the family business continues under the direction of the third generation.

In 1923, L. E. Sauer Sr. decided to go into business for himself. Two friends he met at Centenary Methodist Church provided the financial backing he needed to get started. After three successful years, he felt he wanted to form his own company. His two partners agreed. One partner took his share in cash. The second partner and Sauer Sr. agreed to flip a coin to see who would get each piece of equipment or the equivalent amount of money in cash. Sauer Sr. won most of the equipment, which enabled him to set up L. E. Sauer Machine Co. The company began operations in an old hotel building on South Fourth Street, next to the MacArthur Bridge.

With about 10 employees at first, the general job shop accepted contracts for all types of machine work. It machined metal parts for a wide variety of industries. As the business grew, it earned a reputation for quality and precision workmanship. It also invited challenges to design tools and parts to solve the special needs of each client. As the size and scope of the business changed, it became necessary to lease additional space on South Fourth Street.

The company was able to survive the Depression of the 1930s and then became heavily involved in the war effort in the 1940s. Work was done on parts that were shipped to England and France before the United States entered the war. After the United States entered the war, new machinery was furnished by the Defense Department. L. E. Sauer Machine Co. primarily did work for the Curtiss-Wright Corporation, which was the predecessor of McDonnell Aircraft (now Boeing). As their

Building I in west St. Louis County

contribution to the war effort, all employees worked 76 hours per week for a period of three to four years.

After the war years, the firm continued subsisting on individual contract work for companies like McDonnell Aircraft, Vickers Electric Division, White Rodgers Electric, Gaylord Container Corp. and other corrugated box plants. Getting through some lean times, it continued on its steadfast path. When Louis Sauer Sr. died in 1952, his two sons, Lou and Bob, picked up where he left off and the company moved forward. One testament to the company's diverse skills stands atop the old General American Insurance building in downtown St. Louis. The globelike weather ball manufactured by the company flashed color weather indicators to generations of local citizens.

Searching for ways to stabilize and grow, thus eliminating slack periods, L. E. Sauer Machine Co. examined various ideas to create a product of its own. Lou Sauer's diligence paid off when he found the solution to a problem presented by a client in the corrugated box industry. He devised a system of rotary die cutting whereby corrugated box manufacturers could substantially increase their production. With the die he designed, a perforated circle could be cut on a box as it ran through the printer-slotter. A significant development in paper box production, it proved to be the product of its own that Sauer sought. The company patented Sauer System Rotary Die Cutting, achieving international recognition.

The company then not only stabilized, it expanded rapidly. Developing more products for the corrugated box industry, it needed a sales force to promote its creations. Centenary Central, named for Centenary Methodist and Central Presbyterian, the churches attended by Lou and Bob respectively, was formed as the sales agency for Sauer Machine. Outgrowing the original building on Fourth Street, the company moved its operation to an industrial park in west St. Louis County in 1966. After developing the application of polyurethane cast parts for the corrugated box industry, it formed a third company, Dynasauer Corporation, to supply these products.

Under Warren Sauer's direction, L. E. Sauer Machine Co. acquired its first laser cutting system in

The original shop on South Fourth Street

1989 and expanded into a new market. By 2001 the company had three 3-axis lasers, two 4-axis lasers and one 5-axis laser. Continuing its tradition of quality and customer service, the company has become a regional leader in job shop laser cutting. Heat treating operations were begun in 1994. Starting as an in-house service for Sauer's corrugated box product line, it quickly expanded to become a full-service heat treating operation that opened yet another new market for the company. And, as it has since 1926, the company continues to provide job shop machining for a wide variety of customers.

Sauer System products for the corrugated box industry

As one example of its community involvement, Sauer contributes sponsorship to the Missouriana Studytour, an annual program that allows school teachers to earn extra credit while familiarizing them with a wide variety of Missouri businesses. Every other year the company opens its facilities to the tour.

In its west St. Louis County location, L. E. Sauer Machine Co. is flanked by Centenary Central, Inc. and Dynasauer Corp. As the new century begins, the company continues to respond to changing times and a competitive marketplace. The Sauer System Companies are now a successful, third-generation, family-owned business. Each generation has increased business volume and applied state-of-the-art technology to meet the needs of its customers. Louis Sauer Sr. would be proud.

Ralcorp Holdings, Inc.

Headquartered in downtown St. Louis in offices providing a majestic vista of the Gateway Arch, Ralcorp Holdings, Inc. is a leading supplier of U.S. private-label food products. Since its spin-off from a then century-old, St. Louis-based major corporation, Ralston Purina Company, Ralcorp Holdings, Inc. continually seeks new and synergetic acquisitions.

Entering 2001, Ralcorp's four food producing companies included: Ralston Foods, the nation's largest supplier of private-label cereals; Bremner, Inc., a leading producer of a wide array of private-label crackers and cookies; Nutcracker Brands Inc., a top producer of private-label snack nuts and high-quality chocolate candies; and Carriage House Companies, Inc., a leading private-label provider of a variety of wet-filled products including salad dressings, jams and jellies, peanut butter, table syrup, ketchup and other sauces. In addition to its interest in the food industry, Ralcorp Holdings, Inc. maintained its 21.6 percent equity investment in Vail Resorts, Inc., a premier North American mountain resort.

Bremner, Inc. products

The chronicle of Ralcorp Holdings, Inc. emanates from the origin of Ralston Purina, originally a producer of animal feed dating back to 1894. Founded and based in St. Louis, Ralston Purina evolved with new products and subsidiaries, including companies that manufactured food for human consumption. On April 1, 1994, 100 years after its emergence, Ralston Purina spun off its human food companies to form an independent Ralcorp

Holdings. Ralcorp, a custodian of the people-food businesses of Ralston Purina, then began its transformation into a leader in private-label foods.

The first companies under the umbrella of Ralcorp Holdings included Ralston Foods, Bremner, Inc., Beech-Nut Nutrition Corporation and the Keystone

Breckenridge ski resorts. In 1997 Ralcorp sold Keystone/Breckenridge ski resorts for cash and an equity interest in Vail Resorts, Inc. Later in 1997 Ralcorp sold its branded Chex cereal and snack mix business to General Mills. The following year, due to an intensely competitive market, it sold Beech-Nut, a baby-food producer.

Ralston Foods, an original Ralston Purina institution, continues its legacy as a manufacturer of high-quality ready-to-eat and hot cereals under the helm of Ralcorp Holdings. With plants in the midwestern and western United States, Ralston Foods now produces quality store-brand ready-to-eat and hot breakfast cereals and breakfast bars in addition to three national brand cereals. Its national brands include Sun Flakes, Ralston 100% Wheat Hot Cereal, and 3 Minute Brand Oats. Sun Flakes is a multi-grain cereal sweetened with NutraSweet that is popular with diabetics and calorie conscious consumers.

Bremner Inc.'s history predates that of Ralston Purina. Founded in 1865, it is the nation's leading manufacturer of private-label crackers and a growing supplier

Ralston Foods products

of private-label cookies. Bremner is also well known for its RyKrisp brand specialty crackers. Ralcorp added Wortz Cracker Company in 1997, adding to Bremner's private label cracker line. Later, Bremner acquired Sugar Kake Cookie Company Inc., which specializes in the production of sandwich creme cookies, the largest-selling private-label cookie type. The purchase of Ripon Foods, Inc. in 1999 further enhanced Bremner's cookie capabilities, in the manufacture of wire-cut and enrobed cookies as well as sugar wafers. In late January 2000, Bremner penetrated the in-store bakery cookie segment by purchasing Cascade Cookie Company, Inc.

By the dawn of 2001 Bremner, Inc., with over 60 different cracker and cookie products, became a private-label industry leader. Almost all of Bremner's crackers and cookies are kosher-certified by the Orthodox Union.

Diversifying into the private-label and value-brand snack nut field in 1998, Ralcorp acquired Flavor House Products, Inc. and then Nutcracker Brands, Inc. It further advanced its presence in the snack nut industry by obtaining Southern Roasted Nuts of Georgia, Inc. the next year. Then, in May 2000, it added chocolate candy to its snack nut business by purchasing James P. Linette, Inc. Ralcorp now operates its snack nut and chocolate candy business under the name Nutcracker Brands, Inc.

In addition to selling nuts under store brand labels, Nutcracker Brands Inc. also markets its products under the Nutcracker, Flavor House and Southern Roasted Nuts brands. Its offerings include dry and oil-roasted peanuts, cashews and mixed nuts. James P. Linette, Inc. complements Nutcracker Brands with its quality branded and private-label chocolate products. Linette primarily manufactures private-label peanut butter cups, caramel cups and mint cups.

Entering the private-label mayonnaise and salad dressing sector in 1999, Ralcorp acquired Martin Gillet & Co., Inc, a high-quality producer of dressings and mayonnaise. It then made a substantial investment in the wet-filled category by purchasing the well-respected Red Wing Company Inc. in 2000. The combined companies formed The Carriage House Companies, Inc. As a leading manufacturer of private-label, shelf-stable, wet-filled products, Red Wing

Nutcracker Brands, Inc. products

broadened the Carriage House product mix with syrups, preserves and jellies, peanut butter, specialty sauces, tomato-based sauces, cocktail mixes and sauces. Late in January 2001, Ralcorp announced its acquisition of the wet products portion of Torbitt & Castleman Company, LLC. This expanded Carriage House with similar food products, including preserves and jellies, syrups, Mexican sauces and barbecue sauces.

Carriage House can combine its use of high-quality vegetables and fruits and other choice ingredients with plants from coast to coast to efficiently service all of the nation's food retailers.

Ralcorp Holdings Inc. plans to further develop its private-label food businesses. A member of the Private Label Manufacturers Association, it recognizes that private labels now represent a key part in the modern food market. No longer stigmatized by the history of poor quality associated with the generic brands of yesteryear, private-label and store brands now offer high quality, attractive packaging and lower pricing.

As a key producer of food products, Ralcorp Holdings, Inc. strives to provide meaningful hunger relief by contributing a considerable amount of those products to charities in the communities that host its facilities. That covers over 20 cities in the United States. In St. Louis its grant dollars go to the St. Louis United Way, the St. Louis Area Food Bank, the Regional Commerce and Growth Association, and the St. Louis Art Museum.

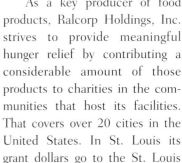

The Carriage House Companies, Inc. products

Sensient Colors Inc.

The artistry of Sensient Colors Inc. is seen in bright swirls of icing, vivid candies and confections, pastel pharmaceutical tablets, eye-catching makeup and ink-jet print. The world's foremost creator of color, Sensient Colors blends art and science to add razzle-dazzle to a world that might otherwise be rather lackluster.

The company's colorful history began in 1905 when Ralph Warner and George Jenkinson founded it to produce extracts for fountain drinks, ice cream and other popular products of the day. By 1911 both men had left the business and William F. Meyer was at the helm.

Meyer, in a move that proved to be a turning point, hired Dr. Harold Johnson as Warner-Jenkinson's first chemist and took the company into the production of food colors. Within two decades, Johnson had created three important, long-standing colors — FD&C Red No. 4, Green No. 3 and Yellow No. 6 — and the lemon-lime flavor used in Seven-Up.

In powder, liquid, granule and plating forms, Warner-Jenkinson's soluble dyes offer certified food colors for products including soft drinks, dry mixes, dairy goods, nuts and sausage casings. Pre-measured coloring systems and dust-reducing products also are available.

Warner-Jenkinson went beyond soluble dyes in 1959 when the Food and Drug Administration approved Lake

Pigments — previously restricted to use in drugs and cosmetics — as food colors. It immediately began producing Lakes, insoluble pigments based on dyes that color by dispersion, to replace two important oil-soluble yellows that had lost FDA-approval.

Lakes' versatility has garnered the pigments a reputation in the industry for solving problems. Among other applications, these certified and safe coloring agents are used in products unsuitable for dyes. Sometimes Lakes and dyes join forces to achieve novel effects, such as blue gum that results in a green tongue. Lakes color food, drugs, cosmetics, personal care products and packaging materials.

The company's creation of Lakes Superior in 1976 increased the importance of these pigments. Lakes Superior, ultra-strong and extremely affordable, used particles no more than 10 microns in size as opposed to the 50-micron particles of standard Lakes. The smaller structure increased the amount of reflected light to yield more color per pound with a bright, clean appearance. Subsequent advances have brought even greater color efficiency, and the average particle size now hits the optimum of .5 micron.

Along with Lakes technology, Warner-Jenkinson also improved dispersion methods for these pigments. In 1981 the company capped 20 years of research with the introduction of Spectracoat, a highly advanced method of delivering Lakes that reduced streaking, prevented cross contamination and addressed other issues of the manufacturing process.

While the development of Lakes played a critical role in driving Warner-Jenkinson's growth and success, the formation of its Color Service Lab in 1964 truly set the company apart from the competition by reinforcing its commitment to customer service and placing it squarely on the path to becoming a pre-eminent color manufacturer. The Color Service Lab, a highly qualified and market-oriented team of chemists, provides unparalleled assistance and an unlimited palette to customers, who

The Color Service Lab at Sensient Colors works with each customer to create the perfect color to meet its needs.

value the group's assistance in conceptualizing new products, preparing them for introduction, troubleshooting problems and engineering cost reductions.

Warner-Jenkinson expanded through the decades — beginning in 1964 with the opening of a color plant in Mexico to serve the Latin American market — and now spans the globe as Sensient Colors with 19 warehouses, offices and manufacturing plants, including the world's three largest dedicated to food colors. In its continuing search for new markets, the company is casting a keen eye at Asia and Eastern Europe.

A growing European demand for natural colors prompted Sensient Colors to develop those agents. In 1984 the company created the first consistent source for carmine, an ancient coloring agent ranging from dark to bright red derived from dried female insects. The company leads the industry in shades of carmine, an extremely stable food, drug and cosmetic color and the only organic pigment FDA-approved for use around the eye. Other Sensient Colors natural colors include: Annatto, an orange originating from the seeds of a shrub, used in foods and drugs; and anthocyanin, primarily derived from grape skins, commonly used in beverages.

Responsive and outstanding technical support and customer service remain the focus at Sensient Colors, which offers no-cost color audits that analyze a company's color usage and recommend changes. Boasting the industry's largest group of food, drug and cosmetic color chemists, the company adeptly applies custom blends, dispersions, dyes, Lakes, natural colors and other agents to contribute to superior finished products and enhance operational efficiency.

A staunch supporter of the United Way and a sponsor of corporate scholarships, Sensient Colors sales grew from $1.5 million in 1960 to $300 million in 2001. The company employs 400 people at its headquarters in St. Louis, 700 worldwide and is part of Sensient Technologies Corp., a Wisconsin-based company.

The company occupies a strong position in the cosmetic color market due in part to its 1991 acquisition of a regulated color company with hair dye technology. It is also a key supplier to ink jet ink manufacturers since its 1997 purchase of a distribution buisness serving a variety of markets. Sensient Colors' broad focus encourages cross-germination. For example, the technology used to put pigments in ink also applies to coloring pharmaceuticals.

Sensient Colors has been meeting the demand for natural coloring agents since 1984, when it developed the first consistent source for carmine.

Confections, candies, cosmetics and pharmaceuticals are among the products enhanced by Sensient Colors colors.

Sensient Colors nurtures strategic relationships with the world's top food and pharmaceutical companies. It serves most major manufacturers of candies, cereals, baked goods, snacks, personal care products, cosmetics, pharmaceuticals, dairy goods, beverages, desserts, puddings, pie fillings, processed meats, spices, cordials and pet foods. To ensure product quality and safety, the company holds ISO 9001 certification, conducts HACCP programs and undergoes annual auditing by the American Institute of Baking.

Through its unique combination of outstanding technical service, responsive customer service and manufacturing superiority, Sensient Colors is bound to color the world for decades to come. Constantly reinforcing its reputation for innovation and creativity, the company will continue to discover the right shade to enhance each product and seek out new markets for its colorful wizardry.

The Young Group Ltd.

At The Young Group Ltd., time-honored values and traditions ring true in the modern world. Longtime employees — and there are many — still receive watches commemorating career milestones. Teamwork and quality workmanship are points of pride. Although no longer family-owned, Young retains a family atmosphere and culture of caring thanks in great measure to Todd McCane, its CEO, and several other managers who purchased the company in 1998 from the Young family.

Founded by Christian Young in 1895 to provide roofing services, the company in 1937 began a series of expansions through acquisition that moved it into new geographic areas and into other aspects of specialty contracting.

Today, Young divisions scattered throughout the Midwest and South offer: industrial roofing and sheet metal; the installation, fabrication and distribution of mechanical insulation; industrial metal wall and roof systems; scaffolding; and fabricated products, such as lockers and partitions. In 2001 *Engineering News-Record* (ENR) ranked Young as the nation's 18th-largest roofing contractor. Overall, with the revenue from all the divisions considered, ENR ranked the company 241st of the 600 top specialty contractors in the nation.

Young's management group, full-time employees themselves who meet three times annually to set business strategy, made two key decisions following the acquisition to ensure the company's continued success. They increased Young's focus on becoming an aggressive sales organization, capitalizing on its reputation for quality products and services, and they established Young in a fast-growing market typically unaffected by downturns in construction by purchasing a company that manufactured lockers and other similar units.

Young's Fabricated Products Division, which sells internationally, now sets the standard for strong and durable partitions, lockers, vanity and laboratory tops, baking oven liners, furniture and other items used worldwide in laboratories, schools, hospitals, health/athletic facilities and military bases. Young's products are made from phenolic, a nearly indestructible, laminate-like material imported from Holland consisting of resin-soaked cellulose fibers that are thermally fused and compressed into solid panels. Trademark goods include Design-Tec® solid phenolic locker systems; DesignRite® partitions of solid phenolic material; and DesignLine™ solid phenolic cabinets. Considered a growth market for Young, the company plans to develop more products using this amazing material.

Roofing remains a solid market for Young with four divisions installing all types of built-up, modified bitumen and single-ply roofing systems and providing guaranteed roof assemblies from all major manufacturers for up to 20 years. The company specializes in architectural sheet metal, custom standing-seam metal roofs and all configurations of flashings as well as historical slate, tile and shingle roofs. An industry leader for over 100

The Edward Jones Dome is one of the many projects The Young Group Ltd. has worked on in St. Louis.

years, Young boasts the expertise to success-fully complete projects regardless of size or complexity.

Young entered the industrial insulation business in 1939 and its Insulation Divisions are recognized throughout the industry for quality, performance and expertise. Among the products and services supplied are insulation, metal lagging, fireproofing, firestopping and scaffolding for commercial, industrial and governmental projects. Young's trained per-sonnel, approved applicators for lightweight fireproofing, have extensive experience in sprayed or poured concrete fireproofing as well as in the application of intumescent-type products.

In addition to supporting Young's insulation and fireproofing groups, the Scaffold Division rents, sells, man-ufactures, erects and dismantles scaffolding on a turnkey basis for other crafts, such as pipe fitters, boilermakers and electricians. Backed by the latest technology, Young quickly customizes scaffolding based upon strict controls for quality and safety while designed to accommodate work site conditions.

Through five Distribution Services Divisions, Young distributes and fabricates insulation products. The company is well known — particularly among the boiler room and chemical plant set — for its standard and custom Insul-flex removable covers, which allow easy access to valves, pumps and flanges while protecting pipes and ductwork.

Young's Industrial Wall and Roof Systems Division supplies and installs conventional industrial metal and plastic wall and roof systems, foam panels, firewalls, draft curtains, explosion venting systems, retrofit standing seam roofs, conveyor covers and other products. Its employees are trained to work with and around hazardous materials and in explosive atmospheres.

Since 1950 Young has fabricated metal products for clients in industries including mining, smelting, manufacturing, power generation, chemical, petroleum, automotive, paper and agriculture. Considered a "trail-blazer in environmental control," Young's two Blow Pipe Divisions focus on reducing industrial air pollution by creating and installing state-of-the-art collection, ventila-tion and fume eradication systems. Technical knowledge, versatility and quality workmanship coupled with

prompt delivery and virtually no work stoppages makes Young tops in this field.

Clients benefit in cost-savings due to Young's ability to provide multiple disciplines on a project. Awarding a single contract for several craft functions also gives the owner a single source for responsibility. Young's commitment to providing total quality management in conjunction with clients is evidenced by its outstanding record for on-time and within-budget projects.

The company's comprehensive safety program and availability of material safety data sheets and safety manuals at the work site help reduce accidents and safe-guard those present as does mandatory training in safe construction procedures and hazard communication for all workers. Young's management and supervisory personnel participate in lengthy OSHA programs and hold weekly meetings at the job sites, which are routinely inspected by the company's safety department. In many cases, Young's safety standards actually exceed those set by the Occupational Safety and Health Administration. Additionally, most employees hold American Red Cross certification in first aid and CPR. Young belongs to the National Safety Council, the Safety Council of Greater St. Louis and the American Society of Safety Engineers.

The company, which holds an annual golf tournament to support nonprofit organizations in the community, owes the success of its first century to the foresight of its leaders in expanding upon old markets and capitalizing on new ones. That time-proven strategy will serve Young well during the next 100 years along with the values and traditions it has carried into the 21st century.

(Above left)
Young has the capacity to fabricate metal to any size or specification.

Young's Fabricated Products Division manufactures lockers, shower stalls and other units from state-of-the-art materials.

Merisant Company

erisant Company is the undisputed world leader in the low-calorie tabletop sweetener business. Its leading tabletop brands, Equal® and Canderel®, are enjoyed by consumers in more than 100 countries around the world.

Merisant, founded in 2000, is continuing to build on the legacy of Equal and Canderel, born from the 1965 discovery of a unique sweetening ingredient. Fourteen years later, in France, the first new sweetener appeared based on this discovery in tablet form — Canderel! — and soon became a real success. Two years after that, the U.S. Food and Drug Administration granted approval and individual packets of Equal Sweetener began appearing in stores. Like Canderel, Equal became an instant success and one of the leading tabletop sweetener brands in the nation. In March 2000 Merisant purchased the tabletop sweetener business from Monsanto Company and by this time, the product line included over 20 brands of sweeteners used in over 100 countries.

The transition of the business from a small division within a large corporation to a stand-alone company with global operations was not without challenges. Arnold Donald, Merisant's Chairman and CEO, played a key role in guiding the company through the many hurdles encountered during this critical transition period. The former Monsanto executive kept both day-to-day operations and the transition on track, capitalizing on his gift for recruiting and retaining highly talented people. Today, St. Louis-based Merisant employs more than 700 people worldwide. Merisant is also a strong believer in a diverse workforce, with people of color holding about 17.5 percent of management positions and women about 33 percent.

Merisant is very optimistic about its plans for growth, which include reaching more households in the United States as well as around the globe, expanding geographically into Central Europe, China and India, developing new sweeteners and extending existing product lines. In 2002 the company took yet another step when it licensed Equal for use in Perfect Pleasures, a line of sugar-free candies sold in the United States.

Merisant's core products, Equal and Canderel, make a real difference in the lives of consumers, helping people enjoy the great taste of the foods they love in a way that is better for them. The company shows a strong commitment to healthier living and promoting wellness, especially among those with diabetes or those at a higher risk of developing it, and features hundreds of recipes on its Web site. The Equal Sweetener Foundation supports diabetes education and research through organizations including the American Diabetes Association, the United Way, Speaking of Women's Health and the International Rett Syndrome Association. Merisant employees participate in walkathons, AIDS fund raising, literacy and tutoring programs, and food drives. Donald, an active member of the community, serves on numerous boards.

Merisant's employees are excited about its future. As more people choose healthier eating habits and as an aging population faces the challenges of managing health, Equal and Canderel are being seen more and more as a simple way to enjoy great-tasting foods and beverages in a way that's better for you.

Equal Sweetener is enjoyed by the entire family.

Sara Lee Bakery Group

BREAD AT ITS BEST, FIRST IN DESSERTS.

Sara Lee Bakery Group, a division of consumer goods powerhouse Sara Lee Corporation, is a premier international baking company headquartered in Clayton. In the summer of 2001, Sara Lee Corporation bought The Earthgrains Company, uniting a leading bread baker and superior frozen baked goods manufacturer. Today, Sara Lee Bakery Group is a leader in the United States, Western Europe and Australia, competing in the fresh, frozen and refrigerated baked goods categories.

Sara Lee Bakery Group is:
- a leading frozen baked goods producer in the United States, marketing cheescakes, pies and pound cake under the family favorite Sara Lee Brand
- the second-largest fresh bread and baked goods producer with leading brands across much of the United States, including Sara Lee, Earth Grains, IronKids, Grant's Farm and Colonial
- the largest U.S. manufacturer of store-brand refrigerated dough products, such as biscuits, cinnamon and Danish rolls, crescent rolls, dinner breads and cookie dough
- No. 1 fresh sliced bread company in Spain
- No. 1 refrigerated dough producer in France and Western Europe
- No. 1 in frozen desserts, pastries and super-premium ice cream in Australia

A rapidly growing company with more than 600 employees in St. Louis and 28,000 worldwide, Sara Lee Bakery Group's success is rooted in making high-quality and innovative products for consumers, providing top-notch and innovative service to retailers and consistently creating value by improving our business for the benefit of consumers, retailers, employees and Sara Lee Corporation shareholders.

The company's bread business, which dates to 1925, provides sliced and whole-loaf breads, buns, rolls and bagels that satisfy varying tastes in the popular, premium and superpremium segments. In 1975 the Earth Grains line of superpremium products was created to offer heartier and denser breads to receptive consumers. In 1991 the company introduced IronKids Bread, the first sandwich bread developed specifically for children's tastes and nutritional needs. Still the No. 1 bread for youngsters nationwide, IronKids has the soft texture of white bread but all the fiber of whole wheat bread and as much calcium in two slices as a glass of milk. In the 1990s Earth Grains introduced a very successful line of shelf-stable bagels and in 2001 two whole-grain Earth Grains loaves began carrying the FDA-approved heart-healthy nutrition claim.

Sara Lee Bakery Group's frozen bakery business, best known for delicious cheesecakes and pies, dates to 1949 when veteran Chicago baker Charles Lubin named his first product, a cream cheesecake, after his 8-year-old daughter, Sara Lee. Consolidated Foods Corporation bought Lubin's Kitchens of Sara Lee in 1956 and the Michigan-based Chef Pierre Inc. pie business in 1978. Consolidated Foods chose its most respected brand name when the corporation changed its name in 1985 to Sara Lee Corporation. Today, the corporation's baking division, Sara Lee Bakery Group, is a leader in the frozen desserts and pies segment. Innovative new products include frozen Sara Lee cheesecake, brownie and carrot-cake Bites, which can be eaten right out of the package thanks to no-thaw technology.

Bread at its best, first in desserts — that's why "Nobody Doesn't Like Sara Lee."

(Bottom left) CEO Barry Beracha raises the Sara Lee Bakery Group flag at the company's headquarters in Clayton for the first time after Sara Lee Corporation acquired The Earthgrains Company in August 2001.

Sara Lee Bakery Group is a leading global maker of fresh, refrigerated and frozen baked goods, including breads, bagels, cheesecakes and pies. Sara Lee Bakery Group has more than 80 bakeries and plants in the United States, Europe and Australia.

Select Artificials Inc.

lowers flare in riotous color, herbs burst from pots, ivies drip down walls and trees rise from the floor in the everlasting paradise that is the St. Louis showroom of Select Artificials Inc. The preferred supplier to thousands of florists, interior designers and retailers, Select serves the wholesale market by importing fine-quality permanent flowers, foliage, trees and Christmas decor.

Classic designs dominate Select's product line and cater to its primarily Midwestern clientele and large number of "mom and pop" customers. The company's botanically correct flowers and plants — consistently among its most popular items — honor nature by duplicating subtle details and proper shading. On the other side of the spectrum, Select's fashion flowers mirror contemporary decorating trends.

Founded in 1964, Select is rooted in the inspiration and determination of its founder, J. Robert Fry, who at age 40 left his job as a high-ranking salesman with a gift company to follow his intuition that a market would emerge for artificial flowers and plants. Fry purchased the wares through direct importers until he forged his own alliances with foreign, typically Asian, manufacturers.

Early on, Fry realized that Select's future hinged upon the ability of its suppliers to manufacture highly desirable permanent flowers and plants, and upon the success of its customers in reselling those items. Fry nurtured beneficial relationships with each group, offering Select's market savvy to manufacturers during product development and the company's professionally designed floral arrangements as samples for clients to duplicate and sell. Fry also encouraged the rise of new businesses by allowing them to establish credit in stages.

Select's line of over 6,000 flowers, plants and other artificials use silk, plastic, a combination thereof or other materials to achieve the most genuine look. Items may incorporate natural elements, including twigs and pine cones, or contain extensive wiring to increase overall flexibility and permit the individual shaping and placement of leaves and petals. Permanent Christmas trees and holiday decor have come a long way over Select's history. Polyvinyl chloride (PVC) has given manufacturers a greater ability to duplicate very fine pine needles and other details.

Select's flowers, fruits and plants have appeared in movie sets, department store displays and even at the White House and the Biltmore Estate in North Carolina. Museum gift shops, well-respected florists and top-notch designers are among Select's local customers.

July 5, 2001, marked a sad milestone in Select's history with the passing of Fry, who at age 77 still actively ran the company he loved. Julie Fry, his wife and business partner, now heads Select, a woman- and minority-owned business, and continues her husband's proud tradition of offering a large selection of high-quality goods combined with outstanding service. Select, firmly grounded in the practices that brought its past success, is advancing confidently into the future, secure in the knowledge that more and more people seek beauty with permanence.

The Wenzel Company

The Camping Company™ — that succinctly describes Wenzel. Since the company's late-19th-century inception, the name Wenzel arose as a leader in the camping gear industry. Serving American families on the go from the onset with wagon covers, tents and tarpaulins, it now offers an extensive line of quality products to enhance the outdoor experience from the backyard to the campgrounds and beyond. Tents, canopies and gazebos, packs, sleeping bags, airbeds, hammocks, lighting products and camp stoves made by Wenzel fit with modern society's appetite to commune with nature in comfort.

Home to Wenzel headquarters, St. Louis owes that company's presence to German immigrant Hermann Wenzel. A sail maker arriving in America with the equivalent of 50 cents in his pocket, he soon applied his skills to start an awning business in St. Louis in 1887. With the help of his wife and children, Hermann's business surmounted the first difficult years and shifted its expert use of canvas from awnings to tents and tarps. It then became H. Wenzel Tent & Duck Company.

With zeal to be the best, Hermann Wenzel sought methods to improve his goods and the company excelled. Following his leadership of 40 years, his legacy of innovation and perfection persisted. The company he founded prospered to become international with offices in Canada and Japan. Its products, some of European design, are sold through retailers in stores throughout the United States, in other countries and over the Internet. Now simply called The Wenzel Company, it continually adapts to ever-evolving consumer needs.

For camping comfort, Wenzel's own research and development (R&D) formulates today's materials to be water resistant, lightweight and allow easy set up. Wenzel further employs R&D to accommodate fashion trends by designing products in pleasing contemporary colors. Always seeking ways to improve its offerings, Wenzel introduced its UV ARMOR™ tent — made of a fabric designed for durability, strength and dryness — as it

progressed into the 21st century. By 2002 its sleeping bag collection included a center zip series devised for easy access and exit, plus bags with "chameleon" hoods for added warmth and coziness. Its Wenzel Insta-Bed™ won the honor of top-five finalist for the prestigious 2001 NASDAQ Sports Product of the Year Award. The following year it unveiled the improved Insta-Bed™ II.

With the great outdoors as a major business concern, Wenzel's civic-minded efforts center on its preservation. Company representatives travel to Washington annually to lobby for conservation. Wenzel is a strong proponent of the CARA Bill (Conservation And Reinvestment Act) and an active member of the Outdoor Industry Association (OIA). It even provides the public with useful camping tips and information on various camping areas.

Early American settlers traveled in covered wagons, and today's families find adventure camping. Wenzel supplies gear for this economic family vacation, which grows more appealing every year. It mans an 800 help line seven days a week to assist customers in the use of its products. And as current lifestyles focus on backyard activities, many camping-related items suit that setting. In the modern world those accoutrements will likely bear the familiar name: Wenzel.

Quality canvas tents and covers built Herman Wenzel's business, which began in St. Louis in 1887.

Now recognized as America's family camping brand, Wenzel offers a full array of products for outdoor enjoyment, including exemplary tents.

...St. Louis continues to be a shopping mecca for the Midwest region.

MARKETPLACE

The only constant is change. And nowhere else is this age-old observation more poignant than in terms of our country's swelling population and capricious demographics. From the beginning of the last century, millions of people found themselves seduced from the quiet restlessness of the countryside to the allure of big-city promises. After World War II, though, growing families broke away from their crowded tenement lifestyles and found a new kind of comfort in the spacious, rolling suburbs. But eventually many would be lured back by the provocative buzz of the city again, rebuilding and repairing what their parents' generation had left behind. The population's insatiable search for new homes, better schools and jobs has dramatically transformed the demographics of virtually every rural hamlet and metropolis across America.

St. Louis has been a forerunner of this movement and local retailers will testify that as the swelling population has shifted, so have the habits and routines of area shoppers. Farsighted retailers, who themselves operate in a perpetual state of retail locomotion, are constantly reinventing themselves as they update storefront curb appeal and tirelessly tweak the shopping landscape, attempting to interpret the needs and tastes of today's sophisticated shoppers.

Once mom-and-pop stores reigned King and Queen in the St. Louis area, along with a host of local and regional chain stores. Neighborhood residents, who generally only shopped as far as their feet or mass transit would take them, were faithful customers. But as the suburbs grew and rolled out over miles of new winding highway and interstate, enclosed malls and strip center complexes became the shopping innovation of the future. As it turned out, this idea of a centralized cluster of stores drawing people from all points of the compass was one in perfect sync with St. Louis' newly mobilized postwar suburban lifestyle. For the first time in history, the automobile and the expanding road network empowered discriminating shoppers as never before, allowing them to freely choose where and when they would spend their money.

St. Louis continues to be a shopping mecca for the Midwest region, drawing visitors from Missouri, Iowa, Arkansas and Illinois, serving every economic level of shopper from high-end specialty stores to mid-range department stores while providing a wide variety of regional and national discount chains.

Convenient locations coupled with a diverse display of stores and merchandise, all under one roof — along with restaurants, movie theaters and other forms of entertainment — seem to have squarely struck the pulse of shoppers and safely secured the mall's future. This along with a generous portion of pioneering independent businesses and eclectic strip-store complexes — offering everything from organic produce to fine leather furniture — makes St. Louis a haven for the discriminating shopper.

MARK H. ZORENSKY
President • Hycel Properties Co.

Brown Shoe Company, Inc.

George Warren Brown, a traveling salesman for his brother at Hamilton-Brown Shoe Company, came up with an idea in 1878. With the shoe market consisting of generally black, genderless, styleless choices, he thought the St. Louis market was ripe for a change.

Along with two partners, Alvin L. Bryan and Jerome Desnoyers, he began Bryan, Brown & Company in St. Louis as a manufacturer of stylish, fine shoes, primarily for women. The company recruited five skilled New England shoemakers as its first employees. Fifteen years later, in 1893, its name changed to Brown Shoe Company.

Overcoming financial obstacles in the early days, Brown Shoe grew from sales of $110,000 in its first year to $4 million by the turn of the century. By that time, the company's shoes had gained a reputation for quality craftsmanship and were being sold in every state in the union.

St. Louis businesses began planning for the 1904 World's Fair, and Brown Shoe helped back the enterprise with a contribution of $10,000. The fair brought many people to St. Louis, including Richard Fenton Outcault, who came to sell the rights to his cartoon characters. He sold character rights to more than 200 companies, including Brown Shoe, which adopted the Buster Brown character as mascot for its children's line.

The popularity of Buster Brown and his dog, Tige, had children asking for the shoes. Live "Buster Browns," accompanied by Tige, toured the country from 1904 to 1915 and from 1921 to 1930, playing in theaters and stores.

In 1943 Buster Brown went coast to coast with the Smilin' Ed McConnell show using the slogan, "I'm Buster Brown, I live in a shoe! That's my dog Tige — He lives there too!" In 1951 the Buster Brown gang moved to television, where the show ran until 1955.

On New Year's Day in 1907, the growing Brown Shoe Company moved to new offices at 17th Street and Washington Avenue. The building was to be known for the next 46 years as the "White House" due to the front façade, which was made of shiny white tile. In 1913 Brown Shoe was listed on the New York Stock Exchange.

During World War I, the company secured large army contracts for footwear and did its best to stay on schedule, with employees sometimes traveling all night in order to deliver shipments on time.

Naturalizer, the company's flagship brand, was born in 1927. At that time, women's footwear was either stylish and uncomfortable or functional and orthopedic-looking. The Naturalizer line offered both style and comfort, as it still does today.

In the late 1930s a Brown Shoe vice president, Clark Gamble, came up with a "gamble" of his own. Instead of salesmen carrying samples of all shoes from town to town, he gave each salesman responsibility for one or two brands. Each brand developed its own identity and advertising campaign. The idea worked. Sales jumped, and soon other shoe manufacturers followed suit.

With World War II, wartime production began once again at Brown Shoe. The plant superintendent at the time, Monte Shomaker, instituted many ideas that helped modernize the factory system, such as planning for a steady stream of orders and supplies and striving to be as self-supplying as possible. After the war, the company built new, efficient, one-level

At leading stores all over America October 1st-9th

Naturalizer "Fit Parade"

The shoe with the beautiful fit

$6.95

plants with air conditioning and humidity control, which helped to attract quality workers.

In 1951 Brown Shoe merged with Wohl Shoe Company, which operated leased shoe departments and retail stores across the country, and the corporation began to grow again. It moved its headquarters from downtown St. Louis to Clayton and in 1954 acquired Regal Shoe Shops' 110 stores. Regal had been known for its innovative "one price" sales marketing before World War II.

In the 1970s Brown Shoe began to diversify, acquiring such companies as Cloth World, Eagle Rubber and Hedstrom. In 1972 the company changed its name to Brown Group, Inc., and in 1981 it acquired the 36-store Famous Footwear chain. Shortly thereafter, it began divesting non-footwear related businesses.

In the 1980s imported shoes were changing the face of the American shoe industry, and domestic manufacturing threatened the company's ability to compete. Brown Group acquired Pagoda Trading Co., a shoe import company, and began building alliances with foreign factories.

Domestic plants could not match the lower costs and flexibility of overseas manufacturing, and the company embarked on the decade-long task of closing its U.S. factories. In most cases, Brown Group found other manufacturers to take its buildings, thus preserving employment in many small towns.

In 1952, after 74 years in downtown St. Louis, Brown Shoe Company moved its headquarters to suburban Clayton.

Today, the company once again calls itself Brown Shoe. Naturalizer remains its flagship brand, and Buster Brown continues to be a favorite with children. Famous Footwear has grown to more than 900 stores, making it the No. 1 brand-name, value-priced chain in America. The company's LifeStride, Connie, AirStep and Dr. Scholl's footwear brands continue to be important mainstays.

The company owns more than 1,400 retail shoe stores in the United States and Canada with brands also being sold to department stores, mass merchandisers and specialty stores. International offices around the world supply a global market.

Brown Shoe employees and the Brown family have carried on the tradition of George Warren Brown by giving generously of their time and money to help enrich St. Louis.

Brown's widow endowed the George Warren Brown School of Social Work at Washington University (built in 1925), and employees remain leaders in raising money for the United Way and March of Dimes.

The company also pledged funds to help start KMOX Radio in 1926 and has contributed to the building of virtually all cultural centers that now define St. Louis as a great community. Through Brown Shoe's Charitable Trust, Brown Shoe continues its generous support of St. Louis cultural institutions, scholarship programs and community activities.

The first home of Bryan, Brown & Co. was located on South Eighth Street in St. Louis.

Dynamic Vending, Inc.

A modern maverick with $60 and ambition, Joshua Koritz of rural Washington, Missouri, started a business venture in 1986. Building on his tenacity and eagerness to learn, he foresaw a future without limit. Today, the company he founded controls the largest vending contracts in the St. Louis area and reaches as far as Columbia, Missouri. Surpassing $12 million in annual sales in 2002, the company's profits continue to rise due to its "dynamic" owner's homegrown business philosophy of enriching others to enrich one's self.

The story of Dynamic Vending captures the essence of the resourceful energy that built St. Louis. Josh Koritz proves that it is still possible to realize the American dream. With an itching to get into the real world after college, Koritz worked at various jobs, finally driving a tow truck. One Christmas Eve, his truck broke down,

> **Dynamic still sells soda, now offered in the popular 20-ounce plastic bottles, but today its machines vend a variety of cold and hot drinks, all types of snacks, fresh fruit and sandwiches, and even hot French fries.**

leaving him stranded on Interstate 55. At that point, he experienced an epiphany, concluding that he could and would find a better way to make a living. Before long, a for-sale sign on a used soda vending machine caught his imagination. He convinced the seller to take $60 down on the $250 purchase price. Sixteen years later, that simple transaction resulted in a St. Louis vending company with nearly 3,500 machines.

It was a long hard climb for Koritz, but he never looked back. With some knowledge of the vending business, he encountered obstacles and setbacks, but learned from each experience. Stocking his first machine with soda, he quickly earned enough to pay off the rest of the $250 and started showing a profit. Using that money to invest in more machines, he worked at other jobs to support himself. He rented a warehouse for $60 a month — the same figure as his initial investment. Recognizing a market for more than just soft drinks, he then formed a

> **Striving to provide the best service possible by investing in both quality workers and the latest equipment, Dynamic Vending sets powerful standards in business management.**

partnership with snack vending. The alliance was short lived, but it convinced Koritz to start buying snack machines. After two years of struggling, his seedling company began to emerge as a promising contender.

By then understanding that new equipment required less maintenance and impressed customers, Koritz took a calculated risk and invested in 30 new cold drink machines. That bold decision exhausted his finances and forced him to give up his Soulard neighborhood apartment. The business being a priority, he had obtained more space at $500 a month for his company's garage and storage. So, making the logical move, he used his company garage as his living quarters, at first sleeping on his desk. His self-sacrifice paid off, and he no longer lives at his business premises.

> **Annually, Dynamic donates large amounts of funds to area charities and has given some of its products to local homeless shelters.**

> ## Throughout the rise of Dynamic Vending, the company always considered, and often tried, new and innovative ways to increase efficiency and bolster sales as well as service.

Koritz continued fueling his company with new equipment using sales earnings, and by 1993 it became necessary to move the operation to a 20,000-square-foot building — which it eventually outgrew, necessitating an additional 10,000 feet at a second site. Realizing the need for extra help, Koritz convinced Kevin Highley, a long-time trusted friend, to come to work for him. Highley not only earned his paycheck, he eventually rose to the position of general manager at Dynamic Vending.

Steadily adding trucks and employees to accommodate its growing customer base — which by the mid-90s included mid-size accounts — Dynamic invested in an efficient accounting software program and a reliable security system. In 1997 it dived into the major markets when Koritz's diligence landed a contract with 13-hospital system, BJC HealthCare. Now, with about 65 employees, Dynamic Vending services a number of other area hospitals and schools, federal and local government buildings, Lambert-St. Louis International Airport and many other large businesses. Dynamic's 40 vehicles are serviced by its own mechanics, and its service technicians maintain the vending machines.

Dynamic still sells soda, now offered in the popular 20-ounce plastic bottles, but today its machines vend a variety of cold and hot drinks, all types of snacks, fresh fruit and sandwiches, and even hot French fries. Dynamic's sales acumen gives the public the products they crave and creates interest in new items. Offering coupons for free selection from any Dynamic Vending machine to existing and prospective customers encourages repeat interest in its vending items.

Striving to provide the best service possible by investing in both quality workers and the latest equipment, Dynamic Vending sets powerful standards in business management. In this streamlined operation, Koritz maintains a simple personal profile, sinking profits back into his company rather than indulging in flamboyant displays of wealth. He calculated early on that volume was the name of the vending game. Cutting into the profit margin by purchasing premium products for his machines in large quantities — as opposed to buying less of cheaper items — constitutes the crux of Dynamic's financial success. Dynamic constantly examines new technology to further strengthen its presence in the industry

Throughout the rise of Dynamic Vending, the company always considered, and often tried, new and innovative ways to increase efficiency and bolster sales as well as service. Its drivers have two-way radios and pagers, and the company monitors its machines to ensure placement of appropriate products through the use of a tool called a planagram. Eventually it will use more sophisticated devices for remote monitoring of both the trucks and the machines.

Everyone works hard at Dynamic, including the owner. With pay raises based on performance, its workers earn above the industry average. It has relatively low employee turnover, which contributes to its high retention rate of existing customers. CEO and sole owner Josh Koritz considers himself a frugal businessman. Yet he is generous to both his employees and his business associates. Annually, Dynamic donates large amounts of funds to area charities and has given some of its products to local homeless shelters.

Following the acquisition of a large competitor in 1999, Dynamic began to contemplate consolidation of its two warehouses. The 21st century ushered in plans for expanding its product line with cold milk machines with a cow motif and possibly establishing its own food preparation facility. Like its owner, Dynamic Vending, Inc. knows no limits.

> ## Surpassing $12 million in annual sales in 2002, the company's profits continue to rise due to its "dynamic" owner's homegrown business philosophy of enriching others to enrich one's self.

Enterprise Rent-A-Car

*I*n 1957 St. Louis-native Jack Taylor was working as the sales manager of a local Cadillac dealership when he had an idea. Leasing cars, he thought, was an easy and convenient option for individuals looking for a new vehicle. Jack took a chance on his idea and founded a company that has grown to become an industry leader — Enterprise Rent-A-Car. Initially named Executive Leasing, the company began as a small, seven-car operation. But even from the beginning, Taylor's mission was clear: provide customers with exceptional service, employees with respect and ample career opportunities, and profitability will inevitably follow. Today, that philosophy continues to guide Enterprise and its now 50,000 employees.

Jack Taylor returned from World War II as a decorated combat naval aviator and ran a thriving truck service until 1948, when he accepted a sales position at a Cadillac dealership. Always professional and hard working, he quickly worked his way up to sales manager of the dealership's downtown St. Louis location. Jack soon decided that leasing presented opportunities for a fast-growing business and told the dealership's owner, Arthur Lindburg, that he wanted to start a car-leasing company. Arthur saw the idea's potential and helped Jack get Executive Leasing off the ground.

Executive first operated in the basement of the dealership next to the body shop. Though the quarters were cramped and filled with the noise of clanking tools, the office's overall environment was professional and business-like. Jack knew that while he couldn't change the appearance of the office, he could ensure that he and his people presented a professional image. He knew that a professional appearance would help gain customers' respect, and all employees dressed accordingly.

Jack expanded the company's services in the 1960s to include auto rentals after some of his leasing customers needed replacement vehicles while their cars were being repaired. The company's rental business began with a fleet of just 17 cars and soon began to expand. As operations grew outside of St. Louis, he learned that the name "Executive" was not available everywhere, so Jack changed the name of his company to Enterprise Leasing after the *USS Enterprise*, an aircraft carrier on which he served.

Enterprise continued adding locations in the 1970s, all devoted to the same philosophy of customers and employees first. Each branch operated as a separate business, with employees earning a base salary and a percentage of the profits based on their branch's performance. This system enabled employees to think of the branch as their own business. During that time, a creative manager in Florida initiated the practice of providing customers with a free ride to the office.

This eventually led to a companywide practice now made familiar by the company's motto: "Pick Enterprise. We'll pick you up."

During the 1970s, Jack and his team realized the opportunities that existed in a relatively unexplored niche segment of the car rental market. Rather than focus on the airport business, already inhabited by large rental car brands, Enterprise concentrated on providing replacement rentals to people in their hometowns. If you needed a car while yours was undergoing repair work, or you needed an extra car for a special occasion, Enterprise became the rental car provider of choice.

By 1986 Jack and his son, Andy, who was named president of the company in 1980, made the strategic decision to begin a nationwide expansion, and Enterprise began opening offices throughout the country at a rapid rate. With Andy at the helm, the customer pick-up service became standard practice, and Enterprise strengthened its standing within the industry by marketing rentals to local body shops and insurance companies that needed replacement vehicles for their customers. In 1989 they changed the company name to Enterprise Rent-A-Car to reflect what had become its core business.

By 1996 Enterprise had surpassed its closest competitor to become the largest rental car company in America. By 2001 the company was operating more than 600,000 vehicles and had nearly 4,800 offices in the United States, Canada, the United Kingdom, Germany and Ireland and was the single largest buyer of new cars and light trucks in the United States. Enterprise is now the largest rental car company in North America, with offices that are located within 15 minutes of 90 percent of U.S. households.

While still a private company owned by the Jack Taylor family, Enterprise leads and continues to grow the

Enterprise employees, many of whom start as management trainees, are provided with training and ample opportunities to grow their careers.

local rental car market segment, which is now nearly equal in size to the airport car rental segment. Enterprise began expanding into the airport market in the late 1990s, and although a relative newcomer to the market, the company ranked first in a national airport customer satisfaction survey three years running (1999-2001).

Named by *Black Collegian* magazine as the nation's largest recruiter of college graduates, Enterprise builds the careers of its employees through a management training program that allows its people autonomy in learning the business from the ground up. Enterprise employees are empowered to learn and grow their careers, and Enterprise has a promote-from-within policy that ensures that motivated employees are rewarded for their success. In fact, nearly 100 percent of Enterprise's senior officers started as management trainees.

Enterprise employees are involved with their communities, and the company actively participates with many organizations, including the National Urban League and the United Way. The Enterprise Rent-A-Car Foundation is the company's charitable arm and recognizes that its employees' lives are entwined with the communities in which they live and work. To that end, the foundation provides grants to community organizations important to employees. Jack Taylor's daughter, Jo Ann Kindle, serves as president of the foundation, an organization that contributed over $5 million to worthy causes in the year 2000.

Although Enterprise is now an international company, the Taylor Family never lost sight of the qualities that made the business a success — superior customer service, respect and opportunities for employees. It was that way when Jack Taylor founded the company, and that's the way it will always be.

Enterprise celebrated its 40th anniversary in 1997. Shown here are Enterprise President and CEO Andy Taylor (left), Enterprise Chief Operating Officer Don Ross (right) and Enterprise founder and Chairman Jack Taylor (back) participating in activities during the company's 40th-anniversary celebration.

Equity Corporate Housing

Relocation is particularly stressful the first night in a new town. After the rigors of travel, all a person really wants to do is spend a quiet night at home. Equity Corporate Housing transforms that dream into reality. An Equity guest doesn't check into a dreary hotel room. He or she simply goes home — albeit in a different town — and with the turn of a key, finds a welcome refuge where place settings gleam on the dining room table and ingredients for a spaghetti dinner beckon from the kitchen counter.

Equity guests find plenty of light and space to get the job done.

Savvy business people are making Equity a leader in the corporate housing industry. The company offers homes in about 35 cities nationwide for guests staying over 30 days. Growing primarily through acquisition, Equity in 1999 purchased Castleton, Inc, a St. Louis company already adept at serving the area's corporate housing needs.

Equity's St. Louis operation provides fully furnished temporary housing in Missouri and Illinois to individuals and families. Its typical customer is a working professional on a temporary or permanent assignment. The company offers an inventory of about 250 units in over 20 apartment communities and annually places at least 1,000 clients.

Equity manages many of the time-consuming, stressful tasks associated with a major move. It organizes utilities and cable television service, obtains furniture and decorates the home. Among other amenities are full-size kitchen appliances and private bedrooms.

David Hoguet, CEO, and Blair Neller, its president, founded the Ohio-based company during the early 1980s to rent residential furniture. Over the years, the temporary housing industry emerged as its largest client and, noting that trend, the two men in 1996 took the company public to raise capital for expansion into that market. Castleton Inc. quickly captured their attention as a possible acquisition.

The company, founded by Tim Duggan in 1987, leased, decorated and furnished apartments, then rented the units to businesses with workers relocating to St. Louis. Duggan's foray into entrepreneurship derived from his belief that people in temporary living situations want amenities, like kitchenettes, and the fact that apartment communities usually have vacancies. Living in an apartment also costs less than other accommodations and allows the resident to fully experience the neighborhood.

Castleton grew slowly until the early 1990s, when businesses began to understand and embrace the concept of corporate housing. Business flowed into the company, which developed a loyal following and numbered among its clients Anheuser-Busch Companies Inc. and McDonnell Douglas, now Boeing. During Operation Desert Storm in 1991, the Army Reserve Personnel Command in St. Louis called up 19,000 soldiers to duty domestically and in the theater, causing an influx of military personnel into the area. Many found a Castleton home awaiting them here.

The company in 1994 began operating in other metropolitan areas through franchising and internal expansion. At its peak, Castleton was in seven cities and employed nearly 45 people in the St. Louis headquarters.

Fully equipped kitchens bring home-cooking to people in temporary living situations.

The company around that time received a U.S. Chamber of Commerce and MassMutual Blue Chip Enterprise Award for inspirational achievement in business.

Downsizing during the 1990s fueled interest in corporate housing as workers relocated for jobs. The decade was one of consolidation in most industries, and Duggan found his company at a crossroads. With three major purchase offers on the table, he decided to sell Castleton and retire rather than to raise capital for acquisitions.

Equity employs 25 people locally and about 1,000 nationwide. St. Louis Rams personnel, corporate titans, workers retooling assembly plants and Saudi Arabian pilots are among those that utilize the company's services in St. Louis.

Equity homes are available in all price ranges. Average nightly charges range from $45 to $65 for a one-bedroom apartment and $60 to $90 for a two-bedroom unit. The company also can locate houses or condominiums. A budget package offers apartments in older communities with fewer amenities, like pools or clubhouses. Since services are a la carte, a guest can tailor a package to meet financial needs. Most guests opt for weekly housekeeping. Those declining the service receive a cleaning kit and vacuum.

Equity requires a 30-day minimum commitment from its guests. Pets pose no problem and the company strives to accommodate specific geographic requests, like

The homey atmosphere of an Equity home invites relaxation.

being near a park or a shopping center. Sports fans and entertainment buffs often ask for big-screen televisions, and guests from other countries sometimes want special kitchen equipment, like rice cookers.

Equity's reputation for excellence shines through in the special touches, like the care taken in decorating and furnishing each apartment. The company aims to consistently surpass people's expectations, and image is the cornerstone of its corporate philosophy. Employees are trained to consider image first, even before profitability, in making decisions.

The region reaps significant economic benefits from Equity's presence. Apartment communities, cable and telephone companies, and local shops gain business. The company contributes to a public view of St. Louis as a desirable city for relocation. Equity guests enjoy living here and their employers are impressed that the region offers such excellent corporate housing.

Equity employees support the community by collecting food and clothing for pantries and shelters. The company frequently replaces its inventory, donating used kitchen items, linens and bedding to outreach centers for distribution to those in need.

Equity plans to offer corporate housing worldwide; by 2010, it hopes to expand into major international markets like London, Singapore, Frankfurt and Zurich. Cyberspace also offers new opportunities. One day, Equity guests will be able to select, furnish and book apartments online.

Equity excels at bringing convenience and comfort to people in temporary living situations. The company goes the extra mile so business travelers keep coming home to Equity no matter where they go.

Equity homes offer comfort and convenience, making the company a leader in the corporate housing industry.

Saint Louis Galleria

*I*t's been nearly two decades since Hycel Properties Co. took stock of the retail climate in the St. Louis area. And after much deliberation, thoughtful examination of the needs and requirements of area shoppers, and securing the civic support of the city of Richmond Heights, it put together a skilled team of architects and builders to engineer a master plan, thus creating one of the area's most unique shopping experiences.

Saint Louis Galleria's thoughtful design, meticulous selection of stores and above all, its timeless décor, sets it apart from all other regional shopping centers. Its tasteful and sophisticated appeal transcends short-lived fads and trends while conspicuously catering to the eclectic tastes and varied economic backgrounds of its ever-loyal and valued patrons.

Phase I of Hycel's master plan was launched in 1984 and included razing the antiquated Westroads Shopping Center (circa 1955). In its place, Saint Louis Galleria would boast 90 new specialty stores and restaurants, fine marble flooring and cherry-wood finishes, an abundance

of skylights, along with a newly remodeled and expanded flagship Dillard's department store. The new center celebrated its grand opening in 1986 with much accolade and praise.

With any such undertaking the risks are abundant, and development of Saint Louis Galleria was no exception. But its fabulous location and timing were perfect and reflected in its immediate success, which quickly attracted the attention of other well-known national retail chains. One of the first eager to come on board in 1991 was the May Department Stores as part of the Galleria's spectacular Phase II expansion — a $337 million-dollar building project that would more than double the Galleria's size to nearly 1.2 million total square feet. As 80 new shops and restaurants were completed, bringing the total count of specialty shops to 165, Saint Louis Galleria also added to its illustrious roster Missouri's first Lord & Taylor and proudly became the flagship location for the Famous-Barr department stores.

Conveniently located in the heart of St. Louis and just minutes from downtown and the airport, with easy access from major highways Interstate-64/Highway 40 and Interstate-170, the lavishly appointed Galleria services the area's 2.5 million residents and the surrounding region.

Designed by the St. Louis-based architectural firm, Hellmuth, Obata & Kassabaum Inc., Saint Louis Galleria offers a classic "open" design featuring a skylit courtyard — The Garden Court — lush landscaping and a terraced reflecting pool. And shoppers can bask in the warmth of the sun as well as the nocturnal glow of the moon and the stars as they stream through the semicircular glassed roof.

Resembling European-style winter gardens, the thoughtful but casual interior landscape design features several ornamental fig trees, overflowing hanging plants, unique topiaries and a variety of selected palms. The Galleria's team of architects worked closely with specially appointed landscape professionals, to the extent of traveling to Florida to personally select complementary plant varieties. In addition, patterned marble floors, articulated skylights, natural cherry wood and brass accents further enhance the Galleria's rich and inviting atmosphere.

As a special gift to the St. Louis community, Saint Louis Galleria also invested in the acquisition and installation of several exquisite pieces of original art produced by six internationally recognized artists. The magnitude and artistic expression of these delightful pieces offers shoppers the rare opportunity to view classic art one-on-one, all the while in a casual environment without pretense or governed by special privileges. Their free-flowing artistic expressions energize the lavish space of the Galleria while giving to the community something entirely unique and fresh.

And nowhere else in the St. Louis area or the surrounding region can selective shoppers wander through such a unique blend of specialty stores and major retailers — all under one roof. Each year over 10 million visitors to Saint Louis Galleria experience the ultimate in shopping, entertaining and dining.

Known as "Where the best stores put their best store," the Galleria has earned the reputation for attracting the best in upscale as well as moderately priced retailers and dining establishments. Cartier, Brooks Brothers, The Cheesecake Factory, Mark Shale, Restoration Hardware, Club Libby Lu, Swarovski, Chico's, M-A-C, Banana Republic, Eddie Bauer, Ann Taylor, The Sharper Image and Z Gallerie are just a sample of the unique stores that

make up the Galleria. Of the 165 specialty shops and restaurants that make up Saint Louis Galleria, nearly 50 stores are exclusive to the St. Louis area. But because St. Louis unarguably represents the pulse of the entire nation, innovative and savvy retailers have also recognized the Galleria as the perfect testing ground for new or select retailing concepts such as: Eddie Bauer Home, Build-A-Bear Workshop®, Brooks Brothers Women and Gap Women, before expanding their efforts nationwide.

But over the last 15 years, the Galleria has established itself as much more than St. Louis' favorite place to shop. Its philanthropic efforts and sense of civic duty have developed special bonds with the people of the St. Louis community that reach far beyond the retail world and help to nurture a sense of civic pride and purpose.

Saint Louis Galleria continues to build on this commitment while supporting a generous list of community events and special fund raisers. Each year it donates thousands of dollars to charitable and nonprofit agencies, in addition to hosting and supporting activities that collectively raise tens of thousands of dollars directly benefiting the St. Louis community. The Girl Scouts of America, Saint Louis Symphony Orchestra, Washington University School of Art, St. Louis Ballet, Forest Park Forever — along with many St. Louis-area food pantries — to name just a few, have all benefited immensely due to the generosity and tireless efforts of the people of Saint Louis Galleria.

Whether it's a day shopping, playing, dining or simply just to get away from it all — Saint Louis Galleria is a great destination — any time of year.

The May Department Stores Company

BEGINNINGS

Long a staple in downtown St. Louis, the stately white marble Railway Exchange Building at 6th and Olive Streets is home not only to Famous-Barr's downtown department store but also to The May Department Stores Company, one of the nation's oldest and largest retailers.

May's history goes further back than its St. Louis roots to the days of the Old West when westward expansion provided new opportunities for the nation's business visionaries. May's success at meeting customers' wants and needs began in 1877 when a young German immigrant named David May opened his first store in the boomtown of Leadville, Colorado, to sell sturdy, practical clothing to silver miners.

Famous-Barr, the leading department store in its markets, provides an exceptional combination of merchandise selection and customer service. Famous-Barr operates 43 stores in seven states, including 11 stores in the St. Louis metropolitan area.

Lord & Taylor is one of the oldest and most respected names in retailing and is a fashion leader in its markets. It operates more than 80 stores in 20 states, including two in the St. Louis market.

The success of that venture led to clothing stores in Denver and the beginning of what today is The May Department Stores Company. As the business developed, May slowly expanded merchandise offerings, branching into shoes, furnishings and women's clothing. A few years later, May purchased The Famous Clothing Store in St. Louis as well as a department store in Cleveland, Ohio, and established the retailer's corporate headquarters in St. Louis.

Moving toward becoming the powerhouse it is today, the company incorporated as The May Department Stores Company in 1910 and was first listed on the New York Stock Exchange in 1911.

That same year, David May acquired another St. Louis department store, the William Barr Dry Goods Company, and combined his two local stores to create Famous-Barr Company, which is today the leading department store in the St. Louis market. In 1913 May moved its corporate headquarters and its Famous-Barr store into the Railway Exchange Building, the location both occupy today.

From its offices in St. Louis, May continued to expand with the acquisition of numerous retail stores across the United States. As department store companies were acquired, May adopted a regional philosophy, retaining the local store's name and strengthening the company's roots in each community. May was also one of the first retailers to open department stores outside of the traditional downtown location, and one of the country's first suburban stores was in St. Louis.

David May's sons, Morton J., Tom and Wilbur D., served in prominent positions in the company's history. Grandson Morton D. "Buster" May was the last May family member to head the company. Visionary leaders in the industry have followed as CEO, including Stanley J. Goodman, David E. Babcock, David C. Farrell and since 1998, Gene S. Kahn. Each has played the key role in positioning May to be one of the leading retailers in the nation.

TODAY

Current Chairman and CEO Gene Kahn keeps the company focused on merchandising to meet customers' expectations and providing innovative customer service.

The company is also focused on recruiting and developing the best talent in retailing to further strengthen May for the future.

Today, May's annual sales are approximately $14 billion, and the company operates stores in 44 states, the District of Columbia and Puerto Rico. May's department store companies operate under 11 trade names in cities nationwide and are headquartered in the following cities: Lord & Taylor in New York City; Hecht's in Washington, D.C.; Strawbridge's in Philadelphia; Foley's in Houston; Robinsons-May in Los Angeles; Filene's in Boston; Kaufmann's in Pittsburgh; Famous-Barr in St. Louis; L.S. Ayres in Indianapolis; The Jones Store in Kansas City; and Meier & Frank in Portland, Oregon.

In 2000, David's Bridal, the largest retailer of bridal gowns and special occasion dresses in the country, became part of May. After Hours Formalwear and Priscilla of Boston joined the company in 2001. May continues to open new stores, further expanding its markets, and it plans to add approximately 15 new department stores and 30 new David's Bridal stores each year. May also continues to update, remodel and make improvements in its stores to ensure they are exciting places to shop, full of fresh ideas and ever-changing merchandise.

MAY AND ST. LOUIS

May contributes approximately $235 million in payroll to the local economy and employs approximately 8,000 associates in its stores — Famous-Barr, Lord & Taylor, and David's Bridal — and its corporate and operations facilities.

In 1993 May moved its May Merchandising Company (MMC) to St. Louis from New York City. Today, May Merchandising represents nearly 700 of May's 2,700 jobs in downtown St. Louis. It is the division that identifies trends in color, fashion and style for all of May's department stores and is responsible for developing May's proprietary brands and private label programs. Also in 1993 May consolidated two of its regional credit centers into one new facility located in suburban St. Louis that now has grown to more than 1,500 jobs.

In 2000 David's Bridal became part of The May Department Stores Company. It is the largest retailer of bridal gowns and special occasion dresses in the country.

MAY AND THE COMMUNITY

May and its associates play important roles in each of the areas where May operates. The May Department Stores Company Foundation contributes approximately $15 million annually to nonprofit organizations in the communities May serves. May employees also make personal contributions through their participation in community events and as volunteers for hundreds of nonprofit organizations.

May has served in a particularly supportive role in St. Louis, providing major sponsorship for leading St. Louis nonprofit organizations that enrich the community's life. In the past decade, May's support has totaled more than $1 million to each of the following organizations: United Way of Greater St. Louis, St. Louis Science Center, the YMCA, Washington University, the St. Louis Symphony, the Missouri Botanical Garden, The OASIS Institute and St. Louis 2004.

Other major support has been given by May, as well as Famous-Barr and Lord & Taylor, to hundreds of other organizations ranging from The Saint Louis Art Museum, The Muny outdoor theatre and Craft Alliance, to the United Negro College Fund and Junior Achievement, to the Jewish Federation, the Nursery Foundation and the Susan G. Koman Race for the Cure.

May senior executives also provide leadership as executive board members for a variety of St. Louis organizations such as Washington University, Bames-Jewish Hospital, the St. Louis Science Center, United Way of Greater St. Louis, the YMCA, Junior Achievement, The OASIS Institute and the Academy of Science.

Lion's Choice

reshly prepared sandwiches made with top-round beef, slow-roasted on premise — that initiated the loyal patronage of the Lion's Choice restaurants. Operating under the corporate name of Red Lion Beef Corporation, the privately held company originated in 1967 when three young men collaborated on a business venture. At a time when increasing numbers of women entered the work force, Marv Gibbs, Art Morey and Clint Tobias determined that tasty, nutritious and inexpensively priced quick-service restaurant food would be a substantial draw.

Starting with one store in Ballwin, Missouri, they named it the Red Lion Beef House. Their food earned both devoted followers and revenue, inspiring them to open a second restaurant two years later. Seeking a national trademark, they changed the commonly used Red Lion name, reconfiguring it to Lion's Choice before unveiling that Creve Coeur, Missouri, store. As profits allowed, they established more locations throughout metro-St. Louis — in Cape Girardeau, Saint Charles and Kansas City, Missouri; and in Warrenville, Illinois, near Chicago.

Nearing its 35th anniversary with 18 stores, including three franchises, Lion's Choice continues selling honest food to intelligent, health-conscious citizens who appreciate value and taste. Its premier beef sandwich is still prepared to order with thinly sliced roast beef, not processed like those made by lesser-quality fast food restaurants. To keep it hot and moist, each sandwich — stacked high with layers of beef on a sesame seed bun — gets a burst of steam just before it is wrapped. Rounding out the menu over time, Lion's Choice added more sandwich choices such as turkey breast, lean ham and even hot dogs. Like the beef sandwich, they contain much protein and are low in calories and cholesterol. Side dishes include skin-on French fries fried in canola oil, chips, slaw, soups, and exemplifying the emphasis on nutrition — vegetable sticks and dip. Bakery cookies and creamy ice cream treats satisfy the craving for dessert.

Finding a niche in the industry, Lion's Choice is not in direct competition with other fast food restaurants. Its employees earn higher wages and stay on longer than the average food worker. Near the end of 2001, its original store still employed one person who started there when it opened. Lion's Choice's cultlike following amazed construction workers when remodeling activities at one site necessitated its closure for several weeks. Climbing over mounds of dirt, hungry customers braved the construction debris hoping to find the restaurant open.

Owing its success to its quality food and work force, Lion's Choice offers exemplary employee benefits, including profit sharing and tuition reimbursement. Its average store manager tenure of 12 years demonstrates its employees' loyalty and dedicated service. Sharing its resources with the communities it serves, it makes donations to about 500 nonprofit groups yearly.

Always a cut above the others, Lion's Choice set a trend that became law — inoculating all employees for hepatitis A. While others drew business with promotions, it kept its pricing comparable, selling on reputation. Focusing on the future, it redefines itself as fast-casual, planning to enhance the experience of its ever-growing list of patrons.

Lion's Choice, originally Red Lion Beef House, began with one store in Ballwin, Missouri. Parked next to that store, in this photo snapped in May 1968, is Clint Tobias' 1960 Ford.

This photo of the grand opening ceremony of the Ballwin store shows (left to right) Clint Tobias' wife, Leta, now Leta Vogel, co-owner; Clint Tobias, one of the original founders; Robert Jones, then Ballwin's mayor; Arthur Morey, another of the three original founders; and an unidentified employee.

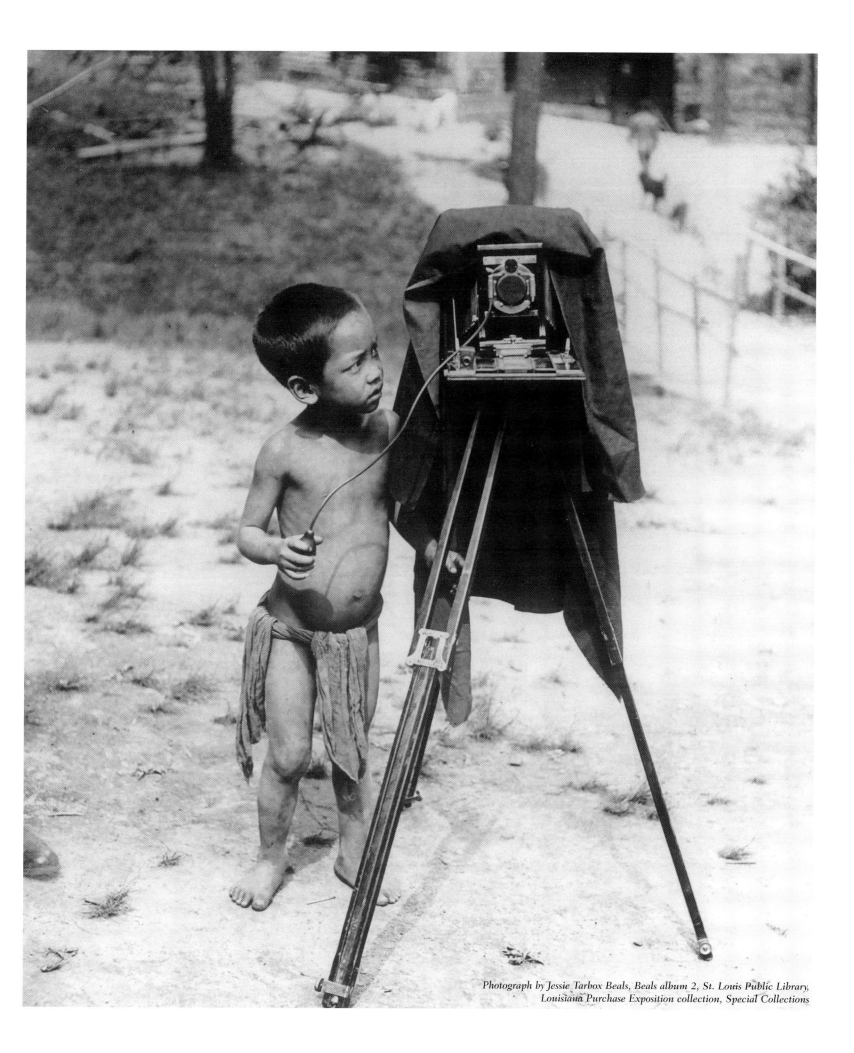

Whether it's people, information or services, it is a unique network of utility, communications and transportation companies that keeps St. Louisans in stride with the ever-changing world in which they thrive.

NETWORKS

St. Louis is constantly moving. Whether it's people, information or services, it is a unique network of utility, communications and transportation companies that keeps St. Louisans in stride with the ever-changing world in which they thrive.

Since before the Civil War, St. Louis has been at the hub of transportation as a link for the expanding railroad system over the Mississippi River. The development of a passenger rail system in the city in 1875 provided area residents mobility they had never dreamed possible. Later, the invention of the airplane helped those dreams soar even farther.

Air travel has been very close to the hearts of many St. Louisans and is an integral part of the history of the city. From the time that airplanes first dotted the skyline, the ability to travel efficiently and safely has been the focus of growing numbers of transportation providers throughout the city. These contributions to the world of transportation helped make St. Louis a leader in the movement of people and communications across the country and around the world.

An essential component to the success of St.Louis as a hub of growth, with an intricate network of service providers, is access to the elements that allow people to work more efficiently and comfortably. While St. Louis was thrilling its residents and visitors with the wonders of electricity at the 1904 World's Fair, local government and businesses worked diligently to secure sufficient water sources for consumption as well as energy.

St. Louis utility companies have provided area residents and businesses with the most cutting-edge and efficient access to all the resources necessary to keep homes and businesses running smoothly. Whether providing electricity or water, information or outstanding customer service, these pillars of the St. Louis business community provide the very services that allow people to interact with the whole world from the comfort of their own homes.

St. Louis' tradition of innovation has earned the "Gateway to the West" the reputation as an ideal location for the establishment and growth of companies that specialize in keeping people informed and connected, businesses plugged in and products and services moving in the limitless directions that still lie ahead.

SBC Communications Inc.

SBC Communications Inc. (NYSE: SBC) has transformed itself from the smallest of the "Baby Bells," formed in 1983 in St. Louis, into one of the world's largest, most dynamic companies in the telecommunications market. As America's pre-eminent provider of DSL Internet service and one of the nation's leading Internet Service Providers, SBC is shaping the future of telecommunications with its deployment of state-of-the-art broadband infrastructure and creation of innovative applications that are capitalizing on broadband's potential to dramatically change the way people work and play.

Reliable ... trusted ... committed ... all are words that come to mind when thinking of SBC and its rich heritage.

One SBC Center in downtown St. Louis
Photo by Jay Baker/fkphoto.com

SBC is rooted in the Bell Telephone Co., one of the companies founded between 1877 and 1880 to control Alexander Graham Bell's patent rights and the only one to remain in business when those patents expired during the 1890s. Serving St. Louis since 1877, Bell Telephone and other regional phone companies combined to form Southwestern Bell, SBC's direct predecessor, in 1917. Since 1927, when the company's exchange on Pine Street began offering dial service, SBC has revolutionized communications.

GROWING AN INDUSTRY LEADER

Under the leadership of Chairman and CEO Edward E. Whitacre Jr., appointed in 1990, SBC has mounted an aggressive expansion strategy, tripling in size over the past five years and increasing its product line to bring *more* people *more* communications solutions.

While San Antonio, Texas, is now home to company headquarters, SBC is a major presence and top employer in St. Louis. Thousands of employees are based at SBC's office complex downtown, including the One SBC Center building, which has contributed significantly to the area's revitalization.

Today, SBC offers local and long distance service, voice and data services, e-business community and network integration, Web site and application hosting, e-marketplace development, paging and messaging, and directory advertising. In 2001 SBC allied with Yahoo! Inc., the world's leading Web destination, to provide co-branded Internet service nationwide as well as customized products and services, which will include many optimized for broadband.

SBC provides wireless services through Cingular Wireless, of which it is the majority owner. While both wireless and long-distance provide substantial growth markets, broadband is SBC's future.

DELIVERING THE FULL PROMISE OF THE INTERNET

Broadband's high speed gives it the power to deliver the full promise of the Internet with a futuristic array of applications designed to save time and enhance life. SBC is dedicated to deploying broadband, thereby laying the foundation for its broad adoption, and is developing cutting-edge products and services for broadband-enabled homes and businesses. Already, broadband delivers conveniences such as distance learning, entertainment on demand and real-time video conferencing.

SBC's contributions to the Internet date to the 1980s, when it began developing the end-to-end infrastructure needed for the Internet's evolution into a platform for broadband applications.

Over the years, SBC has expanded its infrastructure and developed faster technologies. The company leads the industry in deploying broadband access networks to support advanced applications such as streaming video and continues to expand capabilities through DSL Internet access.

Through its $6 billion network transformation initiative, SBC today has a vast broadband network that can deliver high-speed broadband access to 25 million households and businesses nationwide, with millions more within SBC's reach in the near future. Since deployment began, more than 2 million miles of fiber optic strands have been placed across SBC's 13-state region, enough to circle the earth at the equator more than 85 times if each strand were placed end to end.

PROVIDING ACCESS TO ADVANCED TECHNOLOGIES

Developing and implementing new technologies is only one way SBC has impacted the digital revolution. The primary commitment of the company's philanthropic arm — the SBC Foundation — is creating and supporting programs for underserved populations that educate, train or provide access to advanced technologies.

At the St. Louis County Metropolitan Education Center, the SBC Foundation helped establish the Midwest Telecommunications Prepatory Academy. The $1.3 million public-service venture ultimately hopes to boost diversity in the highly skilled telecommunications work force by training young adults for technical jobs.

Under Whitacre's vision and leadership, SBC has emerged as one of the nation's top 10 corporate givers and maintained a steadfast commitment to the communities it serves. For example, SBC's $10 million donation to help establish The Women's Museum: An Institute for the Future in Dallas was the largest single corporate contribution in history to any women's campaign, organization or program.

In addition to financial support, more than 190,000 SBC employees and retirees donate approximately 7 million hours each year on community projects involving education

SBC employees working in the company's Network Operations Center use state-of-the-art technology to provide cutting-edge services to customers.
Photo by David Bateman/David Bateman Photography

and technology. They are members of the SBC Pioneers, the nation's largest company-sponsored volunteer group.

EXCELLING AS A FULL-SERVICE PROVIDER

The late 1900s opened the telecommunications industry to full competition. Once restricted to local service, SBC has become a data powerhouse, capturing a leadership position in the long-distance voice and data markets.

SBC has telecommunications investments in 28 countries and boasts annual revenues that place it among the largest Fortune 100 companies. One of the metropolitan area's largest employers, SBC also endows the region with a state-of-the-art infrastructure that helps attract and retain businesses.

Considered one of the world's leading corporate citizens, SBC has received many awards for its commitment to promoting diversity, encouraging employee advancement, providing high-quality customer service and investing in communities. For the past five years, SBC has been named the World's Most Admired Telecommunications Company in *Fortune* magazine's annual ranking, a recognition that underscores the company's commitment to excellence.

SBC is delivering it all — a full range of data products, responsive and professional customer service, and the expertise to capitalize on emerging technologies. Just as it created innovative and practical products and services revolving around the telephone, SBC will parlay the potential of broadband and other technology advances into extraordinary time-saving and life-enhancing applications that today may be unimaginable, but will one day be as commonly used as the phone itself.

Terminal Railroad Association of St. Louis

*F*ew organizations symbolize the importance of St. Louis as a national railroad hub more than the Terminal Railroad Association of St. Louis — established in 1889 to help coordinate burgeoning westbound and eastbound railroad traffic traveling through the metropolis where the mighty Mississippi River divides the nation.

Today, the Terminal Railroad Association of St. Louis' (TRRA) main function is handling freight cars between St. Louis and Southwestern Illinois. The TRRA owns, operates and uses over 51 miles of main track and 140 miles of yard tracks and sidings located on both sides of the Mississippi. The organization also made an important contribution to the region's future public transportation needs in 1988 when it donated the rail tunnel under downtown St. Louis to the city of St. Louis. The tunnel is used by the region's light rail system, Metro-Link, to transport commuters between Missouri and Illinois.

In 1989 the TRRA made an even trade of the Eads Bridge and its approaches with the city of St. Louis for the MacArthur Bridge and its approaches. The trade gave TRRA control of both railroad bridges connecting freight and passenger rail operations in Missouri and Illinois, as well as affording the Metro-Link light rail system bridge access over the Mississippi.

The TRRA's roots, however, stretch back almost 150 years to rail travel's early days before the Civil War. At

that time train lines originating on the East Coast could only travel as far west as the east bank of the Mississippi River, just across from the growing city of St. Louis. When westbound travelers and cargo reached the Mississippi, they had to be transported across the river by ferry to board awaiting trains in St. Louis in order to

> **The Terminal Railroad Association of St. Louis has played a significant role in the history and development of the city of St. Louis, providing important links over the Mississippi River in the transcontinental railroad system at the St. Louis Gateway.**

continue the journey. In 1853 one of the Terminal Railroad's predecessor companies, the Wiggins Ferry Company, was established to both haul passengers and freight and to set up railroad facilities on both sides of the river. Later on, Wiggins built heavy-duty ferryboats that could haul loaded railroad cars across the river, eliminating the need for unloading and reloading goods.

The years between the Civil War and the beginning of the 20th century were ones of great change on the St. Louis riverfront. The Fourth of July in 1874 saw the completion of both the Eads Bridge, a project of the St. Louis and Illinois Bridge Company that allowed trains to cross the Mississippi River for the first time, and the Tunnel Railroad of St. Louis' 4,800-foot tunnel, which passed underneath downtown

The TRRA owns, operates and uses over 51 miles of main track and 140 miles of yard tracks and sidings located on both sides of the Mississippi.

St. Louis. Other companies secured charters to build railroad facilities on both riverbanks. These facilities tied the bridge and tunnel to the principal railroads operating on the Illinois and Missouri sides of the river.

Another company, Union Depot Company of St. Louis, was formed to build a passenger rail station at 12th and Poplar streets in St. Louis. These facilities were used by the railroads from 1875 until September 1, 1894, when Union Station, located to this day at 18th and Market streets, was completed. As the bustling city of St. Louis outgrew these facilities, the Terminal Railroad of St. Louis and the Terminal Railroad of East St. Louis were incorporated in 1880 to purchase additional ground and to build more railroad tracks and infrastructure.

The TRRA's roots, however, stretch back almost 150 years to rail travel's early days before the Civil War.

However, these efforts were not adequate to fill the booming region's needs.

To satisfy the demands, a new corporation — the Terminal Railroad Association of St. Louis — was created on July 30, 1889. The new company was formed by consolidating several terminal companies operating on both sides of the Eads Bridge and by taking over the lease of the Eads Bridge and the tunnel beneath St. Louis from the Missouri Pacific and Wabash Railroads.

In October of that year, the Terminal Railroad Association of St. Louis entered into an operating agreement with seven railroad companies including what are now CSX Transportation, Union Pacific Railroad, Norfolk Southern Railway Company and Consolidated Rail Corporation. Under the agreement's terms, the Terminal Railroad would be responsible for maintaining and improving existing terminal facilities on both sides of the river as well as building new ones on behalf of the railroad companies. Three years after a second bridge, the Merchants Bridge, was built across the Mississippi in 1890, the Terminal Railroad Association of St. Louis acquired control of it. About a decade later, the Association acquired Wiggins Ferry.

Over the next 13 years the Terminal Railroad Association of St. Louis grew into what was recognized as the largest individual terminal organization in the country. Since 1889 its properties and facilities have been expanded through the purchase of many acres of land and the construction of many miles of tracks. Its terminal facilities served the important industrial areas of metropolitan St. Louis.

Today, there are 28,812 shares of TRRA's capital stock outstanding, which are owned by five proprietary companies. The stock is issued to the proprietary companies only as evidence of membership in the association, but does not pay dividends. Each of the five companies has representatives on the TRRA's board of directors. The board must approve certain issues, such as property transactions, capital expenditures and corporate policies.

The Terminal Railroad Association of St. Louis has played a significant role in the history and development of the city of St. Louis, providing important links over the Mississippi River in the transcontinental railroad system at the St. Louis Gateway. TRRA's influence in the St. Louis region continues not only through its business operations, but also through its corporate participation in many community organizations promoting the betterment of St. Louis and the surrounding areas.

AmerenUE

*B*iting into a hot dog, licking an ice cream cone and switching on a light are ways to sample some of the excitement generated at the 1904 World's Fair, the St. Louis event that introduced America to the hot dog bun, the waffle cone and the joys of electricity. Union Company, AmerenUE's original name, powered the fairgrounds, inspiring Charles Alma Buers to hail the event as "the electrical fair" in a 1904 edition of *The American Inventor.*

The fair prompted a flurry of home wiring, and Union, founded in 1902, turned up the current to begin a tradition of providing low-cost, reliable energy that continues today through AmerenUE. AmerenUE is an operating company of Ameren Corporation, the parent of energy trading and marketing, and fuels procurement companies, plus an Illinois-based electric and natural gas utility, AmerenCIPS.

AmerenUE supplies electricity to 1.2 million customers and natural gas to 123,000 people in Missouri and Illinois, making it Missouri's largest electric company and the state's third-largest natural gas distributor.

The company paid its first, now uninterrupted, cash dividend in 1906, then spent the next three decades expanding territories, acquiring plants and completing Bagnell Dam on the Osage River. By the 1940s Union Electric's production outstripped demand, so with other power companies, the company built a multistate system of power transmission lines that links Ameren with 30 other providers. Ameren is now the nation's second-most connected utility company.

Expansion continued over the next 40 years, including a move into Missouri's gas market and the construction in 1984 of the state's only nuclear power plant. Near Fulton, Missouri, Callaway Nuclear Plant has set national records for safety, efficiency and production in its 17-plus years of service.

The first power plant of what is now Ameren Corporation was in downtown St. Louis, near what is now Laclede's Landing. The plant built in 1902 has been a landmark in the city since 1972 and was sold to Bi-State Development Agency in 1983.

Ameren's largest plant at 2,300 megawatts — Labadie Plant in Franklin County just outside St. Louis — set multiple records in 2000, burning 9 million tons of coal and generating more than 15.7 million megawatt hours of power.

Union Electric merged with CIPSCO Incorporated in 1997 to form Ameren Corporation. The resulting organization provides energy services to more than 1.8 million customers in Missouri and Illinois. At that time, St. Louis-based AmerenUE had a generation capacity of 7,900 megawatts from one nuclear, five fossil-fuel and three hydroelectric generating plants. The merger prepared both utilities for competitive markets, resulting from provider choice legislation enacted in 1997 in Illinois. Today, Ameren's generating capacity has reached 12,600 megawatts and is growing with capacity additions in Illinois.

AmerenUE has built its generating strength while reducing emissions, protecting wildlife habitats and investing in research. Among the prestigious awards the company has received are a 1998 Missouri Governor's Pollution Prevention Award; a 1997 Marlin Perkins Award for supporting a program to install hatching boxes for songbirds on utility poles; and the 1993 Edison Award, the industry's most prestigious honor, for its response to devastating Midwest flooding.

AmerenUE offers assistance with energy bills to low-income customers, and long-life, high-efficiency lighting to community parks, schools and sporting venues.

About 100 years ago, Union Company powered the region's charge into the age of electricity. This century, AmerenUE stands ready to lead the industry in developing cleaner methods for generating power while consistently meeting its customers' needs for low-cost, reliable energy.

Lambert-St. Louis International Airport

Scenes from aviation history pepper the early years of Lambert-St. Louis International Airport. In 1910 Teddy Roosevelt departed from Kinloch Field, as the site was then known, and became the first president to fly. Seventeen years later, Charles Lindbergh left Lambert in the locally sponsored *Spirit of St. Louis* on the first nonstop transatlantic flight.

Aviation industries came to the fore in the area during World War II, and Lambert supported McDonnell Aircraft Company and two other manufacturers in their delivery of airplanes for the war effort. McDonnell, which became McDonnell Douglas and more recently merged with Boeing, later produced the Mercury and Gemini spacecraft at Lambert as well as the F-4E Phantom and other aircraft.

The airport's contributions to aviation history are well known. Yet few people realize that Maj. Albert Bond Lambert is largely responsible for establishing St. Louis as an aviation center. Lambert, who acquired Kinloch Field in 1920, developed the airport, then sold the facility, which was providing passenger and freight services, to St. Louis at his cost in 1928.

Now one of the world's busiest airports and a key hub in the nation's aviation system, Lambert served over 30.5 million passengers in 2000 with about 500,000 takeoffs and landings.

Boasting an excellent reputation for safety, Lambert has grown with the demand for air travel. The 1970s brought a $290 million expansion project. A $1.1 billion expansion, slated for completion in 2006, is adding a new runway and lengthening another to accommodate simultaneous takeoffs and landings. The project, which has a high level of minority participation, will bring the annual operational capacity to 705,000 and also includes roadway relocations, terminal improvements and the acquisition of land for future growth. Airport Director Leonard L. Griggs Jr., a retired Air Force colonel, spearheaded each of these expansions, and with the latest, he has charted a course that will carry Lambert well into the future.

The region and the nation benefit when Lambert expands. The 1970s project added $2 billion to the local economy. The latest expansion, expected to pump $4.7 billion into it through construction alone, should boost the region's economy by $7-10 billion during the first 10 years, with Lambert contributing $125-180 billion to it over 20 years. Analysts predict the expansion will create nearly 86,000 new jobs at Lambert and related businesses, which together employed over 53,900 people in 2001. Nationwide, reduced delays at this centrally located airport should save $5 billion over 10 years.

Lambert's wide variety of carriers — including American Airlines, Delta Air Lines, Southwest Airlines and United Airlines offer a large number of flights, many of which are direct. This easy access to the skies draws businesses to the region as does Lambert's convenient location near major highways in the metropolitan area.

St. Louis has supported aviation since the first planes rose from Kinloch Field. Today, Lambert supports the region. Expansion promises new jobs and economic benefits as well as improvements to air travel nationwide.

Lambert Field as it looked in the 1930s

When photographed in 2001, Lambert was undergoing a major expansion of its facilities.

Missouri-American Water Company

*P*roviding the highest-quality water and world-class customer service to over 1.2 million residential and commercial customers across the state, Missouri-American Water Company is the largest water utility company in Missouri. Its parent company, American Water Works, is the most geographically diverse water utility company in the United States, operating in 23 states and serving more than 1,000 communities nationwide.

In February 1999 American Water Works officially acquired St. Louis County Water Company, whose roots trace back to 1902.

In St. Louis County before 1900, water for its 50,000 residents came from wells and cisterns or in some cases, a nice bubbling spring. There was no unified source of water supply but farsighted citizens could already see the need developing. An attorney, John H. Bothwell; an engineer, J.B. Quigley; and a construction man, John C. Walker, joined together to form a company that would come to operate under the name of St. Louis Water and Light Company. They built a water treatment facility at a point in the Missouri River called "Howard's Bend," about 14 miles west of St. Louis near Olive and Hog Hollow Roads.

Pumping stations were developed and water from the river was pumped by steam engines through a 12-inch

main and initially supplied about 2,000 users. The plant had about a 1.5-million-gallon-per-day capacity. By 1925 the customer base had swelled to 20,000 and required nearly 8 million gallons of water per day. At about the same time, the company officially began operating as St. Louis County Water Company.

After sustaining continued growth through the remainder of the 20th century, today the company operates four water treatment plants in St. Louis County serving area residents in St. Louis, St. Charles and Jefferson Counties.

Missouri-American is proud to continue the tradition of St. Louis County Water as a leader in promoting economic development while partnering with the communities it serves. The company proudly sponsors numerous community activities and programs throughout the St. Louis metropolitan area. Among the many programs it has partnered with are: the NCAA Women's Final Four; the St. Louis County Fair and Air Show; the Habitat for Humanity Build Blitz; and the Governor's Economic Summit for Women.

For the new century, Missouri-American plans to continue to provide excellent customer service by focusing on new and innovative solutions for the water resource needs of its customers, as well as its dedication to providing the highest-quality and most reliable water for the residents of the St. Louis region.

One of the Moon innovations of the year is this new Cabriolet roadster. The deck lid opens up a fully upholstered rear seat "a deux." With the lid down the car is a closed roadster. Concealed compartment for golf bag and other luggage. Rear window may be lowered for communication between passengers. (Patents applied for)

A HEAD of its day with a distinct and different smartness, Moon enjoys an amazing preference wherever smartness is a *sine qua non.*

For pride of possession is the chief satisfaction of the Moon family. Pride in its dauntless performance. Pride in its distinguished appearance. And as the miles roll up, a feeling almost of affection for its clock-like regularity.

So, in the metropolitan style centers, where most of the motor-wise live, you find Moon selling away ahead of its price class, outranking in registrations many of the makers who build more cars than Moon.

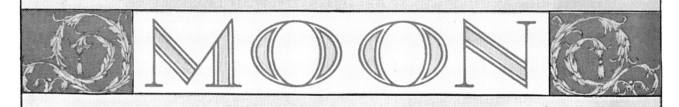

MOON MOTOR CAR COMPANY ᐟ ST. LOUIS ᐟ U. S. A.

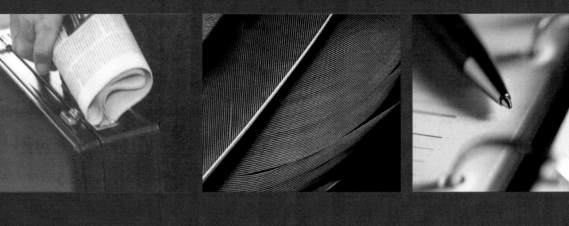

...St. Louis has earned its reputation as a community that fosters business success.

PROFESSIONAL SERVICES

As the birthplace of many of the world's most prominent professional service firms, St. Louis has earned its reputation as a community that fosters business success. Through the decades, St. Louis has helped scores of entrepreneurs launch, nurture and grow their enterprises.

Today, our region serves as home base for dozens of world-class organizations representing such diverse fields as accounting, advertising, architecture, business consulting, law and public relations. The area also serves as a regional hub for hundreds of renowned national and international organizations.

Factors contributing to St. Louis' success as a business incubator include its convenient location, plentiful resources, hard-working people and exceptional quality of life.

Because of its close proximity to the nation's population center, St. Louis serves as a convenient, practical and efficient location for conducting business throughout the world.

By air, road, rail or river, the Gateway to the West is indeed a gateway to the world, offering a diverse and efficient infrastructure for moving people and packages to their destination. Business trips to and from most other U.S. metropolitan areas can be made in a single day. And the region's location in the central time zone means it's a convenient and logical hub between both coasts.

People are the lifeblood of any professional services firm, and St. Louisans are bred with a Midwest work ethic and a commitment to excellence. The region's roster of top-notch colleges and universities help develop young talent and deliver a steady stream of well-qualified candidates.

Talented folks from outside the area are attracted to the region's reasonable cost of living and family-friendly environment. They also treasure the city's thriving cultural institutions and icons, including the symphony, opera, theatres, art museum and botanical garden. And of course, our celebrated professional sports teams are the ideal means for instilling civic pride.

As the Midwest and world economies continue their transformation from manufacturing to service and technology, St. Louis is poised to capitalize on its rich heritage as a welcoming and nurturing location for seizing the global marketplace.

GYO OBATA
Co-founder • Hellmuth, Obata + Kassabaum (HOK), Inc.

Global Vision Strategies, LLC

*W*orking toward world peace one attitude at a time is what Global Vision Strategies, LLC sets out to do each and every time it embarks on a training session, speaking engagement, or a global business facilitation project.

Linda Jacobsen, president, CEO and founder of Global Vision Strategies in St. Charles, believes that every time the company alleviates a global business challenge, facilitates a key relationship, trains a professional to enter a business situation in another country, or helps a relocating family adapt effectively to a foreign culture, it is touching someone in a positive manner.

Jacobsen is originally from Canada. Besides studying in France to earn a master's degree in teaching English as a second language (ESL) and bilingual education, she has lived and worked abroad in several countries. She has taught ESL from the elementary grades through the university level and has extensive experience in refugee resettlement. Over the years, Jacobsen has accumulated a wealth of knowledge regarding business and cross-cultural interactions in foreign countries. Her experiences have endowed the company with a rich depth of cultural understanding, which is evident in the business.

The global management consulting and training company now has 20 employees domestically and around 300 associates and service providers in 93 different countries. All associates have a working knowledge of the cultures that they represent, are at least bilingual, and have lived and worked in a foreign country. Each team is trained to provide consistent high-quality services to all clients in all countries. However, the booming company began with just one person in 1993.

While teaching ESL at a local community college, Jacobsen began working with large, local corporations training employees in foreign languages and preparing them for assignments abroad, and Global Vision Strategies was born. The company's primary mission is to provide strategic training, insight, knowledge and advice to its clients to help them maximize their effectiveness in all of their international and intercultural dealings. Through its efforts, the company strives to create socially responsible global organizations dedicated to global peace and prosperity.

Global Vision Strategies customizes solutions for each client based on express requirements. Some of the services provided by the company include cross-cultural training, global management training, global strategic planning, global business development consulting, foreign language and ESL training and relocation assistance. The company provides 24-hour support seven days a week and encourages clients to call should a challenging situation arise during business interactions. The training programs are designed primarily for employees who are operating or living in foreign countries, managers of expatriate employees, managers or employees of foreign descent and/or the team responsible for providing support services to a company's expatriate and international business operations. The key is to train and empower each level of the organization in order to achieve maximum productivity with minimal mistakes.

How Global Business Affects the Global Economy panelists at the invitation of the Working Woman Network and Business Women's Network International in Washington, D.C. Women from more than 75 nations were present.

Linda Jacobsen, Global Vision Strategies president and CEO (third from right) was the keynote speaker at the invitation of the International Federation of Women Entrepreneurs in New Delhi, India. Heavy press coverage in India led to many interviews and nationally televised discussions with Jacobsen.

Jacobsen asserts that employees who go into international business with the right knowledge set will be able to work in a more effective and expeditious manner. Cultural knowledge helps empower negotiators to think about the other side of the table and enables them to become powerful leaders and relationship builders. This has led to the global business development arm of the company, helping clients establish or grow exporting and manufacturing in foreign markets.

Forging and maintaining the right relationships is the most essential skill for successful international business development. Over the years, the company has developed a wealth of key government, business and community relationships in different countries around the world. Such contacts are of great benefit to clients looking to enhance or develop their global business operations. Most companies find that timely strategic advice and relevant management training makes their international business operations highly effective and profitable.

The company's clients have included various Fortune 500 companies whose identities are protected due to the sensitive nature of global business. The company is committed to the long-term success and satisfaction of its clients via an ongoing system of communication, which ensures the dissemination of information to all the relevant levels in the organization.

Domestically, Global Vision Strategies also works with companies and organizations to provide diversity training and to lead them toward communication solutions that result in better cross-cultural integration and understanding. To this end, Jacobsen chairs a Diversity Task Force in her home county of St. Charles to explore ways to welcome and expand the growing multicultural population.

Due to the nature of the company's vision and a strong corporate philosophy of giving back to society, company employees often donate their time and skills as speakers and facilitators at community events and charitable fund-raisers. Furthermore, Jacobsen serves on many boards and committees, including the World Trade Center, St. Louis; the YMCA of O'Fallon; SIAS University in China; the University of Missouri Extension Council; The Chancellor's Committee for International Issues at the University of Missouri; and PAYBACK, a juvenile restitution program. The company is also active in the local chapter of the World Affairs Council and other industry organizations such as the Society of Human Resource Management (SHRM), the SHRM Global Forum and the Employee Relocation Council.

Global Vision Strategies received the SBA Exporter of the Year award in 2000 and the Working Woman Network's Entrepreneurial Excellence Award in 2001. Jacobsen has spoken at numerous international conferences and venues in many different countries, such as the Global Conference of Women Entrepreneurs in New Delhi, India, and has represented U.S. small business interests in trade talks under two presidents.

In today's economic scenario, businesses big and small are eventually required to operate on a global scale in order to remain competitive. Differences in managerial environments, cultures, languages, behavior and attitudes create substantial challenges for key management and human resource professionals. Global Vision Strategies strives to continue its quest toward better cross-cultural understanding and more efficient global business relationships, one attitude at a time.

Linda Jacobsen accepts the Exporter of the Year award from the SBA. The Missouri House of Representatives Honorable Patricia Secrest, left, acknowledges this honor with a surprise Resolution from the Missouri House as well.

Global Vision Strategies signs historic Letter of Agreement with a Canadian company at a U.S./Canada Trade Summit. (Left to right in background) Sergio Marchi, Canadian minister of International Trade; Aida Alvarez, administrator of the U.S. Small Business Administration; and Ambassador David Aaron, undersecretary for International Trade, U.S. Department of Commerce. Signing with Linda Jacobsen is FGI President Allon Bross of Thornhill, Ontario, Canada.

Maritz Inc.

*E*dward Maritz, a master engraver and jewelry maker, opened a small firm at his home near Tower Grove Park in south Saint Louis in 1894. At the time, no one could foresee the tremendous growth and change the company would experience beyond the next century. Today, Maritz Inc. is the world's single largest source of performance improvement, travel and marketing research services. A pioneer in the concept of non-cash incentive awards and a leader in the use of information technology, Maritz now employs approximately 6,000 people and maintains its expansive headquarters in St. Louis County.

Originally calling his enterprise E. Maritz Jewelry Manufacturing Company, Edward Maritz operated as a wholesaler and manufacturer of fine jewelry and engraved watches. He earned a reputation for quality workmanship and moved his business within St. Louis several times to accommodate its steady growth. By the early 1920s, wholesaling imported watches became its primary business, and the company name changed to Maritz Watch and Manufacturing Company. It began importing Swiss watch movements for insertion in Maritz-designed watch cases. Adding wristwatches — timepieces previously used only by the military — proved a wise business move, as the new fashion erupted in popularity.

The year 1929 proved pivotal for the Maritz company. Founder Edward died and the stock market crashed. With their family's business in jeopardy, Edward's sons James and Lloyd developed an ingenious plan to save it. They began selling watches, jewelry and merchandise to large corporations to use as sales incentives and service awards. The unique idea of improving employee productivity by offering something other than cash caught hold. The following year they produced the first national "prize book" for a St. Louis hat manufacturer and began operating the program under their newly formed division, Maritz Sales Builders.

The sales incentive business not only revived the company, it became its major concern. Weathering the Great Depression and World War II, Maritz continued to prosper, but in 1950, the brothers split the company and parted ways. Lloyd took the jewelry business, while James continued with Sales Builders, which flourished into the next decade.

The growing incentive business served some of the country's largest companies with programs that included award catalogs offering a variety of merchandise that employees earned by accumulating points. The company added group travel to its repertoire of performance and recognition awards when it bought a small Detroit travel company in 1958.

James' sons, James Jr. and Bill, took on leadership roles with Maritz in the 1960s, and the company began to outgrow its office space, by then located on Forest Park Boulevard. The corporate name was shortened to Maritz Inc., and in 1961 the company planned an ambitious move to its current campus near Fenton, in St. Louis County. Beginning with a new merchandise distribution center it completed by 1965, Maritz continued building more offices on the site, which included more than 200 acres.

During the 70s, Maritz expanded and diversified with the addition of communications and marketing research businesses. In 1974 it initiated its move into the international market, opening a full-service motivation agency near London, England. It also opened a travel office in Mexico City. In 1981 it started a series of acquisitions that established Maritz as one of the nation's largest corporate travel suppliers.

That same year, James Maritz Sr. passed away, leaving his sons, James and Bill, to lead the company. When James Jr. retired in 1983, Bill took over as president and CEO. Maritz continued to invent unique incentive products and became a leader in automotive marketing research. In the 90s it extended its international scope by forming Maritz Canada and adding offices throughout Western Europe.

Today, a world leader in performance improvement, travel and marketing research, Maritz is headquartered on a 210-acre campus in southwest St. Louis County.

Maritz' Fenton headquarters continued to grow as well, soon adding a building on the other side of Interstate 44. The company linked the two sides by constructing a 510-foot-long pedestrian bridge over the highway. Now during the winter holidays, travelers along I-44 enjoy the company's sensational holiday lighting display illuminating both sides of the road.

By the time Bill Maritz passed away early in 2001, the small family jewelry company begun by his grandfather had not only gained global recognition in its three main businesses — performance improvement, travel and marketing research — but had emerged as a major innovator of Internet technology. In 2000 Maritz was ranked 28th among the top 500 users by *InformationWeek*. Its eMaritz Internet service is an example of how the company uses technology to deliver products and solutions to new markets.

Throughout its history, Maritz has been generous in sharing its success and resources with the community. It uses its motivation expertise and spacious facilities to train the staff and volunteers of United Way of Greater St. Louis, the area's principal charity fund-raising organization. Bill Maritz' legacy — which prompted the *St. Louis Post-Dispatch* to honor him with the title of Citizen of the Year for 1998 — continues to enrich the metropolitan area where he lived and worked. In 1989 he initiated

the incentive program called "Be There," designed to raise attendance figures in the city's public schools. He also played important roles in the development of the St. Louis riverfront's Laclede's Landing and in the founding of Fair St. Louis, the city's annual spectacular Fourth of July celebration held on the grounds of the Gateway Arch.

As chairman and CEO, Steve Maritz is now the fourth generation of the Maritz family to lead the company as it proceeds into a third century. Constantly reinventing itself to adapt to changing times, Maritz forever seeks new ways to improve its operations and motivate its own employees. The *St. Louis Business Journal* cited Maritz as one of the "Best Places to Work in St. Louis." Maritz Inc. owes its success to a philosophy bequeathed by James Maritz Sr. and expanded by Bill Maritz — "Work hard, have fun, get the job done."

Maritz Sales Builders, a company that pioneered the concept of using merchandise and travel as sales incentives, was originally located on Forest Park Boulevard in St. Louis.

McMahon, Berger, Hanna, Linihan, Cody & McCarthy

"McMahon, Berger," as it is frequently known to the general public, is a 29-member firm that despite its humble beginnings is one of the largest firms in the United States dedicated to the exclusive representation of corporations and other employers in the field of labor and employment law. Notwithstanding its Midwest location, the firm represents employers literally from coast to coast.

In 1955 Lee McMahon, the founder of the firm, left a secure and prestigious career as the Regional Director of the National Labor Relations Board in St. Louis when he recognized that employers in the area were in need of aggressive and creative legal representation in dealing with organized labor, both at the negotiating table as well as in remaining union-free. McMahon's success enabled him to add Alan Berger to his office in 1959, and Berger added scholarship to the practice as well as a subtle

negotiating style that served as an alternative to McMahon's more forceful demeanor. Following several years with the NLRB, Tom Hanna joined the firm in 1966 to bring his litigation experience to McMahon, Berger. Mike Linihan joined the firm in 1968 after his discharge from the U.S. Army following service as an infantry officer in Korea. Bill Cody first worked for a client of the firm in a human resource capacity, attended law school, worked for the NLRB and then joined the firm in 1970. Tom McCarthy, who has the distinction of being the firm's only engineer, joined it in 1974 after working for the NLRB.

During the firm's early years, its practice was confined primarily to negotiations, union campaigns, arbitrations, unfair labor practice and representation cases before the NLRB, occasional wage and hour cases, and state court claims. The firm takes great pride in the fact that its

The partners at McMahon, Berger bring decades of experience to their clients.

efforts on behalf of management enabled many employers to remain competitive and to maintain operations in the St. Louis area as an alternative to moving elsewhere.

In the 1960s the construction unions in St. Louis began to assert their muscle by engaging in unlawful secondary strikes and jurisdictional disputes. The firm subsequently sued several unions for damages and secured damages for clients in what was, in all probability,

> **Few firms can offer the same depth of experience as McMahon, Berger. The firm's clientele, both large and small, numbers in the thousands.**

the first of such actions brought in the Eastern District of Missouri. Secondary strikes and jurisdictional disputes now have become almost extinct since those judgments were rendered and upheld on appeal. McMahon, Berger attorneys also have successfully litigated a number of labor and employment cases that have set precedent on a national basis, including before the U.S. Supreme Court.

The 1970s and 1980s brought forth new legislation and consequent litigation in the fields of discrimination because of race, sex, religion, color and national origin (Title VII and related state and federal laws), age (ADEA), disability (ADA) and safety (OSHA, MSHA). Benefits became subject to federal regulation and the subject of liability and increased litigation (ERISA). Employers also were affected by federal requirements to announce plant closings (WARN) and in the 1990s, to provide family medical leave (FMLA). These new laws resulted in voluminous new regulations, not all of which were consistent with the new statues and congressional intent.

At the same time, corporations began merger, sale and acquisition activities requiring skilled advice both in dealing with unions as well as the examination of labor and employment issues during the due diligence phase. All of these added new dimensions to the practice and the addition of new attorneys to assist employers in adapting to the new laws and, when necessary, litigating disputes. These laws also demanded that labor contracts

harmonize with the new legislation. At the same time, the late 1970s and early 1980s were times of great inflation, which made contract negotiations at first difficult and later, when recession set in, created the need to reform contracts to adapt to market conditions that had changed radically and threatened the viability of many businesses.

To meet these challenges, new attorneys were trained and they demonstrated such great proficiency at the work that they soon became principals themselves: Bob Stewart joined in 1977; Jim Foster in 1980; Dan Begian in 1982; John Renick and Pat McFall in 1985; Kevin Lorenz in 1987; Fred Ricks in 1988, Tom Berry in 1989; Shelley Roither in 1991, and Stan Schroeder and Geoff Gilbert in 1992. Twelve associate attorneys are now working toward greater status within the firm and two distinguished lawyers have joined "of Counsel."

The 21st century presents new challenges and opportunities in employment law. Litigation continues to expand dramatically but now arbitration has become a more readily available replacement for expensive and draining litigation in state and federal courts. The pros and cons of presenting arbitration agreements to prospective and current employees as a method of settling employment disputes is a subject many employers are considering to determine whether arbitration will achieve a real economy in defending against employment claims. Further, employment agreements with restrictive covenants and other non-compete clauses are becoming a common fact of life in the business world. McMahon, Berger has, collectively, decades of experience in these areas and has taken a leadership role in advising clients on these and other new developments in the law and business employment practices.

Few firms can offer the same depth of experience as McMahon, Berger. The firm's clientele, both large and small, numbers in the thousands. Its clients' businesses are local, national and international in scope and encompass every type of endeavor, both public and private. The firm does more than its fair share of litigation in every venue, but it also works with clients on a daily basis with advice designed to avoid expensive litigation wherever possible. McMahon, Berger has learned its trade by long experience and can give any employer the benefit of that knowledge and experience. The law firm also publishes a quarterly newsletter, conducts seminars for clients and other members of the business community and maintains a Web site.

The Mash Group

With a little entrepreneurial spirit, a lot of ingenuity and $10,000, longtime designer and graphic artist Joseph Mash founded The Mash Group in 1984.

What started as a small company in a rented warehouse quickly grew as Fortune 500 clients were attracted to the creative solutions and exceptional customer service that the company has delivered since day one.

The company's primary business is designing and building exhibits for trade shows, conventions, museums, corporate meetings and special events — and having fun while doing it.

With headquarters in St. Louis, The Mash Group has a second location in San Antonio, Texas. Employing about 60 people, it now handles more than 1,000 projects each year from coast to coast. Some projects are large and complex displays, while others may be to provide small or simple

Joseph E. Mash, chairman and CEO of The Mash Group, relaxes in one of his favorite "collectible toys," the original "Weasel" auto from Walt Disney World's "Mr. Toad's Wild Ride."

solutions. From overseeing development, troubleshooting the processes, monitoring costs, documenting progress and ensuring successful completion, The Mash Group applies its full attention to each and every detail of each and every project, no matter the size.

Designs include portable display units, trade show islands, traveling exhibits and permanent displays (museums, corporate reception areas and theme parks). The company is also known for its innovative staging, sound, lighting, sets and decorations.

Using computer imagery, clients can see a concept come to life before construction begins, and with the aid of 3-D technology they can "stroll" through the display and visualize what results they will get. Changes in colors or setup can be manipulated on screen, displaying different options at the touch of a button.

But the company doesn't stop with design. With the advent of high-tech companies, The Mash Group has completed projects for such companies as Acterna, Inc. (a manufacturer of telecommunications testing equipment) and Citrix Systems, Inc. (a producer of computer server hardware). Artists and craftspeople at The Mash Group fabricate the displays and have created projects for such companies as AT&T, Anheuser-Busch, General Electric, Parke-Davis, Purina Mills and a General Electric display at EPCOT in Orlando, Florida.

Parts are machined directly from AutoCAD drawings, and the full-service graphic department can handle any graphic file from any platform. In-house printing, mounting and laminating capabilities enable The Mash Group to produce all graphic requirements for the exhibits, including signage, banners and full-color reprinting on a full range of materials, such as vinyl or light-box transparencies on Plexiglas.

Clients can view sketches and setup drawings on the company Web site and can make changes and comments online. Keeping maximum efficiency and cost control in mind, The Mash Group also provides an FTP service so customers can easily transfer files electronically.

Named as a finalist in the Ernst & Young Entrepreneur of the Year program for 2001, Joe Mash continues to expand services including the addition of computer tools, using the Internet for archiving, and researching new innovations in construction and computer services. He recognizes how much the talented people he employs have contributed to building the company from a small startup to its present status with multimillion-dollar annual sales. Mr. Mash says that he may get the recognition in the public arena, but without the company's sales force, great designers, exceptional engineers, the best shop craftsmen, wonderful client-service coordinators and dedicated support staff, he would still be at a drawing board somewhere. He says they all have his perpetual appreciation.

His philosophy throughout the tenure of the company has been to make the customer feel special. He believes that outstanding customer service keeps people coming back, and The Mash Group has retained clients that have worked with the company since its beginnings.

The Mash Group's dedication to leadership, integrity and innovation has made it a leader in its field, and exceeding expectations is its hallmark. It fulfills its mission to provide customers with the best creative solutions and to exceed expectations without exception. The company prides itself on the fact that clients receive the greatest possible return on investment, which helps ensure mutual growth and profitability.

An internal promotion display used by The Mash Group represents the creative process at exhibitor shows. It includes a variety of moving parts, along with bells and whistles, smoke and mirrors, and a bubble machine that manufactures "creative juices." This display is just an example of the elaborate and inspirational heights that The Mash Group's design/construct team has reached with displays for its many clients.

Anheuser-Busch's trade show exhibit included a second-floor conference room and functional taproom. The elaborate Lipitor display contains areas for testing cholesterol and educational libraries. The Mallinckrodt exhibit was adjustable and could be adapted to different sizes for different shows.

Permanent exhibits and displays at the The Humane Society of Missouri Learning Center, the Purina Mills Research Farm Visitors Center, the Monsanto Insectarium at the St. Louis Zoo, and a history and mission exhibit at the University of Missouri-Columbia Alumni Center also have the "Mash" touch. From beginning to end and everything in between, Mash stresses continuity and attention to detail.

In 1981 Joe Mash and one of the company's account executives were two of the four founders of The Gateway Insiders, which is still active as a networking, lead-generating and market trends business-to-business information source.

The company is a member of the St. Louis Downtown Rotary, The Convention and Visitors Commission, The Business Marketing Association, The St. Louis Advertising Club, the St. Louis Ambassadors and St. Louis Regional Commerce and Growth Association. Joe Mash has been a member of the prestigious group, The Executive Committee (TEC), for nearly 10 years.

The Mash Group donated time and labor for staging, decorating, design and set up of the 1994 regional Olympic Festival. It was the primary sponsor of the SIDS Golf Tournament in 1996 and 1997 and has been active in special staging for functions such as the Salvation Army Tree of Lights and the United Way kickoffs.

Long-term goals include continuation of the pattern of growth the company has experienced for the last seven years. The implementation of diversified marketing strategies and utilization of opportunities that the contemporary business market presents are also a part of the company's future plans.

One of The Mash Group's recent booths that was first used at Supercomm 2001, the 50-foot-by-50-foot Acterna Exhibit was constructed for a trade show setting and features multiple levels, live presentations and product environments.

The Mattson Jack Group

MISSION: THROUGH ENHANCED DECISION-MAKING SUPPORT, ACCELERATE CLIENT GROWTH

*F*ounded in 1986 by William R. Mattson Jr. and Dr. William Jack, The Mattson Jack Group (MJG) is devoted exclusively to delivering high-quality consulting to the health care industry, particularly the pharmaceutical segment. As experienced professionals in the pharmaceutical industry, Bill Mattson and Bill Jack realized the possibility of creating a unique and highly effective client-service organization using a balanced combination of scientific and commercial capabilities. Their entrepreneurial spirit echoes that of millions of American pioneers. One impetus for national development westward was the challenge of surmounting the frontiers of the undiscovered. That pioneering spirit still exists in America today and is especially true of the pharmaceutical/biopharmaceutical industry.

To serve that industry, MJG started with just Mattson and Jack at inception, quickly growing to add five employees, and employed over 90 individuals in 2001. Although the companies it serves are generally based on either the East or West Coast, MJG maintains its corporate headquarters at its newly renovated and expanded offices near Westport in St. Louis County in

recognition of the ease with which clients from either coast or throughout the world can be served from such a central U.S. location. At the same time, MJG's satellite offices in Kansas City, Northern New Jersey, Philadelphia, Phoenix and London allow it to extend a personal touch to clients while effectively serving the global marketplace. In addition, through its affiliates in Japan, MJG reaches the world's second-largest pharmaceutical market behind the United States.

The Mattson Jack Group corporate mission statement declares "accelerating client growth" as its mantra. MJG's consultants are a unique mix of professionals with advanced, relevant scientific degrees and extensive corporate backgrounds with experiences that enable MJG to employ a dynamic team approach — applying critical mass — to meeting clients' needs, continually raising the performance bar relative to client projects. This focus, determination and work ethic directly reflect solid, positive Midwestern values.

Pharmaceutical industry analysts have declared that now is the "golden age" of medical and scientific discovery. In recent memory, terms like *aspirin, penicillin* and *heart transplants* became part of the collective vocabulary. Current research is consistently adding to this lexicon terms like *gene-targeted medicines, molecular scalpels, antiviral vaccine,* and *biological response modifiers.* MJG serves an industry that, having moved from symptom management to a science-based, disease-modifying focus, shapes positive changes to the quality of life for billions on a daily basis.

Both Bill Mattson and Bill Jack stress the importance of investing in long-term partnerships with clients, an interesting challenge in the transforming face of pharmaceuticals, which has experienced over 40 mega-mergers since the launch of MJG in

Co-founders William R. Mattson Jr. and Dr. William Jack

1986. In the first nine months of 2001, the industry saw $30 billion in robust consolidation activities. Throughout these breakneck shifts, MJG has grown aggressively to meet client needs. With Research and Development (R&D) spending in the pharmaceutical industry rising to $22 billion, MJG provides a concentrated outside resource that enables companies to

A Mattson Jack Group team conducts a Forecast Modeling Workshop.

make far-reaching and fast-moving decisions on effective deployment of R&D expenditures and commercial planning and implementation activities.

The pharmaceutical industry as a whole is increasingly global in scope. Combined with a need for increased R&D spending, this has resulted in the current era of consolidation, which is focused on creating long-term value to individuals, society and the health care system. Companies must carefully invest R&D dollars only in those medicines or treatments that bring the greatest benefit, thereby improving patient care and lessening the ultimate impact of price to the consumer. As a consequence of this stringent investment outlook, many of the world's pharmaceutical companies routinely seek MJG's specialized assistance to provide input into decision-making.

The pharmaceutical industry can spend up to $500 million to bring a single drug to market, so it is crucial to know where and how a drug is to be used and the benefits it offers relative to other drugs available for treating the same condition. One of the ways MJG uses its knowledge of diseases and drug therapy to assist clients in their decision-making is to capture the logic of a market within a computer-based model in order to evaluate the market potential of a new drug. With these detailed analyses, MJG's clients can increase the probability that their investments are targeted toward promoting the greatest benefit to the largest number of patients — in the United States, Europe, Japan and elsewhere.

In 2001 MJG reached two noteworthy milestones: the company celebrated its 15th anniversary, and it was awarded the St. Louis Regional Fast 50 Technology Award for the sixth consecutive year — a significant achievement realized by only two other companies in the region. MJG continues to succeed in this measure, despite the fact that as the company grows each year, it becomes inherently more difficult to achieve such an honor.

From St. Louis for the past 15 years, MJG has successfully assisted its clients worldwide by providing the broadest spectrum of services possible, running the gamut from corporate development services, forecasting and market research to promotional response modeling and product life-cycle management. MJG not only supports its clients around the world, but it also plays a role in support of the St. Louis region as a founding member of the Technology Gateway Alliance and as one of the corporate sponsors for the BioDiscovery Symposium. MJG's president, Bill Mattson, serves on the Washington University School of Medicine National Council. Additionally, several of MJG's staff serve on Washington University's Human Studies Committee and Saint Louis University's Institutional Review Board. These groups evaluate research conducted with human subjects at their respective institutions to safeguard patients in clinical trials and to facilitate the transformation of empirical knowledge into scientific medicine.

As Eero Saarinen's inspired design, the "St. Louis Arch," symbolically spans the Gateway to the West, The Mattson Jack Group's unique blend of expertise spans the breadth of the pharmaceutical/biopharmaceutical industries on the new frontier of medicine.

Arteaga Photos LTD

*T*he award-winning work of the Arteaga family began when their founder, Bob Arteaga, discovered his love of photography. Bob is still known today for his photographic interpretation and devotion to the St. Louis community. His commitment to quality is proudly carried on by Wayne, Eldon and Brad Arteaga. Over the last 75 years, Arteaga Photos has captured a complete photographic history of the St. Louis region. Its subjects have included business leaders, company products, sports stars and media personalities.

Photos by Arteaga Photos LTD

Bryan Cave LLP

From small beginnings to the height of the legal profession, Bryan Cave LLP has been at the center of St. Louis business for 128 years. What began as a three-lawyer office has now grown to become the largest law firm in Missouri. Bryan Cave is among the 50 largest law firms in the United States and one of the 100 largest in the world, with more than 600 lawyers.

Major expansion for the firm has occurred since 1973. Since that time, it has grown from one office to 18 and ventured further into areas such as antitrust, international trade, environmental law and product liability.

With offices flanking the breadth of the country from New York to California as well as in several foreign countries, including England, Saudi Arabia, Kuwait, United Arab Emirates and China, the firm represents clients across the globe in a progressive, diversified manner.

The firm believes that globalization means much more than simply being located in more than one country. The blending of a one-firm approach — consistent service to local and global clients — with true client service integration provides a high level of client service that transcends cultural differences. With the use of eCave, the firm's Intranet, the one-firm goal is

> **The firm's client base encompasses many different business types, including high-tech firms, manufacturers, and governmental and nonprofit organizations.**

being accomplished. By tying together all locations, knowledge can be shared internally, and with eCave extranets, externally, unifying practices and information worldwide.

Current technology, accessibility to clients and excellent legal services keep Bryan Cave abreast of the ever-changing needs of modern clients. With Web site development as an additional means of delivering legal services, the firm continues to be innovative and responsive in building and maintaining long-term client relationships.

> **Bryan Cave is among the 50 largest law firms in the United States and one of the 100 largest in the world, with more than 600 lawyers.**

The firm's client base encompasses many different business types, including high-tech firms, manufacturers, and governmental and nonprofit organizations. Client Service Groups that specialize in specific areas such as health care or other industries and areas of the law provide the basis of a well-rounded firm capable of meeting the needs of a diverse clientele with varied and individualized needs.

The recent development of two web-based solutions has further thrust Bryan Cave into technology-based, proactive services. "NoZone" offers clients interactive harassment-compliance training for supervisors to help protect against discrimination and harassment cases filed by employees. "TradeZone" is an integrated system offering answers to U.S. international trade law questions.

Bryan Cave has consistently provided professional pro bono public service whenever possible as a matter of "doing the right thing." Providing lawyers and investigators to high-profile cases, the firm's involvement is based on its reputation for integrity, efficiency, probity and ability. This reputation is its most important asset.

With its deep roots in St. Louis, the firm continues to support the enhancement of life in the region with its St. Louis partners serving on the boards of many nonprofit organizations.

St. Louis has become the beneficiary of a rich fabric of humanity and cultural experiences.

QUALITY OF LIFE

While a native of St. Louis and undoubtedly biased in my feelings about our community, I have observed that those who move here are delighted to discover that we offer the advantages of living in a big city combined with the warmth and convenience typical of most small towns. It is this magnificent dichotomy that allows transplants to St. Louis to adapt so quickly and become active members of our community.

St. Louis has been blessed with a rich heritage of successive migrations of ethnically diverse peoples starting with the French and Spanish in the 18th century, followed by American settlers moving westward into the Louisiana Territory in the 1800s, and western European immigrants (Germans, Italians, Irish) during the late 19th and early 20th centuries. More recently, St. Louis has become home for immigrants from Southeast Asia, Russia, Eastern Europe and the Middle East. These individuals all came to our community seeking new opportunity and better lives for their families. In fulfilling their dreams, St. Louis has become the beneficiary of a rich fabric of humanity and cultural experiences. This can be witnessed today in unique neighborhoods like the Hill, Soulard, south St. Louis City, the Central West End and the Loop. Each wave of immigrants has also brought religious diversity, strong faith and the unique sense of human and family values that characterizes our close-knit community.

St. Louis also has much to offer educationally including 115 public school districts, outstanding urban magnet schools, over 300 of the finest private schools in the nation and 80 technical and vocational schools. Our primary and secondary educational system is complemented by 12 universities and colleges that draw top undergraduate and graduate students from around the world to take advantage of the knowledge base and expertise embodied in our community. Eight junior colleges and numerous professional schools also enhance the quality and skills of the region's work force. Finally, the level of medical care in our community is second to none, thanks to superb clinical resources, innovative scientific research and excellent training programs.

Cultural attributes of St. Louis include a world-class symphony, an outstanding zoo (one of only two free zoos in the country), a nationally recognized opera theatre, the uniqueness and beauty of Laumeier Sculpture Park, the internationally renown Missouri Botanical Garden and a fantastic art museum that boasts the highest per capita visitor rate of any art museum in the United States.

The St. Louis region also offers a plethora of parks, trails, natural preserves and riverways for hiking, biking, boating and simply enjoying the outdoors. Finally, St. Louis is well known for its enthusiasm for sports. Our children have a passion for participating in school and other organized athletics including soccer, hockey, tennis and baseball and we have the good fortune to enjoy some of the best professional sports teams in the country.

So it is easy to understand why generations of families make St. Louis their home and why people who move here and discover our community also establish their roots. Simply put, St. Louis is a great place in which to live!

DR. JIM CRANE
Vice Chancellor • Washington University Medical School

University of Missouri-St. Louis

The University of Missouri-St. Louis is a dynamic, metropolitan institution of higher learning. With 15,000 students, 966 faculty members and more than 60,000 graduates, UM-St. Louis has, in just 40 years, taken its place among the great universities of the St. Louis area. With institutional accreditation by the North Central Association Commission on Accreditation and School Improvement and professional accreditation by 15 national academic associations, UM-St. Louis offers a quality education on par with its three sister institutions in the University of Missouri System. That quality is reflected in the success of its alumni, the recognition of its faculty and the growth of its campus.

UM-St. Louis is now the third-largest university in Missouri. The campus, located in northwest St. Louis County, has grown dramatically since its inception in 1963. From one building and 660 students, UM-St. Louis has developed into the vibrant public research university envisioned by its founders. It now encompasses 328 acres and more than 60 buildings. Among its facilities is the Millennium Student Center, a unique, 175,000-square-foot, three-story edifice that houses all student-related services. The newest addition to the campus is the 128,500-square-foot Performing Arts Center. This new performance venue includes a three-level, 1,600-seat performance hall, a 300-seat music and theater hall, a glass-enclosed, two-tiered atrium lobby with promenade, and state-of-the-art technical facilities for sound, lighting and set production.

UM-St. Louis provides quality teaching, research and service programs of national and international scope. It currently offers 47 undergraduate, 31 master's, one professional and 11 doctoral programs. These programs, along with their computer components and international elements, are designed to ensure that UM-St. Louis graduates are ready to compete in an increasingly global and technological world. The wide range of programs reflects the diverse needs of Missouri's largest community.

The University is proud of the diverse nature of its student body. More than 50 percent of UM-St. Louis students are non-traditional, meaning they are older than the typical 18- to 22-year-old student, and many hold full- or part-time jobs.

Sixty percent of UM-St. Louis' students are women. Twenty percent are minorities, and UM-St. Louis enrolls and graduates the largest number of African-American students of any university in the state.

The University also boasts an exceptional faculty. The 500 full-time faculty members who teach at UM-St. Louis hold advanced degrees from some of the world's most prestigious universities, and a large number of full-time faculty hold doctoral degrees.

Along with the international components being built into UM-St. Louis' curriculum, the University takes great pride in recognizing individuals who have contributed to the quality of life on a global scale. Its "Global Citizen Award" recognizes people who have effected positive change internationally and its World Ecology Medal goes to individuals who have made extraordinary contributions to conservation.

UM-St. Louis also is home to the Des Lee Collaborative Vision, a program linking 23 of the University's 32 endowed professorships to local arts, civic, cultural and educational institutions in a cooperative effort for the betterment of the St. Louis region.

UM-St. Louis is the largest supplier of college-educated workers in St. Louis. The University is constantly striving to improve its partnerships with area school districts, community organizations, and business and labor leaders to help St. Louis grow economically and socially.

The Millennium
Student Center

The St. Louis Mercantile Library at the University of Missouri-St. Louis

A GATEWAY TO THE IMAGINATION

Today, the Mercantile Library can look back on its heritage as the oldest library in continuing existence west of the Mississippi River. Founded in 1846 by philanthropic business leaders and wealthy citizens for the public good, the Mercantile became not only the city's first library, but also the town's first viable art museum, the town's first theater, an early college of sorts, and a home for the city's earliest scientific and other learned societies.

The Mercantile quickly evolved into a huge collection of books on every subject for the city — early universities used its law and medical book collections. Soldiers like the young William T. Sherman studied the tactics of Alexander and Napoleon in its stacks. Journalists such as Joseph Pulitzer read omnivorously in the library's holdings to learn the craft of writing. Authors like Kate Chopin, Sara Teasdale and Eugene Field studied the classics in the Mercantile's stacks. In the process the Mercantile Library's holdings kept enlarging, and today, the many lesser-known holdings — in art, manuscripts, photos and prints — make the collections a kind of bibliographic laboratory for the history of reading and learning in America.

The library was a great forum, an athenaeum, for the city. Its theater boasted many successful performances by Jenny Lind, Lola Montez and the earliest seasons of the world-famous St. Louis Symphony. The library's lecture hall welcomed Oscar Wilde, William Thackeray, Susan Anthony, Ralph Waldo Emerson and Herman Melville, as well as homegrown talents like Mark Twain. In serious times the library's halls rang with tumultuous speeches such as Sen. Thomas Hart Benton's exhortation on "Westward the Star of Empire" — an impassioned speech on the development of the transcontinental railroad. The library became a bulwark for the Union in the 1860s, a place where the Emancipation Proclamation was read and ratified by the Missouri Legislature. Clearly, the Mercantile Library has lived its share of great historical events.

Eventually the Mercantile decided that the time had come to make its collections even more accessible by affiliating with St. Louis' only publicly supported, land-grant institution of higher education, the University of Missouri-St. Louis. After nearly 150 years in the heart of downtown, the Mercantile moved to a young, vibrant college campus — one committed, just as the Mercantile was in its earliest days, to educating the young people of St. Louis for the future. The newest users of the Mercantile, along with scholars from across the nation and the world, are much like the earliest users of the library. They are young men and women bent on new careers, tempered with a deep respect for the traditions that the new St. Louis Mercantile Library at the University of Missouri-St. Louis preserves for present and future generations. It is a place where time and history can be imagined by everyone on a vast, engaging scale.

The St. Louis Mercantile Library c.1855

The St. Louis Mercantile Library/ Thomas Jefferson Library complex

City of O'Fallon

rtifacts sow the earth in O'Fallon with traces of the past. History rises from the ground in the remnants of a limestone chimney and courses down ancient waterways, 19th-century railroad lines and even modern interstates. The splendors of bygone eras accent the conveniences of the contemporary world in this thriving community. O'Fallon's City Hall is sheltered within the walls of a renovated historic structure and its premier commercial and residential development revolves around neighborhoods, including a walking community that resurrects the vitality of urban living.

Over its history, the O'Fallon area has served as a way station or as a home for countless individuals and families. Its natural beauty and easy access to transportation has lured people since the first humans moved to the area about 10,000 B.C.

ROLLING ON THE RIVER

Before I-70 roared through O'Fallon or the first locomotive chugged up to the sleepy little town, the area's creeks served as liquid highways to and from the Missouri and Mississippi rivers. The first American Indians arrived about the end of the ice age and discovered forests and prairies teaming with mastodons, mammoths and other game, and flourishing with plants for food and medicine. Waterways led to ancient trade routes, and chert, the raw material for sharp tools, provided a commodity as well as a local resource.

Many tribes were using the area as a common hunting ground when Spanish and French explorers laid claims to it in the 17th and 18th centuries. Although most of the early settlers were French, Spain controlled the area until 1800 then returned it to France under a secret treaty. Three years later, the United States acquired present-day Missouri from France as part of the Louisiana Purchase, and in 1812 St. Charles County was formed with an original western boundary of the Pacific Ocean.

Enticed by Spanish land grants and undeterred by the prospect of fighting Indians, Americans began moving into St. Charles County during the late 1790s. Most of these pioneers, including the Boone and Zumwalt families, hailed from Kentucky and followed the Mississippi River north to cross into St. Charles near the confluence of the Mississippi and Missouri rivers. The route allowed them to avoid fording the swiftly moving Missouri and to cross the Mississippi at a relatively shallow point.

Adam Zumwalt's biography, which his son wrote in 1880 at the age of 73, details that family's migration from Kentucky. Adam Zumwalt first hacked a large canoe from a poplar tree, loaded it with furniture and two copper stills, and made the trip. After clearing a site and building a cabin, he returned to Kentucky for the rest of his household. The Zumwalts and their hands, like many other

Fort Zumwalt (pictured here about 1890) sometimes sheltered as many as 10 families during the War of 1812.

Darius Heald (in the buggy) built Stony Point several hundred yards to the northeast of Fort Zumwalt, the home his family had occupied for at least 70 years.

pioneers, drove their livestock through dense forests and across waterways.

Moving to O'Fallon is much simpler today. About a 40 minute drive from St. Louis, Interstate 70 runs through the upper two-thirds of the city and Route 40/61, slated to become I-64, lies near the city's southern border.

SETTLING IN

Two of Adam Zumwalt's brothers, Christopher and Jacob, already were living in St. Charles County when the family arrived in 1800. Of the three siblings, each of whom was a Revolutionary War veteran and experienced Indian fighter, Jacob Zumwalt left the most enduring tangible evidence of their presence. O'Fallon's Fort Zumwalt Park encompasses a portion of the family's property, and the inside chimney of the Zumwalt home stands as a stark testament to the resilience of pioneers in the face of frontier perils. The spring that once quenched their thirsts now feeds a man-made lake.

Zumwalt built the Pennsylvania German-style cabin in 1798 of logs cut from white oak trees, and the structure probably was the first hewn-log house built north of the Missouri River. A stockade protected the spring and the large house at "Zumwalt's Fort," which could shelter as many as 10 families during Indian uprisings. The first Methodist sacrament celebrated in Missouri occurred at the fort.

While Jacob Zumwalt farmed, Adam Zumwalt distilled alcohol from grain ground at Christopher Zumwalt's grist mill on Peruque Creek. He targeted American Indians with his moonshine but they initially balked at buying his wares. Zumwalt won their trade, according to his biography, after drinking with them.

Adam Zumwalt's cordial association with the Indians hunting in the area, including the Sacs, Kickapoos and Winnebagoes, proved to be an asset. He helped James Wilkinson, governor of the Louisiana territory from 1805 to 1807, negotiate a treaty with those tribes and often mediated conflicts between Indians and settlers. However, the Indians' increasing concern over whites occupying the hunting grounds, fanned by the rhetoric of their leaders as well as the British, caused violence to erupt.

Stony Point in Fort Zumwalt Park, shown here after being struck by a tornado in 1915

Zumwalt's biography reports that Indians in 1811 attacked six hunters as they dressed a boar and also killed a family in their home. The attacks set the tone for the War of 1812, with the British paying their Indian allies for scalps in what historians often refer to as the "The Second War for Independence." During the conflict, the settlers banded together to tend crops and lived in the forts until a lull in the fighting would lure them back to their homesteads, where they would stay until the guerilla-style warfare resumed.

Britain's goal in waging war against the United States was to control the fur trade in the Midwest and north of the Ohio River and to disrupt American shipping. Lacking the forces to fight the war on their own, the British incited the American Indians to attack settlers, a move that bottled westward migration east of the Mississippi River. The Treaty of Ghent ended the war in 1814 but fighting between Indians and settlers continued for several months until the United States signed peace treaties in 1815 with several tribes in nearby Portage des Sioux.

The former St. Mary's Institute houses the O'Fallon Municipal Centre. *Photo by Ferman Carillo*

PASSING THROUGH, STAYING ON

The frontier called strongly. A steady stream of pioneers moved through the area during the next two decades and even some established residents left. In 1817 Jacob Zumwalt sold the family's plantation to Maj. Nathan Heald, a War of 1812 veteran, for $1,000 and moved west to Pike County, Missouri.

WingHaven offers a variety of new homes in 22 diverse neighborhoods.

O'Fallon welcomed the new millennium by dedicating a clock tower at the municipal center. *Photo by Ferman Carillo*

Heald added several buildings to the property before dying in 1832, including a loom house where slave women and children wove linsey-woolsey. Around 1890, the Heald family moved into Stony Point, a brick house they built within a stone's throw of the Zumwalt home. The city completed restoration of the Healds' two-story home in 2001.

Many pioneers simply passed through the Missouri River valley but the *Report on a Journey to the Western States of North America* prompted hundreds of German immigrants to settle there. Written by Gottfried Duden, who lived near the Boone family from 1824 to 1827, the book went as far as to provide guidelines for selecting home sites. The German immigrants brought money, knowledge of the mechanical arts, a strong work ethic and a distinct love of freedom with them. They profoundly impacted the area's history, beginning with two brothers, Arnold and Nicholas Krekel, who settled there in the early 1830s with their father and siblings.

Arnold Krekel, over time, held local and federal surveying positions, served as attorney for the city and county of St. Charles, and published a newspaper. Elected to the Missouri legislature in 1852, he left the Democratic Party before the Civil War because the group's pro-slavery tendencies offended him. Although he lived in St. Charles, Krekel invested in property in present-day O'Fallon.

In 1854 Krekel allowed the North Missouri Railroad to extend its line, which began in St. Louis, through his property to Peruque Creek and to put a depot at the "Krekel Addition," as his land was known. Two years later, Krekel renamed the station "O'Fallon" in honor of his friend, John O'Fallon, the railroad's president and well-known philanthropist.

However, it is his younger brother, Nicholas Krekel, who is recognized as O'Fallon's founder because in 1856 he built the first home within the city limits. Krekel, the city's first station agent and postmaster, lived upstairs and operated a store and post office on the ground floor of the building, which is now a daycare center.

BACKING THE STARS AND STRIPES

The Civil War lasted from 1861 to 1865 but the seeds of the conflict were sown over four previous decades of legislative battles beginning with the Missouri Compromise, which in 1821 granted Missouri statehood as a slave state.

The war's onset spurred both factions to attempt organizing militias in St. Charles County. Arnold Krekel commanded the Home Guard, a citizen militia of German immigrants loyal to the Union. The Cottleville-based

regiment, in which Nicholas Krekel also served, guarded the county against southern sympathizers and the Confederate Army. The members of "Krekel's Dutch," the popular name for the militia, opposed slavery despite having coexisted peacefully with their slave-owning neighbors before the war.

The militia protected the North Missouri Railroad, a major artery of trade and passenger service that Gen. Sterling Price had targeted for destruction. At least one blockhouse was built near the vulnerable railroad trestle spanning Peruque Creek, and escaped slaves sometimes joined the forces encamped there.

After the war, Arnold Krekel served as president of the Missouri Constitutional Convention and thus signed the state's ordinance emancipating the slaves. Krekel, whom President Lincoln appointed as a U.S. District Court Judge, then co-founded the Lincoln Institute for Negroes. Located in Jefferson City, the school provided postsecondary education for black students.

The last known former slave in the O'Fallon area died in 1927.

LIVING IN PEACE, SERVING IN WAR

At the behest of 107 householders, O'Fallon in 1912 officially became a fourth-class city governed by a board of alderman, elected by ward, and a mayor, elected at large. Within a year, the city had posted signs restricting car speeds to 8 miles per hour inside its limits.

Fred Jacoby, who brought telephone service to O'Fallon in 1900, was the city's first mayor, but Mayor Paul Westhoff, who served three non-consecutive terms touching four decades, was perhaps the city's most popular leader. At his first meeting in 1939, Westhoff launched an era of progress and expansion when he broke a tie vote to construct O'Fallon's water and sewer systems. The sewer

O'Fallon celebrated its centennial in 1956 with a parade and festival.

project was a controversial issue due, in part, to the Works Progress Administration's involvement in it. Although many of O'Fallon's neighboring communities considered similar WPA projects, most declined the opportunity.

O'Fallon residents fought in World War I and bought Liberty Bonds at home, but the entire city was involved in World War II due to the proximity of the Weldon Springs Ordnance Works. The largest of its kind, the munitions plant occupied 17,239 acres and was capable of producing 1 million tons of TNT daily. So many residents worked at the plant that Highway K was constructed from O'Fallon to Weldon Springs. Initially a dirt road, the highway is now one of the city's major arteries.

In 1942 the army conducted a "test" blackout of O'Fallon in preparation for the unlikely event that Germany would try to bomb the plant, strategically located near the center of the United States. Weldon Springs closed after the war but cleanup of TNT pollution and later contamination from a uranium processing plant on the site continued into the 21st century.

When the city celebrated its 1956 centennial, the population was estimated at 1,327. Around that same time, Interstate 70 hit town and suddenly O'Fallon offered country living within a reasonable commute to jobs across the Missouri River. The highway's impact rivaled that of the railroad but along with the potential for growth, I-70 also brought obstacles to development.

For the first 30 years, only Highway K, a dangerous two-lane roadway, passed underneath the interstate and provided access to it. The situation prompted the city in the mid-1980s to lend money to the Missouri Department of Transportation to accelerate the planned widening and extension of Highway K. By 2001 five I-70 interchanges and two overpasses served the city.

Many of the buildings in this early shot of Main Street no longer exist.

DRIVING GROWTH

The 1960s saw a new migration of residents to O'Fallon, a population trend that continues through the present day. Originally one square mile, the city in 2001 encompassed 26 square miles and claimed about 52,000 residents, up from 8,677 in 1980. As the fastest-growing city in the state's fastest-growing county, O'Fallon officials predicted the city's population would top out at between 75,000 and 80,000 in 2006 and anticipated it could go higher if neighboring areas requested annexation. If the estimate proved correct, O'Fallon would be second only to St. Louis City in population in the region.

The sewer system came to the fore again during the term of Mayor George Mussman, who served from 1977 to 1983. Mussman understood that local control of sewers was critical to managing growth and obtained federal money to develop the O'Fallon Sewer District. The move gave the city leverage in dealing with developers because it has no obligation to provide sewer service outside of city limits.

Mayor Paul Renaud, who began his term in 1995, also tackled infrastructure issues, including road and overpass construction. Additionally, under Renaud's leadership, the city improved parks and developed more recreational opportunities for families.

O'Fallon has about 600 acres of parkland. Civic Park, used since the early 1900s, is located on 40 acres within the original Krekel Addition and offers an aquatic center with two swimming pools, Civic Hall and the O'Fallon Historical Society Museum, which is housed in a log cabin that the society saved from demolition as its 1976 bicentennial project. Among other features, Fort Zumwalt Park has 48 wooded acres and a fishing lake. Schulte Park is a small green space and Dames Park provides a football facility.

The O'Fallon Cultural Arts Center is housed in the city's historic train depot.

The 93-acre O'Fallon Sports Park opened in 1998 with soccer fields for adults and young people. A year later, the Ozzie Smith Sports Complex debuted in the existing 135-acre Paul A. Westhoff Park and offers the T.R. Hughes Ballpark, home to the minor league River City Rascals.

LEARNING, WORSHIPING AND WORKING

Three AAA-rated school districts serve O'Fallon: Fort Zumwalt, which covers approximately 75 percent of the city; Francis Howell; and Wentzville R-4. Three parochial schools and over 30 churches are scattered throughout the community. Two branches of the St. Charles City-County library system operate there. The community supports several fire districts including the O'Fallon Fire Department, the offshoot of the city's original small volunteer fire department, which operated on donations from 1906 to 1970.

About 800 companies are located in O'Fallon. Among them are major corporations and significant employers such as MEMC, PPG Industries, Lear Corporation, True Manufacturing and Wainwright Industries, Inc.

MasterCard's Global Technology and Operations Center is one of the businesses located at WingHaven, a mixed-use community that was planned by a team of city personnel, designers and developers. The completed development, with a projected value of $750 million, is expected to employ about 9,000 people in 4.6 million square feet of commercial space and to provide 2,000 apartments, condominiums and houses — with prices ranging from $70,000 to $750,000 — in 22 diverse

neighborhoods, including a walking community. Among WingHaven's amenities are an 18-hole Nicklaus Design golf course and country club, 500 acres of permanent green space and a state-of-the-art communications infrastructure. The project is slated for completion by 2003, five years ahead of schedule.

MasterCard previously was located in St. Louis County and had considered leaving the region before discovering WingHaven. Mayor Renaud spearheaded the effort to secure the facility for O'Fallon. However, other municipal and state officials, the Regional Chamber and Growth Association, and school districts all played key roles in persuading this major employer to stay in the region.

MARRYING TRADITION AND VISION

The past mingles with the present to create the future in O'Fallon, and nowhere is that more apparent than the place in which the city conducts business. The city purchased and renovated the former St. Mary's Institute, which the Sisters of the Adoration of the Most Precious Blood built after establishing a motherhouse in O'Fallon in 1875. The 100,000-square-foot municipal complex consists of three buildings: the novitiate dating from 1930, another structure built about 1950 and the original junior college dating from 1960s. Over time, the complex has housed a Catholic girls' high school and two colleges. The sisters, a teaching order, have staffed Assumption School in O'Fallon as well as a number of other Catholic schools in St. Charles and St. Louis

The T.R. Hughes Ballpark is home to the minor league River City Rascals.

counties. The *St. Louis Business Journal* in 2000 honored the city with a Laclede Award in recognition of the work environment it created in the municipal complex.

The city's emphasis on preserving the past for future generations also reflects in its renovation and ownership of other historic structures. The train depot (c. 1920s), now the city's Cultural Arts Center, and the Westhoff Mercantile (c. 1870), now McGurk's Public House, are two of the buildings the city has saved from the wrecking ball.

In 2001 O'Fallon became the first city in Missouri to be designated as a City of Character by the International Association of Character Cities. O'Fallon's participation in the program reflects its commitment to high standards and values as well as its intention to promote positive character traits throughout the city.

Since frontier times, O'Fallon-area residents and leaders have embraced goals that initially seemed difficult to attain. They cleared the forest for farming. They protected a critical wartime supply line. They attracted a minor league ball team and they kept a major corporation in the region. Insightful decisions made both in the past and in the present are allowing O'Fallon to embrace growth and to avoid many of the pitfalls that often accompany rapid development.

Before recorded history, the first American Indians discovered a paradise in the O'Fallon area that supplied their every need. Today's residents are finding that O'Fallon fulfills their dreams as well. Once a small farming community, this full-service city now offers a wide selection of housing, numerous job opportunities and a bright future to those who call it home.

O'Fallon's first home, which Nicholas Krekel built in 1856, still stands.

BJC HealthCare

*M*assive changes forecast for the U.S. health care industry during the late 1980s galvanized St. Louis' multiple independent hospitals to adopt new ways of providing patient care. For the visionary leaders behind the development of BJC HealthCare, the pathway to success was clear: gain strength through unity and together continue to create healthy futures for the people of St. Louis and surrounding regions.

The 13 hospitals, five skilled nursing facilities and other community health locations that make up today's BJC HealthCare deliver a full range of health care services to rural, urban and suburban communities primarily in the greater St. Louis, southern Illinois and mid-Missouri regions. BJC's services also include behavioral health, dental care, corporate health services, home care, long-term care and hospice. Through its international health care program, BJC reaches out to the global community with physician exchanges, consulting and medical

BJC HealthCare facilities include 13 hospitals, five skilled nursing facilities and other community health locations in rural, urban and suburban communities in the greater St. Louis, southern Illinois and mid-Missouri regions. Professional Office Building D at Missouri Baptist Medical Center houses advanced clinical services and programs such as the Missouri Baptist Heart Center, the Breast HealthCare Center and an open MRI. *Photo by Elizabeth White*

care. BJC also provides more care to the poor and uninsured than any other hospital or health care organization in Missouri.

BJC is the largest health care provider in the St. Louis area, and in 2001, *Modern Healthcare* ranked the organization the sixth-largest not-for-profit health care organization in the United States. That same year, the *St. Louis Business Journal* ranked BJC, which has 26,038 employees and 3,870 physicians, as the metropolitan area's largest employer. In 2000 BJC reported $2.1 billion in net revenues, 135,866 hospital admissions, 1,757,520 outpatient visits, 279,451 home health visits and 360,089 emergency department visits.

BJC traces its roots to 1993, with the merger of Barnes Hospital and Jewish Hospital of St. Louis with Christian Health Services, which operated seven hospitals in Missouri and Illinois. Each of these medical facilities was highly successful at the time of the merger. However, reductions in Medicare and Medicaid reimbursements, an oversupply of hospital beds in the region and other issues seemed to threaten their long-term viability. By uniting, Barnes, Jewish and Christian — founded in 1914, 1902 and 1903 respectively — could sustain their long-standing reputations for excellence in medical treatment and care while maximizing efficiency and reducing costs.

In 1994 two more outstanding medical institutions joined BJC. Missouri Baptist Medical Center, founded in 1913, gave the organization an expanded presence in west St. Louis County as well as a hospital in Sullivan, Missouri. St. Louis Children's Hospital, established in 1879, enriched BJC with a premier facility for the care of children.

Other hospitals that are part of BJC HealthCare are Barnes-Jewish West County Hospital, Barnes-Jewish St. Peters Hospital, Alton Memorial Hospital and Parkland Health Center. Boone Hospital Center and Fayette County Hospital are leased by BJC; Clay County Hospital is managed by BJC. The Rehabilitation Institute of St. Louis is a partnership with HealthSouth Corporation.

Two of BJC's hospitals, Barnes-Jewish Hospital and St. Louis Children's Hospital, have formal affiliations with the Washington University School of Medicine, which is consistently ranked among the top five medical schools in the country. The School of Medicine, founded in 1891, is known internationally for research in neuroscience, genetics, diabetes, cardiovascular disease and other areas. It has contributed to many groundbreaking discoveries and has been associated with 17 Nobel Laureates.

Barnes-Jewish Hospital and St. Louis Children's Hospital rank among the most highly regarded academic medical centers in the nation. BJC is one of the leading supporters of health care education in the region. In 2000 BJC's hospitals and service organizations assisted in the training of 1,530 future doctors and 753 future nurses and allied health professionals.

U.S. News & World Report ranked Barnes-Jewish Hospital among the top 10 U.S. hospitals in its 2001 survey of "America's Best Hospitals." The ranking marked the ninth consecutive time Barnes-Jewish has appeared on the list.

Barnes-Jewish and Children's hospitals have anchored the city's Central West End with a medical complex since

Caring professionals throughout BJC HealthCare provide a full range of health care services to children and adults both at the hospital and in the community.
Photo by Tim Mudrovic

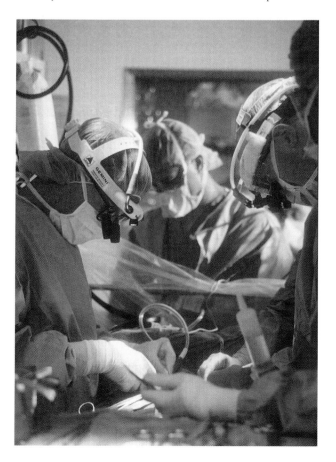

1927. A $320 million renovation and expansion, completed in 2001, brought significant improvements to the campus, including the consolidation of outpatient care in the Center for Advanced Medicine, the Charles F. Knight Emergency and Trauma Center, and the Alvin J. Siteman Cancer Center, a National Cancer Institute-designated treatment and research facility.

Another construction project completed that year was the region's first free-standing rehabilitation hospital. BJC partnered with HealthSouth Corp. to construct The Rehabilitation Institute of St. Louis, a new state-of-the-art facility offering the latest rehabilitation therapy following surgery, trauma or disease. In addition to offering acute inpatient, outpatient and community rehabilitation services, the Institute provides a research setting for physicians affiliated with BJC and Washington University School of Medicine.

Community outreach plays a vital role in BJC's commitment to meeting the health needs of patients throughout the region. The organization annually attracts about 94,000 people to more than 1,200 events, such as health fairs and screenings. BJC sponsors 1,432 youth programs, including immunizations and check-ups, and partners with schools in developing curricula and educational programs.

BJC also offers a continuum of care to older adults through retirement communities and long-term care facilities. The OASIS/BJC Plus Program, which has more than 111,000 members, offers educational and volunteer opportunities and other assistance to senior citizens.

BJC helps people realize the possibilities of a healthy future.

BJC HealthCare's hospitals, physicians and health care providers are recognized as among the best in the region, the nation and the world. International exchanges provide physicians from other countries an opportunity to learn new techniques and utilize advanced technology to care for patients.
Photo by Steve Frazier

Girl Scout Council of Greater St. Louis

*W*here Girls Grow Strong — the tagline introduced by the Girl Scouts in 1999 — clearly characterizes the continuing history of the Girl Scout Council of Greater St. Louis. Its members not only benefit from a broad spectrum of programs that prepare them for tomorrow's world, they also develop the confidence and aspiration to become productive leaders in that realm. Sprouting with one troop of 11 St. Louis girls in 1918, it has grown to list over 50,000 members served by more than 15,000 valuable adult volunteers at the dawn of this new century. The council's jurisdiction envelops 12 adjoining Missouri counties in addition to the city of St. Louis.

Troop 1 of what was originally called the St. Louis Girl Scout Council was organized by Mrs. George Bishop only six years after Juliette Gordon Low founded the Girl Scouts in the United States in 1912. In the inherent Girl Scout spirit of doing a good turn daily, that first group made baby clothes for infants in City Hospital. Several other troops joined the council in 1918, one year before women in the United States obtained the right to vote.

The 1920s brought significant milestones that defined the spirit of the budding organization. Expanding to an area-wide council by including St. Louis County in 1922, the council then received its first charter from the national organization. During those early years the girls started dressing dolls for display and to donate to area children at Christmas. The group acquired the first of its own camps, Camp Cedarledge near Pevely, Missouri, in 1926. Then, in 1928, under the sponsorship of Sumner High School — the first black high school west of the Mississippi — Mrs. Cleotta M.M. Spotts organized Troop A, the first Negro Girl Scout troop to join the council.

During the Depression years that followed, the girls broadened their experience by offering their sewing skills to the local Red Cross. Expanding the range of the girls' learning activities, the first Missouri mariner troop — specifically for girls interested in waterfront sports and recreation — formed in St. Louis in 1937. Though the girls sold homemade cookies earlier that decade to fund activities, they held the first councilwide sale of commercially baked cookies in 1939, selling them for 25 cents a package.

World War II presented ample opportunities for meaningful activities, and the girls contributed to many war-effort projects, including planting victory gardens and selling war bonds. They also conducted drives for much-needed scrap materials. Enhancing its membership diversity in the mid-40s, the council held its first resident camp for the handicapped and its first Catholic Girl Scout interracial communion. Already incorporated as a not-for-profit organization in Missouri by 1948, the group then changed to its current name — the Girl Scout Council of Greater St. Louis (GSCGSL).

In the 1950s, a period of emerging racial equality, the council added Washington, St. Francois, St. Genevieve, Iron, Madison and Jefferson counties to its boundaries. Camp Cedarledge was expanded and a second camp in Gray Summit, Missouri, was established — Camp Fiddlecreek. In 1966 a third camp was added to accommodate its increasing membership — Camp Tuckaho near Troy, Missouri. The next year the GSCGSL boasted the highest member-count in the nation, reaching almost 40,000. Further augmenting its numbers in 1968, it welcomed St. Charles, Crawford, Franklin, Reynolds, Lincoln and Warren county girls to its membership.

Serving its area members from a downtown St. Louis office at the time, the council determined a need to reach the girls in its outlying areas, and in 1977 it introduced the Rural Resource Van. Due to its success in delivering program materials and supplies to local volunteers, the van was later replaced with a motor home in the mid-80s. Today called the G.S. EXPRESS, it is now a 35-foot mobile resource center/shopping unit that travels throughout the council domain.

The 1980s introduced a council calendar and new ideas to further diversify its programs and activities. Introducing the Double Dutch rope jumping sport, which eventually resulted in annual spring tournaments, it also initiated Galaxy of Fun, a series of programs for girls from urban settings. The council launched Classroom Scouting in cooperation with the Boy Scouts in 1986. This in-school program provides opportunities for children with disabilities to learn the principles and values of Girl Scouting, as well as earn badges and attend an annual day camp called Adventure Days.

Early in the 90s the council supported recent immigrants into the United States by organizing a program to help girls new to the country and to Girl Scouting transcend cultural barriers. In 1996, Theresa E. Loveless, an organization veteran of 25 years at that time, became the council's first African American executive director. Under

In 1952, members of Troop 317, the first African American troop in St. Louis to take an international trip, prepare for their trip to Bermuda — the result of two years of work and planning under troop leader Lula Ward Vaughn's guidance.

her direction the council formed its first Girl Scouts Beyond Bars troop. Designed for girls with mothers confined at a correctional center, it gives incarcerated women and their daughters an opportunity to share positive experiences in the safe, supportive environment of a Girl Scout troop meeting. That same year the council published A Rich Yesterday, a Bright Tomorrow, a treasured history of its diversity. Plus, it instituted its first annual Urban Campout, a successful fund-raising gala that annually raises funds for membership outreach programs.

Ever adapting to the changing times with new uniforms as well as programs, the GSCGSL launched Project Anti-Violence Education (PAVE) in late 2000. Developed to help girls avert violence in their lives, the program works through community institutions.

The GSCGSL gets its funding from a number of sources — its cookie and other product sales being the largest. A United Way beneficiary, it also obtains contributions from many individuals and a variety of organizations. The council is working on diversifying its funding sources by developing programs such as the Juliette Low Society (JLS). Established in 1998, JLS membership starts at $1,000 a year and provides special events for members.

With strength in the talents and dedication of its volunteers, the enthusiasm of its large girl membership, and the creativity and innovation of its staff, the Girl Scout Council of Greater St. Louis is a recognized premier organization for girls and young women in the region.

Girl Scouts concluded the "Celebrate 2000: Celebrate Girl Scouting" event in Forest Park on October 20, 2000, with a giant friendship circle.

Landmarks Association of St. Louis, Inc.

An overview of the Cupples Warehouse district
Photo by Robert C. Pettus

equeathed with a wealth of historically and architecturally significant buildings in the time-honored downtown area and in neighborhoods formed in the 19th and 20th centuries, St. Louis owes the conservation and adaptive reuse of much of that inheritance to Landmarks Association of St. Louis, Inc. The history of this private, not-for-profit organization dates back to the late 1950s, a period in American history when venerable structures fell victim to clearance programs and federally financed interstate highways indiscriminately carved paths through established communities. Countrywide discontent brought the National Preservation Act of 1966, a sweeping shift in federal policy that called for an expansion of the National Register of Historic Places to include sites of state and local significance. It also established a review process for federally funded projects.

Incorporating in 1959, Landmarks' founders imparted an unusually broad mission statement that continues to guide the organization well into the 21st century: to preserve, enhance and promote St. Louis' architectural heritage and to encourage sound planning and excellence in contemporary design. Important victories from Landmarks' early years include preservation of the Bissell Mansion and Red Water Tower in Hyde Park, the Chatillon-DeMenil House in Benton Park along with the Wainwright Building and Old Post Office downtown. But in spite of many accomplishments, preservation was seldom considered in context or included in the planning process by government officials. Landmarks embarked on

an ambitious citywide survey to identify important sites and potential historic districts.

With no full-time staff until 1975, Landmarks relied upon a cadre of dedicated volunteers led in large part by long-term President Gerhardt Kramer and architect W. Philip Cotton Jr., who directed the production of a newsletter and devised special events and tours. The pace heightened as the late 1970s brought the first federal tax breaks for renovating historic properties. Listing on the National Register of Historic Places became a financial incentive. Landmarks' small staff — now motivated by Carolyn Toft, executive director for over 25 years — methodically researched, photographed and nominated scores of single sites and districts to the National Register.

By the mid-1980s, St. Louis led the country in historic tax credit reinvestment. Passage of the Tax Reform Act of 1986 severely reduced the number of projects until the state of Missouri passed its complementary historic rehab tax credit program in 1997. Landmarks played a key role in this remarkable collaborative effort, supported and signed by the late Gov. Mel Carnahan. High-profile rescues resulting from this legislation include the Drury Plaza Hotel, encompassing the partly demolished Fur Exchange building; the Westin Hotel, an adaptive reuse of Cupples Station; and the Sheraton St. Louis City Center, ingeniously inserted in the former Edison Brothers (originally J. C. Penney) Warehouse. Without tax

The Chatillon-DeMenil Mansion

credits, these three sites would now be surface parking lots. Not only do such undertakings sustain the city's aesthetic eminence, they demonstrate that rehabilitation creates more jobs than new construction, contributing to the local economy.

Surveys and National Register nominations prepared by Landmarks' staff have also provided essential background for more user-friendly publications including the organization's bimonthly newsletter and series of guidebooks. The most popular, *St. Louis: Landmarks & Historic Districts*, first published in 1988 and reprinted twice, was revised in a greatly expanded version in 2001. That same year Landmarks released the third in its series of multilingual cultural tourism pieces based on public transit. Designed to encourage international tourism and to introduce recent immigrants to easily reached attractions, the full-color brochures were funded in part by the Regional Arts Commission, the Whitaker Foundation and the Gateway Foundation.

In 1991 Landmarks created "What Are Buildings Made Of?" (WABMO) to introduce the built environment to tomorrow's leaders. An acclaimed heritage education program supported since its inception by the Regional Arts Commission, WABMO involves fourth-grade children and their teachers in an unfamiliar downtown setting. Lessons learned travel back to the neighborhoods and schools.

Bohemian Hill near old City Hospital and Lafayette Square is a very different initiative. Designed to demonstrate that good contemporary design can fit comfortably in historic contexts, this effort started in 1999 with Landmarks' supervision of a graduate school studio at Washington University's School of Architecture. Since expanded into a partnership with Youth Education and Health in Soulard's (YEHS) YouthBuild, the Bohemian Hill project realized the construction of three new houses by mid-2001 with a fourth, an accessible courtyard model, in the planning stage. Much of the work was accomplished by at-risk youth whose program combines experience in the building trades with high school equivalency education.

"Raise the Roof" ceremonies at Bohemian Hill complete with a wood model of the new homes, the YouthBuild construction crew and St. Louis Comptroller Darlene Green

Throughout the year Landmarks offers tours and lectures designed to provoke public discussion and arouse interest in local heritage. A flurry of Historic Preservation Week events each May includes a ceremony honoring St. Louis' 11 Most Enhanced Sites. Inaugurated in 1996 to balance the organization's annual compilation of the city's 11 most threatened landmarks, the list of enhanced properties runs the gamut from those privately financed to those requiring every possible public resource. Projects recognized in 2001 ranged in age from an elegant pre-Civil War townhouse to an abandoned 1940 A & P food store and the new addition to the 1920s Central Institute for the Deaf complex — an exemplar of new architecture designed to complement rather than mimic adjacent historic property. The combined investment of all 11 schemes totaled $123 million.

Operating with a handful of paid employees from an office in the heart of downtown St. Louis, Landmarks draws much of its strength from a broad-based membership. The more than 1,500 regional citizens paying dues include architects, attorneys, developers, consultants, historians, neighborhood leaders, bankers and community volunteers who contribute expertise and participate as advocates. Over the years they have encouraged and supported Landmarks, even in the face of great controversy. That is probably the legacy envisioned in 1962 by one of the founders who wrote: "We must encourage continued use and creative adaptation of existing buildings and districts. But it is a mistake to insist that there must be an economic income returned by all buildings. Preservation is often self-justifying on purely cultural terms."

The Lutheran Church ~ Missouri Synod

*F*irmly sustaining the doctrines set forth by Martin Luther, the German monk whose efforts to reform the Church initiated the Protestant movement in the 16th century, The Lutheran Church — Missouri Synod (LCMS) proceeds into the 21st century with purpose and resolve. Formed in the United States by German immigrants in 1847, the denomination has made the most of opportunities and weathered many challenges over time, reaching a membership of 2.6 million baptized members by May 2001. Today, the LCMS serves its worldwide body from its International Center in St. Louis County.

The taproot of the Missouri Synod grew from a group of orthodox Lutherans who fled their native Saxony in Prussia after King Friedrich Wilhelm III, in 1830, decreed a uniform evangelical worship service for all Lutheran and Reformed churches. Seeking the freedom to practice their founder's teachings, they left their home and came to America. The 750 faithful surviving the voyage landed in New Orleans in 1838 and traveled up the Mississippi River, some settling in Perry County, Missouri, and others in St. Louis. In these places they observed and taught the historic Lutheran faith as set forth in the Bible and the Lutheran Confessions, which they maintained to be the true exposition of the Holy Scriptures.

In 1844, a German language periodical, *Der Lutheraner*, edited by one of the Saxon immigrants, circulated among like groups in other states who came to America in search of land or religious freedom or both, acquainting them with each other. Uniting at a convention in 1847, they established the church group of 12 congregations as The German Evangelical Lutheran Synod of Missouri, Ohio and Other States.

The new organization flourished as more German immigrants arrived, often greeted by Missouri Synod Lutherans at the boat docks. A seminary for training pastors and teachers, first established in Perry County, relocated to St. Louis in 1849 and became Concordia Seminary. Another ministry, Concordia Publishing House, established in St. Louis in 1869, is the LCMS publishing arm and currently the nation's fourth-largest Protestant publisher.

Toward the close of the 19th century, the Synod produced an English language periodical, *The Lutheran Witness*, now the denomination's official monthly publication. English became the accepted language, and the group eliminated the word German from its name in 1917. By 1947 it was simply The Lutheran Church — Missouri Synod.

Accepting new technology as a gift from God to spread its beliefs, the LCMS founded KFUO-AM, now the world's oldest continuously operating religious radio station, airing "The Lutheran Hour" since 1930. Its sister station, KFUO-FM, known as "Classic 99," was named America's "classical music station of the year" in 2000 by the National Association of Broadcasters. The Synod also produced the widely acclaimed and longest-running dramatic series in television history, "This is the Life."

Into the 1900s the LCMS steadily increased its membership, owing much of its ministry effectiveness to the devoted efforts of its auxiliary groups: the International Lutheran Laymen's League, producers of "The

Rev. Dr. Gerald B. Kieschnick, president of the 2.6 million-member Lutheran Church — Missouri Synod, offers a handshake after the installation of an assistant. Kieschnick is the 12th man to head the 154-year-old denomination.
Photo by Tim Parker

Lutheran Hour," and the Lutheran Women's Missionary League, organized in 1942. Long before diversity became a catchword, the LCMS eagerly gathered followers from all races and cultures. The church paid special attention to the needs of people with physical impairments.

The 1970s brought the threat of a schism that tested the convictions of LCMS members. The St. Louis seminary's board of control suspended its Concordia president for sanctioning teachings then gaining popularity with other Lutheran groups: questioning the Bible's inerrancy and infallibility and the role of the Lutheran Confessions. This resulted in the walkout of almost all of the school's faculty and many of its students. Ultimately the seminary survived the ordeal with its Biblical principles intact. By 2001 Concordia replenished its student body and faculty to a number equaling that prior to this highly publicized episode.

The following years delivered other trials for the LCMS. Throughout the 1990s it stood firm with its disavowal of any wrongdoing when KFUO was taken to court on employment discrimination charges. In a landmark decision with far-reaching implications on issues of religious freedom, the church and the radio station prevailed, gaining total vindication after a decade of legal struggles.

Toward the close of the 20th century, the ecumenical movement of Christian churches further separated the LCMS from other Lutheran denominations. The Synod's doctrinal positions made it unacceptable to relax or revise those beliefs to accommodate modern societal trends. While other Lutherans joined in fellowship with many Christian churches, the LCMS chose to remain

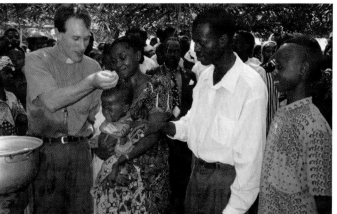

From sweet potato stew to baptismal font.... Rev. Daniel Ramsey, an LCMS missionary in Cote d'Ivoire (Ivory Coast), West Africa, baptizes one of the local children from a cooking pot. He and his wife, Suzanne, are among more than 400 missionaries serving The Lutheran Church — Missouri Synod in some 40 countries worldwide. *Photo by LCMS World Mission*

independent rather than simply "agreeing to disagree" on key matters without reaching full accord. Its centuries-old tradition requires commitment to the message of eternal salvation by grace alone, through faith alone, based on Scripture alone.

The LCMS cannot compromise its position on major moral and religious issues facing today's world. It does not condone abortion or homosexuality. Although women hold many prominent positions in the organization, its Biblical understanding disallows them as clergy.

Despite its positions that some view as unbending, the LCMS not only survives in today's frantic environment, it thrives. After directing its main operations from several downtown St. Louis locations, it christened its beautiful International Center (IC) building in St. Louis County in 1982, adding the north wing in 1988. Further expanding to house the Lutheran Church Extension Fund and LCMS Foundation, it later acquired a building across Interstate 44 that one can easily view from the magnificent three-story-tall glass-panel window in the IC chapel.

From these offices the LCMS upholds its convictions and preserves its solid financial endeavors. Its elementary and secondary schools constitute the largest Protestant school system in North America. Ten LCMS colleges and universities span the United States, along with the church body's highly regarded seminaries in St. Louis and Fort Wayne, Indiana. The Synod, the ninth-largest Christian denomination in America, comprises more than 6,100 congregations and 150 social-ministry organizations and supports missionaries in 40 countries. It uses its pulpits, schools and contemporary communications to radiate the timeless message of the Gospel reasserted by its founder, the Great Reformer, Luther. Its foundation is its strength.

Concordia Seminary, St. Louis, is one of 12 seminaries and universities owned and operated by The Lutheran Church — Missouri Synod. Since its inception in 1839, Concordia, St. Louis, has provided theological education and leadership training to more than 10,000 professional workers in the church. *Photo by Concordia Seminary, St. Louis*

Maryville University of Saint Louis

For almost 130 years, the name Maryville has been synonymous in the St. Louis area with education rooted in Judeo-Christian ethics and values that prepare students to be intellectually sound and vital members of their communities.

Today, Maryville, an independent coeducational university with its main campus in West County, offers more than 50 undergraduate and graduate programs. While wide ranging in content, all programs are grounded in the liberal arts tradition that has continued to be the linchpin of Maryville's existence through the years.

The Maryville Experience began in 1872 on the corner of Meramec and Nebraska in south St. Louis, when the Religious of the Sacred Heart order of nuns opened a boarding school for 80 young women. There also was a free school for underprivileged children, some 70 in number, and a novitiate for 11 young ladies who had chosen the religious order as their vocation. Just one year later, the first degrees were conferred. At that time, the plan of studies was the six-year French Lycee pattern, where the two highest classes were the equivalent of junior college work today.

Before moving to West County in 1961, Maryville, then a college, was located at Meramec and Nebraska in south St. Louis. Maryville University's 130-acre campus at Highway 40 and Woods Mill Road sits at what is now the population center of the St. Louis metropolitan area.

The 1920s proved to be a pivotal decade in Maryville's long and storied history. In 1921 the institution officially became a junior college with the state of Missouri fully accrediting its two higher classes and the lower classes becoming known as academy classes. The following year, 1922, marked Maryville's 50th anniversary and also saw the construction of a gymnasium, made possible through a gift of the alumnae. In 1923 Maryville became a full four-year college. Two years later, the first bachelor's degrees were granted at its first college graduation ceremony. Also during 1925, Maryville, along with Webster and Fontbonne colleges, became a corporate college of St. Louis University in order to be accredited by the North Central Association of Colleges and Secondary Schools. The decade ended with Maryville College and its Academy separating in 1929, with Academy classes moving to Villa Duchesne.

Maryville received its first president in 1937, with the appointment of Sister Odeide Mouton, who would serve in that post for the next 19 years. A residence hall on Maryville's campus now bears her name. In 1939 Sister Marion Bascom, a 1935 Maryville graduate, established the college's first honors program. Today, the Bascom Honors Program challenges Maryville's academically gifted students to expand their horizons through seminars and other special activities that promote critical thinking, analysis and debate.

In 1941 Maryville received independent accreditation from the North Central Association. The first year of the 1950s brought significant changes to the college's appearance, as Duchesne Hall was dedicated. It contained a student lounge, dining room, faculty room and theater. But 1957 brought the news that altered the course of Maryville's history forever. In that year came the decision by college officials to leave South St. Louis for a new home in West County. Alumnae spearheaded a $1 million campaign to fund the move.

On April 23, 1961, Cardinal Joseph Ritter dedicated the new Maryville campus in West County, located off of Highway 40. In May of that year, the last commencement, with 64 graduates, was held at the Meramec and Nebraska campus. The college president at the time was Sister Mary Blish, a 1949 Maryville graduate who was the youngest college president in the country when she was appointed in 1960.

1968 was a watershed year at Maryville, as it was in that year that the decision was made to make the college co-ed. An equally significant decision was made in 1972, Maryville's centennial year, when ownership of the college was transferred from the Religious of the Sacred Heart to a lay board of trustees. In 1977, Dr. Claudius Pritchard became Maryville's first lay president.

The 1980s started in a big way as two new buildings were added to campus: The John E. and Adaline Simon Athletic and Recreation Center and the Charles M. Huttig Memorial Chapel. In 1981, Maryville's under-graduate education programs were accredited by the National Council for the Accreditation of Teacher Education. Over the past 20 years, the School of Education has grown into one of the most respected teacher education schools in the nation.

Also in 1981, Maryville made history by launching Weekend College. For the first time, St. Louis-area working adults could complete entire degree programs solely on the weekends. In 1983, ground was broken for the first building in Maryville Centre, a sprawling business complex adjacent to the college. Through the years, Maryville and Maryville Centre have formed numerous partnerships that have mutually benefited Maryville students and the Centre's corporate clients.

The remainder of the 1980s proved to be a period of growth as more academic programs were added and new buildings, including a University Library, were constructed, along with athletic fields. This spurt of expansion

In 1997 Maryville University launched Building for Leadership, a $26.5 million capital campaign that led to construction of the Art and Design Building, the Anheuser-Busch Academic Center (pictured), the University Auditorium and the University Center.

resulted in Maryville College becoming Maryville University on June 1, 1991. The following year, Keith Lovin was named Maryville's eighth president, a position he still holds today.

In 1993, reflecting its change to University status, Maryville was reorganized into four academic units: the College of Arts and Sciences, the John E. Simon School of Business, the School of Education and the School of Health Professions. In 2000 the College of Arts and Sciences was renamed the School of Liberal Arts and Professional Programs, symbolizing Maryville's commit-ment to meet the changing academic and career needs of its student population.

In 1997, Maryville launched its most ambitious fund-raising program to date. Building for Leadership was a $26.5 million capital campaign established to fund building construction and program enhancements. This campaign produced four new buildings: the Art and Design Building, which opened in 1998; the Anheuser-Busch Academic Center, which also opened in 1998; a 450-seat University Auditorium, which opened in 2001; and the University Center, which houses the bookstore and snack bar, as well as office space for student organizations, and study and recreation areas. The University Center also opened in 2001.

These new structures represent, in a very tangible way, Maryville University's ongoing commitment to meet the needs of its students and to make the "Maryville Experience" a satisfying and fulfilling experience for each person who steps onto the Maryville campus.

Recognizing the special needs of working adults, Maryville University introduced the St. Louis region's first Weekend College in 1981 and continues to offer the widest selection of evening and weekend degree programs.

Rawlings Sporting Goods

Bob Clevenhagen (pictured at Rawlings plant in Washington, Missouri) carries on the tradition for innovation established by past designers, including Harry Latina and Rollie Latina, whose work earned each a place in the Sporting Goods Hall of Fame.

awlings Sporting Goods fills stadiums, gyms, playgrounds and ballfields with the sounds of fun: the sharp crack of a hard line drive, the satisfying plunk of a game-saving catch and the echoing drumbeat of a dribbling basketball. The choice of little leaguers and pros alike, Rawlings produces a wide array of performance-enhancing athletic equipment as well as the uniforms donned by numerous professional baseball players and the authentic team apparel sported by millions of amateur athletes — both male and female.

Recognized as "The Mark of a Pro," Rawlings dates to 1887 when two brothers, George and Alfred Rawlings, founded a store to sell fishing tackle, guns and sports equipment. The brothers ventured into manufacturing shortly thereafter, enticed by the growing demand for baseball equipment and frustrated by insufficient quantities of those items.

Rawlings established itself as an innovator in 1920 with the introduction of the Bill Doak Glove. A team effort between Rawlings and Doak, a spitball-throwing, southpaw St. Louis Cardinal, the glove's multi-thong web design and natural, deep pocket revolutionized the national pastime and became the predecessor of modern gloves. In 1941 Rawlings again set the standard for Major League Baseball (MLB) with the Trapper Mitt,

a three-finger glove with a deep-well pocket attractive to fielders. By 1946 the company was manufacturing gloves tailored for each position.

In 2002 Rawlings again pushed the frontier of glove technology forward with the Vise. Featuring a three-finger design that closes with the strength of a clamp and an expanded pocket for enhanced control, the Vise helps players catch and maintain a firm grip on the baseball.

Rawlings gloves have graced the hands of baseball greats past and present, including Mickey Mantle, Stan Musial, Reggie Jackson, Mike Schmidt, Mark McGwire, Ken Griffey Jr. and Sammy Sosa. Today, more than 50 percent of professional baseball players and millions of amateurs put their faith in Rawlings gloves, which are available in 134 models and in all price ranges.

The company began supplying the St. Louis Cardinals with uniforms in 1906, became the official MLB uniform supplier in 1987 and typically outfits about eight teams annually. Additionally, Rawlings supplies consumers with authentic MLB apparel and corporations with special products customized for promotional purposes. The official baseball supplier to the American and National leagues since 1976, Rawlings has been producing bats since it purchased Adirondack in 1970 and now offers a wide selection of wooden and aluminum bats.

Although Rawlings continues to bear its founders' name, the Rawlings family sold the business early in the 1900s. Publicly traded since 1994, Rawlings boasts a strong U.S. brand with a proud history unmarred by financial difficulties.

Over the decades, Rawlings has received hundreds of patents for sports equipment, and the company's success owes much to the efforts of talented designers such as Harry Latina and his son, Rollie, whose glove designs earned each a place in the Sporting Goods Hall of Fame. Today, the company continues to design and manufacture baseball gloves at its facility in nearby Washington, Missouri.

Rawlings began outfitting the St. Louis Cardinals in 1906. Pictured is the seamstress operation around that time.

Of the many people who helped keep Rawlings at the top of its game throughout the years, one man leaps to the fore. Oscar Roettger, a native St. Louisan with baseball credits that included pitching for the New York Yankees during 1923 and 1924, joined Rawlings after World War II. The personable Roettger drove the brand's growth through the 1970s by cementing its relationships with MLB and professional baseball players.

During that same period, Rawlings initiated a tradition of recognizing baseball's top defensive players. Each year since 1957, the company in partnership with MLB has awarded the Rawlings Gold Glove Award to the finest fielders in both leagues, with a record 11 Gold Gloves going to Hall of Famer St. Louis Cardinal, Ozzie Smith.

While baseball and softball is Rawlings' largest market, the company's commitment to innovation and quality extends to football and basketball. The company sells numerous models of footballs for youth and adult teams, college football shoulder pads and other protective equipment.

Rawlings was instrumental in the development of the NCAA Men's and Women's championships and provided the official basketball for those tournaments for 15 years. In 2002 Rawlings shot the sport into the future with the introduction of a 10-seam basketball. The Ten, featuring two additional seams to shorten the distance between these seams, improved gripping and thus enhanced handling and shooting control.

Headquartered in St. Louis County, Rawlings employs over 1,000 people and operates its distribution centers in Washington, Missouri; a tannery in Tennessee; and five manufacturing plants in the United States and Costa Rica. The company also distributes and sells some goods manufactured in Asia and has licensed the brand for sportswear, shoes, socks, sports bags, toys and other items. Rawlings together with its licensing partners annually distribute over $350 million in products worldwide.

(Far left)
Rawlings has supplied the official baseball to the American and National leagues since 1976.

Over 50 percent of professional baseball players use Rawlings gloves. Pictured is retired St. Louis Cardinal Ozzie Smith, who received 11 Rawlings Gold Glove awards for outstanding fielding.

Rawlings, which owned the No. 1 market share in 75 percent of its product lines during 2002, is the leading supplier of competitive team sports equipment, including batter's helmets and protective gear for catchers and umpires. The official baseball supplier to Major and Minor League Baseball, Rawlings serves professional, collegiate, interscholastic and amateur organizations worldwide. Among other groups, the company actively sponsors the Women's Basketball Coaches Association, the American Baseball Coaches Association and the Young Boys of America.

The Rawlings brand is the company's greatest asset. In addition to allowing the company to retain dominance in established markets, high name recognition will allow Rawlings to easily enter new ones, an increasingly important business strategy as more sports emerge to challenge traditional sports, such as baseball, for America's leisure hours. In 2002 Rawlings identified apparel as one such growing market and began expanding those lines to strengthen its position in that area.

Rawlings products — truly "The Finest in the Field" — inspire the dream of true sport. Well-known as a longstanding American brand noted for innovation and pride in workmanship, the Rawlings brand continues to garner respect as the company develops new products and grows to meet the challenges of the 21st-century marketplace.

Saint Louis ConnectCare

A professional staff delivers high-quality health care services with respect and in a timely manner at Saint Louis ConnectCare.

Dr. Larry Fields guides Saint Louis ConnectCare in its mission of serving uninsured and underinsured patients.

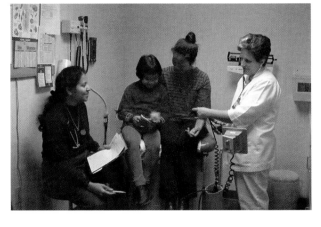

The mission is in the name at Saint Louis ConnectCare, which in 1997 began linking people in need with health care providers after the city's last public hospital closed. ConnectCare anchors a health care safety net with four community-based clinics, offering services ranging from pediatrics to adult medicine and from dentistry to podiatry. The Delmar Medical Center houses a primary care clinic, specialty clinics, an emergency department, a Ryan White Title III Program for HIV patients and a 24-bed hospital. Two facilities provide dialysis.

ConnectCare is joined in spirit with the St. Louis public hospitals preceding it. The Delmar Medical Center is located in the former St. Louis Regional Medical Center and two health centers are named after Homer G. Phillips and Max C. Starkloff hospitals. The other centers are Florence Hill and Lillian E. Courtney.

ConnectCare's history is associated with that of the now defunct Homer G. Phillips Hospital, which grew out of a hospital that the city established in 1918 to care for black patients and to train black physicians and nurses. When that facility became inadequate, Homer G. Phillips, an African-American attorney, spearheaded the development of a new one. Sadly, he was murdered before the hospital's 1937 dedication.

Thousands of African-American medical professionals trained at Homer G. Phillips, which transferred its last patients to Max C. Starkloff in 1979. When Starkloff closed a few years later, the city and county founded Regional to treat poor residents. Regional's 1997 closing dealt a devastating blow to its population. Officials and health care professionals quickly formed a consortium to address the issue. St. Louis Mayor Clarence Harmon's chief of staff, Mike Jones; other area leaders; and Larry E. Fields, MD, MBA, the city's chief health officer, provided instrumental guidance in the evolution of ConnectCare as a way to bridge the gap in health care access while leaders sought a sustainable solution.

In the past, hospitals and other providers offset the cost of charity care with payments from insured patients. Lower reimbursement rates mean less money to help those in need. Population movement from the city to the suburbs also contributes to the financial pressures of public health care providers. People moving from the city typically have insurance; those remaining often are uninsured, receive little preventive care and are at greater risk for developing serious medical conditions.

In October 1998, BJC Health System, the area's largest health care system, agreed to assist with ConnectCare's management for the first five years. The move made certain BJC resources available to ConnectCare.

Fields became ConnectCare's president and CEO in February 1998 while also the city's health commissioner and health department director. In May 2000 he left those posts to devote his expertise to ConnectCare's goal of delivering first-rate services with respect and compassion to people who face numerous hardships.

Personnel from the mayor's office constituted the system's first board of directors, but the city's involvement ceased within the first year with the organization of a formal board. Current directors include a medical school dean, a newspaper publisher and representatives from each of the area's hospital systems. Patients, community leaders and others provide input through an advisory council and an ombudsman.

The Community Advisory Council, formed to lend a voice to the community, played a major role as ConnectCare's board transformed a vision — access to quality health care for all people — into a reality. With the council's input, a model for community-based health care emerged that includes primary and specialty care, outside referrals, health promotion and education, and a network of support services.

In addition to receiving patients from its community-based health centers, ConnectCare receives referrals from external sources for specialty care and testing. Patients see other participating providers for intensive inpatient care, highly specialized testing or mental health services. Because many low-income people have transportation problems, the system operates a shuttle, and each center staffs a pharmacy and laboratory.

ConnectCare treats each patient as a whole person with individual needs, linking patients with social services and providing case management. A community's overall wellness is tied to its financial health so the system works with faith-based coalitions and other organizations, including St. Louis 2004 and Civic Progress, working to improve local economic conditions.

ConnectCare's staff of 493 people, including 36 physicians, serves a population estimated at 80,000 and treats about 52,000 people annually. The system in 1999 logged over 200,000 visits, 39,000 shuttle rides and 191,505 prescriptions filled. Forty percent of its patients

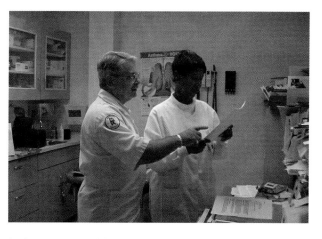

Saint Louis ConnectCare ensures access to health care for all area residents, regardless of ability to pay, and focuses on the patient's total support system to achieve better outcomes.

lack insurance although many work; 54 percent receive Medicare or Medicaid; 6 percent have other health insurance.

State money accounts for half of ConnectCare's annual budget of about $40 million. The remainder derives from insurance billings, city and county payments, and grants like one received in 2000 from the Episcopal-Presbyterian Medical Charitable Trust Fund that endowed the Dr. William E. Smiley Fund with $500,000 to offset pharmaceutical costs. ConnectCare annually spends at least $6.5 million on medicines and supplies for its patients and those from other health centers.

Focus St. Louis in 1999 honored ConnectCare with a "What's Right with the Region" Award and the College of American Pathologists conferred accreditation on its medical laboratories. Technology also moved to the forefront that year with the automation of pharmacies, health centers, the medical center and medical management offices.

Area leaders are analyzing other cities' public health care systems as they customize a sustainable solution to the problems of health care access in St. Louis, an increasingly difficult task. The Balanced Budget Act of 1997, which reduced Medicare and Medicaid payments, greatly challenged and contributed to the demise of some systems that had been operating successfully but were unable to bear additional financial strain.

In an ever-changing world, one issue remains constant. Poor people lack complete access to health care services. For over 40 years, Homer G. Phillips Hospital combated the health care injustices inflicted on African Americans. Now ConnectCare battles to guarantee quality health care for all people as leaders struggle to develop fiscally sound solutions despite a diminishing flow of revenue.

Saint Louis ConnectCare offers a full complement of services, including an on-site pharmacy.

Saint Louis Symphony Orchestra

The Saint Louis Symphony Orchestra and Powell Symphony Hall have long shared a symbiotic and singular relationship. The former is the crown jewel in St. Louis' rich cultural and artistic heritage, while the latter is the cornerstone of the city's premier performing arts district.

Indeed, chandeliers glittered and champagne flowed the night the Saint Louis Symphony Orchestra christened elegant Powell Symphony Hall as its permanent home in 1968. Constructed and opened in 1925 as the St. Louis Theatre, Powell Symphony Hall was the result of a two-year, $2 million transformation of a historical building destined for demolition. A perfect marriage of form and function, the former movie theater and vaudeville house offered incredible acoustics and a European ambiance appropriate for showcasing America's second-oldest symphony.

All Saint Louis Symphony musicians live in the community.
Photo by Dan Dreyfus

The Saint Louis Symphony Orchestra dates from 1880, when Joseph Otten, a 28-year-old organist, formed the St. Louis Choral Society. The first few years were met with mixed reviews, but nevertheless Otten initiated consecutive concert seasons that have continued uninterrupted to this day. Max Zach, the conductor from 1907 to 1921, dramatically improved the quality of performances and broadened the repertoire.

However, it was when gifted French conductor Vladimir Golschmann took the podium in 1931 that the Orchestra evolved into a truly world-class musical organization. It was during his 27-year tenure that the ensemble made its Carnegie Hall debut in 1950.

During Golschmann's reign, the Orchestra met its first real financial threat in the face of the Great Depression. The Society may have disbanded if not for the financial generosity and leadership of Oscar Johnson

Jr., the young heir to the International Shoe Company fortune. Despite a self-proclaimed musical ignorance, Johnson served as president of the Society for 20 years — repeatedly offsetting the Symphony's budget deficits, and later initiating the purchase of the St. Louis Theatre with a $500,000 donation.

Mr. Johnson's initial gift spurred the Ford Foundation and Mrs. Walter Powell, widow of a Brown Shoe executive, to fund the restoration of the theatre — thus preserving a vibrant part of St. Louis' architectural heritage. The theatre was originally built in 1925 when Art Deco was the fashionable design of the times. Forty years later, the renovators found inspiration in Old World luxury, modeling the Hall after the Chapel of Louis the XIV at Versailles with marble floors, crystal chandeliers, gilt accents, a sweeping staircase and lush red carpeting, draperies and seats.

When Powell Symphony Hall opened its doors in September 1968 to Beethoven's *Consecration of the House* overture, the Saint Louis Symphony Orchestra ushered in a new era with a new home, renewed public support and a dynamic conductor on the podium. The 55-year-old Walter Susskind, conducting since he was 20, also was a prodigious pianist and prolific composer. He was as complete a musician as he was a maestro. Besides his sophistication and international reputation, Susskind also brought to the Symphony Society an enormously talented protege, Leonard Slatkin. Susskind immediately assigned Slatkin a significant number of concerts, and as a result, Slatkin rapidly developed style, confidence and control.

Leonard Slatkin left St. Louis with his mentor in 1975, only to return in 1979 on the cusp of the Symphony Society's centennial birthday. He was the Orchestra's first American-born music director and, coincidentally, the son of a former first violinist in the Orchestra. Always confident, Slatkin took an active role in programming the Orchestra's repertoire and selecting soloists. The personable young conductor often introduced pieces from the podium with informal and engaging commentary and was known to mingle with audiences after concerts. Slatkin left his St. Louis post in 1996, but not before both he and the Orchestra had risen to international acclaim.

From 1996 through 2002, the Orchestra's outstanding tradition continued under the distinguished baton of acclaimed Dutch conductor, Hans Vonk. The maestro's diverse repertoire made him a sought-after guest conductor, and he appeared with many of the world's prestigious orchestras and major opera houses. Before stepping down from the podium due to health reasons, Vonk succeeded, masterfully, in making the Orchestra as much at home in the European classics as it had grown to be in the 20th century works.

Performing free of charge more than 250 times per year — in schools, in churches, in nursing homes — the Saint Louis Symphony Orchestra is an integral part of the community. For instance, the Symphony broke new ground in 1994 when it established the Community Partnership Program (CPP), which aims to reach new audiences and foster a love of orchestral and choral music through programs featuring musicians as teachers, mentors and performers. The core of the program is its IN UNISON program, a partnership between the Orchestra and more than two dozen African-American churches. The IN UNISON Chorus, composed of IN UNISON churches and other local singers, presents concerts throughout the season and regularly appears with the Orchestra.

The Symphony is a vital partner in music education with area schools. Through the example it sets for young musicians; through the Kinder Konzerts and Young People's Concerts performed for nearly 60,000 youngsters from more than 600 schools; through the Youth Orchestra, which includes musicians from more than three dozen schools; through the Des Lee Fine Arts Education Collaborative, which involves 62 schools in 10 districts throughout the region; and, through the personal involvement of individual musicians, the Symphony is an invaluable asset to those who teach music and encourage students' participation.

All 92 members of the Saint Louis Symphony are rooted in the community. Concertmaster David Halen is one of nine native Missourians in the Orchestra and all the musicians live in the St. Louis community — a distinctive trait of the ensemble, as many cultural organizations import their artists. In fact, St. Louis Mayor Francis Slay recently offered a proclamation with the comment that the Symphony "is the only hometown team whose players all live and work here year-round."

The Saint Louis Symphony Orchestra — which Placido Domingo recently called "one of the treasures of the orchestral world" — boasts six Grammy Awards and 56 Grammy nominations as well as six awards for adventuresome programming from the American Society of Composers, Authors and Publishers. The Orchestra's wide range of recordings reflects a strong commitment to contemporary composers, particularly Americans. Its recordings of Barber, Gershwin, Schumann, Bernstein and Piston are considered definitive.

To preserve the Symphony's top-tier status, the Jack Taylor Family, owners of Enterprise Rent-A-Car, stepped forward with a $40 million challenge in December 2000. The Taylor family's unprecedented pledge, which must be matched by December 31, 2004, helped bridge an uncertain future brought upon by an insufficient endowment. Inspired by the Taylor Family Challenge, the Symphony is in the midst of an unprecedented fund-raising effort to match the Taylors' $40 million, raise the endowment beyond $100 million and sustain the Symphony's operations for years to come.

With the community having stepped forward in dramatic fashion, the Saint Louis Symphony Orchestra continues to shine the international spotlight on St. Louis — just as it has done for 122 celebrated years.

Saint Louis Symphony musicians enjoy teaching and performing in the region through the Community Partnerships Program.

Maestro Hans Vonk conducts during the 2000-2001 season. *Photo by Dan Dreyfus*

Sisters of Mercy Health System

healing ministry that a young woman began in 19th-century Ireland flourishes today in the Sisters of Mercy Health System (Mercy), an organization of physicians, health care facilities and related services that operates in seven states. Mercy, headquartered in St. Louis, follows the tradition of Catherine McAuley, who in 1831 founded the Religious Sisters of Mercy to serve the poor and the sick.

The Roman Catholic sisters — known as the "walking nuns" because they left their convents to care for others — had reached America by 1854 and in 1871 they opened a 25-bed infirmary in St. Louis. Over the next century, the Sisters of Mercy of the St. Louis Regional Community extended their ministry to other states, including Arkansas, Oklahoma, Kansas, Texas, Mississippi and Louisiana.

Despite a strong health ministry, the last half of the 20th century brought challenges that threatened the sisters' sacred tradition of service. Fewer women were choosing the religious life, and independent hospitals like those the order operated were becoming difficult to maintain under health care reforms. The nuns prayed, consulted Scripture and analyzed the industry to find a solution that

would preserve and strengthen their ministry. In 1986 they created Mercy, joining together Sisters of Mercy hospitals located throughout their multi-state region.

Today, Mercy continues its historic tradition of sponsoring hospitals while extending its ministry to include outpatient facilities, physician practices, and other health and social services programs. In fiscal year 2000 the system reported 171,443 inpatient admissions, 5,247,035 outpatient visits and 345,687 home health visits.

In 2000 *Modern Healthcare* magazine ranked Mercy, by net patient revenue, as the nation's 11th-largest health care system and the ninth-largest not-for-profit system. Many of the organization's 25,000 employees and 4,000 physicians serve in St. Louis, the location of Mercy's largest hospital, St. John's Mercy Medical Center.

Sister Mary Roch Rocklage, chair of the Mercy board, served as the organization's first president and CEO. Always focused on improving access to health care, she was instrumental in establishing Mercy Health Plans. The managed care organization in 1994 became available in St. Louis and Springfield, Missouri, and Laredo, Texas. Mercy also partners with Arkansas Blue Cross and Blue Shield in developing insurance plans to meet various needs.

Sister Rocklage's dedication to improving health care was recognized in 2000 when the American Hospital Association board of trustees elected her to serve as chair-elect the following year and as chair in 2002. Ronald B. Ashworth already had succeeded Sister Rocklage as president and CEO of Mercy after an eight-year tenure as executive vice president and chief operating officer. Ashworth has served on the Mercy board of directors since its inception.

As a faith-based system, Mercy's ministry stretches beyond merely providing traditional health care services. In fiscal year 2000 it provided over $300 million in charity care, community outreach programs, education and research, and charitable contributions. The organization brings assistance to some of the nation's poorest areas, like Mound Bayou in the Mississippi Delta. A former slave, Isaiah Montgomery, founded that town in 1887 in the hope of creating a self-sufficient African-American community. In the late 1990s Montgomery's dream seemed dead, as unemployment hovered at 20 percent

The childbirth center at St. John's Mercy Medical Center, Mercy's largest hospital, is well respected throughout the region.

and only about half of the junior high students went on to earn diplomas. Mercy is reviving hope in the community through programs offering educational and recreational opportunities.

The system's St. Louis-based facilities, including St. John's Mercy, support poor and underserved people living in the St. Louis metropolitan area in many ways. St John's Mercy Neighborhood Ministry strives to improve the quality of life for inner-city residents through programs that target problems ranging from lack of transportation to violence. The Meacham Park Health Center in St. Louis County offers medical and dental services on a sliding scale and St John's Mercy Neighborhood Health Center brings family medicine and social services to a neighborhood populated by immigrants from around the world. Employees contribute to community projects and helped build two Habitat for Humanity houses in 1999 and 2000.

Mercy leaders actively participate in local and regional organizations emphasizing increased access to health care and also monitor pertinent legislation, like the Balanced Budget Act of 1997. That measure, in part, slashed Medicare and Medicaid reimbursements and left many hospitals struggling financially. Patients suffered the effects in reduced services and closures. Mercy and other health care providers in 1999 successfully lobbied Congress to increase reimbursement rates slightly and they continue to advocate additional relief from the act.

Mercy promotes literacy and addresses other issues in the areas it serves.

Technological advancements are changing health care, both administratively and in clinical settings. *Information Week* magazine in 2000 ranked Mercy 286th in its list of 500 innovative users of information technology in recognition of the organization's current capabilities as well as upcoming e-health strategies, including the implementation of a systemwide clinical data repository. Mercy was also ranked as one of the 100 "most wired" health systems by *Hospitals and Health Networks* magazine in 2001.

Customer service is the heart of Mercy, where each patient is treated with dignity and fairness. Mercy's focus on service is an outgrowth of its core values, which along with service and dignity include justice, excellence and stewardship. In modeling these values, Mercy seeks not only to meet the expected needs of clinical excellence but also to exceed expectations for personal service and care.

Catherine McAuley, who died only 10 years after founding the Sisters of Mercy, probably would be surprised at the way Mercy delivers health care services but undoubtedly she'd be pleased that the Sisters found a way to continue helping the poor and sick despite changing times. Perhaps there has never been a greater need for Catherine McAuley's tradition of service. The U.S. Census Bureau in September 2000 estimated that over 42 million Americans lacked health insurance.

As Mercy carries Catherine McAuley's legacy into the future, it will focus even more on the needs of its partners: patients, families, employees and physicians. Further integration of its regional health care networks is likely, the goal being to lower costs while raising the bar on quality clinical services. Although open to expansion opportunities, Mercy will pursue growth only as appropriate in meeting the needs of defined service areas.

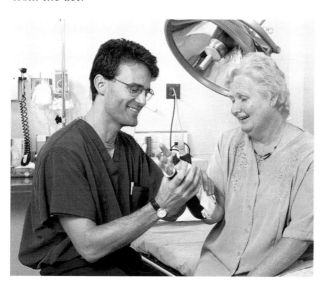

Mercy offers inpatient and outpatient services, physician practices, and other health and social programs.

SSM Health Care - St. Louis

ather than simply being a health care provider, SSM Health Care - St. Louis is the continuation of a healing mission first established more than 130 years ago. That model of quality, compassionate health care remains strong and vibrant. The caretaker of this vision is the network's parent organization, SSM Health Care, also based in St. Louis.

The essence of SSM is best expressed through its mission statement developed with input from employees, physicians, volunteers and trustees, which reads: Through our exceptional health care services, we reveal the healing presence of God. SSM Health Care - St. Louis, through its seven hospitals and affiliated physicians, fulfills its mission by delivering high-quality, compassionate care.

SSM Health Care's origin is inseparably linked to its sponsoring congregation, the Franciscan Sisters of Mary. When their predecessors arrived in St. Louis in 1872, they immediately began to care for smallpox victims. Eventually, they established hospitals that today are part of SSM Health Care, one of the largest Catholic health care systems in the United States. SSM Health Care - St. Louis was formed in 1994, combining three physician groups (SSM Medical Group, SSM DePaul Medical Group, and SSM St. Charles Clinic Medical Group) with the seven St. Louis-area SSM facilities: SSM Cardinal Glennon Children's Hospital, SSM DePaul Health Center, SSM St. Joseph Hospital of Kirkwood, SSM St. Joseph Health Center (St. Charles), SSM St. Joseph Hospital West (Lake Saint Louis), SSM St. Mary's Health Center and SSM Rehab.

Recognized by the *St. Louis Business Journal* as among the "best places to work in St. Louis," SSM Health Care - St. Louis attracts topflight, committed, dedicated professionals in a highly competitive health care environment that is experiencing increased demand. SSM's focus on diversity dovetails with its commitment to quality to earn recognition as a workplace of choice in the St. Louis health care market. Each of its entities shares a chapter in St. Louis' history and works in unison to answer the health needs of St. Louis.

Opened in the mid-1950s, SSM Cardinal Glennon Children's Hospital honors the wishes of its namesake, Cardinal John J. Glennon, who served as Archbishop of St. Louis from 1902-1946. As the only freestanding Catholic pediatric hospital in America, it is nationally renowned for advanced medical care, education and research to benefit all children in need. While Cardinal Glennon's clinical achievements include many "firsts" in treatment and therapy, its child/parent-friendly facilities and services bid "welcome." Both will be enhanced through a $46 million modernization project significantly expanding emergency and outpatient services while improving comfort and convenience for patients and families.

As the first hospital west of the Mississippi, SSM DePaul Health Center is the oldest continuously operating Catholic hospital in the United States. Serving St. Louis since 1828, DePaul has become one of the fastest-growing hospitals in St. Louis, reflecting the confidence of an expanding population. While both a community and comprehensive health care facility — with leading-edge heart services, women's services and nationally emulated emergency/ trauma care — DePaul also places emphasis on senior and behavioral health services. With its

(Above) SSM Cardinal Glennon Children's Hospital delivers quality health services for children from birth through adolescence. With "Glennon Care for Kids" sites throughout the region, pediatric expertise is available close to home.

SSM Health Care - St. Louis hospitals are committed to caring for seniors. Services go beyond inpatient care to include dedicated outpatient centers that provide transportation, access to physician specialists, wellness programs and health screenings.

newly opened "Fragile Care" unit, DePaul introduced the first dedicated, in-patient geropsychiatric unit for the St. Louis region.

A neighborhood treasure in suburban southwest St. Louis County, SSM St. Joseph Hospital of Kirkwood opened in 1939. Skilled, family-friendly physicians and staff have developed a caring environment well known for exemplary service. While community-oriented, St. Joseph Hospital features a full array of advanced, comprehensive services and fully equipped facilities. In an innovative collaboration linking expertise with location, St. Joseph Hospital of Kirkwood opened St. Louis' first independent outpatient cardiac catheterization lab, managed by a group of leading area cardiologists. The hospital's location accentuates a focus on wellness and outpatient care.

Generations of St. Charles residents have entrusted their health to SSM St. Joseph Health Center, founded in 1885. The hospital, a centerpiece in historic downtown St. Charles, earned the first-ever MissouriPro Quality Award for its recognized commitment to quality care. Due to St. Charles County's phenomenal growth, SSM St. Joseph Medical Park, an expansive ambulatory/surgery center, will extend the convenience of St. Joseph's high-quality care to central St. Charles County. SSM St. Joseph Health Center continues as the oldest, largest and most comprehensive health care provider in St. Charles, Lincoln, Warren and Pike counties.

Conveniently located off Interstate 70 at Lake Saint Louis, SSM St. Joseph Hospital West has answered the swiftly expanding medical needs of the area's growing "Westplex" region since 1986. Honoring its excellence, efficiency and overall performance, the HCIA-Sachs Institute designated St. Joseph Hospital West as one of the 100 Top Hospitals™ in the country. The population growth in western St. Charles, Lincoln, Warren and Pike counties led to the dramatic expansion of St. Joseph Hospital West's Emergency & Trauma Center. Nearly tripling in size and space, it is now the largest emergency care facility in its service area.

Since 1924 SSM St. Mary's Health Center in Richmond Heights has been a major tertiary care hospital, including a regional heart services and surgery program. As home for the Department of Obstetrics and Gynecology for St. Louis University's School of Medicine, St. Mary's provides advanced high-risk maternal/fetal medical care with a family-centered focus. A strong commitment to senior care is also reflected in St. Mary's dedicated

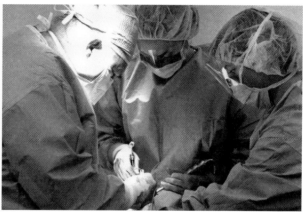

SSM Health Care - St. Louis has been honored as one of the "Best Places to Work" by the *St. Louis Business Journal*. The publication has cited SSM for its "impressive array of benefits and work scheduling options" and for being among the most "family friendly" places to work in the St. Louis area.

SSM Health Care - St. Louis hospitals offer exceptional medical care, close by. SSM's community-centered hospitals maintain state-of-the-art, advanced-level care in such areas as orthopedic surgery, heart services, women's health, cancer care and more.

Knee & Hip Center for total joint replacements, an innovative pain management program and a Senior Care Coordination Center.

Originally known as Mount Saint Rose Throat and Chest Hospital when it opened in 1900, SSM Rehab has grown, diversified and focused its mission to become the only not-for-profit rehabilitation hospital in St. Louis. Rehabilitating individuals with brain and spinal cord injuries, stroke, cancer and orthopedic conditions, SSM Rehab also offers a premier program for those with complex cardiac and respiratory conditions. SSM Rehab inpatient services are located in acute care hospital settings to provide patients immediate access to medical and urgent care. SSM Rehab also provides neighborhood sites throughout the St. Louis area to deliver convenient access to outpatient physical therapy, work injury management, sports rehab and other specialty rehab services.

SSM Health Care - St. Louis constantly strives to make a difference in the lives of the people it serves by upholding the five values attached to SSM's mission statement. They are: Compassion, Respect, Excellence, Stewardship and Community.

St. Anthony's Medical Center

A tradition of caring for St. Louis' sick started by the Franciscan Sisters in 1873 seemed destined to die after nearly a century when the order announced it would close St. Anthony's Hospital. Instead, the dedication to serving the community gained a new life under lay ownership.

Before deciding to close their hospital, the nuns had considered moving it to land they owned in rural South St. Louis County. The lay board in 1969 voted to proceed with that plan although many people at the time considered building a hospital in the sparsely populated area to be a risky venture. The wisdom of the board's decision became evident in 1975, when St. Anthony's became 90-percent occupied one month after opening. In 2000 the hospital accounted for 155,000 patient days and projected a future annual growth rate of 5 percent.

The 794-bed facility, a level-two trauma center, remains South County's only hospital. It offers a broad continuum of health care services as well as strategic centers of excellence for childbirth, orthopedics, cancer, cardiology, behavioral health, hospice care and surgery. The emergency room logs more than 70,000 visits annually, has 46 treatment rooms and serves 10 ambulance districts. St. Anthony's also operates two separate urgent care facilities in south county.

This sprawling 80-acre campus is home to St. Louis' third-largest medical center.

The medical center's impressive array of services and facilities is due, in part, to the efforts of three original board members: the late Robert Hyland, Norbert Siegfried and Joseph Lipic.

Hyland, on the board from 1967 to 1992, believed St. Anthony's should provide comprehensive health care. He was a driving force behind the Hyland Center, which opened in 1977 for the treatment of chemical dependency. The facility became a leader in the field, and its successor, Hyland Behavioral Health, now offers 126 inpatient beds as well as outpatient programs for the treatment of addictions and psychiatric disorders in people of all ages.

Siegfried, chairman of the board of St. Anthony's, led the hospital through the extensive campus renovations that made it the metropolitan area's third-largest medical center. Lipic spearheaded the development of the hospital's Fern and Russell F. de Greeff Hospice House, Missouri's only freestanding inpatient hospice, and placed the final link in the continuum of care.

St. Anthony's Cancer Center opened its doors to patients in June 2000.

CANCER CENTER

Three lay CEOs also have been critical to the success of St. Anthony's. Under the leadership of George P. Casey, the hospital moved from the city to the county. Richard Grisham initiated growth and brought financial stability to the medical center. David Seifert, the current CEO, expanded its ministry on and beyond its campus despite a challenging health care climate and drove the development of the Cancer Center.

The medical center's commitment to oncology dates back to 1957, when St. Anthony's became one of the first in the area to offer cobalt cancer treatment. The Cancer Center opened in 2000 to provide physical, emotional and spiritual care for cancer patients as well as education, screenings and other services.

Recognizing a growing need for cardiology services among its population, St. Anthony's has partnered with its doctors to develop a state-of-the-art Cardiology Center. Slated for completion in 2002, the Center will be an integral part of a strategy to increase the number of heart surgeries performed annually from 600 to 800 and will be part of a $30 million medical office complex.

When the Cardiology Center is completed, St. Anthony's plans to consolidate women's and children's services in an area previously used for offices. The hospital already boasts a new Childbirth Center equipped with nine labor-delivery-recovery suites, two Caesarean birth rooms, 16 postpartum rooms and three antenatal rooms.

The medical center's acute rehabilitation unit assists people who have suffered disabling injuries and illnesses such as strokes, fractures or amputations. A transitional apartment allows the patient and family to practice skills in a homey environment, and supervised trips prepare patients to re-enter the community. An extensive array of physical and occupational therapy services coupled with this unit forms the core of St. Anthony's sophisticated neurosciences services.

Over 1,000 knee replacement surgeries are performed at the medical center each year. According to HCIA Inc., which studies the health care industry, in 1999 St. Anthony's was one of the 60 best performing U.S. hospitals for knee replacement and was listed as one of HCIA's 100 Top Hospitals.

Missouri's only freestanding inpatient hospice

Fern and Russell F. de Greeff Hospice House

People are the heart of St. Anthony's. The medical center's reputation for excellence, combined with a challenging array of cases, attracts highly qualified medical personnel. Its large volunteer program — about 1,300 strong — hails to 1945, when the hospital became the first civilian facility west of the Mississippi to use Red Cross Gray Ladies.

St. Anthony's Medical Center's 80-acre campus has received awards for its beauty from the Landscape Critic Council of Missouri and area garden clubs. The hospital's administrators are proactive in advancing programs that mirror the needs of the community.

A desire to serve the community prompted the Franciscan Sisters in 1873 to open a small hospital in St. Louis and compelled them to bravely care for thousands of polio patients during epidemics of the disease in the 1940s. Their example sets the bar at St. Anthony's, where commitment to community and compassionate health care always come first.

The chapel's beautiful stained glass windows were part of the original hospital located at the corner of Chippewa and Grand.

St. Louis University High School

For the generations of commuters who for the past five decades have driven by it every day on Highway 40, St. Louis University High School has been an institution in the city in the physical sense, even for those who hadn't a clue what goes on behind its doors. The main building has been an imposing presence on Oakland Avenue since 1924.

Through the years, much has changed in the neighborhood and the school itself. The original eight acres have grown to 24 and in that time, a gymnasium, a library, a football and soccer stadium, and a 600-seat performing arts center have been added.

What hasn't changed is the school's status as a St. Louis institution in the spiritual sense; a place that has turned out generation after generation of leaders in the commercial, professional and spiritual life of the community. That has been a constant, and continues now.

The building that can be seen from Highway 40 has its beginnings in a school founded in 1818 called St. Louis Academy. In 1832 the campus grew to include university classes, and St. Louis University was born. The preparatory school remained a part of the university until 1924, when it merged with two other Jesuit high schools and moved to a separate location.

Anna Backer built the new facility as a tribute to her husband, George, who was an 1869 graduate of the school. The main building, Backer Memorial, is named in his honor. Many others have contributed to the building and expansion of the school as it is today.

AS IT IS TODAY

St. Louis University High School is a private Roman Catholic school operated by the Society of Jesus, the Jesuits. Religious life is a part of daily life at the school.

Eleven members of the faculty have religious vocations and the remainder, about 120 in all, are devout and enthusiastic subscribers to the philosophy of Jesuit education, preparing young men for life through growth in personal competence, responsibility and commitment to justice, love and peace. About 21 percent are themselves graduates of St. Louis University High School, and all are highly qualified academically. More than 90 percent have advanced degrees. Faculty members live their faith, acting as role models in their effort to mold young men who develop their gifts for the service of God and others.

With an average of 1,000 boys each year and 120 faculty members, class sizes are small and individual attention is abundant.

As one of 46 Jesuit high schools in the United States, St. Louis University High School is recognized as one of the top schools in the system, ranking 9th overall in average American College Test scores among all schools in the nation.

Graduates go on to attend such prestigious universities as Boston College, Notre Dame, Georgetown and Harvard. Seventy-three percent of the students receive scholarship assistance. Many enter college as sophomores

Students study together in one of the common rooms at St. Louis University High School.

after passing placement exams. Graduates enter fields such as education, law, medicine, science, business, engineering, social work and religious ministry.

An important component of the school's philosophy is that what takes place outside the classroom is just as important as what takes place inside it. Clubs, sports organizations and, especially, community service, get as much attention as academics.

In an undertaking known as Senior Project, SLUH seniors contribute three weeks of community involvement that may include service work around the St. Louis area or, in some cases, around the world at Jesuit missions in Belize, Brazil and elsewhere. Community service performed during the first three years of high school builds toward this final project. This focus on community service sets the tone for lifelong community involvement.

St. Louis University's sports teams are known as the Billikens, and St. Louis University High School's teams are the Junior Billikens. Baseball, basketball, cross country, football, golf, soccer, swimming and diving, tennis, volleyball, water polo, wrestling, hockey, lacrosse and racquetball are all a part of the sports curriculum. There is also a wealth of clubs and activities including the Association for Cultural Enrichment, Dauphin Players Theater, Dauphin Yearbook, Karate Club, Model United Nations, Outdoor Experience Club, Pastoral Team, Sisyphus Literary Magazine and a Pep Band. The school's basement houses a billiard room that is probably the largest "pool hall" in the area.

The school is one of the largest private schools in Missouri with about 270 freshmen entering each year. Students compete to be accepted into the limited available positions. Acceptance is based on academic ability as established through standardized testing as well as leadership potential and a commitment to a Catholic education and to helping other people. Students are geographically, socially and economically diverse, coming from more than 80 different zip code areas.

A total of about $1 million per year in annual financial aid is available, and more than one in every four students receives aid. Acceptance to the school is on a need-blind basis. Financial aid is made possible through donations made by alumni and friends of the school, in addition to the annual "Cashbah" fund-raising dinner and auction.

Graduation ceremonies at another St. Louis institution, Powell Symphony Hall, complete the high school experience for SLUH students, and commence the final leg of the school's mission: sending "men for others" out into the world with critical minds and compassionate hearts.

Tenet Saint Louis

Operating five acute-care hospitals and maintaining the second-largest hospital network in the city of St. Louis at the dawn of 2001, Tenet Saint Louis has proven a leader in redefining health care delivery. Each of its components — SouthPointe Hospital, Forest Park Hospital, Saint Louis University Hospital, Des Peres Hospital and St. Alexius Hospital — holds a history intertwined with the roots of the region it serves.

After its national parent company acquired Lutheran Medical Center in 1984, Tenet Saint Louis evolved with the acquisition of four other area hospitals in recent years. The St. Louis operation has since emerged as an industry vanguard that offers a broad range of health care services.

Beginning as Lutheran Hospital in two rooms of a private residence, SouthPointe Hospital's history spans almost one and a half centuries. Founded in 1858, the original medical facility provided care for the many immigrants pouring into St. Louis at the time. Located on the corner of what is now Broadway and Geyer on the city's south side, it defied the 19th-century concept of a hospital as a place where people went to die.

Moving to its present location in 1878, Lutheran Medical Center grew tremendously through the years. It is now an 11-building complex known as SouthPointe Hospital.

SouthPointe Hospital's Continent Ostomy Program offers the option of the Barnett Continent Intestinal Reservoir (BCIR), an internal appliance for patients

undergoing — or who have undergone — total removal of the colon. Other specialized services include New Start (a program for surgical weight reduction), the Center for Physical Rehabilitation and an extensive psychiatric program.

Forest Park Hospital's background dates back to 1889. First run by two Deaconess sisters and two physicians, it moved to its current location near Forest Park in 1930. It operated there as Deaconess Hospital and then as Deaconess Central Hospital. Purchased by Tenet in 1997, it later adopted the name of the vast city park easily viewed from its premises.

Forest Park Hospital's Oncology Program features a multidisciplinary approach, which includes The Breast Center, medical oncology, radiation oncology and surgical procedures. The hospital's recently renovated Cardiac Catheterization Lab employs some of the latest equipment and techniques. The hospital's many other services include its obstetrics unit and its Wound Care Center.

Saint Louis University Hospital was originally named Firmin Desloge Hospital for the benefactor who donated substantial funding for the first building, officially dedicated in 1933. That structure still remains part of the complex, with a Gothic roof of copper-covered lead that tops the 250-foot building of modified French Gothic architectural design.

Today, as an academic medical center, Saint Louis University Hospital treats some of the region's most ill and injured patients. Through its partnership with SLUCare — the physicians of Saint Louis University — the hospital is a leader in advancing medicine. Saint

Louis University Hospital currently ranks among the best in the nation in 10 medical specialties, according to *U.S. News & World Report*. Its medical staff has pioneered many medical breakthroughs, and the hospital serves as the area's only Level I Trauma Center certified by both Missouri and Illinois.

In October 2000 Tenet and Saint Louis University announced the creation of the Saint Louis University Cancer Center. The facility will serve as a dedicated center for cancer prevention, education, research and treatment.

Des Peres Hospital was built in 1974 in response to the growing health care needs of the rapidly increasing populations of west and south St. Louis County, and to better serve residents of Jefferson and Franklin counties as well as other nearby communities.

Forest Park Hospital overlooks vast Forest Park.

Originally called Normandy Osteopathic Hospital-South, its name changed several times since it opened. It became part of Tenet Healthcare in July 1997 and was named Des Peres Hospital in 1999.

True to its heritage, Des Peres Hospital continues to provide quality medical and surgical care through the efforts of its physicians and other qualified health care professionals. Medical Staff members represent both the allopathic (M.D.) and osteopathic (D.O.) systems of medical practice as well as other accepted traditions. Diverse services and programs include Heart Care, Orthopedics and Sports Medicine, a Senior Care Center, Geriatrics, Psychiatric Care, Emergency Department and Comprehensive Rehabilitation.

St. Alexius Hospital, the newest member of the Tenet Saint Louis family, was named after a 5th-century

Roman saint who devoted his life to serving the poor. The hospital was founded in 1869 by the Alexian Brothers, a healing order of Catholic men who carried on the mission of St. Alexius. Located in south St. Louis on what is now South Broadway, the hospital was originally named Alexian Brothers Hospital. Over the years, it expanded, was rebuilt in 1979 and was renamed St. Alexius Hospital in 2000. In late 2001 St. Alexius Hospital became part of Tenet Saint Louis.

Today, the 203-bed hospital's services include a behavioral health network, around-the-clock emergency services, a 40-bed skilled nursing unit, 16-bed acute rehabilitation inpatient unit and 12-bed intensive care unit.

Saint Louis University Hospital's tower is as familiar to the central city skyline as the arch is to the riverfront.

Des Peres Hospital serves west St. Louis county and its surrounding counties.

Moving forward, Tenet Saint Louis hospitals play a leadership role in dealing with the problems of providing medical care for the area's poor and indigent who do not have health insurance or medical coverage. As valuable assets to the community, Tenet's hospitals contributed more than $53 million in taxes, charity care and unpaid medical care during the 2000 fiscal year.

Cooperating School Districts of Greater St. Louis Inc.

*H*ungry for interaction with each other but isolated in rural communities, St. Louis County school district superintendents in 1928 decided to "do lunch" occasionally. From those feasts of conversation and food sprang the Cooperating School Districts of Greater St. Louis, an educational collaborative now serving members throughout the metropolitan region.

CSD operated informally for 25 years and quickly expanded beyond networking opportunities. By the 1930s it had wielded cooperative purchasing power for the first time and had created a shared, mobile film library.

Today, CSD operates educational channels, sponsors professional development activities, lobbies lawmakers, and maintains research and recruitment resources. CSD's Insurance Trust brokers the lowest possible rates for members, researches benefits and notifies participants of changes.

Only public school districts may join and govern CSD — 49 in 2001 — but private and parochial schools may access services a la carte. CSD derives support from dues, fees for services, grants, foundation funding, and state and federal money.

At no extra charge, any Missouri school may order from CSD's online catalog of over 40,000 supplies and services. The organization boasts annual purchases of about $33 million, screens vendors for statutory compliance and processes orders from schools, even handling refunds and exchanges.

CSD's programs and services ever evolve to mirror the current educational environment.

The advent of computers in schools prompted CSD to offer technology classes, and in 1981 it held the first annual Midwest Education and Technology Conference. Concern about the deterioration of basic values brought the implementation of a program in 1988 to help educators instill positive character traits in children. Since that time, CHARACTERplus and CSD's academy for character education have garnered national recognition.

The organization also houses the St. Louis Regional Professional Development Center (RPDC), which offers many seminars and academies, and is one of only nine such centers set up statewide by the Missouri Department of Elementary and Secondary Education. Principals at one academy hone leadership and management skills and study new educational strategies while aspiring principals attend another to learn about the position and prepare for the state examination. Nationally known reading specialists share their expertise with teachers and principals at literacy academies.

The 1993 passage of Missouri's Outstanding Schools Act profoundly impacted education by raising the bar for student achievement and mandating rigorous assessments. CSD quickly responded to the new challenges by cross-referencing each of its over 6,000 videos to state standards and adapting professional development offerings to meet changing needs.

At the behest of human resource managers, CSD created the Regional Educational Application Process in the late 1990s. The searchable online system provides a standardized application for candidates seeking teaching and administrative positions, and streamlines recruitment for CSD members. About a dozen other states have purchased the system and CSD's management of it.

Like many excellent ideas, CSD was born over lunch, and luncheon meetings remain a happy tradition. History has seen CSD shift from providing direct services to brokering services in furtherance of its goal to positively impact student learning, academics and personal growth.

CSD has a long history of coaching teachers on ways to integrate computers and software into the curriculum.

CSD offers hundreds of professional development opportunities each year.

Medical Transportation Management Inc.

eg and Lynn Griswold founded Medical Transportation Management Inc. (MTM) on a good idea and a great ideal. Capitalizing on their entrepreneurial spirit and willingness for hard work, the Griswolds have parlayed opportunities in the St. Louis area into a successful business that has raised the bar for medical transportation in Missouri and other states. Their networked system of non-emergency medical transportation uses strict standards to ensure quality customer service and vigilant oversight to reduce fraud. By improving access to heath care for Medicaid recipients, MTM ultimately encourages preventive care and promotes wellness.

The Griswolds' interest in the world of para-lifts, non-emergency ambulances and other vehicles began while Lynn Griswold was employed by a managed care organization. While working on the company's proposal for serving Missouri's Medicaid recipients, he discovered a line requiring HMOs to provide access to care.

Peg Griswold researched the idea and found that non-emergency medical transportation was basically unorganized, with small companies competing for a limited amount of work. That realization gave a new dimension to the Griswolds' dream because a management company networking existing and new transportation services would dramatically improve the situation.

In 1995 six St. Louis HMOs awarded MTM contracts to manage non-emergency medical transportation. MTM's business grew incrementally as Medicaid managed care expanded statewide. Two years later, MTM began serving the Medicaid recipients outside of managed care through a Missouri state contract. MTM now operates in several states and averages 250,000 trips per month, including about 6,500 in the St. Louis area.

Customer service representatives confirm eligibility, then assess each passenger's needs. Some people require a wheelchair lift, stretcher, non-emergency ambulance or an attendant. Others can use a med-car or public transit. MTM's social service staff assists passengers with special needs, such as dialysis or behavioral concerns. A gasoline-reimbursement program encourages people to drive themselves or go with a friend. A meals-and-lodging program helps with long distance and overnight trips. MTM's automated system utilizes custom software containing information about its carefully screened vendors to determine the appropriate mode of transportation and most cost-effective vendor.

MTM, which dispatches around the clock, builds good vendor relationships through ongoing training and assistance in meeting quality standards covering everything from confidentiality to equipment. It conducts quality assurance visits as well as periodic audits and investigates complaints. It reconciles each trip, randomly verifies medical appointments and scrutinizes all long-distance, expensive or frequent trips. MTM notifies authorities of suspected Medicaid fraud, actions that in the past have resulted in prosecution.

MTM's system is receiving attention. An extensive Robert Woods Johnson study on Medicaid transportation ranked MTM among the country's "best practices." A good corporate citizen, MTM provides service at no charge to St. Louis 911 Plus, which handles non-emergency calls.

As technology evolves, MTM's operation will maximize satellite and Internet enhancements. The company's future growth seems assured, as an aging population increasingly relies on non-emergency medical transportation to remain independent, and as federal and state systems continue to support quality access to medical care.

MTM manages approximately 3 million non-emergency medical trips annually.

MTM's executive staff: (front, left to right) Lynn Griswold, Peg Griswold, James M. Sebben; (back, left to right) JB Bowers, Brenda Battle

Metropolitan Association for Philanthropy

The Metropolitan Association for Philanthropy (MAP) was founded in 1970 by a group of St. Louis-region corporations and foundations interested in increasing the effectiveness of their grantmaking. MAP was designed to bring together grantmakers to share information and enhance philanthropic impact and to provide regional grantmakers access to a concentrated source of information about local nonprofit organizations and community needs. Dedicated to strengthening the philanthropic community by supporting new and increased philanthropy, MAP encourages partnerships that expand the impact of philanthropy.

In 1980 MAP established the Funding Resource Center to serve as a self-help library for grant seekers. It also tackled challenging community issues and was instrumental in forming the St. Louis Regional Educational Partnership in 1988 with the goal of improving student learning.

Responding to members' interests in the 1990s, MAP developed a Children and Youth Focus Group to engage donors through relevant information and educational programming. It then established the annual Gene Schwilck Award for Outstanding Service to Youth in St. Louis, given to an individual who notably improved the quality of life and opportunities for success for children and youth.

That same decade, MAP joined forces with the Forum of Regional Associations of Grantmakers, a national organization working with grantmaker associations across the country. Additionally, it developed The Library Partners Program to provide nonprofit organizations information and training related to fundraising. MAP provided critical services to members during the great flood that ravaged parts of the St. Louis region. It published issue alerts to keep members apprised of community and victim needs related to the flood and tracked contributions and in-kind donations.

Broadening its 90s efforts, MAP launched three new initiatives: a project in conjunction with the *St. Louis Business Journal* to identify and share best practices of nonprofit/business partnerships in the region; a neighborhood development focus group; and the Teen Pregnancy Collaborative. In 1995 MAP continued its focus on youth with the development of The Teens Care Fund, providing grants of up to $500 to youth for community service projects. In 1999 it published The Philanthropic Landscape of St. Louis, benchmarking local giving trends.

MAP celebrated its 30th anniversary in 2000 with membership of over 70 corporations and foundations. Adding satellite library collections for public use at local public libraries in Kirkwood and St. Charles by 2001, it planned the third satellite branch in East St. Louis. Since then, the New Americans Interest Group was formed to study the impact of the regional influx of refugees and immigrants. The Neighborhood Funders Group organized to examine implications of concentrating funding geographically.

Refocusing its mission, MAP engaged in new efforts to enhance philanthropy. Gateway to Giving, a partnership of 20 organizations convened by MAP, was launched to increase philanthropy in the region and received a three-year national grant from New Ventures in Philanthropy. MAP increased nonprofits' access to fund-raising resources through a partnership with the St. Louis Public Library, which now houses The Foundation Center's regional collection. And a new Education Interest Group was created to focus on philanthropy's role in improving schools. With a rich history and an exciting future, MAP continues providing critical leadership for philanthropy in the St. Louis region.

Riverview Gardens School District

Overcoming challenges is the hallmark of the Riverview Gardens School District, whose history courses like a river that grows and shrinks and grows again. The 12-square-mile district, primarily bedroom communities, offers a primer on raising student achievement with a limited tax base.

Established in 1926, Riverview Gardens quickly began to grow. During the first 25 years, it built one elementary school, annexed another and opened a high school. Between 1951 and 1965, it expanded four schools and built 10.

In the 1970s enrollment dropped but began a 15-year upswing in the late 1980s. Between 1996 and 2000, the district built an elementary school and expanded eight others. All projects were completed on time and on budget. In 2001 the district had about 7,800 students and more renovations were slated through 2005 to accommodate future growth.

The district was in the spotlight for much of 2001. President George W. Bush visited one of its elementary schools, commending its Success for All reading program. The Missouri Center for Safe Schools proclaimed Riverview Gardens a "showcase" district for safety plans and training. The high school became an A+ School, a status Missouri grants only to schools that have increased performance and graduation rates. Students in A+ schools who meet certain criteria receive college financial assistance.

Also in 2001, three schools adopted First Things First. The federal initiative teams teachers and students in small learning communities for several years and reduces teacher-student ratios by putting administrators in classrooms.

Riverview Gardens has worked aggressively to improve student achievement, and by 2000, students were reaping the benefits of that vigilance. Scores improved dramatically in 18 of 24 categories on Missouri's rigorous standardized tests that year. Additionally, the state recognized three elementary schools on its "most improved schools" list.

A $2 million National Science Foundation grant is training teachers in a hands-on approach to science education. The grant expanded an ongoing initiative that has been credited for a double-digit increase in one school's science scores.

Transience is a difficult issue for the district. At one school, three out of four children who start the school year move before it ends. To provide stability, some schools keep teachers with classes for two grades. To meet the students' non-educational needs, the district partners with numerous institutions and agencies to obtain free dental and eye exams, health screenings, uniforms and other items.

Riverview Gardens selects strong leaders as principals, pays well for teachers with advanced degrees, and offers professional development opportunities and tuition reimbursement. Its success in recruiting and retaining quality teachers recently earned it a Missouri Best Practices award while the outstanding cooperation between labor and management and the district's collaborative, interest-based bargaining were commended by the United Auto Workers Union and the Saturn Corp.

For more than seven decades, Riverview Gardens has surmounted difficulties with its single-minded focus on student achievement. This proves that quality education depends less on a large tax base or stable population and more on the talent and dedication of educators.

Student achievement, in academics and in life, is the focus at Riverview Gardens.

Riverview Gardens boasts ever-increasing graduation rates.

Schrader Funeral Home

Frederick Schrader, a German-born carpenter and cabinetmaker, settled in the St. Louis County community of Ballwin, Missouri, in 1846. Using his trade skills to support his family, he began crafting caskets for area residents by 1868. That was the beginning of the funeral business that he cultivated to sustain his descendants throughout the following century and into the next. The enterprise he started is now the St. Louis area's oldest family-owned funeral home, as well as Ballwin's oldest business.

Frederick's son, William, helped with the family business, known in those early years as "undertaking," which included making the necessary arrangements for burials. By 1910 William became a licensed embalmer and built a proper funeral parlor about a block west of the original location on Manchester Road. As horse-drawn vehicles became obsolete, he fashioned a hearse body for a motorized vehicle for his operation. The enterprise passed on to William's son, Harry, who like his father, ran the business and lived in that same building, which eventually expanded to meet the needs of the growing community.

By the time Harry retired in the 1960s, the small operation begun by his grandfather had become a full-fledged funeral home. Harry's son, Harold "Skip," and daughter, Ruth Schrader Arft, fourth-generation owners and funeral directors, saw the progression of additions to the building beginning with the chapel garages and the premier visitation room, the Williamsburg, in the 60s. The next decade brought completion of the east wing, incorporating the beautifully appointed Wedgwood and Rose Rooms. The smaller, more intimate Canterbury Room rounded out the accommodations along with the large chapel featuring colonial design pews.

Although the building, now surrounded by the 1990 added atrium, no longer houses a family dwelling, fifth-generation Schraders continue the tradition — Skip's son, Steven, and Ruth's daughter, Peggy Arft-Goethe, are part of the current staff of 31. Steven's wife, Cathy, Ruth's husband, Hank Arft, who played first base for the American League St. Louis Browns for five years, and his son-in-law, Dennis Goethe, also hold positions at Schrader.

Earning its third consecutive Pursuit of Excellence Award, given by the National Funeral Directors Association in 2001, Schrader continually strives to benefit the living. It encourages families to celebrate the loved one's life by individualizing services with photographs, videos, music and personal mementos. The funeral home also sponsors the Schrader Sunshine Club, a grief support group established in the 1990s.

Sharing its good fortune with the community that supported it over the years, Schrader sponsors several community youth sports teams. In 1998 it established an annual scholarship award to benefit students in the Funeral Service Program at St. Louis Community College. Each year it holds a communitywide Christmas Memorial Service with the lighting of a tall Christmas tree in its grand foyer, followed by Schrader family members serving refreshments to those in attendance. Additionally, Schrader's on-staff grief specialist, John Avery, often provides support to area schools in times of need.

Starting a two-year building renovation in 2001, Schrader Funeral Home anticipates another century of dedicated service to the St. Louis area.

The Schrader, Arft & Goethe families

Sunshine Ministries

Like other disciples of Jesus Christ, Edward Card started as a fisherman. In 1903 he moved to St. Louis where he started a rescue mission. Financed by a group of Christian businessmen, the soup kitchen and gospel mission on Market Street was named Sunshine Mission. Under the leadership of the man affectionately known as "Daddy" Card, the mission offered rays of hope to encourage the destitute and downtrodden people on the city's streets. Sunshine Mission later grew to include an overnight shelter for homeless men and eventually added a long-term resident program designed to help men recover from substance abuse and other destructive behaviors that kept them from leading productive lives.

In the 1980s the mission began to serve the "near-homeless" in the St. Louis community. Reflecting this expanded outreach, it later changed its name to Sunshine Ministries. From its headquarters, now on 13th Street near downtown St. Louis, it continues to serve homeless men as well as operating family and youth services programs. In 2000, after acquiring 80 acres of land in Foristell, Missouri, it opened Eagle Lodge — a camp and retreat center designed to expose inner city youth to a natural, rural setting.

Sunshine Ministries operates with a staff of approximately 25 employees, plus many volunteers, and seminary students. The overnight men's shelter provides food, clothing, shower facilities, comfortable beds and spiritual guidance to nearly 50 men each evening. The program is designed to treat the men with honor and respect in a clean, safe environment.

The men in the long-term Resident Program make a 13-month commitment to their personal rehabilitation. Through spiritual and practical counseling, the men begin rehabilitation by learning to respect themselves and realize their potential as God's creation. Living a structured life that includes work responsibilities, they receive basic life-skills training, computer-based skills assessment and job training to prepare them for a successful entry into the mainstream. Upon completion, they move to Sunshine's transitional program where they begin their journey toward independence.

Sunshine Ministries' Family Services help men, women and children whose poverty-level incomes force them to live in crime-ridden neighborhoods. Required to register and attend monthly meetings, they receive food, clothing, spiritual encouragement and emotional support from the caring staff. They can also attend many educational and vocational programs designed to help them improve their lives.

Since it is easier to mold a child than to mend an adult, Sunshine Ministries provides many programs for at-risk youth. The Kids Club and Teen Club offer after-school and summer programs set in safe, loving environments. Through mentoring and tutoring, the young people are equipped to seek happy and successful adult lives.

Relying totally on private funding supplemented by donated food and supplies, Sunshine Ministries' life-blood is its donors and volunteers. Drawing recognition from U.S. Vice President Dick Cheney during his visit to St. Louis, the mission became a national model of faith-based ministries that provides a hand up rather than a handout to those in need. Every day Sunshine Ministries carries out its mission statement by offering healing from the past, help for the present and hope for the future.

Edward "Daddy" Card founded Sunshine Mission in 1903.

Jim and Carol Clarkson, Sunshine Ministries' current directors, oversee the mission's outreach to the poor and needy of St. Louis.

University of Missouri-Columbia

Memorial Union, with its distinctive gothic clock tower, was built after World War I to honor MU faculty and students who have given their lives for their country in war. The Union also is a favorite place for members of the Mizzou family to gather for meetings, studying and snacks.

ermeated in a rich tradition of offering quality higher education to Missourians while intently pursuing knowledge to further that heritage, the University of Missouri-Columbia embodies the essence of learning. Founded in Columbia, Missouri, in 1839, it was the first public university established in the Louisiana Purchase territory. Today renowned as Missouri's largest public research university, it is also a major land-grant institution. Known as MU, or simply "Mizzou," by legions of alumni from St. Louis and throughout Missouri, the United States and over 100 other countries, its unique offerings result in achievements vital to global well being.

MU initially arose through the earnest efforts of its local Boone County citizens, who envisioned public education as the vehicle to a better way of life. Its first graduating class of 1843 included two students. Now its total enrollment surpasses 23,000. In 1867 it added a College of Education and began to admit women. The real impetus for growth occurred in 1870 when it was awarded land-grant status under the terms of the Morrill Act. MU then inaugurated its College of Agriculture and in 1888 set up the Agricultural Experiment Station on Sanborn Field in Columbia, which continues today.

During those early years, MU also added schools of law and medicine and its College of Engineering. Undaunted by a disastrous fire in 1892, it rebuilt around all that remained of its first academic building, the now famous Columns. Into the 20th century Mizzou blossomed as a major research university, increasing its programs, including an interdisciplinary graduate school. Founding the world's first School of Journalism in 1908, it initiated its legacy of developing exceptionally skilled talent for careers in the media. Following World War II, MU's enrollment escalated, partially due to the GI Bill. It became fully integrated in 1950 when it opened its doors to African-American students. By 1963 the University became a four-campus system with flagship Mizzou as its largest university member.

Now in its third century and stronger than ever with 20 colleges and schools, MU is one of only six universities in the country with medicine, veterinary medicine and law all on one campus. It is an invited member of the Association of American Universities, the most prestigious group of public and private research universities in the nation, and the only public member in Missouri. MU also ranks in the first tier of America's fastest-growing research universities. As part of a campus master plan, MU designs new buildings to blend harmoniously with the remaining time-honored originals. Recently earning a national award for landscaping, its campus is now a botanic garden. Rounding out the college experience since it fielded its first football team in 1890, it is the only institution in Missouri operating all of its sports in NCAA Division I-A, the nation's highest level of intercollegiate athletics.

Mizzou's roster of notable alumni encompasses every conceivable field of endeavor and spans every decade of its existence. Never resting on past laurels, MU began construction on a major research complex in 2001 — the Life Sciences Center. Its continued dedication to learning fortifies its founders' vision of seeking the means for a promising future.

One of the most photographed sites in Missouri, the six 43-foot Ionic Columns that stand in the center of Francis Quadrangle represent the core of MU's pride and tradition. They are all that remain of Academic Hall, completed in 1843 and destroyed by fire in 1892.

St. Louis, Gateway to the West, is a portal for the technology-driven economy.

TECHNOLOGY

St. Louis, Gateway to the West, is a portal for the technology-driven economy. We enjoy an extraordinary history of innovative technology leadership along with colleges and universities, major research centers, a remarkable concentration of engineering talent and solid economic growth.

The Gateway City boasts a long history of blending business and technical solutions. St. Louis businessmen sponsored Charles Lindbergh's 1927 solo, trans-Atlantic flight that made aviation history and led to the region's development as a leading aerospace industry and defense community. Unique employment opportunities attracted some of America's brightest engineers, who helped establish our region's technological leadership. This exceptional pool of talent, combined with deep-rooted civic leadership, facilitated decades of beneficial collaboration between industry, research and government interests.

The St. Louis metropolitan area understands, produces and applies advanced technology to enhance workflow processes. Our businesses eagerly utilize technology solutions to boost productivity and increase profits, resulting in local economic stability. Alan Greenspan, Chairman of the Federal Reserve, explained to a St. Louis audience at the National Summit on High Technology, June 15, 1999, "An economy that 20 years ago seemed to have seen its better days is displaying a remarkable run of economic growth that appears to have its roots in ongoing advances in technology." Local employers invest more than $2 billion annually in research and development, with a primary focus on agriculture, nutrition, improved food quality and disease prevention. Known as the "BioBelt," the St. Louis region is an internationally recognized world leader in plant and life sciences research. Researchers embrace the challenges of solving critical problems from increasing world food production to unlocking mysteries of the human body. For example, St. Louis is the current home of the United States Human Genome Research Project and the birthplace of pioneering work in Asynchronous Transfer Mode (ATM) technology and Positron Emission Tomography (PET) Scanners.

"Information innovation lies at the root of productivity and economic growth," according to Alan Greenspan. The St. Louis area is a powerhouse that produces innovative information technology and applies sophisticated IT solutions to business problems, favorably positioning local business to maintain our strong regional economy. Additionally, the metropolitan area offers an outstanding quality of life that includes short commutes, affordable housing and a low cost of living.

I am proud to say, "The Gateway City, my home, has always welcomed those pioneering spirits that seek an open door to the future and a better life for all."

GREG SULLIVAN
CEO and Founder • G.A. Sullivan

Insituform Technologies, Inc.

A maze of infrastructure exists below the surface of every city, equally as complicated and vital to a region as the one above, yet not often noticed or even thought about.

Insituform Technologies, Inc. is in the business of ensuring that this intricate web continues to remain silent and invisible by updating and revitalizing aging sewer, water and other underground pipes using special technologies that allow the company to perform its work without digging or disruption.

In the years since such original pipe structures were put into place, many aboveground buildings, streets and houses have been added that make it difficult to completely dig up and replace the old systems. In 1971, Eric Wood, an innovative individual in London, first implemented a process that would be not only less disruptive, but also quicker in the rehabilitation of deteriorating sewer systems. This idea was the birth of the Insituform® proprietary process, which expanded to North America in 1980.

Now headquartered in Chesterfield with a 60,000-square-foot research and development facility, Insituform (from the Latin, "to form in place") serves locations in the United States from coast to coast, in addition to communities worldwide.

Over the years, the company has evolved with technology, offering newer, even more efficient processes that also make Insituform a more cost-effective choice for repairs to pipes such as sanitary sewers, storm sewers, force mains and service laterals.

Industrial applications include the repair of process effluent sewers, recirculation pipes, raw water intake pipes, product transfer pipes and cooling water systems, as well as sanitary and storm sewers. The Insituform process offers particular benefit to those with difficult-to-access pipes.

The company's first initiative is to fully assess job sites for existing conditions and to troubleshoot or prevent problems from occurring with Insituform's personnel ready to assist with any public concerns. Vertical integration gives the company the opportunity to manage projects from engineering and manufacturing through completed installation.

The special process is a unique, yet simple application. Existing pipes are utilized as the "form" of the new Insituform® pipe. After careful, project-specific, customized engineering work, the company manufactures a felt tube that is coated on one side with a permanently bonded, continuous polyethylene layer. During the manufacturing process, the tube is put through a series of separate quality tests and made to exact size and length specifications. Prior to installation the tube is impregnated with a thermo-setting resin.

During the installation, water pressure is applied, turning the tube inside out using a patented Controlled Head Inversion Process (CHIP). Hot water is then circulated throughout the pipe to cure the resin, resulting in a structural and jointless Insituform® pipe within the original host pipe. With the use of closed-circuit television, visual inspection is accomplished before and after installation. Service laterals can be restored internally with the use of robotically controlled cutting devices. The tubes have a minimum design life of about 50 years.

The procedure is safe and effective, and all Insituform processes are ISO 9001 certified, ensuring the best quality control throughout the entire project. The company prides itself on the quality of all aspects of its products and services and provides the most advanced and versatile pipeline rehabilitation technologies available. A centralized management system maintains consistent products and implementation throughout all of Insituform's operations.

Insituform's Chesterfield headquarters comprises a 60,000-square-foot research and development facility, training center, engineering, local operations facility, as well as centralized human resources, accounting and marketing.

Technologies include cured-in-place rehabilitation, fold-and-form rehabilitation, tunneling and microtunneling, pipebursting, sliplining and repair of deteriorating pipes in the oil, gas and mining industries.

Insituform's processes are used globally in water, wastewater and industrial markets, as well as providing solutions for markets such as airports and military bases. Tens of millions of feet of pipeline have been installed using Insituform's processes, bringing clean water in and taking wastewater out of many locations around the world, including Europe, Asia, Israel, New Zealand, South America and West Africa.

Insituform's crews are composed of the company's own certified and internally trained employees. Training focuses on providing the utmost in quality service, improving productivity and managing change through formal in-house training classes. Insituform employs approximately 1,700 people worldwide and about 200 in the St. Louis area.

The company's primary customers are cities and townships, engineering consulting firms, industrial plants and may be recommended by local government. It has been honored with many trade journal "Projects of the Year" awards.

Due to Insituform's diversification, it offers many solutions that can be adapted to meet specific needs. Growth, products and services that offer cost-effective customer value remain major goals of the company, while providing outstanding quality, safety and speed, as it keeps public inconvenience to a minimum.

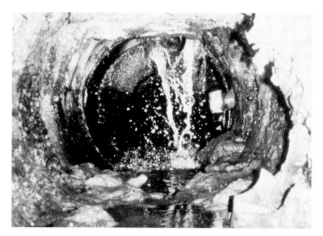

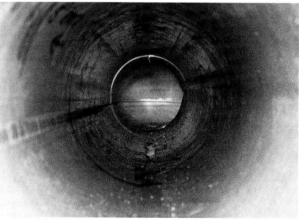

It is a challenge to repair aging sewers without disturbing the neighborhood, roads and office buildings above the surface. That is the specialty of Insituform Technologies, Inc. Its business is rehabilitating, repairing, maintaining and installing underground pipes. (Top) Deteriorating concrete sewer. (Bottom) Pipe rehabilitated with the Insituform® process.

SUBSIDIARIES

Affholder®, Inc., a tunneling company that installs pipelines, rehabilitates deteriorating pipes and bores large underground tunnels for growing communities, solves a variety of underground problems using various methods such as new tunnel construction, wet mix and dry mix shotcrete rehabilitation, epoxy resin grouting and manhole rehabilitation.

A major milestone for the company was its acquisition of Kinsel® Industries, Inc. in January 2001. Kinsel provides the company with greater capabilities to perform trenchless technologies such as pipebursting, microtunneling and sliplining. Pipebursting enables the replacement of pipes with newer pipes that are of the same or larger diameters. It is a trenchless technology using a pipebursting tool, which bursts the old pipe into pieces as a new pipe is pulled into place. The process increases capacity of existing sewer and water lines without major digging or public disruption.

Insituform's TiteLiner® division offers the world's leading internal solutions for protecting pipelines from abrasion and corrosion. These solutions are used globally throughout the petrochemical and mining industries.

COMMUNITY OUTREACH

Insituform also remains active in the St. Louis community. As a joint Gold Sponsor with its Affholder subsidiary for the Salute to Excellence Scholarship Awards Banquet, the company has assisted youth throughout the area.

Special relationships with Mathews-Dickey Boys' and Girls' Club, Beaumont High School, Lincoln University and other children's and young adults' organizations, provide Insituform venues for major contributions to the community. Over the past few years, the company has provided needed appliances and funding, sponsored educational programs and awarded scholarships to such organizations in St. Louis and throughout the country.

Monsanto Company

onsanto is a technology leader in the agricultural industry with a history of science-based innovation going back more than 100 years. The company consists of creative and dedicated people from around the world who share a vision of abundant food and a healthy environment and who are fully committed to the communities in which they serve.

Monsanto produces seeds for important food crops, including wheat, corn, soybeans and grain sorghum. The seeds are marketed under the Asgrow, DEKALB, Hartz and Quantum brands.

Monsanto's agricultural researchers are working to create imaginative new possibilities that will improve farmers' productivity and efficiency. Monsanto believes in the benefits of biotechnology and pledges to pursue those benefits with respect, openness and honesty.

The roots from which the current Monsanto has grown, began in 1901 when John F. Queeny founded the Monsanto Chemical Works, naming the company after his wife, Olga Mendez Monsanto. Queeny established the company to make products for the food and pharmaceutical industries, beginning with the artificial sweetener, saccharin. Since then, Monsanto has evolved through many stages to become a technology leader focusing on new ways to create more abundant, nutritious food and a healthier environment.

Queeny started with a single product, but his new company grew quickly. In 1917 the company began producing aspirin and by the mid-1940s its offerings included agricultural products as well as a variety of essential ingredients for making rubber, soaps and detergents, phosphorus, fibers, plastics and resins. In 1960 Monsanto formed a separate agriculture division, allowing the company to concentrate on emerging technologies, and in 1981 it began construction of a major research facility in Chesterfield, Missouri, firmly establishing biotechnology as a strategic focus.

During the next 20 years, Monsanto achieved significant success in the field of agriculture. Roundup became the world's most used herbicide and soon the company launched the world's first genetically enhanced crop. In 1987 Monsanto scientist John Franz was awarded America's highest honor for technical achievement, the National Medal of Technology, in recognition of his discovery of the active ingredient in Roundup. Then in 1998 four more scientists at Monsanto were given this same award for their work in plant biology and biotechnology. In 2001 Dr. William S. Knowles, retired from Monsanto, was awarded the Nobel Prize in Chemistry for work that resulted in a new treatment for Parkinson's disease.

During the 1980s Monsanto began to focus more and more on life sciences, agriculture, pharmaceuticals and food. In the 1990s Monsanto acquired several related companies, eventually merging with Pharmacia and Upjohn. The merger split the agriculture division into a separate company that is now the current Monsanto Company.

If one thing stands out as a symbol of the company during the last century, it has to be its history of innovative people. These people served as the backbone of the company as it navigated through a century of tumultuous challenge. Now in a new century, Monsanto begins a new

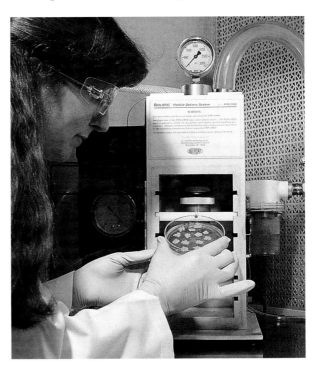

life as a new company, retaining its heritage of remarkable people. The new company is focused on agriculture, using its scientific resources to contribute to feeding and clothing people around the world.

Today, the 14,700 people of Monsanto are working to create imaginative new possibilities that will improve farmers' productivity, and efficiency. They are committed to developing thoughtful, responsible science and to producing products and services that are safe and reliable and that help answer the world's growing need for food and fiber.

As part of its ongoing commitment to serve communities, Monsanto has actively engaged in the civic and cultural life of the communities in which it operates. The Monsanto Fund was created in 1964 with the goal of improving people's lives by helping to bridge the gap between their needs and their resources. The fund focuses on areas of agricultural abundance, the environment, science education and local communities. It has been an important contributor to a variety of projects including the Buhle Farmer's Academy in Delmas, South Africa; the Phinizy Swamp Nature Park in Augusta, Georgia; the Tangerang Milk Program in Jakarta, Indonesia; and the Maria Ofelia V. Pedrosa Elementary School in Sao Jose dos Campos, Brazil.

In St. Louis, the fund has contributed $50 million toward the founding of the Donald Danforth Plant Science Center and has donated 40 acres of land, some of which will be used for a 12,000-square-foot greenhouse. The Danforth Center is dedicated to training scientists for work in developing countries and will conduct full-scale efforts to better understand how plants can contribute to human health. In addition, the fund has supported the Monsanto Insectarium at the St. Louis Zoo, the Missouri Botanical Gardens, Queeny Park in West County, renovations in Forest Park, the St. Louis Symphony, the Repertory Theatre and many more.

The Nidus Center for Scientific Enterprise is another beneficiary of Monsanto's investment. Nidus is a plant and life sciences incubator offering a place for people with new ideas to come for help in developing those ideas into successful businesses. Its primary goals are to build an entrepreneurial culture that supports and nurtures young companies in the plant and life sciences, to help make necessary capital available through venture capital funds, to ensure a progressive business climate that fosters and sustains the growth of plant and life sciences in the

St. Louis region and to make laboratory space available to companies that need it. The Nidus Center primarily serves agricultural and medical biotech clients.

As a new independent company, Monsanto has committed itself to a new Pledge. The elements of the Pledge are focused on five areas of behavior. The company pledges to dialogue and listen to diverse points of view; to be transparent to insure that information is available, accessible, and understandable; to respect religious, cultural and ethical concerns of people around the world; to share knowledge and technology; and to deliver benefits in the form of high-quality products that are beneficial to customers and to the environment.

Monsanto's business is to create simple solutions in agriculture from a deep and respectful understanding of nature. The company's goals are to reduce the need for pesticides in crop production, to offer farmers around the world new ways to become more successful and self-sufficient, and to help meet the world's growing demand for food and fiber while helping protect the quality of the world's land, air and water.

Talisen Technologies

With $3,000 and the support of the St. Louis County Business Incubator, George Brill launched a high-tech company based upon a need he observed while working for a major aerospace manufacturer. Now Talisen Technologies, formerly AeroTech Service Group, is rocketing into the global marketplace with a supply chain management infrastructure serving industries as diverse as manufacturing and health care, and Brill, the company's CEO, serves on the business incubator's board of directors.

A former engineer for the U.S. Navy and located at McDonnell Douglas (now Boeing), Brill in 1991 founded AeroTech Service Group to facilitate the transfer of technical data, like specifications and drawings, between Boeing and its suppliers and clients. The company, which initially received economical office space and support services through the St. Louis County Business Incubator, dealt primarily with hard-copy records at first, but changes were in the works.

To reduce paperwork and increase efficiency, Boeing had created a system providing secure electronic access to its technical data. Brill in 1993 piloted that system by bringing two suppliers online, and Boeing granted AeroTech Service Group at the time the right to connect others.

Boeing's system used the Internet, a Department of Defense invention that researchers, academics and those connected with the government had been using for over two decades. A physicist at CERN, the European Organization for Nuclear Research, began creating the World Wide Web in 1991 but access to it remained limited until 1994, when the release of a Windows-based Web browser opened the information superhighway to the masses.

Boeing and Talisen Technologies formed a strategic alliance and adapted Boeing's system for the Web. Talisen Technologies then commercialized that technology to develop its own Virtual Factory Enterprise™ (VFE) in 1996. The infrastructure, designed for manufacturers, facilitates supply chain transactions, offers a common platform for e-business applications in real-time and provides other advantages.

VFE catered to changes in the heavy manufacturing industry favoring collaboration and the use of digitally controlled equipment, both of which require electronic submission of data. The Virtual Enterprise™ evolved from VFE as a product with wide marketability to other industries. Both combine software and services to provide one secure gateway into a company's databases and applications, allowing customers, partners and suppliers to access them as determined by individual user profiles. The systems provide centralized authentication and account management.

Talisen Technologies integrates VE and VFE to accommodate specific programs and legacy applications. The products work on common computer platforms such as mainframes, UNIX workstations and personal computers; they are available with a Web interface or for X Windows systems. Talisen Technologies also rents time on its infrastructure, a popular option among small businesses, and offers services including information systems consulting.

The development of VE put Talisen Technologies at a crossroads with three paths — consulting, brokering information or marketing

Talisen Technologies' clients benefit from the extensive experience that its owners — Bruce Draper, George Brill and Paul Schwetz — bring to each project.

VE exclusively — and the situation was featured in a Harvard Business School case study and a *Harvard Business Review* story, both published in 1996. Harvard's interest in Talisen Technologies validated the company in the eyes of the business world.

Talisen Technologies' decision to focus on VE, rather than pursuing its other options, allowed for speedy expansion. Supply chain practices apply even in the health care industry, where insurance companies are paying customers and health care providers are suppliers. For organizations struggling to comply with federal mandates governing the secure electronic maintenance, transmission and accessibility of patient records, VE is the answer because it already meets stringent Defense Department requirements. VE ensures secure access to patient, customer and vendor information, streamlines workflow processes, and reduces paperwork and costs.

In 2000 Talisen Technologies began implementing VE in health care organizations and branching out into other non-defense-related industries. Its commercial customers include Anchor Glass; Riverwood International, a paperboard and packaging company; and Celox Networks, a manufacturer of high-speed telecommunications switches.

Brill, who serves on the advisory board for Parks College of Engineering and Aviation, owns Talisen Technologies with two partners, Bruce Draper and Paul Schwetz, who joined the firm in 1995 and 1997 respectively. Draper, chief technology officer, has an extensive knowledge of technology fundamentals and a natural teaching ability that enables him to convey that understanding to others. Paul Schwetz, president, uses his business and financial expertise to guide Talisen Technologies in navigating the global market and negotiating complicated alliances.

In 1998 Boeing offered Talisen Technologies a low-risk opportunity to expand into foreign markets through a program that seeks to offset the price another country pays for aircraft by seeding economic growth there. Transferring technology is one means to that end so Boeing began buying Talisen Technologies' products and services for foreign companies. In time Talisen Technologies forms a joint venture or strategic partnership with each company. Scandinavia, the Netherlands and the United Kingdom are among the areas Talisen Technologies serves through this type of business relationship.

About 3,000 manufacturers rely on Talisen Technologies' goods and services, among them GKN

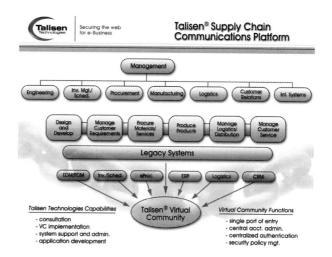

Talisen Technologies' Virtual Enterprise™ provides an e-business solution applicable to any supply chain.

Aerospace, British Aerospace, Northrop Grumman, Rolls-Royce and Smith Industries. The company operates nationwide and in other countries including Australia, Israel and Japan.

Deloitte & Touche in 2001 ranked Talisen Technologies as 23rd in its regional Technology Fast 50 List, recognizing the company's growth of 250 percent over five years. In 1998 Talisen Technologies ranked 393rd in the national Technology Fast 500 List and boasted 728-percent growth over five years.

Talisen Technologies works closely with civic agencies to raise awareness about technology. Staff members visit schools during National Engineering Week and participate in recruitment fairs. The company helped supply computer-aided drafting and manufacturing systems for the Cornerstone Partnership, which offers job training to at-risk youths and laid-off workers.

Profitable from inception, Talisen Technologies grew without debt during its first decade. The privately held company in 2001 began attracting outside financing to fuel international expansion and to further marketing efforts in the health care industry.

Talisen Technologies' story is one of a metamorphosis. The company has transformed from a "mom and pop" shop into a respected business entity with a global presence. The Internet has changed in a similar fashion. Once the purview of a select few, it now links people and businesses around the world. However, security concerns temper the freedoms of e-commerce. Talisen Technologies connects business, suppliers and customers with peace of mind.

Charter Communications, Inc.

With a nationwide broadband network providing immediate information and resources from anywhere in the world to customers in their homes, businesses and even on the road, Charter Communications, Inc. is fulfilling Chairman of the Board Paul Allen's vision of a Wired World.

Founded in 1993 as a cable television company and headquartered in St. Louis, Charter has grown into the fourth-largest broadband communications company in the United States with more than 7 million customers and 17,000 employees in 40 states.

From the start, Charter has focused on high-quality service, the latest technology, and a range of programming and availability — all at a reasonable price.

Allen acquired Charter Communications in 1998, and in keeping with his Wired World vision, today the company provides many innovative programs and is equipped to handle the expansion of future technology. This is accomplished through its broadband infrastructure made up of fiber-optic lines and coaxial cable.

Undertaking an aggressive upgrade and rebuild, Charter has built a state-of-the-art architecture that allows the company to continually add new services and products for entertainment, communication and data services as well as a wider range of television programming.

Charter's industry position has not resulted solely from its reliable products and services, but is due largely to its dedication to customer service and acquisition of suburban cable systems. The company's national footprint linking smaller communities with larger ones throughout the United States has allowed it to promptly offer leading edge services to all of its customers.

Two years of multiple acquisitions doubled the size of the company by the end of 2000, and it reached a major milestone of 1 million digital cable customers, adding more than 17,000 new users each week. The customer base for high-speed Internet services tripled, allowing users to download files and access Web sites much faster than when using conventional phone lines, offering a constant connection with no dial-up time.

A Charter 2001 initiative established customer care centers strategically located across the country. These centers give customers prompt, quality service and support the newest products.

Personalized television may sound futuristic, but Charter provides an interface to access all services such as video programming, the Internet, video on demand and communications through a television set today. Services are personalized to each individual's tastes. The latest technology also includes Internet protocol telephony in which telephone communications are also provided via the broadband cable.

Charter is a Fortune 500 and NASDAQ 100 company and has received many prestigious awards including the Outstanding Corporate Growth Award, the 2001 R.E. "Ted" Turner Innovator of the Year Award from the Southern Cable Telecommunications Association and the 2000 Innovator Award for Technology from *Cablevision Magazine*.

Charter Communications supports the local communities in which it resides through such programs as Cable in the Classroom, providing free cable connections and programming to more than 8,000 schools nationwide, and VH1 Save the Music Foundation, an initiative designed to raise awareness of the positive impact of music participation. The Charter-sponsored Web site, KIDSNET, encourages media literacy in children. Charter offers free Internet access through WorldGate to schools and some homes to give students opportunities, regardless of economic status.

Entering the 21st century, Charter Communications continues its quest to provide broadband service availability to virtually everyone and help to create a Wired World that makes everyone's world more accessible and just a little bit smaller.

Gary Vaughn (left) and Jeff Young, Charter Communications technicians from the St. Louis system, work on the upgrade and rebuild of the original St. Louis system. Charter is among the nation's largest broadband communications companies and is currently serving some 7 million customers in 40 states.

Koplar Communications International, Inc

oplar Communications International, Inc. (KCI) is a privately held company whose reach extends worldwide. While KCI's affiliates engage in various businesses including commercial property management and distribution of animated television programming, the company's future direction is focused on the development of interactive media and entertainment.

Throughout the company's history, creativity, vision and innovation have turned bold ventures into successful enterprises. In the 1920s eighth-grade-educated Sam Koplar parlayed a brick salvaging business into a construction company that built some of St. Louis' enduring architectural landmarks, including Powell Symphony Hall and The Park Plaza Hotel. After Sam acquired the adjacent Chase Hotel, his architect son, Harold Koplar (HK), constructed a grand lobby connecting the two properties, creating the Chase-Park Plaza. HK continually enhanced the hotel, personally designing and building numerous additions including The Khorassan Room and Starlight Roof. His ability to attract top-name talent made The Chase Club one of the nation's legendary nightclubs and made "The Chase — The Place" in St. Louis from the 1940s through the 1970s.

Seeking to expand his entertainment empire through the new medium of television, HK launched his station, KPLR-TV, in 1959 with St. Louis' first-ever live telecast of a Cardinals baseball game. HK created popular shows such as "Wrestling at the Chase," and KPLR-TV became known for technological innovations such as the "Videocruiser," St. Louis' first remote production vehicle.

In the 1960s HK designed and built The Lodge of Four Seasons in Missouri's Lake of the Ozarks. His hotel, crown jewel of one of the premier resort communities in the Midwest, is a powerful catalyst for economic growth in the Lake Region. H.K.'s daughter, Susan Brown, and her husband, Peter, direct the ongoing development of these properties. With the recent addition of The Porto Cima Community featuring Missouri's only 18-hole Jack Nicklaus Signature Golf Course, the area has become a world-class resort destination.

By the mid-1970s HK's son, Edward J. (Ted) Koplar, had begun to chart KPLR-TV's future. He focused on excellence in programming and made KPLR-TV the country's first station licensed to use satellite technologies. Ted's initiatives kept KPLR-TV consistently ranked among the top five independent stations in the United States from the late 70s through the 1980s. After acquiring the local broadcast rights for Cardinals baseball, KPLR-TV ranked No. 1 until the station was sold in 1998.

World Events Productions, Ltd., founded by Ted in 1981 to produce television programming, achieved overwhelming success when its first series, "Voltron, Defender of the Universe," became the nation's No. 1-rated children's show during 1984-85. "Voltron" and subsequent series are distributed worldwide. To develop and promote local talent, in the early 1990s Ted created Team 11, an ethnically diverse troupe of young entertainers who perform for audiences locally and throughout the country. A number of Team 11 alumni are enjoying successful professional careers in the entertainment industry.

Today, Ted's combined interests in technology and entertainment are realized in his company, VEIL™ Interactive Technologies. Working with leading networks, advertisers, technology partners and studios, VEIL offers limitless possibilities for television's future. The company's global vision, merging interactive technologies and entertainment, will transform the way people around the world view television.

Sam Koplar,
Harold (HK)Koplar;
Chase-Park Plaza Hotel;
KPLR-TV's Earth
Satellite Station;
Edward J. (Ted) Koplar;
Susan and Peter Brown;
The Lodge of
Four Seasons

Sigma-Aldrich Corporation

DNA's double helix and constellation of proteins beckon to Sigma-Aldrich Corporation like an inviting finger. At the frontier of science, the company supports researchers unlocking the secrets of life written in the human genome by supplying high-quality research chemicals and products, such as synthetic DNA.

Sigma-Aldrich's commitment to leadership in the emerging markets of life sciences and high technology is evidenced by its investments in facilities. Near its St. Louis headquarters, a $55 million world-class Life Science and High Technology Center enhances the company's discovery capabilities and furthers its innovative leadership in the dynamic life science, biotechnology and high technology areas. In Wisconsin a $28 million facility specializes in organometallic chemistry and allows the company to seize opportunities in high technology that promise large-scale applications in industries like electronics and petroleum.

Sigma-Aldrich's history flows from two sources. Sigma Chemical dates back to the founding of Midwest Consultants in 1934 by two brothers, Aaron Fischer and Bernard Fischlowitz. Aldrich Chemical Company was established in 1951 by Dr. Alfred Bader.

Sigma initially manufactured products as diverse as ink and saccharin. Its focus narrowed with the production of adenosine triphosphate, the universal energy molecule, and other high-quality research products. Biochemical sales snowballed during the 1950s, and Sigma also entered the diagnostics market with the first ready-made reagent kits.

The research conducted at Sigma-Aldrich's Life Science and High Technology Center in St. Louis ultimately benefits people around the world. The new $55 million facility, housing 240 scientists and staff, offers state-of-the-art laboratories and a 300-seat conference/learning auditorium.

Sigma-Aldrich's unparalleled scientific knowledge, strong collections of biotechnology capabilities and quality products with a wide range of chemical applications make it the leading supplier of the life science and high-technology markets as well as the pre-eminent manufacturer and supplier of biochemical and organic chemical products and kits.

During its first two decades, Aldrich became a respected supplier of organic chemical compounds. The merger of Sigma and Aldrich in 1975 blended two unique product lines.

Sigma-Aldrich, with 15 worldwide distribution centers, derives about 45 percent of business from the United States and 40 percent from Europe. The company produces about 40,000 of the over 85,000 unique products it lists. In 2001 sales approached $1.2 billion.

Among its offerings are biochemical and organic chemical products, research and laboratory kits, and chemicals for the production of computer chips. Products for cell signaling and neuroscience aid the study of Parkinson's, Alzheimer's and other diseases. Sigma-Aldrich supports the discovery, testing and production of pharmaceuticals.

The company's success arises from quality workmanship, dedicated employees and outstanding leaders including Dan Broida, Tom Cori and David Harvey.

Broida, an early Sigma employee, took it into the biochemical market and developed a reputation for customer service by welcoming collect calls at any hour. In 2000 Sigma's chemists answered over 1 million technical inquiries.

Cori, Sigma-Aldrich's leader from 1975 until 2000, established it in the global markets and managed acquisitions and expansion. The company grew to 6,000 employees in 33 countries under his leadership.

Harvey, the current chief executive, aligned Sigma-Aldrich's entities under four business units (scientific research, biotechnology, fine chemicals and diagnostics), instituted a cohesive corporate culture and updated technology. The company's Web site offers online sales and outsourcing and technical data.

Sigma-Aldrich has the right chemistry to be a global market leader in life science and high technology while maintaining its niche in the diagnostics market. As in the past, the company's obsession for service and passion for process improvement will drive its future success.

BIBLIOGRAPHY

MONOGRAPHS

Berg, A. Scott. *Lindbergh*. G. P. Putnam's, 1998.

Billon, Frederic Louis. *Annals of St. Louis in its Early Days Under French and Spanish Domination*. St. Louis: Nixon-Jones Printing Co., 1886.

Boernstein, Henry. *The Mysteries of St. Louis: a Novel*. Translated by Friedrich Munch; a modern edition by Steven W. Rowan and Elizabeth Simms. Chicago: Charles H. Kerr, 1990.

Boyer, Paul. *Urban Masses and Moral Order in America, 1820-1920*. Cambridge, MA: Harvard University Press, 1978.

Broeg, Bob. *The One Hundred Greatest Moments in St. Louis Sports*. St. Louis: Missouri Historical Society Press, 2000.

Bryan, John Albury. *The Riverfront at St. Louis: Gateway to the West*. St. Louis: Jefferson National Expansion Memorial, National Park Service, U. S. Department of the Interior, 1942.

Charlton, Thomas Lee. *The Development of St. Louis as a Southwestern Commercial Depot, 1870-1920*. Austin: University of Texas at Austin, Ph.D. Thesis, 1969.

City Plan Commission of St. Louis. *St. Louis After the War*. St. Louis: Nixon-Jones Printing Company, 1917.

City Plan Commission of St. Louis *A Plan for the Central Riverfront, Saint Louis*. St. Louis: Nixon-Jones Printing Company, 1928.

Civic League of St. Louis. *A City Plan for St. Louis*. St. Louis: Nixon-Jones Printing Company, 1907.

Clamorgan, Cyprian. *The Colored Aristocracy of St. Louis*. Columbia: University of Missouri Press, 1999.

Clevenger, Martha, ed. *"Indescribably Grand": Diaries and Letters from the 1904 World's Fair*. St. Louis: Missouri Historical Society Press, 1996.

Corbett, Katharine T. *In Her Place: A Guide to St. Louis Women's History*. St. Louis: Missouri Historical Society Press, 1999.

Corbett, Katharine T. and Miller, Howard. *Saint Louis in the Gilded Age*. St. Louis: Missouri Historical Society Press, 1993.

Cronon, William. *Nature's Metropolis: Chicago and the Great West*. New York: W. W. Norton & Company, 1991.

DeVoto, Bernard. *Across the Wide Missouri*. Boston: Houghton Mifflin Company, 1947.

DeVoto, Bernard. *The Course of Empire*. Boston: Houghton Mifflin Company, 1952.

DeVoto, Bernard, ed. *The Journals of Lewis and Clark*. Boston: Houghton Mifflin Company, 1953.

Early, Gerald Lyn, ed. *Ain't But a Place: An Anthology of African American Writings About St. Louis*. St. Louis: Missouri Historical Society Press, 1998.

Ehrlich, Walter. *Zion in the Valley: The Jewish Community of St. Louis*. Columbia: University of Missouri Press, 1997.

Fivel, Sharon. *From Carriage Trade to Ready-Made: St. Louis Clothing Designers, 1880-1920*. St. Louis: Missouri Historical Society Press, 1992.

Foley, William E. *A History of Missouri, Volume 1: 1673 to 1820*. Columbia: University of Missouri Press, 1971, 1999.

Foley, William E. *The First Chouteaus, River Barons of Early St. Louis*. Urbana: University of Illinois Press, 1983.

Foley, William E. *The Genesis of Missouri: From Wilderness Outpost to Statehood*. Columbia: University of Missouri Press, 1990.

Fox, Tim, ed. *Where We Live: A Guide to St. Louis Communities*. St. Louis: Missouri Historical Society Press, 1995.

Giedion, Sigfried. *Space, Time and Architecture: the Growth of a New Tradition*. Cambridge, MA: Harvard University Press, 1967.

Gray, Rockwell. *A Century of Enterprise: St. Louis, 1894-1994*. St. Louis: Missouri Historical Society Press, 1994.

Greene, Lorenzo J. et al. *Missouri's Black Heritage*. Columbia: University of Missouri Press, 1980, 1993.

Hodes, Frederick Anthony. *The Urbanization of St. Louis: A Study in Urban Residential Patterns in the Nineteenth Century*. St. Louis: St. Louis University, Ph.D. Thesis, 1973.

Honig, Donald. *The St. Louis Cardinals: An Illustrated History*. New York: Prentice Hall, 1991.

Hurley, Andrew, ed. *Common Fields: An Environmental History of St. Louis*. St. Louis: Missouri Historical Society Press, 1997.

Kilgo, Dolores A. *Likeness and Landscape: Thomas M. Easterly and the Art of the Daguerreotype*. St. Louis: Missouri Historical Society Press, 1994.

Lavender, David. *The Great West*. Boston: Houghton Mifflin Company, 1965.

Lange, Dena Floren. *St. Louis: Child of the River, Parent of the West*. St. Louis, 1939.

McCue, George. *The Building Art in St. Louis: Two Centuries*. St. Louis: The American Institute of Architects, 1967.

McDermott, John Francis. *The Early Histories of St. Louis*. St. Louis: St. Louis Historical Documents Foundation, 1952.

McPherson, James M. *Battle Cry of Freedom: The Civil War Era*. New York: Oxford University Press, 1988.

Milner II, Clyde A., Carol A. *O'Connor and Martha A. Sandweiss*. The Oxford History of the American West. New York: Oxford University Press, 1994.

Morrow, Ralph E. *Washington University in St. Louis: A History*. St. Louis: Missouri Historical Society Press, 1996.

Primm, James Neal. *Lion of the Valley: St. Louis, Missouri 1764-1980*. St. Louis: Missouri Historical Society Press, 1998.

Reese, De Anna J. *Intertwining Paths: Respectability, Character, Beauty and the Making of Community Among St. Louis Black Women, 1900-1920*. Columbia: University of Missouri, Ph.D. Thesis, 1996.

Reichler, Joseph L. *Baseball Encyclopedia: The Complete and Official Record of Major League Baseball*. New York: Macmillan, 1982.

Rowan, Steven W., translator and editor. *Germans for a Free Missouri: Translations from the St. Louis Radical Press, 1857-1862*. Introduction by James Neal Primm. Columbia: University of Missouri Pres, 1983.

Sandweiss, Eric Todd. *Construction and Community in South St. Louis, 1850-1910*. Berkeley: University of California at Berkeley, Ph.D. Thesis, 1991.

Spencer, Thomas Edwin. *Story of Old St. Louis*. St. Louis: Press of Con. P. Curran Printing Company, 1914.

Spencer, Thomas M. *The St. Louis Veiled Prophet Celebration: Power on Parade, 1877-1995*. Columbia: University of Missouri Press, 2000.

Stevens, Walter B. *St. Louis: The Fourth City, 1764-1911*. St. Louis: S. J. Clarke Publishing Co., 1911.

Stockton, J. Roy. *The Gashouse Gang and a couple of other guys*. New York: A. S. Barnes and Co., 1945.

Teaford, Jon C. *Cities of the Heartland: The Rise and Fall of the Industrial Midwest*. Bloomington: University of Indiana Press, 1993.

Troen, Selwyn K. and Glen E. Holt, eds. *St. Louis*. New York; New Viewpoints, 1977.

van Ravenswaay, Charles. *St. Louis: An Informal History of the City and its People, 1764-1865*. Edited by Candace O'Connor. St. Louis: Missouri Historical Society Press, 1991.

Wiebe, Robert H. *The Search for Order, 1877-1920*. New York: Hill and Wang, 1967.

Wilson, Laura. *The Great Fire of St. Louis in 1849*. St. Louis: Jefferson National Expansion Memorial, National Park Service, U.S. Department of the Interior, 1938.

Winter, William C. *The Civil War in St. Louis: A Guided Tour*. St. Louis: Missouri Historical Society Press, 1994.

Wright, John A. *Discovering African-American St. Louis: A Guide to Historic Sites*. St. Louis: Missouri Historical Society Press, 1994.

Young Men's Christian Association of St. Louis and St. Louis County. *A Century of Progess*. St. Louis: The Association, 1953.

JOURNAL ARTICLES

Abbot, Mark. "Déjà vu all over again? St. Louis Master Plans and the Dream of a Democratic Community." Gateway Heritage 19 (4) Spring 1999.

Adams, Patricia. "Fighting for Democracy in St. Louis: Civil Rights During World War II." Missouri Historical Review, 1985.

Adler, Jeffrey S. "Yankee Colonizers and the Making of Antebellum St. Louis." Gateway Heritage 12 (3) Winter 1992.

Allen, Michael. "'Row, Boatmen Row!': Songs of the Early Ohio and Mississippi Rivermen." Gateway Heritage 14 (3) Winter 1993-94

Cassella, William N. "City-County Separation: 'The Great Divorce' of 1876." Bulletin of the Missouri Historical Society, 15 (2) January 1959.

Chaky, Doreen. "Fossils and the Fur Trade: The Chouteaus as Patrons of Paleontology." Gateway Heritage 19 (1) Summer 1998.

Corbett, Katharine T. and Mary E. Seematter. "'No Crystal Stair': Black St. Louis, 1920-1940." Gateway Heritage 8 (2) Fall 1987.

Crets, Jennifer Ann. "'Water of Diamond Transparency': The Legacy of Chain of Rocks Waterworks Park." Gateway Heritage 15 (1) Summer 1994.

Cutrer, Thomas W. "'McCulloch Had Made a Clean Platter in Missouri': Ben McCulloch and the Battle of Wilson's Creek, August 10, 1861." Gateway Heritage 14 (1) Summer 1993.

Dyreson, Mark. "The Playing Fields of Progress: American Athletic Nationalism and the 1904 Olympics." Gateway Heritage 14 (2) Fall 1993.

Faragher, John Mack. "'Well in Halth bu Deep in Markury': The Autumn Years of Daniel Boone." Gateway Heritage 13 (3) Winter 1993.

Foley, William E. "Galleries, Gumbo and 'La Guignolee.'" Gateway Heritage 10 (1), Summer 1989.

Gerteis, Louis. "St. Louis Theatre in the Age of the Original Jim Crow." Gateway Heritage 15 (4) Spring 1995.

Gilbert, Judith. "Esther and Her Sisters: Free Women of Color as Property Owners in Colonial St. Louis, 1765-1803." Gateway Heritage 17 (1) Summer 1996.

Gitlin, Jay. " 'Avec bien du regret: The Americanization of Creole St. Louis." Gateway Heritage 9 (4), Spring 1989.

Hammerstrom, Kirsten. "The St. Louis Scene: History, Place and the St. Louis Arch." Gateway Heritage 19 (2) Fall 1998.

Hurley, Andrew. "On the Waterfront: Railroads and Real Estate in Antebellum St. Louis." Gateway Heritage 13 (4) Spring 1993.

Jellison, Charles. "Farewell Words with Frankie Frisch." Gateway Heritage 20 (4) Spring 2000.

Kohl, Martha. "From Freedom to Franchise: The Debate over African American Enfranchisement, 1865-1870." Gateway Heritage 16 (4) Spring 1996.

McConachie, Scott. "Public Problems, Private Places." Bulletin of the Missouri Historical Society, 35 (2) January 1979.

McPherson, James M. "From Limited to Total War: Missouri and the Nation, 1861-1865." Gateway Heritage 12 (4) Spring 1992.

Miller, Howard S. "The Politics of Public Bathing in Progressive St. Louis." Gateway Heritage 9 (2) Fall 1989.

Moore, Robert. "A Ray of Hope, Extinguished: St. Louis Slave Suits for Freedom." Gateway Heritage 14 (3) Winter 1993-94.

Piott, Stephen L. "Modernization and the Anti-Monopoly Issue: The St. Louis Transit Strike of 1900." Bulletin of the Missouri Historical Society 35 (1) October 1978.

Olbrich, William L. "The Anzeiger Clique, St. Louis Germans and the Question of Slavery, 1836-1850." Gateway Heritage 16 (4) Spring 1996.

Rammelkamp, Julian. "St. Louis Boosters and Boodlers." Bulletin of the Missouri Historical Society, 34 (4) July 1978.

Rohrbough, Malcolm J. "The Art of Nostalgia: Bingham, Boone, and the Developing West." Gateway Heritage 11 (2) Winter 1990.

Roediger, David. "America's First General Strike: The St. Louis 'Commune' of 1877." Midwest Quarterly 21 (2) Winter 1980.

Rosen, Richard Allen. "Rethinking the Row House: The Development of Lucas Place, 1850-1865." Gateway Heritage 13 (1) Summer 1992.

Rowan, Steven. "'Smoking Myriads of Houses': German American Novelists View 1850s St. Louis." Gateway Heritage 20 (4) Spring 2000.

Rygelski, Jim. Baseball's "Boss President: Chris von der Ahe and the Nineteenth-Century St. Louis Browns." Gateway Heritage 13 (1), Summer 1992.

Smith, Gary N. "The Charles A. Lindbergh Trunk: A Time Capsule of His St. Louis Years." Gateway Heritage 16 (1) Summer 1995.

Smith, Jeffrey E. "A Match Made in St. Louis: Andrew Carnegie and the Eads Bridge." Gateway Heritage 17 (3) Winter 1996-97.

Smith, Jeffrey E. "A Mirror Held to St. Louis: William Marion Reedy and the 1904 World's Fair." Gateway Heritage 19 (1) Summer 1998.

Spencer, Thomas. "Power on Parade: The Origins of the Veiled Prophet Celebration in St. Louis. " Gateway Heritage 14 (2) Fall 1993.

Staley, Laura. "The Suffrage Movement in St. Louis During the 1870s." Gateway Heritage 3 (4) Spring 1983.

Tap, Bruce. "Reconstructing Emancipation's Martyr: John C. Fremont and the Joint Committee on the Conduct of War." Gateway Heritage 14 (4) Spring 1994.

Thorne, Tanis C. "'Liquor Has Been Their Undoing': Liquor Trafficking and Alcohol Abuse in the Lower Missouri Fur Trade." Gateway Heritage 13 (2) Fall 1992.

Williams, Christine. "Prosperity in the Face of Prejudice: The Life of a Free Black Woman in Frontier St. Louis." Gateway Heritage 19 (2) Fall 1998.

Winter, William C., ed. "'Like Sheep in a Slaughter Pen: A St. Louisan Remembers the Camp Jackson Massacre, May 10, 1861." Gateway Heritage 15 (4) Spring 1995.

Wrest, Renee. "No Contradiction Here: Beauty and Utility During St. Louis' City Beautiful Era." Gateway Heritage 14 (1) Summer 1993.

Young, Dina. "The Silent Search for Voice: The St. Louis Equal Suffrage League and the Dilemma of Elite Reform, 1910-1920." Gateway Heritage 8 (4) Spring 1988.

Young, Dina. "The St. Louis Streetcar Strike of 1900: Pivotal Politics at the Century's Dawn." Gateway Heritage 12 (1) Spring 1991.

INDEX

INDEX OF
PARTNERS & WEB SITES

continued on following page